History on the Edge

For Gabrielle —
fondly,
Michelle.

MEDIEVAL CULTURES

SERIES EDITORS
Rita Copeland
Barbara A. Hanawalt
David Wallace

Sponsored by the Center for Medieval Studies
at the University of Minnesota

Volumes in the series study the diversity of medieval cultural histories and practices, including such interrelated issues as gender, class, and social hierarchies; race and ethnicity; geographical relations; definitions of political space; discourses of authority and dissent; educational institutions; canonical and noncanonical literatures; and technologies of textual and visual literacies.

For more books in the series, see p. vi.

History on the Edge
Excalibur and the Borders of Britain
1100–1300

Michelle R. Warren

Medieval Cultures
Volume 22

University of Minnesota Press
Minneapolis
London

Parts of chapters 1 and 2 originally appeared as "Making Contact: Postcolonial Perspectives through Geoffrey of Monmouth's *Historia regum Britannie*," *Arthuriana* 8, no. 4 (1998): 115–34; reprinted courtesy of *Arthuriana*. Parts of chapter 6 originally appeared as "Designing the End of History in the Arming of Galahad," *Arthuriana* 5, no. 4 (1995): 45–55; reprinted courtesy of *Arthuriana*. Parts of chapter 6 also appeared as "Marmiadoise of Greece: The Fall of Ancient History in the *Estoire de Merlin*," *Romance Languages Annual* 9 (1997): 141–48; copyright Purdue Research Foundation, reprinted with permission, all rights reserved.

Published by the University of Minnesota Press
111 Third Avenue South, Suite 290
Minneapolis, MN 55401-2520
http://www.upress.umn.edu

Library of Congress Cataloging-in-Publication Data

Warren, Michelle R., 1967–
    History on the edge : Excalibur and the borders of Britain, 1100–1300 / Michelle R. Warren.
      p.   cm. — (Medieval cultures ; v. 22)
    Includes bibliographical references and index.
    ISBN 0-8166-3491-2 (alk. paper) — ISBN 0-8166-3492-0 (pbk. : alk. paper)
    1. Great Britain—History—Medieval period, 1066–1485—Historiography.
2. France—History—Medieval period, 987–1515—Historiography.
3. British—France—History—To 1500—Historiography.   4. Scottish Borders (England and Scotland)—Historiography.   5. Great Britain—History—To 1066—Historiography.   6. Welsh Borders (England and Wales)—Historiography.   7. Great Britain—Boundaries—Historiography.
8. Ethnology—Great Britain—Historiography.   9. France—Boundaries—Historiography.   10. Arthur, King—Influence. I. Title. II. Series.
DA175 .W35   2000
941.02'07'2—dc21   99-050861

Contents

✤

MEDIEVAL CULTURES

Preface

✢

This book has been through many shapes since, during the first months of graduate school, I laughed at the news that the Excalibur Hotel would soon open in Las Vegas. I have redrawn its boundaries innumerable times as I struggled (vainly, it seemed) to manage a seemingly amorphous group of materials united by a single word. The present shape of this book owes much to the cumulative impact of many disparate encounters. For their generosity and occasionally strategic interventions, I am grateful to Rebecca Biron, Frank Brandsma, Brigitte Cazelles, Richard Dienst, David Dumville, SunHee Kim Gertz, Sepp Gumbrecht, Kathleen Hobbs, Patricia Clare Ingham, Lesley Johnson, Seth Lerer, Reg McGinnis, Stephen Nichols, Hugh Thomas, and David Van Meter. I owe special thanks to Tom Goodman, Gabrielle Spiegel, Robert Stein, and Paul Strohm for offering invaluable advice on drafts of the manuscript.

My research has been supported by several grants from the University of Miami. In addition to travel and material expenses, these awards supported a succession of undergraduate research assistants who managed my often cumbersome relations with the library and the copy machine; I am especially grateful to Angelique Ruhi and Maytee Valenzuela for their cheerfulness and resourcefulness. Finally, I could not have completed this book without the good services of the interlibrary loan departments at both the University of Miami and Bennington College.

One of the great challenges of writing about translation and adaptation is to avoid tedious repetition. I hope readers will indulge the iterative spirit of medieval historiography wherever I have failed the expectations of the modern genre. One of the other challenges has been the languages of history, themselves innovative at every turn. Much of what is new in this book derives from labors of language, and I have personally translated all citations while profiting from the insights of those more experienced: Lewis Thorpe for Geoffrey of Monmouth's *Historia regum Britanniae*; Frederick Madden, Rosamund Allen, and W. R. J. Barron and S. C. Weinberg for Laȝamon's *Brut*; and Neil Wright for the *Gesta regum Britanniae* (whose lively translations I have amended only slightly).

For readers' ease, I have regularized the spelling of proper names and tried to render readable English prose versions of the concepts and turns of phrase that first captured my attention. Almost certainly I have made mistakes and some questionable choices along the way; if readers find that these matter, I will count myself lucky.

Prologus historiarum Britanniae

❖

"The trouble with the Engenglish is that their hiss hiss history happened overseas, so they do do don't know what it means." These stuttering words are spoken by the character Whiskey Sisodia, an Indian impresario living in London, in Salman Rushdie's *Satanic Verses*. Sisodia articulates here the fundamental dynamics of postcolonial subjectivity, which equivocates between memory and amnesia (the English *do* and *don't* know their history) while hovering between the familiar and the foreign (literally, *over seas*).[1] The menace (*hiss hiss*) of the English past has taken place overseas precisely because that past has been shaped by colonial ambition. The English themselves originally came from overseas, inspiring in others the amnesia they themselves would later suffer. Indeed, Sisodia's comment echoes the judgment leveled against the Scots in the ninth-century *Historia Brittonum*: they don't know their origins ("nescientes originis sui") (60). In both of these contexts, postcolonial amnesia witnesses the complex role of origins in colonial history. The English and the Scots have in fact both forgotten the original people of Insular history, the Britons. Nonetheless, the ghosts of colonized Britons haunt subsequent formulations of imperial Britain, casting long shadows across European historiography.

In medieval Britain, one of the key moments in the process of colonial contamination was Aethelred's marriage to Emma of Normandy. Through their son Edward the Confessor, William of Normandy claimed to inherit the Insular monarchy, leading to overseas business that the English would rather forget. Rushdie's own portrayal of William stages an instructive encounter of memory and amnesia within a colonial scenario. Rushdie embodies England in the aged Rosa Diamond, an apparently childless widow of eighty-eight who scans the horizon for Norman ghosts, which she defines as "[u]nfinished business" (129). In fact, Rosa prays for nothing less than "the past's return" as she challenges the Normans to come again: "Come on, you Norman ships, she begged: let's have you, Willie-the-Conk" (129). Rosa's desire to confront the eleventh-century Norman conqueror expresses an English desire to de-colonize the national origin.

Rosa's own memory is dominated by visions of the battle of Hastings: "Longbows, maces, pikes. The flaxen-Saxon boys, cut down in their sweet youth, Harold Arroweye and William with his mouth full of sand" (130). Spying something moving on the shore, she is shocked by the idea that Willie might have actually landed again: "What she said aloud in her excitement: 'I don't believe it!' — 'It isn't true!' — 'He's never *here*!' On unsteady feet, with bumping chest, Rosa went for her hat, cloak, stick. While, on the winter seashore, Gibreel Farishta awoke with a mouth full of, no, not sand. Snow" (130). In this moment, Rosa and the reader encounter Gibreel as a Norman zombie, performing Rosa's memory of William at Hastings. His mouth full of snow, not sand, only replaces one incongruity (the presence of William) with another (the presence of snow). In this moment of substitution, the Indian survivor of English colonialism (and an airplane explosion over the English Channel) occupies the place of the Norman conqueror who forcefully overcame the English. Fleetingly, Gibreel embodies the postcolonial ambitions of both English and Indian; fleetingly, time, space, and ethnicity bend around to meet themselves. The contortions amplify when Rosa takes Gibreel in and he masquerades as her dead husband, the chivalric Sir Henry. Homi Bhabha recognizes Gibreel's dual performance as English colonizer and Indian colonized when he concludes: "He is the history that happened overseas, elsewhere" (168). Gibreel is also, however, the Norman colonizer and the English colonized, and thus the force of restless, ghostly, medieval memory.

These memories include the Britons, who occupy important narrative roles in the historiography generated from the Norman Conquest. In this book, I pursue some of their unfinished colonial business through the twelfth and thirteenth centuries—a business that in some senses has barely begun, even though Britain sustained post-colonial cultures (hyphenated to indicate a chronological relation to a specific historical occupation) well before the twentieth century. Trojans, Angles, Romans, Saxons, Danes, and Normans forcibly settled the island; Anglo-Saxons in turn settled the Americas and the Indian subcontinent. Each colonial encounter has engendered new power dynamics and new narratives, including the theories called *postcolonial* (unhyphenated, to indicate concepts not bound to specific histories).[2] As some critics of postcolonialism recognize,[3] the history of colonial ambition presents numerous revelatory continuities, despite changes in venue and technology. Analyses of these resemblances can qualify and quantify the unique dynamics of each meeting of unequal powers. By juxtaposing Rushdie's *Satanic Verses* and the *Historia Brittonum*, then, I do not offer the "discovery" of a new origin of postcolonial desire or nationalist amnesia. Such a proposal would overlook the urgent politics of contemporary struggles against oppression. Rather, I propose that analogies can sharpen the contours of historical difference even as they construct points of contact across time. Postcolonial studies, for example, formulate theories of culture and identity in border communities that speak to the discontinuities of medieval boundaries, even though the legal and political mechanisms differ greatly. At the same time, certain resemblances between medieval and modern cultures dismantle the seemingly impermeable boundary that critics draw on the modern side of the Middle Ages. As medieval studies are making clear, the pre-colonial, pre-national Middle Ages imagined by postcolonial critics reinscribes the cultural homogeneity that colonial discourse analysis seeks to dismantle.[4] My juxtaposition, which might be called a "strategic achronism," thus claims that the familiar and the foreign (the modern and the medieval) are always already mutually contaminated and in the process of decomposition. Postcolonial criticism narrates the traumas of this process.

After the successful conquest of 1066, Norman settlement of Britain provoked not only dramatic shifts in land tenure and the political contours of northern Europe, but also vigorous historiographical action. As R. W. Southern first suggested, the cultural trauma of Norman colonization focused attention on the near and distant past, as both dominant and dominated groups defended their collective identities and sought therapeutic cures for alienation in history. In this process, King Arthur became the most contested of all Britons. The histories of Britain that include Arthur, beginning with Geoffrey of Monmouth's in the 1130s, narrate the long history of Insular colonialism in reaction to various contemporary pressures. In fact, the Arthurian histories made canonical by medievalist criticism all emerged from border cultures and engage the dynamics of boundary formation into the thirteenth century and across the Channel. As writers responded to disruptions in their contemporary landscapes by narrating the histories of Insular jurisdictions, Arthurian historiography took shape as a form of border writing.

I have arrived at this conclusion almost by accident. Having constructed an intractable corpus of Arthuriana from references to *Excalibur* in the available indexes of medieval literature, I eventually focused on narratives that recount Arthur's complete reign in relation to the origins of Insular settlement. I resisted the critical methods (still widely practiced) that determine literary typologies from historical context. Moreover, I avoided treating the Arthurian period in narrative isolation, having discovered firsthand the interpretive fallacies that arise from excerpting. From the beginning, I have been determined that it is not possible, as Eugène Vinaver once feared, to make "too generous a use...of the simple virtues of Excalibur" (526). I have likewise been inspired by Angus Fletcher's intuition that Excalibur, Dante's beatific rose, and the eponymous Pearl of English verse "contain the cosmos of those works where they appear" (229). I discovered the shape of this cosmos while using a map to understand what it meant for Geoffrey to be "of Monmouth" and for Robert to be "of Gloucester." Suddenly, it became clear that every text in my corpus emerged from an identifiable border region. Arthurian historiography, I will now argue, was written most often and most emphatically in relation to boundary pressures. The coercive and often violent nature of these pressures makes the sword, which began in my research as an almost random object, an engaging emblem of historiography in the border.

The itinerary of Arthurian historiography traverses the edges of the island as well as the Continent. The journey begins in the Severn River Valley, in the town of Monmouth. Probably from Oxford, Geoffrey of Monmouth manifested his ambivalent relation with colonial domination by narrating Britain's history for Norman patrons. Almost immediately, Geoffrey's neighbors in Wales revised his *Historia regum Britanniae* as they imagined a reversal of Norman domination. Meanwhile, Insular and Continental Normans could learn the Britons' history in French from Gaimar or Wace and project their own fantasies of justified expansionism against the Insular past (Gaimar's history, however, has not survived). By the end of the twelfth century, back on the banks of the Severn, Laȝamon was translating Wace's history into an English landscape as if it had always belonged there. Shortly afterward, on the other side of the Channel and the French royal domain, the Arthurian prose cycle began to take shape as a vast meditation on the dangers of prestigious history, true to the ambivalent spirit of Geoffrey's *Historia*. Around the *Historia*'s centenary anniversary, a monk in Brittany returned the Britons to their epic origins in the *Gesta regum Britanniae*, moralizing their fate and rejecting the prestige of coercive history. In the later years of the thirteenth century, Arthurian historiography continued to flourish in the Welsh border region where it first emerged—in revisions of Laȝamon's English history, in Robert of Gloucester's English translation of the Latin *Historia*, and in Welsh translations of revised *Historiae*.

This comparative journey exposes the border cultures of Arthur's biographers and lays bare the perils of isolating his history from their landscapes. It takes place at the juncture of textual minutiae, cultural history, and ethnic psychology. The chapters that follow trace the regional, rather than chronological, contours of this journey. This method underscores the fact that border relations do not develop teleologically. Although it means occasionally discussing revisions before their sources, this regional focus opens new perspectives on processes of creation and reception. I begin with a definition of border writing through postcolonial theories, including the sword's role as an emblem of coercive boundary formation. The first section then takes in the Insular landscape: Geoffrey between Monmouth and Oxford (chapter 2), Latin revision and Welsh translation in Wales in the twelfth and thirteenth centuries (chapter 3), and English translation along the Severn in the thirteenth century (chapter 4). The second section follows Arthurian historiography across the Channel: Latin revision and French translation in Normandy in the twelfth century (chapter 5), the French prose cycle in the thirteenth century (chapter 6), and Latin revision in thirteenth-century Brittany (chapter 7). In each region, reactions to domination fail to develop neat chrono-logical patterns from colonial celebration to post-colonial ambivalence to anti-colonial diatribe. Instead, representations of colonial history are bound to dynamic cultural processes that shape surprising resemblances and startling differences across both time and space.

CHAPTER 1

Arthurian Border Writing

Medieval narratives about King Arthur constitute a lengthy catalog of both remarkable originality and inveterate repetition. From Geoffrey of Monmouth's unprecedented account of Arthur's reign in the *Historia regum Britanniae* (completed in the 1130s) to the *Hystoire du sainct greaal* (printed in Paris in 1516), writers composed Arthur's regnal history at varying intervals, from the western edge of Wales to the eastern regions of France (and throughout the rest of Europe). Yet to say that Arthur was popular does not explain why he attracted attention in these particular forms, places, and times. Writing about the history of the Britons, in fact, served the cultural and political needs of a variety of groups, with conflicting purposes and values. Although unified by a common appeal to what I will call "Briton history" (so as to avoid the imperialist connotations of *British*),[1] these groups considered themselves distinct from one another. I contend in this book that the historical Arthur attracted writers specifically engaged with pressures to defend, maintain, or expand the identity of their region. These historians wrote from peripheral positions, usually in border areas.

The historical use of the Arthurian reign is only one aspect, but an especially notable one, of historiographical responses to the boundary pressures created by the Norman conquest of 1066. Norman colonization focused attention on the Insular past partly because, in general, cultural trauma inspires defenses of collective identities. Colonization shifts boundaries radically, provoking colonizers and colonized alike to demarcate new limits. In border regions especially, imaginative boundaries of all kinds need periodic reconstruction. Post-colonial societies reorder boundaries in relation to land tenure, as well as symbolically in relation to culture. Since swords literally enforce the new political borders, violence dominates the processes of boundary formation. In the twelfth century, the *Gesta Stephani* explicitly locates the establishment of a new boundary between Wales and England in the edge of the sword. Just after introducing Wales as a country nearly equal to England in delightful productivity (thanks to Norman colonization), the narrator turns to the Welsh rebellion that began in 1136. Seizing the area of Gower, the rebels overpowered the king's knights "in ore gladii" (with the edge of the sword); the Welsh proceeded to retake most of the country (14–

20). This very boundary—perhaps even in the same year—generated Geoffrey's *Historia,* the first account of the Britons' history to narrate Arthur's reign along with his sword. Similar border pressures inspired iterations of this narrative through the next two centuries.

Arthurian historiography is only a particularly cogent, not a unique, example of a practice that can be called *border writing.* In the medieval period, any number of writers can be located in border cultures (Gerald of Wales and Orderic Vitalis come immediately to mind, as does the author of *Fouke le Fitz Waryn*); they, however, responded to boundary pressures without writing histories of Arthur. Likewise, many Arthurian narratives do not engage the identity issues indigenous to border cultures. Nevertheless, I will argue that complete histories of the Arthurian reign, tied to the origins of Insular dominion, were conceived most often at the edges of regional differences. The principal historiographical versions of Arthur's reign represent the historical tensions attendant on the formation of spatial, ethnic, linguistic, and temporal boundaries. Historical narration itself performs limits symbolically, interacting with contemporary tensions by forming and transforming the past. These limits engage force, and are thus conjoined to symbols of coercion.

By beginning at the edges rather than the centers of power, the dynamics that shape identity through resistance and accommodation gain clarity. Throughout this book, I explore the consequences of pressing the edges. As Homi Bhabha hopes to read "from the nation's edge, through the sense of the city, from the periphery of the people, in culture's transnational dissemination" (170), I read Arthurian historiography from the regional edges where it was most often written, in an effort to understand its engagements with the dynamics of domination. To substantiate this mode of reading, I draw widely on postcolonial analyses and social anthropologies because they sharpen the contours of cultural continuities and disruptions.

A theory of the border offers a method of historical analysis that confronts the paradoxes that inhere in limits and boundaries. The figure of paradox inhabits all boundary concepts because the line of the limit seeks to institute an absolute difference at the place of most intimate contact between two spaces (or concepts, or peoples, or times, or...). Border writing figures history as a space shaped by blood and ink, by sword and chronicle. This is similar to the writing Michel de Certeau associates with the arrival of Europeans at the land across their western ocean, a writing that enacts "a colonization of the body by the discourse of power: this is *writing that conquers*" (xxv; emphasis in the original). At the same time that border histories articulate the victors' will to dominate, they also engage the desires of the vanquished. Arthurian border histories thus represent Insular colonialisms in order to stake a multitude of territorial claims—over space, ethnicity, language, and time.

Navigating Landscape

From the earliest versions, histories of Britain begin with a physical description of the island and its natural resources. Usually aestheticized, the topographic *descriptio* identifies the land as worthy of possession. Landscape description thus works as one of the defining tropes of border writing: the *descriptio* conquers land symbolically, making the landscape metaphor an agent of history. On an island, the landscape metaphor is fraught with paradox because the shore forms an immutable yet permeable boundary: the land definitely ends, but ships carrying new settlers from overseas easily land. The shore embodies the general paradox of boundaries, where absolute differences occupy the places of most intimate contact.

Border narratives write the history of the land's shape as an argument for its present and future shape, foregrounding the determinations of place fundamental to all historiography. The narration of landscape symbolically conquers space, for both colonial settlers and resisting colonized subjects. Edward Said, for example, has shown how colonial settlers and colonized subjects both territorialize their identities, celebrating wholeness and condemning partition (85). After colonization, land is first retaken in the imagination; for Said, the anti-imperialist imagination is essentially *cartographic* (77–79). The *descriptio* of Britain, which I analyze in detail in later chapters, provides for this same possessive desire; in some ways, the aestheticized landscape makes the viewer its predator.[2] Projected onto entire groups of people, this predatory desire makes the cartography of border writing quite poignantly a social cartography. In this way, the narration of topography becomes what Bhabha calls the "inscape of national identity" (143). In the history of the kings of Britain, the "inscape" of collective identification prefaces the story of how the land gained its shape through forceful settlement. Caught in the cartographic imagination, the representation of Insular space equivocates between the fantasy of hegemonic dominion (a land without borders) and the fragmentation that clearly endures in the landscape. Rushdie captures this equivocation in images of mobile topography, such as the Insular coastline that has "moved a mile or more out to sea" (129) since the Norman Conquest, and the rebellious cartography of London, "changing shape at will and without warning" (327).

The genre of landscape narrative shares many of the social effects of landscape painting. Arguing forcefully in favor of this analogy, Jonathan Smith defines space as a geography of cultural signs. According to Smith, the landscape genre promises an escape from time by effacing the painful prospects of the future (80); "[t]he landscape mediates social communication, and privileged landscapes are designed to hide whatever defiles" (85). In contrast to this colonial fantasy, post-colonial landscapes (like

Geoffrey of Monmouth's *descriptio*) encode portents of the violence that will destroy the aestheticized ideal, such as crumbled buildings set among fertile fields. These shadows of the future also reconfigure history, defying the corollary promise to "raise a wall that blocks the past" (Smith 80). Post-colonial landscapes dismantle this wall, ironically contrasting social ideals with historical transgressions. The founding description of the Insular landscape exposes this irony by actually identifying the hidden sites of threats and aggression. Smith concludes, "When closely observed, every self-image humans have written into the landscape will betray its pretensions with ironic affirmations of an order that is both wider and weirder" (87). The irony of Insular landscape description lies specifically in its invocation of an order that belies the Britonic glory implied in the subsequent narrative. As such, the *descriptio* performs what W. J. T. Mitchell calls "the 'dreamwork' of imperialism": it discloses "both utopian fantasies of the perfect imperial prospect and fractured images of unresolved ambivalence and unsuppressed resistance" (10). Throughout the twelfth and thirteenth centuries, the Insular *descriptio* positions histories of Britain within these dynamics—as imperial fantasies, nightmares, or dismissals.

The land, as landscape, is not simply natural space but also territory. Territory itself constitutes communication, what Robert Sack calls "the basic geographic expression of influence and power, [which] provides an essential link between society, space, and time" (261). Paul Zumthor has shown in *La mesure du monde* that the measure of space defines many different kinds of communal belonging in medieval literature. Gilles Deleuze and Félix Guattari investigate territorialization in broader social terms in *A Thousand Plateaus*. Through their theory of the refrain, they link territoriality specifically to the ritual repetition of patterned discourse, which shapes "melodic landscapes": to repeat verses is to territorialize history and fabricate time (318–49). The echo of Arthurian historiography across the centuries constitutes what Patricia Clare Ingham has called a "colonial refrain,"[3] a repetition of patterned discourse that defines the limits of territorial possession. Several of the histories I will discuss in fact call directly upon the audience to repeat the narrative. If audiences respond, their oral refrains iterate the written refrain of historiographical repetition, extending the territory of historical possession to a perennial "here and now."

While concepts of territory articulate the ways in which social and imperial identities work the land, physical topography itself engages the paradox of boundaries, thereby contributing to the cultural pressures that generate border writing. Many boundaries inhere in the shape of the planet surface, such as mountain ranges, rivers, and oceans. Indeed, human cultures have most often traced their own differences along these topographical lines, establishing legal limits to jurisdiction and group identity according to the physical shape of land. Topography does not,

4

however, provide stable grounds for difference. Like all boundary concepts, topographic limits sustain paradox. The topographical paradox most pertinent to Insular history concerns boundaries marked by navigable waterways—what the narrator of the *Estoire del saint graal* calls "les mers ou barges poent corre" (the seas where boats can run) (339). The shore, for example, separates land masses immutably while the waters that lap its edge easily convey ships from distant lands. Geoffrey's *Historia* presents the Channel specifically as the part of the island that facilitates navigation to France ("absque meridianae plagae freto quo ad Gallias navigatur") (73). The water itself contains the unfathomed depths of uncertainty that characterize boundary identity. The physical perils of navigation mirror the perils of transfers between stabilities, of the process itself of identity construction among shifting edges. Insular space thus paradoxically sustains and resists colonizing maneuvers: the open shore facilitates the initiation of conquest while impeding colonial resolution.

Within the island itself, rivers embed instability in the permanent features of the landscape. Navigable rivers flowing to the sea provide easy pathways for conquering foreigners. In the interior, rivers may mark boundaries between the domains of different groups or lords, facilitating lateral communication. The intensity of activity along rivers makes them politically attractive (literally), and they typically draw people together more than they separate: in order to enhance safety, the inhabitants of the bordering lands seek control over both sides of the water. The ebb and flow of these efforts, as the two sides alternately succeed and fail, renders the aquatic frontier the most unstable of geopolitical boundaries.[4] While rivers do commonly mark political limits (most famously in the medieval period in the Treaty of Verdun of 843 that set the limits of the Carolingian empire), the actual zone of stability is usually displaced to one side or the other.[5] Water, then, invites cultural and political disruption as the ocean conducts ships to the shore and then up the rivers that perforate it.

Medieval cartography represents graphically the dominance of water in the conception of Insular space. On Gerald of Wales's map of Britain, broad river bands separate England from Wales (the Severn) and England from Scotland (the Humber and the Scottish Sea) (see figure 1). As I show in chapter 2, the conception of Britain as a land divided by the Severn and the Humber inaugurates a structure of nearly permanent political instability; the narratives analyzed in chapters 2, 3, and 4 all respond to the dynamic paradoxes that flow along the Severn (and which do so well into the seventeenth century, when Milton resurrects the river's eponymous founder Sabrina as a virgin nymph of British unity).[6] In contrast to Gerald's schematic division of the island, Matthew Paris represents veritable aquatic labyrinths, suggesting the near impossibility of travel without water (see figure 2). The fourteenth-century Gough Map and an anonymous fifteenth-century map also represent the land's permeability by

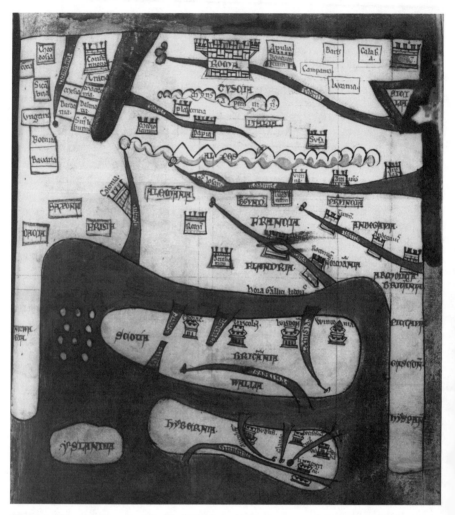

Figure 1. Map of Europe by Gerald of Wales, c. 1200. Courtesy of the National Library of Ireland, MS 700; reprinted with permission.

portraying the island as a series of sculpted edges, many curving almost all the way through the (supposedly) solid center.[7] These maps manifest the depth of the challenge posed by navigable water to the Insular border, a challenge that shaped Britain well into the modern period.[8] Historical writing itself engages the instability engendered by aquatic boundaries, attempting to fix limits in narrative that cannot be satisfactorily fixed in the landscape.

The shores of islands and rivers only become boundaries, of course, as a result of human groups' efforts to create and maintain political differences. A boundary is a legal effect, a *logos* imposed upon the *topos*

Figure 2. Map of Britain by Matthew Paris, c. 1250. Courtesy of the British Library, Cotton MS Claudius D. vi, f. 12v; reprinted with permission.

7

For much of the Middle Ages, this imposition was discontinuous and often multilayered.[9] The practice of performing homage in border areas
blatantly exploits the paradoxes of discontinuity. Acts of homage "in
the border" (*in marchia*) affirm the place where powers clearly separate;
the very act of meeting, however, demonstrates that they also overlap.
The border is thus not a neutral zone but a multiple zone. Whether an
homage of peace after war or a formal declaration of tenancy (or both),
homage in the border is an act of concession between two powers that
creates dependency while affirming independence.[10] On the island, the
borders between Wales and England sustained some of the most complex
boundary engagements (discussed in chapters 2, 3, and 4). The fragmented nature of the Welsh March, as with many places of border contact, heightened jurisdictional consciousness and encouraged the development of border laws (*lex Marchie*) distinct from Welsh and English
law.[11]

On the Continent, the dynamics of homage in border areas dominated Norman-French relations into the thirteenth century (as I discuss
in chapter 5). All known acts of homage between the duke of Normandy
and the king of France between 911 and 1140, for example, took place in
border areas, affirming the duke's autonomy in matters of peace while
maintaining the significance of the king's initial concession of the land.
These homages occurred most frequently along the river Epte, plausibly
because the waterway made it the most unstable frontier between Norman and French royal interests. Jean-François Lemarignier argues further
that as land tenure issues became the primary motivation for homage,
the border became a less important space. The duke thus fulfilled the
legal requirement of homage at the *domus* of his lord by appearing in
Paris for the first time in 1149. The move from the border to the city (from
the edge to the metropolitan center) signals a reduction of the duke's
autonomy as well as a fundamental change in the status of the border itself. Elsewhere on the Continent, Brittany and Champagne also witnessed significant border conflict — and produced significant Arthurian
historiography (discussed in chapters 6 and 7). Champagne-Blois provoked
special measures for balancing power among aristocratic, ecclesiastical,
and royal authorities, for it nearly surrounded the French royal domain.
In these areas, the bridge of the river Natiaux served as a frequent meeting point for lords of overlapping and changing jurisdictions.[12]

Historical writing from these borders performs a jurisdictional accommodation similar to homage and other codified border practices. Border
historiography claims space while seeking to transform symbolically the
identity of that space, and sometimes the nature of the claim. As spaces
of paradox, borders serve important central functions from the margin;
they are edges where centers can meet. Like justice and territorial conquest, marches are carved out and defended with the edge of the sword
(*ora gladii*). This defense takes place on the land, but the swords are han

dled by people. The differences defended thus ultimately concern the collective identities of peoples as much as the actual spaces of their contact.

The Ends of Genealogy

If concern for the land makes border writing cartographic, its concern for peoples makes it genealogic. For Britain, ethnic genealogy begins with the Trojans who became the Britons. Their descendants (Welsh and Breton) and their descendants' conquerors (Anglo-Saxons and Normans) all actively constructed Trojan-Briton history as part of their own identity. These genealogical constructions strategically deploy ethnic and family resemblances while defending social and political differences. This combination maintains genealogy within the bounds of paradox. The *Historia* and the narratives it inspired scrutinize genealogical strategies (such as exogamy and endogamy) along with the maneuvers that disrupt them (such as adultery, rape, sodomy, and fratricide) as they interrogate the limits of collective identification.

Ethnic identity is defined as a boundary concept by Fredrik Barth in the introduction to *Ethnic Groups and Boundaries.* Barth argues that the "shared traits" usually used to define ethnic groups result from strategies of social interaction rather than from inherent characteristics. Barth's method shifts attention away from the seemingly autonomous "cultural stuff" that constitutes the internal history of separate groups to "ethnic boundaries and boundary maintenance" (10–17). Boundaries may be maintained, even accentuated, in multiethnic encounters even while the "cultural stuff" changes. Barth underscores the fact that human groups are usually in contact with each other, and thus always organized around boundary maintenance: border regions only magnify the focus. John Armstrong has pursued Barth's boundary approach across the *longue durée* of ethnic history in *Nations before Nationalism.* Armstrong identifies ethnicity as only one of a range of conceptual strategies he calls "symbolic boundary mechanisms" (8), that is, the nontechnical and legal mechanisms that groups use to perceive the boundary between themselves and others. Armstrong locates the significance of boundaries for human identity at the center of a synthetic study of group relations: "The boundary approach clearly implies that ethnicity is a bundle of shifting interactions rather than a nuclear component of social organization" (6). Border writing actively performs the work of what Armstrong calls symbolic "border guards" (6) by ascribing differences and staking out resemblances. In borders, historiography itself becomes a mechanism for policing difference.

The politics of difference are especially poignant in situations of colonial contact. For a colonial subject, a politics of strategic difference and resemblance constitutes an itinerant ethnicity. Bhabha, for example, underscores the partiality of ethnic identification in borders, where presence is never total and being—"the overlap and displacement of domains of difference" (2)—perpetually crosses contradictory limits. The in-between subject is always split between here and there, between self and other. Bhabha concludes that the hybridity of border communities engenders "an insurgent act of cultural translation" that defies fixation (7).[13] From a similar perspective, Mary Louise Pratt calls border identities "interactive" and "improvisational" (7). The partialities of medieval ethnicities, firmly recognized by many historians, thus resemble postcolonial border subjects in important ways. The performative multiplicity of border identity means that we cannot reason Norman blood from a Norman name or Welsh blood from a perceived political bias toward the Welsh, and that biological parentage works as only one identifying element jostled among many partial contacts.

Barth's and Bhabha's approaches to the edges of identity contrast methodologically with investigations of shared "cultural stuff" by Anthony Smith in the *Ethnic Origin of Nations* and Benedict Anderson in *Imagined Communities*. Where Smith defines *ethnie* according to peoples' shared characteristics and sense of solidarity (22–31), Anderson identifies nationalism as a set of shared affective ties and sense of group belonging (5–7). Medievalists have taken easily to these models of national community because they do not depend absolutely on the technology of the modern nation-state. Yet Smith and Anderson both imply sociological homogeneities that submerge the characteristics of communities imagined through difference (as Kathleen Davis has shown in detail for Anderson). Blindnesses to discontinuities (in genealogy, time, and space) pose substantial methodological problems not only for analyses of modern post-colonial cultures, as Bhabha argues (159), but for medieval cultures, where discontinuous borders are indigenous. By deconstructing social homogeneity and working through difference, cultural theories like Barth's or Bhabha's enable historians to cross the boundaries that define differences without effacing them.

In different ways, Barth, Armstrong, and Bhabha demonstrate that struggles for group identity play out most intensively in border regions. In the eleventh and twelfth centuries, the most active struggles for ethnic and family identity deployed Trojan ancestors. By the end of the twelfth century, many of the ruling families of Europe had traced their genealogies back to Troy. The process did not create bonds of identification among these families, but rather sought to differentiate each group from its potential rivals. The genealogical use of the Trojans shows how the perception of difference rather than identity structures the boundaries between groups. The Trojans' putative descendants, the Britons, likewise guarded the borders of other ethnic groups. The Britons' history is an ethnic myth, with all of the traits identified by Smith, from landscape to the vision of a golden age (183–200). Briton historiography remained territory for contesting the past for centuries. In that contest, the Britons remained figured as the people who lost their history, only to have it given back by the takers. The writing of Briton history thus takes place (literally takes place) in a colonial dynamic in which the Britons play the role of the "people without history."[14] When Geoffrey of Monmouth provided the master narrative of the Britons' imperial past, he gave them history and thus an identity for the future. The gift (identity through history), however, remained the property of others and therefore contested territory. The writing and rewriting of Briton history thus creates and retrenches the boundary between those with and without their own past.

The Britons did not, however, write this myth for themselves: it was written by and for their conquerors. The Britons become a boundary mechanism of many different groups, the ubiquitous Other of European collective identities expressed in genealogical discourse. Arthur, the most contested Briton of all, is contained through repeated resurrection by those who deploy his history to legitimize their own differences. Although Martin Shichtman and Laurie Finke present Arthur as a "social signifier whose function was to smooth over the ideological conflicts created by the Norman colonization of England" (4), his reception seems to have divided the different peoples who claimed his heritage more often than it unified them. Indeed, James Holt contrasts Arthur's reception convincingly with the elocutionary force of Charlemagne, around whose name the Frankish peoples became French.[15] Except for the Welsh and the Bretons (whose Arthurian historiography I discuss in chapters 3 and 7), Arthur is an effective antecedent but not a unifying ancestor.

Genealogy, of course, strategically deploys ethnic and family resemblance as well as difference. Bloodlines construct continuities across time, militating against historical differences. When the aristocratic imagination turned to family histories in the eleventh century, as Georges Duby has shown, the redactors of genealogical narratives were drawn to the prestige of royal blood.[16] They literally wedded aristocratic families to existing royal genealogies. The Flemish, for example, claimed the Carolingians, while the Angevins joined the Capetians. This practice diffused differences between royal and aristocratic families by exposing their intimate sexual relations. Genealogical discourse thus returns to paradox: it claims vital differences on the basis of shared relatives. The relativity of genealogical difference captures the cultural ambivalence of groups attracted to the powers that dominate them.

The Beginnings of Etymology

The genealogical principle of border writing encompasses an etymological principle, since the history of a people is nearly inseparable from the history of its languages. The symbolic flexibility of language renders it one of the most effective border guards of identity. As Armstrong points

11

out, language does not constitute a presocial identity: in the *longue durée* of ethnic history, "language was more often the product than the cause of polity formation" (241–42). The choice of a particular language for history writing thus allies the historical content with the linguistic communities capable of reading it. This choice may affirm or transgress conventional alliances, reshaping cultural boundaries through narrative form. In this sense, historiography as border writing belongs to the dominated as well as the empowered.

Etymology is an important boundary mechanism, intimately related to territorial identity and genealogy, because it signals relations among groups in the changing forms of their words. The conceptual power of etymology in medieval European culture has been succinctly (and most influentially) expressed by Ernst Robert Curtius, who declared the genre a "category of thought" and Isidore of Seville's *Etymologiae sive origines* "the basic book of the Middle Ages" (495, 496). More recently, R. Howard Bloch has formulated the privileged role of etymology in the narration of group identity in *Etymologies and Genealogies*. The etymology of Britain itself, for example, is closely bound to the cultural translation of Briton genealogy since the land takes it name from the first Briton father. Subsequently, histories of Insular naming trace patterns of conquest and domination into the Norman period.

Etymological narrative, like genealogical narrative and historiography in general, is a diachronic mode of discourse. Etymologies thematize not only word formation but also culture formation across time, expressing what Daniel Rosenberg has called "a rhetoric of temporality" (321–22). Just as genealogies represent relations between peoples of different times, etymologies represent the chronology of relations between words. In treatises devoted to language study, etymology introduces a diachronic element into a synchronic explanation of language. In historical narrative, etymologies introduce an alternate and even competing diachronic reference into an already diachronic structure. This reference depends on an alternate memory, which supplements the memory recorded in the primary narrative. Etymologies thus cogently address the problems of representing memory, not only because they conjure moments outside the scope of the main narrative, but also because they record losses of meaning and form.

Like memory and forgetting in etymology, translation remaps historical knowledge to reflect, or change, relations of domination. Translation actively engages the boundaries of identity because it shuttles between differences and near-resemblances. In colonial encounters, translation can enhance power differences and thus reinforce the boundaries that support domination. Walter Mignolo identifies the forceful displacement of one language by another as "linguistic dismissal" (186), which reflects the efforts of colonizing powers to efface cultural differences by eradicating linguistic variation. Language laws, for example, aim to create homogeneous linguistic communities that will facilitate cultural domination; the cultural attractiveness of dominant groups displaces indigenous languages just as forcefully. Through this perspective, Geoffrey of Monmouth's claim to translate an ancient book in the Briton language becomes what Eric Cheyfitz calls a "fiction of translation" (15) that serves the colonial fantasies of Geoffrey's readers. By claiming to displace the ethnically marked Briton source, Geoffrey defeats the Britons with the Latin of the Romans (who occasionally overpower the Britons in the narrative itself). Geoffrey's translators in turn assert their own cultural sovereignty over his *Historia.* Always already translation, the writing of Briton history effaces difference and affirms continuity from the origins of Insular dominion to the time and language of each writer. Just as territorial acquisition by the sword defines boundaries through violence, translation enacts an imperialism of sources and a colonization of the past. Vernacular translation in particular renders the past familiar and assimilates the foreign to the indigenous. Like the island itself, the story of the past becomes a cultural space to be conquered.

In the border, however, strategies of difference turn easily into resemblance. Multilingualism is the linguistic manifestation of what Bhabha theorizes as hybridity, "the name for the strategic reversal of the process of domination through disavowal" (112). Translation thus "turns the discursive conditions of dominance into the grounds of intervention" (112), undermining (rather than reinforcing) the boundaries between cultures in contact. Postcolonial bilingualism can shape a "subversive poetics" that blurs boundaries and undermines hierarchies, thereby challenging the basic structures of power.[17] Through this perspective, Geoffrey's claim to translate makes the Britons more like his Latin-literate readers — that is, more like everybody engaged in the history of imperial domination. Latin universalizes the Briton cultural experience by diffusing ethnic identification in a common, international language.[18] Latin thus breaks down the discursive barrier between the Britons' past and present, the barrier that stands between them and present cultural legitimacy. In one case, Geoffrey directly challenges the homogeneity of linguistic culture by citing dialogue in Saxon (184), just as Rushdie does by citing Latin (276, 404). Finally, Geoffrey repeatedly displays multilingual transference in onomastic histories. These representations of translation subvert the hegemony of the linguistic power that dominates the colonized.

Tellingly, Geoffrey's Latin history was adapted in Wales (see chapter 3) at the same time that Gaimar set about rendering it in French. Used in this way, border writing disrupts the discourse of the colonizer through an appropriation that overturns the language of domination. The resistance continues in English with Laȝamon's translation of Wace's French *Roman de Brut* (see chapter 4). Laȝamon's prologue, however, presents the languaging of his history as trilingual, drawing from English, French, and Latin. Laȝamon demonstrates cultural contact as a series of language contacts, staging a polyglot performance characteristic of postcolonial discourse, but subsumed in the performance by English. Through his own resolutely monolingual composition, Laȝamon presents a linguistic gloss on post-colonial experience that dismisses the polyglot condition of life, just as Norman conquerors dismissed English. Even at the close of the fifteenth century, the languaging of Arthurian history remains an urgent cultural issue: in the 1485 preface to Thomas Malory's *Morte Darthur,* William Caxton notes that he agreed to print the text because the deeds of the great Arthur could be read in many languages, including Dutch, Italian, Spanish, Greek, and French, but not "in our maternal tongue" (2).

Translation, then, can enact or resist colonialist success, or both. While the *Historia* represents the Britons' loss of history through their loss of language, it also resists their colonization by remembering their past. As a strategy for crossing boundaries, translation remains bound to paradox: it makes the past available to both the powerful (Geoffrey's Norman patrons and translators) and the powerless (Geoffrey's Welsh readers and translators). For both the Normans and the Welsh, however, the past is always already written in another language. New forms repeatedly displace and re-present (in the double sense of *display again* and *make contemporary again*) the origin. Multilingualism accommodates (and challenges) the differences between these contending claims to originary power. The technology of translation thus simultaneously enables memory and facilitates forgetting. In border historiography, descriptions of translation and etymology capture the linguistic dramas lived in encounters among speakers of unequal power.

Taking Time

Genealogy and etymology, as diachronic modes of discourse, shape time as a further boundary concept pertinent to border writing. The identity of the past per se and the shape of its chronology both become instrumental in the imagination of other kinds of borders (between places, peoples, and languages). In processes of colonization, the history of the colonized people is the final frontier of cultural dominion. This process, however, is also paradoxical, since history writing joins the past to the present while simultaneously establishing the temporal divide between past and present realities. As de Certeau argues, historiography creates the past at the same time that it buries and elides it; history writing is the "construction and erosion of units" (98–100). Erosion (a cartographic metaphor) creates new shapes as it erases old ones, especially since the boundaries at work are not only between the past and the present, but also between both and the future. In this sense, border writing both remembers and forgets the founding divisions of history.

14

Bhabha defines this need to forget in relation to the violence of origins, the always traumatic point of departure in genealogical discourse. Through forgetting, people become unified under a "national will"—an idea credited to Ernest Renan in nineteenth-century France.[19] This process reconfigures time: "Being obliged to forget becomes the basis for remembering the nation, peopling it anew, imagining the possibility of other contending and liberating forms of cultural identification" (Bhabha 161). In the history of Britain, the Britons are represented as repeatedly forgetting the island's founding wound, the land's division by Brutus's sons. Yet they can never forget long enough to reconstitute a unified space. Narratives of this process by the conquered forget to forget, commemorating original violence as a resistance to post-colonial hegemony. Narratives by the conquerors, however, remember to remember, imagining the incorporation of past differences into a new whole. Bhabha dreams toward this unity as a new kind of counternarrative from within borders: "For it is by living on the borderline of history and language, on the limits of race and gender, that we are in a position to translate the differences between them into a kind of solidarity" (170). This vision of unity must come from the edge, whether it aims to resist or conquer. This explains in part why edges are historiographically and culturally productive: they actively encompass paradox.

While history writing configures the past, it also narrates toward the future: "the locus that it carves for the past is equally a fashion of *making a place for a future.*"[20] Geoffrey of Monmouth, for example, turns to the Britons and the Saxons—the historical, not the present, ones—while imagining the future of the Normans. Likewise, the past is the site of counternarratives by Welsh and Breton historians who recover the past to resist the future (see chapters 3 and 7). Geoffrey's contemporary Henry of Huntingdon recognized this function of history explicitly: "Historia igitur preterita quasi presentia uisui representat, futura ex preteritis imaginando diiudicat" (History therefore brings the past into view as though it were present, and allows judgment of the future by representing the past) (4, 5). Historiography thus takes place in a temporal border, ambivalent and bound by temporal conflict.

Within historical narratives, the borders between one period and another represent a further way in which time figures as a boundary concept. Geoffrey's *Historia,* for example, originates a new historiographical shape for Briton history by moving the temporal boundary of Briton dominion from the fifth to nearly the eighth century. The history of Arthur himself takes place liminally, as his reign occupies a space between known historical kings. The narration of Arthur thus creates time, redrawing the boundaries of periodization for an audience frequently engaged in armed conflict over Insular dominion.

The boundaries between historical periods and cultures are of course constituted in writing—in history writing. Indeed, de Certeau argues that history writing itself is a liminal concept: "it [history] is the vibration of limits" (37–38); it has the function of *"symbolizing limits* and thus of enabling us to *go beyond those limits"* (85; emphasis in original). Historiography narrates the edges; historiography written from edges does so all the more urgently. Each boundary concept in fact borders the others. Genealogy, for example, traces group identity through time and also in relation to territory. Likewise, etymology locates language diachronically and ethnically. The border, as a figure of paradox, cuts across multiple concepts, joining them indelibly as it separates them irretrievably. Historiography represents the simultaneity of these paradoxes in time. If, as Lee Patterson has argued, the management of paradox constitutes historical consciousness per se in the Middle Ages (210), border historiography represents a hyperconsciousness that textualizes modes of possession.

The imagination of new forms makes border writing both didactic and performative. For de Certeau, this is one of the functions of historiography in general, where the narrative "both describes and engenders" (40). The paradox of this double performance makes historiography an ambivalent form, like a borderline itself (83). Pierre Bourdieu gives a regionalist interpretation of narrative performativity (223), while Bhabha locates it within a nationalist pedagogy (139–52). As *tempus* is laid across *topos*, *logos*, and the *populus* (sometimes a synonym for *regio* in Latin), the writing of nationalist discourse lives in what Bhabha calls "double-time": narrative creates collective identification (the performative function) by explaining it (the pedagogical function). These narratives and counternarratives contest the stability of time and disrupt the homogenization of communities (149). In the contest of narratives, spatial boundaries become the signs of cultural difference; temporal boundaries signify both historical and cultural difference; the people are "liminal," split between subject and object (151). Every category, then, becomes a border.

In ore gladii

Bhabha's pedagogy of difference risks turning all writing everywhere into *border writing.* The border histories of Arthur, however, share one unique trait: they give his sword a proper name. Furthermore, they use the name to identify significant military encounters. The patterns shaped by strategic naming engage fundamental relations between force, territorial possession, and historical judgment. Representations of Arthur's sword engage the historical roles of medieval swords in general, many of which challenge the boundaries between human bodies, inanimate objects, and abstract principles. Physically, force promises the creation and defense of stable boundaries; socially, this creation disturbs the limits of existing relationships. In this way, coercive boundary formation engenders ambivalence. Swords purvey this ambivalence, as their sym-

16

bolic effects belie the certitude of their literal edges. Swords, moreover, formally incarnate the boundary paradox: their edges divide trenchantly while forming the blade's indivisible unity. Swords' intimate relations with human bodies further enhance their liminal ontology. When named, this unity displaces the ordinary difference between objects and human social systems. As an agent of coercive desire, the named sword becomes a vital artifact of the medieval border imaginary, reaching fundamental cultural relations that are thrown into greatest relief at the edge.

The naming of swords extends back to the origins of heroic culture and is an indigenous European practice.[21] Proper names in general, Claude Lévi-Strauss argued, classify social information (285). When applied to inanimate material, proper names assimilate objects to the social logic of human culture. Names structure and contain social information, and so forge cultural and narrative bonds. Through naming, objects acquire the effects of personhood and an implied potential for subjectivity. Indeed, Leo Spitzer suggested that a name in and of itself marks the subjectivity of a sword.[22] When, for example, the scabbard of *La queste del saint graal* promises that its name and that of its sword will be revealed (206), it assures readers that these objects will take their proper place in human society before the end of the narrative.

Personification and subjectivity together furnish the potential for the object's autonomy and its ability to acquire a reputation independently from the heroes who handle it. Even among unnamed swords, examples of autonomous speaking blades abound, from ninth- and tenth-century survivors who bear inscriptions like "INGLERII ME FECIT" (Inglerii made me)[23] to literary voices who describe their own life and history.[24] The distance from speech to physical action is small indeed. In the Dutch *Roman van Walewein,* for example, the Sword of Two Rings leaps out of its scabbard "pommel over hilt" to bow before Gawain, "as if it were a man who had sinned and sought mercy, wishing to do penance" (161). Roland's sword Durendal also asserts its independence when it remains whole despite Roland's efforts to break it.[25] In numerous other examples, blades shatter at the very moment that human warriors most desire their efficacy. Whenever objects fail to meet human expectations, warriors and readers confront the autonomy of material culture.

With or without names, material objects manifest their own social logic. Interpretive archaeologists engage this logic with traditional (colonial) ethnographic methods, by adopting the perspective of the other: "As we interpret self from the perspective of the other, so we also take the perspective of the object: 'The stone defines the hand,' as surely as the hand defines itself."[26] Taking the object's perspective, it is possible to construct what Igor Kopytoff has called a "biography of things." The biography of a sword, for example, begins with forging. Individual swords may also experience inscription, hilting, baptism, naming, bloodstains, envenoming, relic storage, breakage, gifting, refitting, sale, burial, drowning, and theft. Narrative representations of named swords draw from the object's general biography to construct individual histories with unique and dynamic relations to force and legitimacy.

One of the most important elements of a sword's biography is its relation to human warriors. Since the sword is likewise a vital part of the warrior's biography, their relation is synecdochic rather than metonymic: the sword is a part of the warrior, not merely associated with him. Through synecdoche, the sword shares the characteristics and reputation of the hero, and the hero attracts those of the sword. The lethal weapon completes the heroic body, whose grip on the hilt weakens the usual boundary between the flesh and the world of objects. Indeed, in one Welsh triad, swords rather than men determine likeness.[27] Literary heroes, for example, frequently represent their swords as substitutes for their own being or agency;[28] in death, literary and historical warriors share their grave with their steel companion.[29] Synecdochic substitution opens a double communication between objects and men, in which it becomes difficult to determine who substitutes for whom. The sword's desirable battlefield characteristics, for example, become known as the hero's own performance power.[30] And formidable knights become "Longsword," while weak kings become "Soft-Sword."[31] *La queste del saint graal* presents the most complete example of this ontological contamination with the description of King David's sword in the Ship of Faith. The marvelous properties of the hilt turn the hand that holds it into an engine of destruction: one side of the hilt is made from a Calidonian serpent that prevents the man who touches it from feeling too hot, while the other is made from a fish found only in the Euphrates that causes the man who touches it to forget everything except the reason he picked up the sword (202–3). The powers of the hilt define the ways in which humans are naturally ill suited for war, and create in their place a warrior formed in the image of the sword itself: unimpeded by physical or mental discomfort and divested of biographical memory, the man concentrates absolutely on death.

Allegorical interpretations of weapons also assimilate material form to human identity. Extended allegorical interpretations of armor derive from the letter to the Ephesians, who are called upon to put on the "arma Dei" (arms of God): "loricam iustitiae" (the hauberk of justice) "scutum fidei" (the shield of faith), "galeam salutis" (the helmet of salvation), and the "gladium Spiritus quod est verbum Dei" (sword of the Spirit, which is the word of God).[32] Described as elements of the chivalric portrait in medieval narrative, armor invites ethical as well as spiritual interpretations. The Lady of the Lake in the prose *Lancelot,* for example, offers a complete exposition of knightly armor before Lancelot departure for Arthur's court. After explicating the shield, hauberk, helmet, and lance, she pauses at length on the sword, describing the ethical import of its physical possibilities: "Li doi trenchant senefient que

evaliers doit estre serjans a Nostre Signor et a son pueple...la pointe
iefie obedience" (The two edges signify that the knight must be the
geant of Our Lord and of his people...the point signifies obedience)
251–52). In many cases the sword enjoys a distinct advantage over the human
dy—durability. The blade's ability to survive through time, literally
d figuratively, enables the sword to carry historical memory. Because
e artifact can survive beyond the life of any individual hand, it com-
inicates across time with relative ease, like written narrative itself.
e perceived immortality of the object captures the human desire for
rpetual memory, cogently expressed in Annette Weiner's study of so-
lly prestigious objects in *Inalienable Possessions* as well as in Jean
udrillard's *Système des objects*. Durable, antique objects maintain the
esence of the past and connect both present and past to the future. In
is sense, the naming of legendary swords in narrative performs the
emorial mediations of historiography itself.

The memorial capacities of legendary swords like Excalibur or Duren-
l derive not only from their insertion alongside heroic bodies in his-
cical narrative, but also from the social roles of swords in medieval
lture. Like the narratives that tell of Arthur or Roland, swords recall
nquest. When Edward I challenged Earl Warenne to prove the legality
his land titles, for example, Walter of Guisborough reports that the
rl brandished an antique and rusty sword ("gladium antiquuum et
iginatum") (216). Whatever the exact historical status of the gesture
id some historians doubt its reality), the episode forges a narrative
ik between the past (when the sword, wielded by the earl's ancestors,
nquered the lands) and the present. The display of the rusty sword as
jal proof renders the means of conquest a retroactive sign of the legiti-
acy of forceful occupation. The passage in fact begins "Cito post inqui-
iuit rex," evoking the vocabulary of illegitimate disturbance (*inqui-*
itione) that also characterizes the narration of jurisdictional conflict
Geoffrey's *Historia*. The uniqueness of the object protects the earl's
iim from these disturbances. M. T. Clanchy has called the earl's sword
prop "in the theatre of memory" and concludes that the relation be-
reen objects and property attested by the conveyance of title through
mbolic gesture is deeply embedded in post-Conquest thought on legal
jitimacy (38–41). The testimonial power of swords permeates some
storical narratives, such as the Breton *Gesta regum Britanniae*, where
th narrator and characters call swords to witness ("gladio testante")
g., 56, 206) (see chapter 7). The presence of artifacts in all of the
rthurian histories encodes enduring memories, performing the past so
at it can act upon the future.

Medieval swords commemorate submission as well as domination. In
iperial, royal, and chivalric ceremonies, the ritual transfer of swords
tively reconfigures relationships of authority. Receiving the sword

19

from the altar, emperors, kings, and knights take on ecclesiastical and secular service. In the oldest imperial *ordines,* the emperor accepts to defend the Church by taking the sword from the ecclesiastical hand.[33] Some archaeological survivors materialize the sword's service to God with the inscription "IN NOMINE DOMINI" or citations of prayers.[34] Royal coronation rites echo the language of the imperial rite very closely, perpetuating the sword as a sign of ecclesiastical service.[35] The sword, of course, can easily slide from royal submission to royal power, as demonstrated in a French coronation rite that depicts the duke of Burgundy parading the drawn sword throughout the ceremony.[36] Gradually, the ideology of the sword slid from the royal to the comital to the knightly.[37] The blessing of the sword confers on the soldier the same rights and responsibility of defense as that conferred on monarchs, and frequently in the same language.[38] The representation in narrative of the transmission of swords from one hand to another establishes similar bonds of reciprocal dependence — between characters, ethnic groups, and narrative episodes. From *Beowulf* to the *Chanson de Roland* to the *Cid,* named swords bind men to each other, to God, and to their own past actions.[39] They share, moreover, in the organizing force of proper names in general.[40]

Medieval rulers and pontiffs even debated their conflicts over submission and service through sword metaphors. In order to defend their interpretations of relative authority, theologians and lawyers deployed what became known as the "argument of the two swords." This complex exegetical tradition is built on a brief exchange between Jesus and his disciples as narrated in Luke: having learned of Jesus's imminent arrest, the disciples look around for a means of resistance and cry out: "Ecce gladii duo hic" (Look, two swords are here), to which Jesus replies: "Satis est" (That is sufficient).[41] The multiple and competing exegeses of this passage maintained the sword at the center of medieval thought on the representation of power. Ideological tensions between princely governments and the papacy pulled the sword in different directions, but always with a focus on the fundamental dynamics of constraint. The conflicts argued through the allegory of the two swords concern who has the authority, de jure, to legitimately coerce whom, and when.[42] The coercive impact of the figure, in fact, outweighs the relatively benign notion of "spheres of authority" (a concept based on "cultural stuff" rather than boundaries). The "sword pericope" (as Gerard Caspary dubbed it) became a sharp figure for drawing the boundary between spiritual and temporal jurisdiction over the earth, the two broadest jurisdictions of the medieval landscape. The details of the theological and constitutional implications of the arguments are less important here than the fact that throughout the medieval period the most pressing issues of spiritual and constitutional jurisdiction were theorized and "proved" in the image of a sword.

In knighting rituals and chivalric portraits, coronation rites and legal exegesis, battle and burial, swords mediate and signify jurisdictional relationships in human society. They enjoy singular, synecdochic relations with the heroic body; as the hand on the hilt moves to strike or to give, the object engages a broader relation with the social body. In battle, the blade inscribes the answer to jurisdictional dispute indelibly on the body of the defeated. In political theology and ritual, the image of the sword signifies the relation between spiritual and temporal jurisdictions, and the reciprocal obligations of lords (divine, ecclesiastical, and lay) and the men who defend them. When the object moves from one hand to another, it can signify either the plenitude or the limits of the giver's power. These movements occur at the crossroads of social and economic interests, of generosity and coercion. In narrative, they traverse historical relations between the conquered and the conquering.

Caliburn, Escalibor, Excalibur

From a historiographical perspective, Geoffrey of Monmouth gave birth to Arthur's sword. In the *Historia,* the presence of the sword's name organizes Arthur's principal military achievements into a visible group that traces the boundaries of Briton dominion. The sword name focuses the reader's attention on the shape of these boundaries and the means by which they are established. Geoffrey's *Historia* names Arthur's sword before or during three moments of conflict: the battle against Cheldric's Saxon army, the duel with Frollo at Paris, and the battle against Lucius's Roman army. In the *Historia*'s reception, this pattern is never repeated exactly. Writers not only change the distribution of namings within the three episodes, they also add new ones and eliminate inherited ones. These changes to the sword's biography reflect different approaches to the representation of legitimate authority. In each case, the group of episodes defined by the repetition of the name communicates the historical and ideological vision of the narrative as a whole.

Like most names attached to swords, *Caliburn* has provoked etymological commentary. As might be expected, the majority of sword names refer rather transparently to the characteristics of an effective weapon: hard, durable, and resistant.[43] *Caliburn* itself seems derived from a relatively rare Latin noun for *steel;*[44] the prefix *es-* attached to *Caliburn* on the Continent has a seemingly emphatic value.[45] T. Atkinson Jenkins claims further that the prefix originated in "clerical hands" (12) because it also modifies a series of words related to religious practice. Jenkins thus imagines the clerical redactors of the French Arthurian cycle affixing the *es-* to *calibor,* like a new hilt for an old blade, as they appropriate the name for their own ideological purposes.[46] In each case, the act of naming and the name's linguistic form signal the sword's place in a mental landscape of authority, power, and social obligation.

The meaning of the *inventio* of an Arthurian sword bound to Briton imperialism sharpens when compared with the emblems of power and legitimacy associated with Arthur in chronicles prior to Geoffrey's. In the *Historia Brittonum*, Arthur carries an image of Mary across his shoulders (or on his shield) (76); William of Malmesbury interprets the image as integral to Arthur's defensive covering ("armis suis insuerat").[47] In the *Annales Cambriae*, Arthur bears the Holy Cross (or an image of it) (85). Both of these objects (or images) reference the divine sanction of Arthur's battles. They do not, however, literally produce victory as the sword does. By naming the sword, Geoffrey conjoins an offensive instrument to Arthur's traditional defensive symbols, and then displaces them completely.

In the interplay between idea and action, between political theory and its lethal execution, the sword does not merely function as a symbol (the physical embodiment of an abstract principle); it has the physical capacity to enforce the consequences of that principle. The representation of the named sword thus both performs and comments on acts of conquest. Each appearance of the name interrogates the legitimacy of territorial expansion and boundary formation. Legitimacy surfaces trenchantly because the sword may also be manipulated for illegitimate action: its physical capacities may be exercised against its symbolic valence. The named sword, as emblem and artifact, thus incorporates the conflict between force and law that is at stake throughout Briton history. Arthurian historiography stages the actions of the sword in relation to past and future in order to define the limits of legitimacy in the present. Because of the sword's capacity to combine lethal force with abstract theory, the path of conquest marked by its presence expresses attitudes toward the imperial journey: when Caliburn draws blood, the reader can draw conclusions.

Ultimately, swords write borders, in the sense that warfare painfully negotiates the geopolitical contours of the land. Borders, however, also write swords, in the sense that geopolitical instability generates historiography acutely concerned with judging acts of force. The chapters that follow here show how Arthurian historiography writes Arthur's sword and how this historiographical tradition (which tells the history of jurisdictional conflicts) takes shape in disputed regions. I hope to show that while it can be a mistake to make too much of the struggles of medieval historiography, it is also a mistake to make too little of the urgencies and exigencies of writing about the past in the Middle Ages.

Totius insulae

CHAPTER 2

Historia in marchia
Geoffrey of Monmouth's Colonial Itinerary

Arthurian historiography emerges as a mode of border writing with Geoffrey of Monmouth's *Historia regum Brittaniae*. Certainly, Geoffrey is not the first to mention Arthur nor the first to attempt a comprehensive Insular history, but his *Historia* does both on an unprecedented scale. Born of border culture, the *Historia* engages Norman colonization by portraying the Britons' colonial history. Conquered conquerors (like the English), the Britons provoke ambivalent judgments of aggression: each time they embark on colonial expansion, Geoffrey both glorifies and laments their ambition.[1] The *Historia* thus equivocates between the admiration and condemnation of conquering history; it mediates between colonial and postcolonial imaginations. Throughout, the twin effects of memory and amnesia keep the *Historia* on the edge.

Geoffrey's own border identity shapes this history of colonial desire. The epithet *Monemutensis* locates him at the edge of England, in the Welsh March formed by Norman colonization. Located in Wales on the banks of the river Wye just west of the Severn River, Monmouth's castle had been held since 1066 by Breton and Norman lords installed by Norman conquerors.[2] Monmouth thus harbored multiple cultures (Welsh, Breton, Norman, and English), actively communicating in several languages. Scholars have tried to identify Geoffrey as a member of one or another of these groups on the basis of perceived biases and parentage.[3] Yet the interactive and often improvised identifications at work in a colonial border like twelfth-century Monmouthshire impede the deduction of ethnicity from politics or blood relationships. Our understanding of Geoffrey must thus remain in the multiple zone *Monemutensis.*

Geoffrey did not write the *Historia* in Monmouth, however, but in Oxford (upstream from London along the Thames). Geoffrey's epithet from the periphery thus arises once he penetrates an authoritative center, suggesting that border identity matters most urgently in the metropole. Geoffrey's second epithet returns him to the colonial periphery: since 1151, he has been known as "Bishop of Saint Asaph's." Although consecrated, Geoffrey never traveled to northeastern Wales to occupy his seat because disputes among the Welsh prevented access to the region.[4] The literal impossibility of Geoffrey's arrival at the scene of colonization testifies to successful Welsh enforcement of a new boundary between their colonial periphery and Norman colonizing desire. The intimate yet antagonistic dynamics of colonial contact thus arrest Geoffrey's identity in transit, preventing his departure from the metropole (Gerald of Wales will later stumble down a similar path). Suspended in Oxford, Geoffrey's personal itinerary remains haunted by the ghost of the Saint Asaph's episcopacy.

Around the time of Geoffrey's death in 1154, Wace completed a French translation of the *Historia* in Normandy. This *translatio* expanded the range of an already itinerate text. Indeed, with more than two hundred extant manuscripts, the *Historia* has a rich history of Insular and Continental reception that is only beginning to be understood. In recent years, the textual corpus has been under an intense scrutiny that has generated a series of invaluable publications.[5] Although much textual territory remains uncharted, notions of the standard or "vulgate" text have already changed substantially.[6] In reaction to this new research, many scholars have abandoned older editions (by Acton Griscom and Edmond Faral) in favor of Neil Wright's edition of Bern, Burgerbibliothek MS 568. Wright, however, clearly indicates that the Bern manuscript witnesses the *Historia*'s reception in Normandy.[7] David Dumville argues further that the Bern text probably circulated *only* in Normandy (22–25). I will therefore discuss the Bern text along with Norman reception (in chapter 5). Here, I will cite from Faral's critical edition in order to attribute the strongest possible author function to *Galfridus Monemutensis*. Although Faral's text does have flaws, as Wright points out, it nonetheless represents "a better picture of the standard version" than any other edition published so far.[8]

The text's itinerancy is most evident in the three different dedications. Until recently, critics used the dedications to date different textual recensions on the assumption that they must address allies rather than antagonists—and Robert of Gloucester, Waleran of Meulan, and Stephen of Blois were rarely at peace during the 1130s and 1140s. Critics have also argued that the dedications, in conjunction with the *Historia*'s seemingly propagandistic value, represent Geoffrey's allegiances to the monarchy. Uncertainty about the dating of the dedications, however, precludes any certain conclusions about political meaning.[9] Appeals to peace and *quietatione* would be appropriate any time from 1135 (when Stephen, Henry I's nephew, seized the crown from Henry's daughter Matilda) to 1154 (when Matilda's son, Henry II, ascended the throne). Robert of Gloucester initially accepted Stephen, but then supported Matilda (his own half sister) after June 1138.[10] Meanwhile, Waleran, of the powerful Norman Beaumont family, strengthened his attachments to Stephen and received from him the earldom of Worcester.[11] If we imagine Geoffrey completing the *Historia* between 1136 and 1138 (as most critics do) and distributing it until his death, then the period in which Geoffrey controlled some of the text's dissemination corresponds exactly to the tumultuous transition from Norman to Angevin rule. Taken as a group of statements conceived over time by Geoffrey himself, the dedications witness a subtle negotiation that both supports and resists superior powers. By alternately claiming and disavowing his textual authority, Geoffrey unsettles paradigms of domination.

With the first dedication, Geoffrey improvises a discursive relation between Robert and a glorious Briton past. Robert himself had recently improvised an alliance with the Briton present. John Gillingham has shown that after the Welsh prince Morgan ousted Stephen's men from the castle at Caerleon and claimed the kingship of Glamorgan, Robert forged an alliance with the Welsh in common cause against Stephen.[12] Gillingham goes on to argue that the *Historia* provides a venerable history for the Welsh in order to legitimate Robert's otherwise unseemly alliance with the barbarians (115–16). The *Historia* also legitimates Gloucester's antiquity over other earldoms.[13] From this perspective, the *Historia* originates in military conflict over territorial control and proceeds to imagine new boundaries by redrawing their history. Even at a later date, the dedication to Robert serves as a plea for peace, for Robert's bellicosity resulted in a great deal of local destruction.[14] The single dedication thus appeals to Robert to seek peaceful rather than violent solutions to political problems.

Although the idea that the text appeals to peace can be constructed from its interaction with contemporary politics, the dedication itself makes a very specific appeal: Geoffrey invites Robert to correct ("corrigatur") the text so that it no longer appears to come from Geoffrey but rather from one descended ("generauit") from Henry, "illustrious king of the English" (72). In effect, Geoffrey asks that Robert, as a semblance of his royal father ("alterum Henricum"), incorporate Geoffrey's genealogy of kings into the contemporary royal genealogy.[15] By asking Robert to efface the appearance of Geoffrey's anterior authority, Geoffrey invites him to exercise the power of colonization discursively. Simultaneously, Geoffrey subverts the power relation by providing the original text himself: he installs himself as the textual patron and gives Robert the role of "correcting" client. In the asymmetrical power relations of colonial contact, Geoffrey proposes a countersymmetry that empowers him as the originator of a text he claims he hopes to disown. He asserts a didactic authority that turns the *Historia*'s narrative of violent transgressions into an erroneous precedent—from the destruction of Troy through the exile of Cadwallader (strikingly resonate with the name of the newly powerful Welsh leader Cadwaladr ap Gruffydd ap Cynan).[16] Robert's "correction" of the bloody implications of Briton history suggests a political resolution of present civil discord.

The double dedication to Robert and Waleran improvises even more audaciously. Wright has proposed that this dedication postdates Robert's desertion of Stephen and that Geoffrey sought to reconcile the antagonists (*Bern* xv). The address to the earls of Gloucester and Worcester thus represents a form of diplomacy. Referring to Waleran as "altera regni nostra columpna" (our other pillar of the realm) (*Bern* xiii), Geoffrey casts the warring neighbors as twin supports of the realm in an ironic inversion of their twin destruction of the Severn River Valley: in this period, the conflict over England's governance became an almost local dispute in this relatively small corner of southern England.[17] The dedication makes Waleran not only the realm's second support, but a descendent of Charlemagne and the embodiment (like Robert) of wisdom joined to military prowess. By ascribing the *Historia*'s inspiration to Waleran, however, Geoffrey implies that the narrative of civil discord *was* inspired by contemporary strife and that Waleran is responsible for much of it (he had not, after all, honored his oath to Matilda).

Like Robert, Waleran can correct this history by seeking political settlement. Geoffrey appeals directly to his correcting power, asking Waleran to take the work "sub tutela tua" (under your tutelage). Geoffrey disowns the very origin of the text when he asks for protection under Waleran's tree so as to make music on the reed pipe "musae tue" (of your muse) (*Bern* xiii). The idea of Waleran's tutelage may be more than rhetorical flattery, since Waleran did write in Latin and the *Historia* was known in his entourage.[18] Waleran may indeed have adopted the *Historia* as his own colonial refrain. Geoffrey, however, aims to curtail Waleran's territory by deploying a rhetoric of resemblance (*altera*) that subtly accuses the two pillars of the realm. Moreover, Martin Shichtman and Laurie Finke argue that by addressing rivals, Geoffrey seeks to profit from their competition, an antagonistic strategy necessitated by the inherent inequalities of the patron-client relationship (19–20). Yet Geoffrey's request that both Waleran and Robert make the text their own overturns these inequalities (akin to those of colonial relationships in some ways). The double dedication thus exposes the malleability of relations of domination by conflating textual authority with political authority. It turns the differences between Geoffrey and his patrons, and between the patrons themselves, into powerful resemblances.

Geoffrey reconfigures this play of resemblance in the third dedication by naming Stephen in the text previously addressed to Robert, and Robert in the text previously addressed to Waleran. Stephen is now invited to correct the text and, as king, to incorporate its genealogy into the royal line; Robert is now "our other pillar." Geoffrey mobilizes Stephen and Robert's genealogical resemblance by reminding them that they both descend from Henry and that they possess his venerable past as their own. At the same time, Geoffrey maintains himself in a slight difference: when he asks for protection under Robert's tree, he refers to "muse mee" (my muse) rather than "your muse" (*Bern* xiv). By retaining the inspiration for himself, Geoffrey takes full responsibility for the text but asks Robert (in Stephen's hearing) to take responsibility for his per-

son. This dedication rearranges the doubleness of the patron-client relation, just as it rearranges the names in the text. Here, the configuration
of responsibility for the *Historia* (among Geoffrey, Stephen, Robert, and
Henry I) negotiates a settlement of differences between political rivals
and between empires past and present. In a sense, Geoffrey authors (and
authorizes) the reconciliation that he eventually witnessed in 1153 when
Stephen recognized Henry's grandson as his heir.[19]

All three dedications implicate political adversaries with intimate connections in order to censure rather than support their activities. A similar censure, and boundary equivocation, surfaces in the closing historiographical dedication. Here, Geoffrey asserts his own textual patronage
over contemporary historians. He makes them his clients, giving them
a script of Briton history that they may copy but not replace. Repetition
can iterate the refrain Geoffrey established and thereby extend the Britons' historiographical territory. To patrol the border of this territory,
Geoffrey mobilizes the ancient Briton book brought "ex Britannia" by
Walter: lacking this book, Caradoc of Llancarfan is to limit himself to
Welsh history and William of Malmesbury and Henry of Huntingdon to
Saxon (303). These ethnic boundaries imply territorial disputes over the
domain of the past; Geoffrey defines any effort to redraw historiographical jurisdictions as illegitimate. At the same time, according to Valerie
Flint, the epilogue borders on disciplinary parody. Whether serious or
facetious, the epilogue's principle of division accords with the boundary
concerns of the *Historia* itself and the border imagination from which it
emerged.

The ambivalence that characterizes Geoffrey's opening and closing
statements permeates the *Historia*. Narrating the Britons' civil wars and
interactions with invaders from across the seas, Geoffrey invites readers
to consider the legitimacy of successful conquest but without consistently orienting their responses. Often, he makes the judgment of guilt
and innocence difficult, as Robert Hanning has shown with Anacletus:
on the one hand, Brutus coerces him at sword point to betray his people
(both condemnable); on the other, the betrayal liberates the Trojans (the
laudable goal).[20] Similarly, Geoffrey condemns Maximianus's imperial
ambitions because they weakened the island, while defining the Britons'
greatness by their ability to subdue foreign peoples (Geoffrey 167). Hanning argues further that Geoffrey divides his colonial ambivalence toward the Normans among different groups, attributing to him a "dual
vision of history" that shows both human agency and subjection to Fortune.[21] William Brandt has shown that this dualism, or paradox, is typical of twelfth-century imperializing histories. It arises from the conflict
between clerical and aristocratic modes of perception. In the clerical mode, action disturbs norms illegitimately; in the aristocratic mode,
the maintenance of prestige requires action. This "basic incoherence in
the medieval world-view," however, did not create a conscious paradox,

for it was normal to posit quiescence as legitimate for others while seeing one's own actions as legitimately expansionist (79–80). In the *Historia*, peace and stability depend on *quietatione*, while honor and prestige
require a family to increase its holdings — "familiam suam augmentare"
(Geoffrey 238). To augment one's family, of course, one must disturb existing boundaries, creating *inquietatione*. Paradoxically again, peace engenders both the desire for expansion and the resources necessary for effective disturbances. As relations alternate between peace and war,
boundaries remain inevitably unstable.

In the early twelfth century, then, Geoffrey emerged as a "border intellectual"[22] from his own unstable boundary along England's western
edge. From Oxford, he appropriates a central position of authority by invoking Norman patrons in his dedications. These discursive relations
empower him to overturn colonial history, yet his narrative returns repeatedly to scenes of colonizing conquest — the description of the island,
Brutus's arrival there, the Romans' several conquests, the Britons' colonization of Armorica, and the Saxons' colonization of Britain. Each of
these encounters establishes domination through spatial, linguistic, and
erotic desire; each reconfigures the results of strategic resemblance. The
variable consequences of coercive contact demonstrate that no single
model can explain patterns of domination: the results only look predictable
retrospectively. As Brutus surveys the fecund land, or Corineus embraces Goemagog's shoulders, or Vortigern mouths his first Saxon words,
or Arthur dons a coat of human beards, we witness exemplary scenes of
colonial ambivalence.

Descriptio Britanniae

As outlined in chapter 1, border writing foregrounds landscape as a cultural signifier. Geoffrey roots history in the land through the opening
descriptio of the island, and then elaborates spatial signification by signaling the geopolitical consequences of historical relationships. The *Historia's* cartographic representations are typical of colonial literatures, as
recent investigations of nineteenth- and twentieth-century colonialisms
amply demonstrate. Islands in particular signify colonial ambivalence:
they are both "fixed colonial territory" (in an imperialist mode) and a
"dynamic space of becoming" (in a postcolonial mode).[23] In both medieval and modern contexts, land is bound to genealogical and etymological strategies: the *descriptio* is *gentis* and *temporis* as well as *terrae*.

Pointing to the Britons' historiographical erasure, Geoffrey states explicitly that he seeks to remember their forgotten history, which he has
been unable to discover in Bede and Gildas (71). This amnesia has changed
the shape of the past; Geoffrey claims to restore the original shape, preserved in oral memories as reliable as written records (71). These memories extend from the distant past like a refrain, preserving Briton terri-

tory. Throughout the *Historia*, however, alternate memories undermine the integrity of the Briton border and the linear progress of history. Geoffrey's text comes to occupy a double-time between memory and amnesia: it remembers the imperial past of a colonized people who became the indigenous Other of later conquerors. In a postcolonial performance, Geoffrey creates Briton identity in narrative as he teaches its contours. The word *Britannia* at the head of the first sentence after the dedication literally holds the place of this created memory.

Geoffrey goes on to describe the island in terms that evoke what Pratt calls "imperial eyes." Drawing on the landscape narratives of Gildas, Bede, the *Historia Brittonum*, and Henry of Huntingdon, Geoffrey takes possession of the island through writing. The landscape narrative begins as a pastoral countermemory to the violent experience of territorial conquest. The island is the "best" ("insularam optima"), a most "pleasant site" ("amoeno situ") full of natural resources and suitable for cultivation (73). The catalog of admirable qualities implies already a human presence,[24] yet it is a presence forgetful of its own coercive designs. The force of Geoffrey's pastoral will is evident when his *descriptio* is compared with Henry of Huntingdon's. Although Henry also describes the land in aesthetically superlative terms ("beatissima...insularum," "insularum nobilissima") (11, 12), he concludes with a summary of the island's names—witnesses of successive conquests: "quondam Albion nomen fuit, postea uero Britannia, nunc autem Anglia" (Albion was once the name, then Britain, and now England) (12). Geoffrey, forgetful of the past and the present, refers only to *Britannia*.

Geoffrey rearranges his textual inheritance to emphasize the land's generative potential by grouping all the pastoral elements together before describing the cities. Following Gildas, he incorporates the island's principal rivers into the landscape; reflecting the island's eventual tripartite division, he adds the Humber to the list. The emendation, however, turns Gildas's anthropomorphic metaphor of the Thames and the Severn as two arms reaching out to gather in the world's riches (90) into a monster with "tria brachia" (72). Indeed, whereas Gildas makes the island a bride bejeweled with cities ("electa veluti sponsa monilibus diversis ornata") (90), Geoffrey's three-armed figure wears the tattered garb of crumbling cities ("in desertis locis squalescunt") (73). Geoffrey's disintegrating cities break with the synchronic tableau of his sources; his allusions to violent conflict also contrast meaningfully with Bede's harmonious landscape.[25] Just when he has established the aesthetic of time's absence through the pastoral landscape, he exposes the colonial cataracts that trouble his imperial vision. The decrepit cities deconstruct the myth of metropolitan power and the fantasy of durable empire.

Having set the urban blight of the present within the beautiful landscape of the past, Geoffrey turns to the people responsible for the decay. By describing the people last, Geoffrey underscores not only the cultural signification of the landscape (which originates with humans), but also the human source of its destruction. Like the landscape description, the ethnographic outline introduces several troubling temporal disruptions. Recent conquest, for example, prompts Geoffrey to add the Normans to the list of four peoples he inherited from his sources. Geoffrey names the Normans first; he goes on to reverse the order of his sources by naming the Britons before the Saxons, Picts, and Scots (73). The list underscores the filial relation between the most ancient and the most recent peoples (the Normans and Britons at the head of the list) while alluding to the historiographer's perspectival problems. The Normans' history, for example, begins after the *Historia*. And Geoffrey refers immediately to the Britons' submission to the Picts and the Saxons. The list thus testifies to the difficulty of the memory that Geoffrey sets out to create: through the combined countermemories of the Scots, Picts, Saxons, and Normans, the Britons' history has become precarious. In the end, Geoffrey's *descriptio* offers none of the nostalgic comfort proper to the landscape genre. Even at this originary moment, boundary fissures dominate the island's surface.

Promissa insula

Geoffrey does not merely preface the *Historia* with a *descriptio*, he makes the landscape a historical character. When the Britons first arrive at the island, Brutus possesses the land through both force and language, in what R. Howard Bloch calls "an eponymic fusion of names, land, and language."[26] The land's genealogy thus coincides with the Britons'; their divisions become those of the landscape. A unified territory becomes the ideal achievement of a unified people, and its fragmentation a sign of ethnic disintegration. The hunt for land begins in Troy, a space literally "removed from the map."[27] Engaging in the hunt as a married man, Brutus cannot build his patrimony through kinship ties, on the model of the "predatory kinship" that Eleanor Searle discerns among the Normans. Instead, kinship commemorates alliances forged by the sword. Marriages are thus retrospective rather than prospective (with the exception of the Briton proposal to the Roman Maximianus, who subsequently initiates Britain's fall). As a result, the obligation to acquire new land, along with the absence of empty land, repeatedly promotes political instability, just as it often did in medieval societies. From the Britons' first thought of liberty to their last gasp of sovereignty, they imagine their authentic identity through territorial possession.

The defeated and enslaved Trojans express their desire for liberty specifically as a desire for reterritorialization: they ask Pandrasus for land, either in Greece or elsewhere ("aliarum terrarum nationes").[28] When he refuses, the Trojans rebel and defeat him through cunning and force. As victors, the Trojans again demand the right to depart for "alias nationes," with ships, provisions, and Pandrasus's daughter Innogen. *Nationes* takes on a spatial dimension, implying the conquest of already occupied space. The Trojan hunt for land, then, envisages colonization from its inception. Once conquered, this land will be ruled by the descendents of a Greek mother and Trojan father. The Briton genealogy is thus founded on the union of conqueror and conquered. The Briton offspring of this marriage efface the boundary between antagonists, promising a future of peace and reconciliation. In this regard, Brutus's marriage resembles many of those contracted in colonial dynamics, from twelfth-century Britain to nineteenth-century India.[29] Geoffrey's patron Robert incarnates the generative potential of these kinds of colonial intimacy, for his mother is rumored to have been Nesta, sister of the Welsh prince Staffyd ap Rhys.[30] Most of Geoffrey's representations, however, portray the dangers rather than the advantages of such intimate colonial contact.

Before arriving in Britain, Brutus passes over both unoccupied and occupied land. The island of Loegecia, uninhabited and agriculturally rich, presents the peaceful option for settlement. Loegecia's *descriptio* echoes Britain's, with its plentiful game and decrepit cities:[31] both landscapes portray the troubling end of a civilization not yet begun. When Brutus asks the oracle Diana to prophesy the Trojans' destiny, she offers a typical colonial cartography: his realm ("patria sua") is a deserted island ("insula deserta"), empty and free for the taking, where he will build another Troy ("altera Troja"); ultimately, his race will subjugate the world ("[t]otius terrae") (84). Although Diana's description resembles Loegecia itself ("insula in oceano," "deserta"), the Trojans never consider that this could be their new *patria*. As the site of a former civilization whose traces remain in the urban ruins, Loegecia is already inhabited by history. In fact, Loegecia is not *deserta* at all but full of conquered ghosts, and so too crowded for the Trojans.

When the Trojans, augmented by Corineus's men, land in Aquitaine, the *Historia* presents the second option for land acquisition — armed conquest. Having anchored in the Loire, the Trojans explore "situmque regni" (the site of the realm) (85). The description of the land as a *regnum* distinguishes it from all previous references (which include *nationes, locam, terra,* and *patria*). A *regnum* is defined by its boundary (*fines*), which marks the difference between inhabitants and outsiders (*externam gentem*). When the Trojans land at the shore, they thus enter a governed civilization where their explorations constitute trespassing. Accordingly, King Goffar asks whether they intend war or peace, that is, whether they intend to recognize the limits of the realm ("fines regni"): Corineus answers an emphatic *no* by smashing in the head of Goffar's messenger with his bow (85–86). In the war that ensues over the Trojans' trespassing, Brutus seeks nothing less than to empty the inconveniently full land through genocide: "volens infelicem gentem usque ad unum delere" ([he] want[ed] to obliterate the unfortunate people down to the last one)

(88). Since this goal turns out to be impracticable, and since Aquitaine is not the "promissam insulam" (90), Brutus takes advantage of a lull in the hostilities to set sail.

As Brutus arrives at the island with his band of Trojan exiles, Geoffrey again identifies the land as an *amoeno situ*: seeing through Brutus's imperial eyes, he forgets the crumbled cities his own eyes have seen. While in these early contacts Brutus clearly exemplifies Pratt's confident "monarch-of-all-I-see" (204–5), Geoffrey's historical amnesia proves fleeting. He subsequently implies ambivalence in every colonizing gesture. Most important, the island is not deserted (as prophesied) but inhabited by giants. The fact of precedence thus immediately blurs Brutus's imperializing gaze; he is not the origin of Insular civilization but an (at least) second-comer. Brutus and his Trojan companions establish a provisional boundary between themselves and the natives by driving the giants into mountain caves; the giants return, however, and kill a number of Britons (90–91). Brutus reestablishes the desired difference between the ruled and the unruly by slaughtering all the giants except Goemagog, whom he saves for a wrestling match with Corineus, "qui cum talibus congredi ultra modum aestuabat" (who burned beyond measure for such a fight) (91). Geoffrey has already established Corineus's intimate relations with giants by comparing him to one when the Trojans first meet him (85) and explaining that he chose his lands because of their large population of giants, which he delights ("delectabat") in wrestling (91). Corineus's excessive desire to touch indigenous bodies expresses a colonial desire to resemble the native; his particular desire to *wrestle* the native exposes the violent antagonism of this desire for the almost-same. Corineus forcefully exacts dominion from the play of his similarity to giants.

Corineus approaches the encounter "maximo gaudio," "abjectis armis" (with the greatest joy, casting down his arms). With great pleasure, Corineus divests himself of the signs of his civilized difference from the native. The contest begins with their locked embrace: "et alter alterum vinculis brachiorum adnectens crebris afflatibus aera vexant" (and each binding the other by fastening his arms, pressing together, they shake the air with their breath) (91). After Goemagog breaks three of Corineus's ribs, Corineus heaves him onto his shoulders and carries him some distance before throwing him over a cliff: "At ille, per abrupta saxorum cadens, in mille frustra dilaceratus est et fluctus sanguine maculavit" (There, by falling onto broken rocks, he is torn to a thousand pieces and he stained the waves with his blood) (92). The fragmentation of the indigenous body on the shore figures the fatal multiplicity of differences in the border. The stain of giant-blood in the water that conveyed the colonizing settlers to the island marks—but only briefly—the contamination of colonial power. Geoffrey's own mixing of present and past tenses casts the event into double-time, witnessing the split subjectivity of colonial experience. When people subsequently name the place "Goemagog's Leap," they commemorate the split between the old order (Goemagog himself) and its destruction.[32] The name glosses over coercion, however, by implying that the native removed himself voluntarily.

After the destruction of the indigenous giants, the island's colonization continues with land distribution. Once Brutus has divided the *patria* among his men, Geoffrey presents the new boundaries as timeless elements of the landscape by noting the rapid disappearance of signs of conquest: "ut brevi tempore terram ab aevo inhabitatam censeres" (after a brief time you would have thought the land inhabited since forever) (90). This declaration effaces the temporal boundary between the Trojan dominion and all previous ones, appropriating all time for the Trojans.[33] The willful forgetting of prior history, however, has threatened Briton ownership of this past (as the *descriptio* has already indicated). Brutus's laudable achievement thus depends on a historiographic maneuver that Geoffrey will condemn when deployed against the Trojans' descendents.

The change of name from *Albion* to *Britannia* seals the possession of land and time. Geoffrey explains that Brutus intended to preserve the memory of his founding; in the same fashion the men are known as *Britons* and the language (formerly called "curvum Graecum") as *Britannica* (90–91). The narration of these changes, however, presents a troubling alternative memory, for it preserves the older, threatening identities of the giants and the Greeks. Indeed, as Jean-Yves Tilliette observes, "uncurved Greek" is nothing less than the classical tradition (229). The Trojan speakers of "curved Greek" thus distort a history of Greek triumph that Brutus intends to forget. Although Brutus does fuse his genealogy with the new landscape, the old name of his language reminds us that his progeny are half Greek (through Innogen) and thus conceived in an anxious union between conqueror and vanquished.

Equally disturbing to future unity is the fact that Brutus's eponymous achievement does not cover the whole island. Following Brutus's example, Corineus names his land and his people after himself—*Corinea*, "corrupted" to *Cornubia* (91). Cornubia (Cornwall) thus takes shape externally to Britain, yet vaguely included in it. Unifying solutions to divisive strife will repeatedly originate in Cornwall: as O. J. Padel first emphasized, five of the nine major dynasties, including Arthur's, originate in Cornwall (5–8); even in Merlin's prophecies, relief comes from the Bear of Cornwall.[34] Cornwall can reunite the island because it lies both inside and outside of Britain, set out in a cartography of paradox before Britain's own division. Geoffrey's construction of Cornwall as a salvific, independent space, however, collides with the region's contemporary captivity. At the time of Geoffrey's writing, Cornwall was subjected to complicated, and still somewhat obscure, jurisdictional disruptions. According to Judith Green's assessment, Reginald son of Henry I (and therefore Robert of Gloucester's half brother) married the daughter of William lord of Cardinham and drew the county away from Stephen's influence in 1140. Stephen's appointed earl briefly ousted Reginald, but Reginald regained the territory and held it to his death in 1175.[35] Cornwall's contemporary resonances render the region a space of equivocation, typical of Geoffrey's other border constructs. Indeed, it remained, and remains, an unstable margin of British identity.[36] From its inception, then, Insular history occupies fragmented space.

Brutus concludes the island's colonization with urban architecture, building a city on the shore ("littora") of the Thames (92) (the first of the *descriptio*'s three rivers). If the Severn bounds the west and the Humber the north, the Thames represents the boundary of the island per se, the inland expression of the ocean edge. New Troy thus occupies the shore, recalling both Brutus's arrival from across the ocean and Goemagog's burial. Brutus's city inaugurates a recurring practice of architectural innovation as a sign of completed conquest, one that echoes the Norman castle-building practices of the twelfth and thirteenth centuries.[37] Throughout the *Historia*, building projects commemorate the unification of the realm.

The unification contained in New Troy, however, lasts no longer than a sentence. Narrating the name's creation, Geoffrey is drawn into an alternate, prospective chronology that leads directly to fratricidal war. The etymology refers to the conflict that breaks out between Lud and Nennius when Lud tries to change the city's name to *Kaerlud* to commemorate his own civic improvements (92). Lud's renaming threatens to efface the memory of his predecessors, just as Brutus's displaced *Albion*. While Lud (like Brutus) looks to the future, Nennius (like Geoffrey) defends the past. The simultaneity of these perspectives disrupts the chronological thread, introducing discord into the founding moment of peaceful unification.[38] In the compressed time of the etymology, Geoffrey thus thematizes the loss of memory. He holds the narrative in check by deferring to Gildas, who (Geoffrey claims) has already provided a superior account of the war. Since Gildas's history does not in fact contain such a story, the name *Gildas* holds the place of an absent history. The reader, of course, can already perceive that Lud won out, since *Kaerlud* leads to *London* more readily than *Trinovantum* does. As in the *descriptio*, the simultaneity of temporal references problematizes the project of history and the prospect of legitimation.

The suggestion of fratricidal conflict contained in the naming of New Troy introduces the conflicts that will arise from the partition of Brutus's patrimony among his three sons. After Brutus's death, they divide the island, naming each part after themselves (Loegria, Kambria, Albania). Geoffrey's description of this process is fraught with temporal discord, as he marks off Kambria along the Severn (whose origin has yet to be narrated) and refers to the twelfth-century names of both Kambria and Albania (93). Cornwall, of course, is not part of the division, having already been established in a line of descent separate from Brutus's. The division of the island founds a "disunited kingdom,"[39] generating long-term topographical trauma from which the island has yet to recover. While the partition of conquered territory reflects some contemporary Norman inheritance practices,[40] it also recalls their often violent consequences. The rest of the narrative recounts the ambivalent cycle of efforts to erase these lines from the landscape.

The two rivers that mark the boundaries of the three realms, the Severn and the Humber, soon receive their names from the death of figures who transgress boundaries. Humber the Hun disturbs the Insular border when he invades Albania and kills Albanactus. Locrinus and Kamber march against him, and he drowns in the river that comes to bear his name (93). Like Goemagog, Humber is submerged in the water that defines the limit; the boundary again contains and destroys the agent that threatened to displace it. Similarly, the Severn takes its name from Habren, Locrinus's daughter by Estrildis (a German princess from Humber's entourage). Locrinus's Cornish wife Gwendolen kills him in battle and has the mixed-race daughter and her foreign mother put to death in the river (95). She then propagates legislation to name the river after the girl. Gwendolen wants to honor the girl because she was the daughter of her own husband—the same reason apparently that she would want to kill her. This "spatial deployment of collective memory," as Monika Otter calls it (70), literally encodes history in the land. This honor, however, has been both preserved and forgotten, as the "britannica lingua" still calls the river *Habren* but "per corruptionem nominis alia lingua Sabrina vocatur" (by corruption of the name it is called *Sabrina* in another language) (95). Like Lud's "corruption" of *Troja Nova*, the incursion of "another language" effaces Gwendolen's commemorative gesture. Habren herself embodied a union of ethnic differences (Briton and German); her river now marks the limit of Gwendolen's realm (she rules the whole island except Kambria). The aquatic division is thus named for a figure who incarnated division while blurring differences. The river hides the body of the illegitimate child, sign of an unauthorized lineage; the name commemorates the concealment while keeping it visible. The name's corruption reconceals the threat and enables a perfect forgetting—except that the *Historia* preserves Habren's memory in the etymology. This episode illustrates succinctly the complex dynamic of memory and forgetting that shapes the *Historia* into a compelling border text.

Geoffrey's account of the first generation of Britons thus establishes intimate and agonized connections among land, ethnic identity, the language of history, and the possession of time. The cultural politics of these identity issues play out through the rest of the text, repeatedly confronting the original fractured circumstances as Geoffrey underscores again and again the dangers of discord, the gains of multilingualism, and the value of memory. Within each of these boundaries lie coercive force and judgments of legitimacy.

Totam insulam a mari usque ad mare

The hunt for land continues throughout the *Historia*. When rulers achieve Insular unity, they hunt overseas; foreign invaders like the Romans and the Saxons target Britain in their own hunt. The vocabulary of dominion represents the whole island under a single ruler as the ideal, its division a recurring wound. Seven times after Brutus, rulers reconstitute dominion over the whole island, from sea to sea (*totam insulam, a mari usque ad mare*).[41] By encompassing dominion within the limits of the sea, Geoffrey projects political achievement as a measurement of land. The *Historia* nostalgically recalls this original whole and sustains the emerging aristocratic ethos of primogeniture. Implicitly, then, the Britons' decline derives from their willingness to divide the patrimony; their fate illustrates how partibility diffuses ethnic and family power. The divisions tend to return to the unstable lines first set by Brutus's sons along the Severn and the Humber.[42] Since instability inheres in aquatic boundaries, the island's internal borders remain unstable as long as topography defines limits. Only by negating navigation, as the Britons do when they plant iron spikes in the Thames to sink invading Roman ships (130–31), can the Insular boundary stabilize and foreclose dangerous paradoxes. Rulers achieve greater stability when they create architectural space (as Brutus does with New Troy). Paradoxically, condemnable fratricides also establish laudable hegemonies. These homosocial murders, like Gwendolen's of Habren and Estrildis, repeatedly normalize domination by destroying near-resemblances. Eventually, the divisions run so deep that the *insula* cannot recover and dominion resides in the *regnum*. Indeed, as Walter Schirmer first argued, the *Historia*'s hero is the *regnum* rather than the *reges* (the *kings* of the title) (29). The *regnum*, however, is a fallen hero, a sign of territorial loss and a permanently fragmented *insula*.

The most lethal challenge to Insular integrity comes from the Britons' own overseas expansion. Maximianus creates the fatal division with his conquest of Armorica. Across the water, he discovers a second *locus amoenus*, and Geoffrey offers a new *descriptio* in the mouth of the conqueror, addressed to Conanus:

Ne pigeat igitur te regnum Britanniae insulae cessisse mihi, licet possidendi eum spem habuisses, quia, quicquid in illa amisisti, tibi in hac patria restaurabo: promovebo etenim te in regem regni hujus, et erit haec altera Britannia, et eam ex genere nostro, expulsis indigenis, repleamus. Patria namque fertilis est segetibus, et flumina piscosa sunt, nemora perpulchra, et saltus ubique amoeni, nec est uspiam meo judicio gratior tellus. (160)

[Do not therefore grieve that the rule of the island of Britain has been ceded to me, when you had hopes to possess it lawfully your-self, because whatever you have lost there, I will restore to you in this *patria*, because I will promote you to the kingship of this realm, and it will be another Britain, and out of our own people, after ex-pelling the indigenes, we will repopulate it. For this *patria* is fertile with corn, and the rivers with fish; the woodlands are very beauti-ful and the forests pleasant—in my judgment no land is more agreeable.]

From the verbal description of aesthetic possession (which casts the fer-tile ground as compliant, with shades of grateful in *gratior*) to the dis-missal of the natives, Maximianus replicates the founding of Britain. By proposing to recreate the original land and procreate the original people, he imagines a perfect semblance extended through space and time. Nonetheless, the difference from the original is drawn by the Channel that touches both; the very idea of an *altera* to Diana's unique *promissa insula* foreshadows the end of the Briton empire. Moreover, Maximi-anus's conquest leads directly to Britain's invasion by foreigners from overseas. The undefended Briton plebes seek Roman protection in vain. As a result, they inhabit a bloody border bounded by colonial aggression on one side and the nonnavigable sea on the other: "Nos mare ad bar-baros, barbari ad mare repellunt. Interea oriuntur duo genere funerum: aut enim submergimur, aut jugulamur" (The sea drives us to the barbar-ians, the barbarians to the sea. Meanwhile two kinds of death arise: either we are submerged or our throats are cut) (167–68). Murdered or drowned, the Britons play the role of the indigenous giants for a new group of ag-gressive settlers.

These foreign settlements prompt Geoffrey to deterritorialize the mea-surement of rule by identifying Briton sovereignty through the *regnum* and name *Britannia*. Constantine of Brittany, for example, takes on the crown of the *realm* ("diadema regni") rather than the island (170); his successor Vortigern treacherously acquires the justice of the *realm* ("to-tiam justitiam regni") (171). From this point forward, *regnum* displaces territorial measurement and identifies the Britons' loss of Insular sover-eignty. Although Uther briefly reverses the process, wearing the crown of the island ("diadema insulae") (219), Arthur inherits from him a crown of the realm ("diadema regni") (228). And despite Arthur's own spectac-ular territorial achievements, he leaves his successor a crown of Britain ("diadema Britanniae") (278). The name recalls the original founder Bru-tus, but as a nostalgic memory rather than a territorial achievement. As Saxon settlement proceeds, Cadvan wears the crown of the realm ("regni diademate") (285), and Cadwallo the last crown of Britain (297). In the end, neither the Britons nor the English merit any crown at all because each maintains a divided dominion ruled by the three kings (283). While the Britons never recover their pristine dignity ("pristinam dignitatem"), the English also fail to quantify their rule: the Armorican Britons Ivor and Iny promulgate "inquietatione" against the English, limiting their rule to Loegria ("toti Loegriae") (303). Geoffrey thus presents English rule as partial, located neither in the landscape nor in legal concepts. Instead, the ghost of Loegria's eponymous founder, Brutus's eldest son, Locrinus, haunts their dominion.

The displacement of the *insula* by the *regnum* witnesses territorial loss, rendered dramatic by the primacy of landscape in Geoffrey's representation of Briton identity. Indeed, alongside this terminological pattern, Geoffrey deploys landscape and architectural narratives as signs of significant jurisdictional shifts. Where landscape encodes ambivalence toward colonial settlement, architecture promises to resolve troubling paradoxes. The resolutions, however, can sustain domination as easily as they overturn it. Where Belinus and Aurelius consolidate their rule through architectural innovation, for example, similar efforts by the Romans and Saxons solidify Briton losses.

In a unique example of successful Briton architecture, Belinus bolsters his dominion by building roads. His massive construction project aims explicitly to resolve the roads' ambiguous edges and thus clarify the extent of royal jurisdiction ("omne ambiguum legi suae auferre volens") (112). He builds four roads with clearly defined stone borders—one the length of the island ("longitudinem"), one the width ("latitudinem"), and two diagonally ("ab obliquo insulae"). Each road literally carves a limit independent from the natural topography; nowhere does Geoffrey mention the traditional river boundaries. Belinus's roads thus safeguard the stability of the future by resolving spatial ambiguity and dismissing topographic ambivalence. Indeed, Belinus's mastery of the Insular border is so secure that he builds a gate on the banks of the Thames to facilitate the safe crossing from water to land ("Desuper vero aedificavit turrim mirae magnitudinis portumque subtus ad pedem applicantibus navibus idonem") (118). Conceiving of boundaries other than the rivers and the island, Belinus is rewarded with what Geoffrey judges to be the most prosperous reign of all time. When he dies, his citizens commemorate his architectural skill by placing his ashes artfully ("mira arte") atop his gate. His body fuses with his architectural creation rather than with the land, completing his own valuation of constructed space over topography.

Stonehenge represents a second spectacular monument to unified rule, directly predicated on colonialist success. The project begins when Aurelius seeks a suitable memorial for the Britons who died fighting the Saxons: he asks his craftsmen ("artificibus lignorum et lapidum") to design an innovative structure ("novamque structuram") (211). Since they are unable to imagine the novel, Merlin suggests importing the Giants' Ring ("chorea gigantum") from Ireland (212). These stones belonged to the giants defeated by Brutus and Corineus: they thus recall indigenous culture and the coercive origins of Briton dominion, itself now threatened by new settlers. The giants themselves brought the stones from Africa for medicinal purposes (213), implying an ancient history of settlement akin to the Trojan-Britons'. The stones are further linked to colonial ambition because to acquire them, the Britons must invade Ireland. Although the Britons subdue the Irish, they only succeed in conquering the stones through Merlin's superior mechanical skills ("suasque machinationes") (214). The lesson Geoffrey draws—that craft ("ingenium") outmaneuvers strength ("virtuti")—touches Geoffrey's own ingenious engagements with bellicose patrons.[43] The Giants' Ring thus signifies the Britons' (and Geoffrey's) mastery over a lengthy and geographically disparate colonial heritage, as well as their successful defense of Insular dominion against the Saxons. At the same time, however, the Giants' Ring surrounds Briton corpses, the dead traces of successful Saxon conquest. The monument's indigenous origins are ultimately forgotten, as the English ("Anglorum lingua") call it *Stanheng* (280). The stones, then, come to signify Briton defeat.

In this, the giants' stones resemble nearly every other architectural innovation imposed on the Insular landscape. Marius, for example, commemorates his victory over the Picts with a stone inscribed with the story of the battle (142). He then gives northern Albania to the surviving Picts. As a result, this part of the island is alienated from Insular history: "Sed haec hactenus, cum non proposuerim tractare historiam eorum sive Scottorum, qui ex illis et Hibernensibus originem duxerunt" (But no more about this here, since I do not propose to handle their [the Picts'] history or that of the Scots, who descended from them and the Irish) (143). Foreclosing his own narrative entanglements, Geoffrey exposes here the shameful fact that no history of a single people can encompass the whole island—and that any history of the whole island must encompass several peoples. Marius's stone stands on this durable geographical and historiographical boundary, marking a permanent Insular divide.

Two generations later, the Romans build a wall designed to contain the threat of these same northerners (146). Sited to the north of the Humber, the wall manifests (less poetically than Marius's stone) the geopolitical tendency for stable boundaries to be marked to one side of a navigable waterway. Likewise, after Maximianus depopulates the island with his conquest of Armorica, the Briton plebes construct another wall in an effort to stem the tide of foreign settlement (165). Both walls extend from sea to sea ("a mari usque ad mare"), recalling the formula used to describe paninsular dominion but here describing an architectural boundary that forecloses that possibility (both walls are clearly visible on Matthew Paris's map; see figure 2). The walls immure the fantasy of impermeable borders, a fantasy that here turns against the dream of unified Briton dominion.

Architecture turns against the Britons most spectacularly with the beginning of Saxon settlement. When Vortigern refuses to give Hengist a title to go with his farmland, Hengist proposes to quantify a defensive space instead:

> Concede, inquit, mihi, servo tuo, quantum une corrigia possit ambiri infra terram quam dedisti, ut ibidem promuntorium aedificem, quo me, si opus fuerit, recipiam. (178)

> ["Concede," he asked, "to me, your servant, as much as a thong can encompass within the land you have given, so that I can build a fortress to receive me if trouble comes."]

Once Vortigern agrees, Hengist uses the thong like a line on a map to manipulate the scale of topography and encompass a vast territory:

> [C]epit Hengistus corium tauri, atque ipsum in unam corrigiam redegit. Exinde saxosum locum, quem maxima cautela elegerat, circuivit cum corrigia et infra spatium metatum castellum aedificare incepit, quod, ut aedificatum fuit, traxit nomen ex corrigia, quia cum ea metatum fuerat: dictum namque fuit postmodum britannice Kaercarrei, saxonice vero Thanecastre, quod Latino sermone Castrum Corrigiae appellamus. (178)

> [Then Hengist took the hide of a bull and rendered it a single thong. Then he encircled with the thong a rocky place, which he selected with great care, and within the measured space he began to build a castle, which, when it was built, derived its name from the thong since it had been measured with one: thus it was called afterward in the Briton language *Kaercarrei*, in the Saxon *Thanecastre*, which we call in the Latin language *Castle of the Thong*.]

The rawhide thong represents a new technology of conquest, and Hengist a new kind of conqueror in the image of a land surveyor (a "monarch-of-all-I-survey"). As a colonial cartographer, Hengist imagines a boundary with no concrete relation to nature or history: he does not claim the land between two rivers or the land of his ancestors, as others do in the *Historia*. Hengist's acquisition of land represents a mode of colonization without an aestheticized imperial gaze: instead of discovering a *locus amoenus*, Hengist creates a "saxosum locum" (which slyly suggests a *Saxonum locum*). The rocky site is of course strategically prudent ("cautela"), but the space itself is defined by strategic measurement ("spatium metatum"), not the shape of the rocks. Hengist proceeds to build his colonial headquarters on the rocky material of Goemagog's destruction ("abrupta saxorum"), founding his domination on a site that recalls native disintegration. Geoffrey's concluding trilingual naming of the fortification moves through the languaging process of conquest right into the collective present tense of Latin dominance.

Hengist's settlement and construction signal the beginning of the end of Briton dominion, which ultimately comes in territorial and architectural terms. Soon after Hengist completes his fortification, Vortigern's failed tower immures the fragility of dominion and portends the fall of Britain itself; Merlin even prophesies that the warring dragons who disturb the tower's foundations represent the Britons and Saxons (188–91). In the end, as Cadwallader sails into exile in Armorica, he presents a final *descriptio* that ironically disowns the land that Brutus claimed. Addressed to the Romans, Scots, Picts, and Saxons, Cadwallader's speech grants them all the deserted land (repeating *redite* three times) (300). The landscape resembles once again the promised *insula deserta*; at the same time, it is inhabited by most of the peoples of Geoffrey's own *descriptio*. The *Historia* thus opens and closes with an emptied landscape, the natural space of colonial dreams and postcolonial nightmares. In the ultimate paradoxical maneuver, Geoffrey portrays Briton dominion as unstable while rooted in the land, but crushed by the stabilizing effects of architectural innovation.

Alias nationes

The ideal of unified Insular space sustains the ideal of a unified Insular race, a single people possessing a single land through time in a seamless genealogical progression. The fusion of territory and genealogy connects land to reproduction: marriage becomes a territorial strategy, and irregular intercourse (adultery, sodomy, rape, etc.) undermines Insular unity. But just as land acquisition is treated paradoxically (expansion and preservation are both laudable and condemnable), so are kinship strategies: marriages can destroy group cohesion; adulterers and sodomites can create stable kingdoms; fratricide repeatedly enhances Insular unity. Geoffrey deals with these tensions by stating positive ideological interpretations overtly, and then silently eliding the negative consequences. The result is a deeply ambivalent portrayal of expansionism and aggressive settlement.

Several aquatic allegories bridge the conceptual distance between spatial and ethnic identity. As Heinrich Pähler first suggested (80–81), Geoffrey's representation of the marvelous square pool at Loch Lomond captures his approach to ethnic ideology. In a twenty-by-five-foot shallow pool, a different species of fish occupies each corner; none ever visits any other part of the pool (236). The invisible yet impermeable boundaries represent an ideal of ethnic segregation, where the fish represent

43

the four peoples named in the opening *descriptio*. Geoffrey's representation is forcefully ideological when compared with the marvel's description in the *Historia Brittonum*. There, men fish in every part of the pool, catching all kinds of fish from every part ("et aliud genus piscium trahitur ex omnibus partibus"). The marvel, however, is that such a small pool, with no rivers flowing in or out, can support such a great variety of species (81–82). In contrast to this naturalistic wonder, Geoffrey's fishy marvel imagines a perfectly segregated Insular space.

The second aquatic marvel, located along the Severn, also offers an allegory of ethnic relations, this time as a lesson about the dangers of intermingling. Geoffrey explains the marvel with less topographical precision than the *Historia Brittonum* but with the same general import: water flows in but the level does not rise; when the tide goes out, this water is spewed forth, and if anyone in the whole country ("totius patriae") faces it and is touched by its drops, nothing will save him from being washed away, but if his back is turned, he has nothing to fear and will stay unharmed on the shore ("non est irroratio timenda, etiam si in ripis astaret") (237). As an allegory of the Welsh border, the Severn marvel represents how safekeeping depends on turning one's back to outsiders. The Severn and the fish pool both capture the value, and wonder, of segregation. These marvels embed ethnic fantasies in the aquatic landscape, fantasies that resist the mingling actually taking place on land.

From the *Historia*'s very beginning, Geoffrey tries to segregate Briton genealogy from historical multiplicities. Turning his back on the four genealogies of Brutus offered by the *Historia Brittonum* (59–63), Geoffrey gives him a single Trojan father. Geoffrey's genealogical reasoning responds to the new prominence of genealogical discourse in the twelfth-century aristocratic consciousness, expressed succinctly by Francis Ingledew: "British history is...systematically genealogized for the first time at the same moment that it is first systematically imperialized" (678). In a structure of vertical lineage and primogeniture, anxiety about lineage runs high; this widespread twelfth-century anxiety permeates the *Historia*.[44] Exogamy, for example, can extend land holdings, but it also destabilizes group identity by introducing outsiders. Endogamy, by contrast, preserves land holdings but can destabilize allegiances within the group. In the *Historia*, the Britons both find and lose their identity through exogamous marriage. Ambivalent as always, the *Historia* alternates between the value of preservation (primogeniture and endogamy) and the value of expansion (partibility and exogamy). According to James C. Holt, this paradox characterizes the twelfth century in general, as the aristocracy struggled to reconcile the tensions between inheritable patrimony and partible acquisitions.[45] The *Historia*'s patent ambivalence, however, might inflame rather than calm the anxieties it illustrates. Indeed, Brutus's genealogy may be singularly Trojan, but it is also founded on patricide (however accidental).[46] As with many of the *Historia's* patterns, Brutus's lineage is both laudable and transgressive.

Brutus enters further into the shadows of ambivalence with his exogamous marriage to Innogen, daughter of the Trojans' Greek oppressor. Brutus refuses Greek colonial land, as well as Trojan and Greek history, but he takes a Greek wife on his hunt for new land. Paradoxically, the mixed marriage results from the Trojans' refusal to remain immingled ("immixti") with the Greeks (81). Subsequently, Brutus and Innogen's descendants protect their ethnic integrity and police the boundary of their collective identity through endogamy. Ebraucus, for example, keeps his daughters within the extended ethnic family by sending them to marry Trojans in Italy (97). Later, the Britons refuse to marry with the Picts (143)—who nevertheless end up "cum Britonibus mixti" (mixed with Britons) (148). Thus although the lineage is founded on exogamy, it can only be maintained through endogamy.

Conanus states the endogamous principle overtly when he requests women from Britain to complete the colonization of Armorica:

> Cumque sibi cessisset victoria, voluit commilitonibus suis conjuges dare, ut ex eis nascerentur heredes, qui terram illam perpetuo possiderent. Et ut nullam commixtionem cum Gallis facerent, decrevit ut ex Britannia insula mulieres venirent, quae ipsis maritarentur. (162)

> [Once victory had been ceded to him, he wanted to give wives to his fellow warriors, so that heirs would be born to them who would possess the land in perpetuity. And so that they would not commingle with any of the Gauls, he decided that women should come from Britain to be married to them.]

By maintaining the boundary between the Britons and the native Gauls, Conanus envisions a stable possession of land. Like the caves that harbored the giants, the endogamous marriages promise to contain the difference between the Britons and the natives. But the threat of illicit sexual mingling remains, as did the giants—and here there is no definitive solution analogous to the wrestling match. Even more troubling, the seventy-one thousand women sent from Britain never reach Armorica: a storm destroys the ships, and those who do not drown are killed or enslaved on the shores of Germany. Conanus's statement of the endogamous imperative, then, is followed immediately by the silenced suggestion that the Britons must have married Armorican women (carefully preserved from the massacre of the men). *Commixti*, the Armorican Britons embody a genealogical rupture that no Briton can mention. The invisible encounter of Briton men and Armorican women hides the sexual heritage of colonial ambivalence toward the female native. The

Armorican Britons' secret genealogical history threatens their bond with the Insular Britons, as Cadwallo demonstrates when he gives Salomon a lengthy genealogical lesson in order to convince him to help his Insular relatives (293). Cadwallo's genealogical text overlooks all women, establishing a purely Briton agnatic line in defense of ethnic purity.

The danger of colonial sexual compromise invades Brittany during Arthur's reign when a giant abducts the duke's niece Helen and her nurse (255–57). The giant tries to rape Helen, but she dies of fright at the very thought; instead, he violates the old nurse. The substitution ensures that there will be no offspring of native aggression. The giant's sexual desire for the women represents the menace of heterosexual rape to genealogical integrity, and thus to expansionist settlement. When men try to rescue Helen and her nurse, the giant captures and eats them. His cannibalism enacts the native's power to subsume colonizing difference.[47] Cannibalism and rape both force monstrous intimacies; both invade the bodily integrity of difference. Only the valiant Arthur can put an end to this terrifying scene of colonial breakdown. Arthur's victory leads him to the same joy as Corineus, for the mutilated giant-body inspires his laughter ("in risum"). Arthur's victory over resemblance is even greater than Corineus's because he uses a sword (sign of his civilized difference) instead of his hands. As he attacks, kills, and then repeatedly stabs the giant with his steel phallus, he enacts a metaphoric passage from conquest as heterosexual rape to a homoerotics of colonial desire. Indeed, Sara Suleri has argued that colonial rape metaphors derive from an avoidance of colonial homoeroticism (17–23). Arthur in fact pursues the homoerotic subtext by immediately narrating his encounter with the giant Ritho (257). Ritho resembles Arthur in that he wears a royal coat, but its material—the beards of the men he has conquered—declares his difference. When Ritho demanded Arthur's beard to complete his colonial fetish, Arthur refused, and they met in battle: the victor would win the coat and the other man's beard. Geoffrey does not specify whether they wrestled or dueled, but when Arthur takes on the coat made of human beards, he looks troublingly like the native cannibal. The coat itself represents the portability of resemblance, whose transference contaminates the difference between men and giants.

The monstrous ambivalence embodied in native giants takes a tamer, but no less lethal, form in Geoffrey's exposition of the Britons' Roman relatives. As both kin and foreigner, the Romans present a special problem in the interpretation of endogamy and territorial possession. Upon sight of the island from across the Channel, Caesar makes a possession speech that effaces apparent ethnic difference and declares unity through shared Trojan roots ("ex Trojana gente processimus") (126). Caesar goes on to summarize the Britons and Romans' common history (the beginning of the *Historia* itself) and to claim tribute from the Britons because they are inferior. Caesar's reasoning disinherits the Britons by invalidating their ethnic difference, that is, the genealogical and territorial boundaries of their identity. Indeed, the Britons' claim to possess their *patria* depends on a denial of any *pater* before Brutus. Caesar instantly remembers a more distant past and refers to Priam ("antiquam nobilitatem patris nostri Priami"); Cassibellanus counters with a rival father, Aeneas (126). The Roman wars are thus fought between cousins over a conflicting vision of genealogical difference. These fundamentally fratricidal conflicts demonstrate a genealogical doubling that both forms and deforms the boundary of group identity.

Subsequent marriages to Romans turn on endogamous interpretations of the common genealogy (most skillfully illustrated by Caradocus [155–59]), while rebellions against Roman domination turn on exogamous interpretations of these same marriages. The risk of these unions surfaces when Arviragus and Claudius build Gloucester on the banks of the Severn to commemorate Arviragus's marriage to Genvissa (140): the city's liminal position joins Kambria and Loegria, just as the marriage joins Britain and Rome—but at the site of Habren's death, a foreigner who divided realms. The divisive potential of Roman matrimony is clear in the conflict between Geta (son of the Roman Severus and a Roman mother) and Bassianus (Severus's son by a Briton woman): although the Britons initially support Bassianus on account of his mother, after he wins the kingdom they reject him as a Roman (147). Once the lineages mingle in a post-colonial society, any individual can be identified with any group.

The genealogical sign of the Britons' downfall is Vortigern's marriage to Hengist's daughter Ronwen, the first (recognized) exogamous marriage since Brutus and Innogen. The Saxons, in a typical move of predatory kinship, eagerly marry into a new domain. The marriage explicitly provides for the colonization of Briton land by the Saxons, as Vortigern disinherits a Briton in order to give Hengist land in exchange for the girl (179). The marriage not only damages the unity of the ethnic group, it transgresses the boundary of religious difference: the Saxons are not only foreigners ("alienigenis") but Pagans ("pagani"). Indeed, Geoffrey portrays Vortigern's desire for Ronwen as the work of Satan (179): unlike ethnic difference, genealogical reasoning cannot efface religious identity. Initially, the threat posed by the Saxons is in fact more religious than ethnic, as their presence threatens to blur this essential boundary: through intermarriage, it becomes impossible to distinguish Pagans from Christians (180–81). The mixing of blood and religion distills the boundaries of Briton identity, and facilitates Saxon colonization as miscegenation. Aurelius's subsequent efforts to counteract Saxon settlement retrace the boundaries of blood and faith: Geoffrey identifies the combatants as Christian Britons and Pagan Saxons (207).

The Britons ultimately value their ethnic solidarity higher than their Christian identity and refuse to help with the Saxons' conversion: they assert that they have no interest in the Saxons' religion and as much in common with the Angles as with dogs (284). Christianity, however, mediates the Britons' restoration to Britain, for an angelic voice informs Cadwallader that they will return when their relics do (they have been removed because of the Pagan invasions) (301–2). The relics carry the memory of historical dominion; they are the fragmentary signs of divinely sanctioned unity. Through this spiritual manipulation of scale, the Britons are promised a complete reterritorialization and a restoration of all proper boundaries.

De britannico in latinum

The Britons, then, are made strong through endogamy and destroyed through exogamy. Contact with others, whether cousins from Rome or Pagans from Germany, always threatens peace and stability. The most dangerous figures of ethnic conflict are bicultural and bilingual: Hamo (brought up among Britons in Rome) nearly defeats the Britons by using their language (and armor) to infiltrate their army (138–39); likewise, a Saxon knowledgeable in Briton culture uses his bilingualism as a weapon against Aurelius (216). These bicultural aggressors perform the conquest of language implicit in Geoffrey's own project. Geoffrey's claim to translate casts him as a bilingual insurgent, colonizing the Briton past for the future. At the same time, he authenticates the witness of the colonized source: while other Trojan histories derive from Greek sources and thus present an incommensurable textual gap,[48] Geoffrey claims to translate a book with a direct linguistic link to remote Trojan origins. Since only the *Historia* can identify the historical moment when the Trojan language became *Briton* (90–91), Geoffrey alone masters the vicissitudes of Insular translation.

Within the *Historia*, Geoffrey portrays Gildas and Alfred as figures for his own declared translation practice. They first appear as translators of the Molmutine Laws, Gildas taking them from Briton to Latin and Alfred from Latin to English (113); Geoffrey later represents Alfred as the translator of Marcia's Laws ("Merchenelage") (120). Gildas's text turns from the conquered vernacular (Briton) to imperial Latin, which resembles Geoffrey's ostensible production of a Latin text from a Briton source. Alfred, for his part, ratifies English conquest by twice taking Briton laws into his own language, recalling Geoffrey's invitations to Robert and Waleran in the dedications. In both instances, Geoffrey's representation of translation is strategically ideological, since neither the laws nor their translations seem to have existed.[49] Geoffrey thus creates both Gildas and Alfred as figures of the conquering translator. Geoffrey himself combines their ostensible practices of transferal: he turns Bede's villainous Britons into heroic defenders of Christianity and legitimate sovereignty, Gildas's depictions of Briton failures into episodes of triumph, and Roman monuments into Briton edifices.[50] Through these kinds of inversions and negations, Geoffrey conquers his Latin sources for the Britons' greater glory. In these historiographic conquests, the history of conquerors serves the conquered.

Throughout the *Historia*, Geoffrey uses language to take possession of historical territory. At several key moments when the Britons are losing ground historically, Geoffrey reasserts their sovereignty historiographically by reminding readers of Briton place-names. Just as the island reaches its greatest period of Romanization under Constantine, for example, Geoffrey locates the Roman general Trahern in a Briton landscape by having him land near the city "called Kaerperis in Briton"; Octavius marches to meet him at the camp "called Maisuria in Briton" (153). By calling the Briton names to narrative action, Geoffrey presages the return of Briton sovereignty. Geoffrey also avoids referring to the later names of these places, suggesting enduring Briton ownership. Likewise, as the power of the Saxons is about to ascend with the death of Vortimer, Geoffrey describes his burial "in urbe Trinovantum" (182). In the midst of the growing Saxon threat, Geoffrey reminds readers of the city's Trojan origin, even though he has already referred to it as *London*.

Elsewhere, Geoffrey uses language to witness the passing of Briton sovereignty. He signals the Saxons' impending colonization, for example, in Saxon speech. At the feast celebrating the completion of the Castle of the Thong, Ronwen toasts Vortigern in Saxon; he burns for her immediately ("incaluit") (just as Corineus burned, somewhat less aggressively, for Goemagog ["aestuabat"]). Following his interpreter's instructions, Vortigern gives the appropriate reply in Saxon; after Ronwen drinks, Vortigern kisses her and drinks himself. As guests of the royal host, the Saxons should follow Vortigern's custom, yet Vortigern immediately mimics theirs. Born of his desire for the foreign woman, Vortigern's mimicry makes him a partial colonial subject, and creates discursively the Saxons' colonial power: although he is king, he plays the role of the colonized native (which he is, from Hengist's perspective). Like Corineus and Arthur with the giants, Vortigern's imitation creates the "classificatory confusion" typical of colonial "mimic men."[51] Vortigern, however, illustrates the fatal side of this play, where the confusion of power differences overpowers the powerful. Whereas Corineus and Arthur turn the menace of near-resemblance against the natives, Vortigern's desire to resemble the Saxons positions him on the dominated side of power. As the bearers of desirable culture, Ronwen and Hengist take power from Vortigern's attraction. When Geoffrey reports that Vortigern's mimicry originated an enduring tradition for toasts (178–79), he views the Saxon arrival in the double-time of retrospection and prospection: the tradition endures because the Saxons conquered the Britons. Geoffrey subsequently confirms Saxon success when he says that Constantine was buried at a place "called Stonehenge in the language of the Angles" (280), and refers to *Guallias* instead of *Kambria* before the Britons have in fact lost their name and dominion (282).

Etymologies confront directly the coercive origins of linguistic change. In Trinovantum's prospective etymology, for example, Geoffrey signals the Normans' conquest of the English by referring to the new name *Lundres* given by foreigners ("alienigenis") (125). This kind of translation crosses the historiographical boundary of the *Historia* itself, and disturbs history with multiple chronologies. Elsewhere, etymological uncertainty witnesses the potentially permanent loss of origin. Gloucester, for example, is either named after the Roman Claudius or his son Glouis (140): the cultural identification remains the same, but the true origin has been forgotten. Likewise, Geoffrey states that *Altera Britannia* was formerly called *Armorica* or *Letavia* (168). Here, Geoffrey cannot even explain the difference between the possible origins: the two proper names simply mark a forgotten past (reminiscent of *Albion* and *Britannia*). These linguistic disruptions replicate the occasional genealogical disruptions that disturb Geoffrey's narration of royal succession.

The most dramatic case of etymological equivocation concerns the Britons themselves. Whereas their translation from *Trojan* to *Briton* occurs in linear, patronymic fashion, their translation from *Briton* to *Welsh* is fraught with uncertainty: "Barbarie etiam irrepente, jam non vocabantur Britones, sed Guallenses, vocabulum sive a Guallone, duce eorum, sive a Gualaes regina, sive a barbarie trahentes" (As the barbarians grew in strength, they were no longer *Britons* but *Welsh*, a word deriving either from Wallo, a duke of theirs, or from Queen Walas, or from *barbarian*) (303). If named after their duke, the Welsh originate just like the Britons. If named after their queen, they commemorate the fusion of genealogy and territory that connects women to the land. The final option, however, represents the colonial judgment of their conquerors (barbarians themselves at the beginning of the sentence): *barbarie* only refers to *Guallenses* through a silent translation from the English *wylisc*, meaning *foreign*.[52] The shadow presence of English in Geoffrey's already equivocal etymology renders an (at least) triple ambivalence toward genealogy and conquest: Geoffrey cannot decide between the queen and the duke (matrilineal and patrilineal identity), between Welsh self-identification and outside judgment, or between the conquered English and conquering Normans. The sentence itself performs the shifting status of *barbarian* in the twelfth century, from *foreigner* at the beginning to degraded culture by the end.[53] With this ethnic etymology, Geoffrey concludes the *Historia* on the edge between colonial and post-colonial identities.

Ab aevo

All of the representations of identity I have discussed so far implicate time and the processes of history per se. Topography, genealogy, and etymology all measure the time of conquest and colonization. Ingledew has already characterized the *Historia* as "a vast act of spatial as well as temporal colonization" (687), and Otter has compared Geoffrey's imperial relation to the past to Brutus's imperial relation to the island (81–83). Yet, as R. R. Davies points out, Geoffrey's historiographic victory was hollow in that he reclaimed the distant past while giving up more recent history to the English.[54] Geoffrey's historiographic mode is thus simultaneously nostalgic and prospective, caught in an ambivalent double time of past and future.

Geoffrey may value the preservation of a peaceful status quo, but he communicates this value through an aggressive historiographical expansion of Briton dominion. As R. William Leckie Jr. has demonstrated, Geoffrey appropriates over two hundred years of Anglo-Saxon history for the Britons, repositioning the passage of dominion from the fifth to the seventh or even the tenth century. For example, Bede represents Oswald as the first Saxon to unite the island (230), but Geoffrey limits his domain to the north (296) and attributes the first English crown to Aethelstan (303). This new temporal boundary creates historiographical *inquietatione*, whose troubling effects Leckie traces in the historiography of the later twelfth century.

Genealogical revision enables this historiographic colonization of time, and genealogical time provides the *Historia*'s basic temporal structure. Geoffrey, however, calculates time in several ways, undermining the genealogical mode. Moreover, even the genealogies do not accrete value smoothly. The result is a temporal order that witnesses a dissipation of value through the multiplication of reference. The seven periods of Insular unification highlight the *Historia*'s genealogical reasoning, as well as its limits. The first period of unification after Brutus represents an ideal regnal chronology: dominion passes regularly from father to son, and the duration of each reign can be measured in years. Thus the period of unity from Mempricius through Leir can be calcuated as exactly 215 years. One cannot, however, calculate the duration of the second period of unity: apart from Cunedagius's 33 years, Geoffrey gives no duration for any of the reigns. Only the genealogical progression—the names themselves and their relations—provide a sense of continuity. The genealogy itself breaks twice when Geoffrey passes over in silence the parentage of both Sisillius and Gorboduc. Likewise, the fourth period of unity (from Belinus to Elidurus) cannot be measured, and the mysterious Guithelin disrupts the genealogy (120). The worst fragmentations of time and genealogy occur in the fifth period, when Geoffrey provides a long list of successive rulers without any mention of temporal or genealogical relationships (124–25). These discontinuous genealogies disrupt regnal time and cast shadows of illegitimacy over Briton dominion.

Geoffrey keeps time outside the regnal sequence through references to events beyond Britain's shores and through annalistic dates. Synchronic references include allusions to events in Judea, Rome, and Greece. Most occur early in the narrative, anchoring the most shadowy periods of Briton history to recognized Old Testament and Roman events; they often follow conspicuously invented episodes.[55] These very synchronies, however, threaten to unravel Geoffrey's linear chronology because they introduce tangential events that disrupt the boundary of a history defined by a single group and their dominion over a single place. Geoffrey must forcefully exclude contiguous Roman history, for example, to avoid "prolixity" and "diversion" from his purpose (118). Likewise, he consigns the Scots to another historiographical domain (143). The annalistic entries after Christ's birth (Lucius's death in 156, Arthur's in 542, Cadwallader's in 689) introduce a universal scale that invites further disruptive references to other events in these years and other years, irrespective of reign or realm. The keeping of historiographical time thus sustains and weakens Geoffrey's conquest of the past. Temporal boundaries, like others, join differences as much as they separate them.

Caliburno gladio optimo

Geoffrey's most dramatic temporal incursion is the insertion of Arthur's lengthy reign between those of known historic kings, anchored by the annalistic terminus 542 A.D. From within this temporal border, Arthur's reign iterates many aspects of his predecessors' reigns, rendering him both typical and exemplary.[56] He thus crystallizes the *Historia*'s colonial ambivalence. He is born, for example, of Uther's most irregular intercourse with Ygerna (an adulterous union disguised as marital relations by Merlin's magic). His genealogy, moreover, encompasses the island's doubles, descending as he does from Cornwall through his mother and Brittany through his father. Arthur's body thus reunifies prior history, gathering the Britons' temporally and spatially dispersed bloodlines. His own childless marriage to a Roman woman (237), however, forecloses the future of this idealized unification. As a barren couple, Arthur and Guenivere fail to enter into genealogical time. As if to compensate this lack, Arthur relies more on legal definitions of dominion than any other king.

At the beginning of his reign, Arthur receives the only official symbols of kingship mentioned in the *Historia* ("Insignibus itaque regiis initiatus"). He immediately proceeds against the Saxons: "Commonebat etiam id rectitudo, cum totius insulae monarchiam debuerat hereditario jure obtinere" (the righteousness [of his cause] encouraged him, for he should have obtained the monarchy of the whole island by lawful inheritance) (229). Rather than fulminating against Pagans, foreigners, or personal enemies, Arthur rationalizes the legal legitimacy of the attack. His right, rather than originating in territorial possession, leads to it.

His second major encounter with the Saxons adds divine sanction to jurisprudence, as Arthur and the archbishop Dubricius both make speeches before the battle (232–33); royal and Christian reasoning fuse most powerfully in Arthur's arms. The arming description (the only one in the *Historia*) introduces Arthur's regalia and provides the first elements of the biography of the sword that will enforce Arthur's imperial progress:

> Ipse vero Arturus, lorica tanto rege digna indutus, auream galeam simulacro draconis insculptam capiti adaptat, humeris quoque suis clypeum vocabulo Pridwen, in quo imago sanctae Mariae Dei genetricis inpicta ipsam in memoriam ipsius saepissime revocabat. Accintus etiam Caliburno, gladio optimo et in insula Avallonis fabricato, lancea dexteram suam decorat, quae nomine Ron vocabatur: haec erat ardua lataque lancea, cladibus apta. (233)

> [Arthur himself, dressed in a hauberk truly worthy of such a king, bore on his head a golden helmet sculpted in the form of a dragon, and on his shoulder the shield called Pridwen on which was depicted an image of Saint Mary Mother of God, which summoned her to his memory frequently. Girded with Caliburn, the greatest sword and made on the island Avalon, the lance whose name was called Ron adorned his right hand: this lance was hard and broad, apt for destruction.]

Each element obliquely engages boundary thematics and the legitimacy of Arthur's cause. The sculpted helmet, for example, recalls the allegory of the dragonlike star that Merlin interpreted for Uther (217–19). Bearing this image on his head, Arthur supports the center of the realm spanned by the star's vectors. The shield likewise encodes a relation to jurisdictional boundaries, as divine sanction literally defends Arthur by standing between him and his enemy. The sword itself points to a concrete spatialization of dominion through Avalon. An island within an island, Avalon represents a place of creation, where things are *fabricato* in the same way that Belinus's gate, Cadwallo's statue (299), and other important monuments are fabricated as symbolic border guards. Finally, the superlative lance (rendered in rhymed hexameter)[57] reminds the reader of the arms' destructive purpose — to impose the irrevocable boundary between life and death. Together, Arthur's regalia trace the bounds of the heroic body and merge with it, reinforcing the physical barrier between Arthur and the enemy's sharp assaults (the body itself nearly disappears from the final lines).

Arthur's portrait suggests genealogical legitimacy, represents dominion through allegory and topograpy, and foregrounds the role of force in the just formation of political boundaries. Arthur carries this legitimizing matrix into battle and succeeds gloriously with Caliburn. He sets

out explicitly to restore the realm's pristine dignity ("pristinam dignitatem") in terms of the Britons' inherited territorial rights ("paterno-
jure"), which the Saxons have displaced (237). This prosecution of inheritance in legal terms represents a new mode of territorialization in
the *Historia,* one that refers to law and memory before force. Through
Arthur, Geoffrey thematizes the difference between *de jure* and *de facto*
possession. This juridical monarchy represents the most abstracted, and
most stable, mode of dominion—a mode partly communicated through
the sword. Synecdochic double of Arthur, Caliburn signifies the imperial progress of a destroyed (and forgotten) empire.

Inspired by his own force, Arthur sets out on extensive imperial campaigns, subduing foreign kings and installing his own colonial governors
(238–39). In this imperial progress, Frollo's defeat at Paris represents in
compressed form the spatial and cultural engagements of colonizing conquest. First, the Britons and Gauls do not meet as armies. Instead, Arthur
and Frollo engage in a duel. The vast multiethnic composition of the empire is thus reduced to their individual bodies. The site of the duel, an
island in the Seine River outside of Paris, also expresses the containment of conflict. Water bounds the space, isolating it yet also connect-
ing it to the metropolitan capital and territories beyond. Through this
manipulation of scale, Geoffrey constructs a spatial icon of Britain, colonized and colonizing space. Like Britain and Avalon, the Parisian island shapes colonial ambivalence.

Arthur fights and wins the duel with Caliburn in hand. This second
appearance of the sword's name constructs a narrative pair, joining the
defensive maintenance of the Insular boundary to its offensive extension. The decisive stroke itself inscribes an indelible boundary between
the two sides of Frollo's head:

> Manante igitur sanguine, cum Arturus loricam et clypeum rubere
> vidisset, ardentiori ira succensus est atque, erecto totis viribus Cal-
> iburno, impressit eum per galeam in caput Flollonis, quod in duas
> partes dissecuit. (241)

> [Then when Arthur saw hauberk and shield turn red with the flow-
> ing blood, more hotly is his rage inflamed, and raising with all his
> strength Caliburn, he pressed it through the helmet into the head
> of Frollo, which he sliced into two parts.]

The blood presumably obscures the image of Mary, replacing her as
Arthur's inspiration. Cut off from the memory of the divine sanction
that she represents, Arthur now acts autonomously as a warrior-hero of
superlative strength. His success indicates that there is more than one
kind of legitimate conquest—defense of the demesne and augmentation

of its lands. Since Geoffrey sites this resolution in an insular space, it serves as an allegory of the colonization and defense of Britain itself.

This scaled use of space, suggesting allegory, opens the duel to typological interpretation. The site at Paris, conjoined with the naming of the sword, focuses further attention on this last of many conquests as paradigmatic (indeed, Arthur has conquered many lands but this is the first time since the Saxon victory that Geoffrey mentions Caliburn). Typology, like so many colonial issues in the *Historia*, engenders ambivalence because it invites conflicting interpretations. For Geoffrey's Norman patrons, for example, the conquest of Paris might represent the ultimate colonial fantasy; Arthur's installation of Bedver and Kai as lords of Normandy and Anjou certainly supports the image of a Norman-Angevin alliance. Along similar lines, J. S. P. Tatlock and more recently Stephen Knight cast Arthur as a figure for William the Conqueror, and Paris as a figure of Britain.[58] At the same time, however, the Briton conquest of anywhere represents the contemporary resurgence of Welsh power in England. Indeed, Bedver and Kai are two of the most recognizably Celtic names of Arthur's entourage:[59] their lordship of Normandy and Anjou can represent a counteroccupation of the lands associated with recent Insular conquest. Arthur's defeat of Frollo, then, cannot incite Anglo-Norman fantasies without also provoking nightmares.

Arthur's celebration of victory back in Britain performs symbolically his unification of Insular dominion and successful colonization of Europe. The names of the guests outline the empire's geography, while the procession for the crown wearing conjoins the Insular realm to the sword's juridical force: "Quatuor autem reges, Albaniae videlicet atque Cornubiae, Demetiae et Venedotiae, quorum jus id fuerat, quatuor aureos gladios ferentes, ante illum praeibant" (Four kings, of Albany, Cornwall, Demetia, and Venedotia, as was their right, processed before him [Arthur] carrying four golden swords) (245). The kings embody four insular regions, and their swords the authority that patrols their boundaries. The need for patrol surfaces abruptly with the arrival of messengers bearing a letter from Arthur's imperial rival, Lucius of Rome. Lucius complains about the new boundary that Arthur drew when he killed Frollo. The letter refers to injury and injustice ("injuriam . . . Romae," "injustis actibus") and seeks retribution before the Roman senate; if Arthur refuses court, Lucius promises to prosecute his complaint with the sword ("gladiis") (248). In this case, adjudication by the sword will signal the failure of jurisprudence. Lucius and Arthur thus deploy legal reasoning, whereas Caesar and Cassibellanus argued a similar dispute through genealogy. Since the *Historia* grounds genealogy in territory, the difference once again abstracts Arthur from the landscape.

Arthur of course will not *acquiesce* to Lucius's jurisdiction, just as Arviragus refused Cassibellanus's and invited the Romans to Britain in the first place. Arthur characterizes the message as an aggressive disturbance ("inquietudinem Lucii") and proceeds to deconstruct its legal legitimacy. He refers several times to the case's irrationality ("irrationabili cause"), arguing that the claim has no justice ("jure") because the Britons were weakened by civil discord when the Romans first came. Moreover, they took the island by force: no possession taken by violence is just (249). Here, in Arthur's mouth, Geoffrey invalidates force as a legal basis of sovereignty, implying a firm distinction between *de jure* and *de facto* possession. Geoffrey sustains Arthur's ruling at the battle's conclusion in an apostrophe, referring to the unjust disturbance ("injustis inquietationibus") and the unjust demand for tribute ("tributum quod ab ipsis injuste exigebatur") (273). The correspondence in judgment suggests that Arthur's pronouncement corresponds closely to Geoffrey's purposes: to denounce the legitimacy of political boundaries formed with the sword.

Nevertheless, Geoffrey undermines the clarity of Arthur's initial theory when Arthur goes on to assert that the illegitimate Roman claim against him justifies an illegitimate claim against Rome. Arthur concludes that Lucius should in fact pay tribute to Britain because Britons previously conquered Rome (249). Here, Arthur reverses the logic of *de jure* and *de facto*, blurring the distinction between *ratio* and *irratio*. Arthur posits the illegitimacy of violent conquest while pursuing a violent solution that protects his own interests. The argument expresses clearly the ideological paradox of the *Historia* and medieval aristocratic culture in general: *inquietatione* legitimately enlarges one's own rights, but others should remain *quiet*. Hoel's reply sustains the logic of justified reversal: he asserts that those who steal deserve to be stolen from (250). What's more, Hoel begins his speech by praising Arthur's "Tullianian fluidity" ("tua deliberatio Tulliano liquore lite") (250), an allusion that appropriates the rhetorical prowess of the Roman Marcus *Tullianus* Cicero for the defense of the Briton *patria*.[60] The troubling consequences of founding liberation on the oppressor's rhetoric surface when Hoel goes on to cite the prophecy that three Britons would rule Rome, noting that Arthur will be the third: since Arthur himself has just named three Roman emperors from Britain (Belinus, Constantine, and Maximianus), the prophecy seems to condemn rather than fortify Arthur's claim. Auguselus encourages us to forget this paradox by speaking rapturously of war's "sweet wounds." From these legal theories, genealogical principles, suspicious prophecies, and aesthetic pleasures, the war over who has greater right ("maius jus") begins.

Once the Britons and the Romans meet in full-scale battle, Arthur's forces do not achieve immediate success. As Arthur seeks to encourage his men to more effective performance, Geoffrey joins action to symbol and rhetoric:

Ipse etenim, audita suorum strage, quae paulo ante eisdem dabatur, cum legione irruerat et, abstracto Caliburno, gladio optimo, celsa voce atque verbis commilitones suos inanimabat, inquiens: "Quid facitis, viri? Utquid muliebres permittitis illaesos abire? Ne abscedat ullus vivus!" (272)

[Having heard a little before of the slaughter being made of his [men] by [the Romans], he attacked with his division and, drawing Caliburn the greatest sword, raising his voice, with these words he inspired his comrades, crying out: "What are you doing, men? Are you letting these women leave? Don't let any leave alive!"]

As always, the sword operates in the ablative case, as the means by which Arthur accomplishes victory. "Abstracto caliburno gladio optimo" in fact repeats exactly the description of Arthur's charge against the Saxon Cheldric. Against Lucius, however, Arthur draws the sword to verbally incite *others* to military prowess. Displaying his sword alongside his speech, Arthur admonishes the men to use their own swords better. The gesture implies both encouragement and coercion, and recalls Brutus's persuasive speech to Anacletus.

Arthur continues his speech in a highly structured rhetorical pattern. Each of the next three sentences begins with the imperative to remember ("mementote"): first their physical strength ("dextrarum vestrarum"), then their ancestors ("avorum vestrorum"), and finally their own freedom ("libertatis vestrae"). Each element forms part of a complete argument of justified action: they have strength and historical precedent on their side, and they fight to defend themselves. Following these rhythmic appeals to memory, Arthur ends by repeating his opening question and command in reverse order (272). Framed by the interrogative, Arthur's speech leaves the answer to performance: it conjoins memory (the critical faculty of history) to Caliburn and the Britons' own lethal weapons. Arthur himself enforces history in battle, as "Caliburnus" compels the Romans to vomit their souls along with their blood ("cogeret eos animas eructare cum sanguine") (272). In this last appearance, Geoffrey makes the sword the agent rather than the subject of action for the first time. It governs and executes an absolutely effective action. In the end, *Caliburnus* performs the sword's effective autonomy, that is, its direct role in securing the hero's success and its ability to answer fully the rhetoric of imperial counterconquest. It strikes here as the sign of its own legitimate action.

Arthur achieves his military victory over Rome with Caliburn in hand, completing a trio of battles grouped by the name of the sword. With this third naming, *Caliburn* emerges as a sign of imperial success: its presence traces the path of Arthur's expanding empire from Britain through Gaul to Rome. Yet despite the justification of Arthur's cause against Rome and the legitimacy of his Insular sovereignty, he loses both when Mordred steals his island and his wife. Like Brennius, Arthur loses "regnum et sponsa" — after rather than before gaining the right to Rome (274–75). Geoffrey implies that the transgression is sexual as well as territorial by noting that Guenivere has violated the law of her first marriage ("violato jure priorum nuptiarum") and committed adultery ("copulatam") (274). Once again, however, Geoffrey passes over irregular intercourse in silence, this time explicitly: "Ne hoc quidem, consul auguste, Galfridus Monemutensis tacebit" (About this, august lord, Geoffrey of Monmouth says nothing) (274–75). At the line of transgression, Geoffrey names himself as source. He withholds historical knowledge from his patron, refusing to remember the details of sexual compromise. Moreover, as if to protect subsequent narrative from contamination, he reminds readers that what follows comes both from the Briton source and the learned Walter of Oxford (275). Irregular intercourse thus threatens not only political power and genealogical reproduction, but the processes of historiography itself.

As Arthur fights to recover his Insular jurisdiction for the second time, he faces both Pagan Saxons and a relative. This army of indigenous and foreign usurpers ultimately defeats Arthur, but Mordred himself is also defeated: such is the danger of legislating by the sword. In the course of several battles, Arthur's sword never appears by name: its performance is limited to imperial success. Caliburn's absence at the moment of defeat indicates not just the absence of success, but of memory. Forgetting the landed basis of his authority, Arthur left his inheritance open to attack. The defeat demonstrates the fragility of territorial control and conquered gains. Ultimately, the *Historia*'s narrative structure appeals to moderation and *quiet*: expanding the bounds of authority increases the value of the family, but more than modest expansion is impossible. Arthur himself ends in Avalon, the land of Caliburn's origin. This regression negates the intervening imperial progress, circumventing both its past and future with an appeal to an insular border beyond time.

The sword's presence in the *Historia* thus comments on the ideology of territorial expansion. The commentary continues with each new redaction and translation, for the *Historia* achieved its own form of cultural imperialism when it became the focus of ideological expression for subsequent historians. Because the *Historia* controls the shape of Briton history and the pattern of the sword's presence, its literary effect mirrors the desired effect of military conquest; the *Historia* becomes a prescriptive rather than descriptive form of history. In the process, as Lee Patterson has also observed, Geoffrey transmits the instability of his own ambivalent vision (202). Yet as the *Historia* amply demonstrates, conquest incites resistance as the dispossessed seek to reappropriate their territory: Geoffrey's colonizing historiography also invites counterconquest.[61] In the *Historia*'s reception, judgments of cultures past and present can be read through overt apostrophe as well as in the very detailed ways in which the text is "correcta et abbreuiata."[62] The "correction and abbreviation" of landscape, genealogy, etymology, and chronology provide the most cogent examples of how border cultures penetrate the languages of history. In each case, Arthur serves as a boundary figure, and the narrative of his reign as a mechanism for interrogating cultural bounds.

❖

CHAPTER 3

Ultra Sabrinam in Guallias
Resistance to the Past in Wales

The *Historia*'s equivocations between colonial and postcolonial perspectives engage the ambivalence that inheres in border cultures. The fragmentary multiplicity and instability of borders, however, opens border writing to other possibilities as well. Revisions and translations of the *Historia* in fact bear witness to a range of solutions to colonial heritage. Rarely homogeneously "pro" or "anti" colonial, these solutions negotiate complex fields of historical and present trauma. In Wales, for example, resistance to Norman colonization informs a defensive view of Welsh sovereignty that seeks to eradicate ambivalence, but not colonialist ambition per se. Instead, Welsh interpretations claim legitimate expansionism for the Britons only. Although Geoffrey gave the Britons' history while giving it away to their most recent conquerors, the *Historia*'s receptions across the Severn (*ultra Sabrinam*) reclaim the past for the Welsh. So long as Geoffrey's text remains the model, however, traces of the Britons' subjugation remain. Welsh narratives thus express historical sovereignty while also recording the cultural trauma of colonization.

Historians across the Severn avert their colonized eyes from the troubling ambivalences that crisscross Geoffrey's vision. Instead, they focus on the inherent right of liberty. Genealogical arguments are consequently marginalized, and the *regnum* displaces the *insula*. In this vision of rule, tangled arguments de jure give way to decisive de facto demonstrations. Geoffrey's memories, countermemories, and forgettings unravel into a linear (and more Christianized) view of history that promises an eventual restoration for the unfree. The representation of language also shapes an insulated perspective that does not encompass both sides of most boundary issues. Instead, the view stops (most often) just short of the perception of historical difference. By attenuating the cultural force of landscape and boundaries, Welsh receptions resist the paradigms that sustain colonial power. They bolster images of sovereign Welsh freedom, which periodically verged on political reality during the twelfth and thirteenth centuries.

Sub brevitate redacta

In the first half of the twelfth century, the princes of Wales considered themselves on the path to political and cultural restoration. David Crouch's account of the kingdom of Glamorgan, in particular, portrays a sustained revival of Welsh sovereignty beginning in 1136; his maps comparing the contours of Welsh rule in 1130 and 1137 demonstrate vividly the territorial gains made while Geoffrey worked on the *Historia*.[1] Indeed, the redactor of the chronicle *Brut y Tywysogion* is effusive about the supremacy of Owain and Cadwaladr in 1136, and identifies the deceased Gruffydd ap Cynan in 1137 as "prince of Gwynedd and head and king and defender and pacifier of all Wales."[2] In 1141, Welsh princes fought alongside Robert of Gloucester at Lincoln and defeated Stephen; they remained visible in Robert's affairs until his death in 1147 and thereafter bolstered the power of Roger of Hereford (also in favor of the Angevin cause of Matilda and her son Henry).[3] Throughout Stephen's reign, then, the Welsh expressed themselves as a resurgent power. One chronicler even claims that in 1164 the Welsh threw off the rule of the French completely.[4]

Between 1136 and 1155, the period during which Welsh recovery was "undoubted,"[5] Welsh princes frequently claimed parity with their Norman neighbors. Very conceivably the *Historia*, dedicated to one of those neighbors, offered ancient prophecy of this renewal. Based in part on Welsh tradition,[6] the *Historia* could exalt the Britons' historical liberty as an argument for, and reflection of, the present emancipation. Indeed, between 1138 and 1155 a version of the *Historia* known as the First Variant was copied frequently, and almost certainly originated in Wales.[7] Two of the manuscripts contain proper names glossed with their Welsh forms, a copy of the First Variant was added to another only after it arrived in Wales, and a Welsh monk claims responsibility for copying a fourth text.[8] Although these thirteenth- and fourteenth-century manuscripts do not testify directly to twelfth-century copying in Wales, they do show that this *Historia* circulated there and that it appealed to Welsh readers.

With the publication of Wright's critical edition of the First Variant, it is now possible to analyze in detail the text's relation to the *Historia*. Previously, critics have had only a partial picture, since Jacob Hammer's edition is based on a text containing both variant and vulgate material. According to Wright, the First Variant clearly "bears the stamp of a mind other than Geoffrey's";[9] locating it in Wales allows us to imagine what kind of mind. This localization does not necessarily indicate a Welsh redactor (or redactors), since by the early twelfth century many areas of Wales (especially developed areas where history might be written) had become home to colonial settlers from the east.[10] Moreover, Leckie has argued that the First Variant occasionally portrays a bias toward the English; Wright substantiates this conclusion by showing how the First Variant substitutes Geoffrey's reworkings of Gildas with verbatim borrowings from Bede.[11] One redactor clearly implies an Anglophone reader with the comment that *Kareliucoit* is called *Lincoln* in "our language" ("nostra lingua") (139);[12] another (or the same) adds praise for Alfred's English translation of the Molmutine Laws (34). And why would an ethnocentric redactor eliminate the list of Welsh princes who attend Arthur's crown wearing (150)? As with Geoffrey, a perceived ethnic bias, or even linguistic competency, does not constitute a singular identity. Welsh historiography in fact includes both the Welsh history Geoffrey allotted to Caradoc (*Brut y Tywysogyon*) and the Saxon history assigned to William of Malmesbury and Henry of Huntingdon (*Brenhinedd y Saesson*).

There are numerous practical explanations for the simultaneity of Welsh and English perspectives in the First Variant, from a Welshman imitating the English to an Anglophone scribe copying a text imported from a Welsh monastic outpost. Even an Englishman in Wales could conceivably adopt a Welsh perspective while continuing to identify linguistically as an Anglophone, perhaps in one of the many priories that lurked in the shadows of colonial castles or at a Cistercian abbey like Strata Florida, where many historical and literary works were produced.[13] Moreover, Welsh and English views on the Insular colonial past are fundamentally compatible. After the Norman Conquest, both conquered peoples could envision the value of arguments based on liberty rather than territorial possession. And the Welsh could comfortably praise Christian English kings since their dominion over the island had also passed. Whatever the First Variant's origins (and they are probably several), the simultaneous traces of Welsh and English minds witness a textual product of border culture.

One copy of the First Variant, composed by Brother Madog of Edeirnon, performs vividly the destabilizing effects of colonial contact. In a substantial verse preface, Madog asserts the ancient Britons' unrivaled greatness. He then explains his intention to recount some of Britain's difficult battles "briefly" ("breviter"), repeating several lines later that all the facts are "composed with brevity" ("sub brevitate redacta").[14] Madog's insistence on brevity accords with another redactor's conclusion: "Explicit Historia Brittonum correcta et abbreuiata" (Here ends the Briton History corrected and abbreviated).[15] In both cases, the patterns of abridgment amplify Welsh cultural perspectives. In fact, Madog envisions the history itself as a narrative balm for the wounds of lost sovereignty ("nos refovens"), intended to delight rather harm the reader ("Delectura lectorem, non nocitura"). Madog's text, however, is about half unabbreviated "vulgate" material: as a composite abbreviation, his *Historia* is as likely to salt as heal cultural wounds. Even the complete First Variant does not always reflect the moral outlook and historical interests of its redactor.[16] Because the First Variant retains elements that conflict with the obvious changes, it reminds readers that this history is possessed by outsiders. Even in translation, Welsh possession of Briton history remains partial, borrowed as it is from foreign conquerors.

Tocius regni

The First Variant's repossession of Insular colonialism begins with the landscape. From the earliest scenes, the redactors dismiss many of the ambivalences that Geoffrey encodes in the *descriptio*. They suppress, for example, all of the landscape's aesthetic elements, stating factually that there used to be twenty-eight glorious cities but saying nothing of their demise (1). This enumeration blinds Geoffrey's imperial gaze: the narrator does not view the landscape like a conqueror, who takes possession through description, but like an indigenous owner. The redactors are perfectly capable of aesthetic description, for they describe Ireland as an opulent landscape, cultivated and adorned with buildings (40–41). (Geoffrey notes only that the new inhabitants multiplied.) Casting a furtive colonial glance west, the redactors thus emphasize the difference between colonial Irish settlement and indigenous Briton occupation. This representational strategy forgets founding violence and implicitly ratifies Welsh resurgence.

The remainder of the First Variant's opening *descriptio* narrows the *Historia*'s historiographical focus, fulfilling Madog's promise not to "harm" Welsh readers. Summarizing the island's inhabitants, for example, redactors eliminate reference to the Normans and the Saxons (or just the Saxons, if drawing directly from Bede) (1). Redactors thus restrict the population to the conquering and unconquered Britons, overlooking their conquerors until absolutely necessary. The conclusion, moreover, suppresses Geoffrey's recognition of the Britons' eventual subjugation to the Picts and Saxons. Finally, the redactors (drawing from Bede) resurrect the genealogical multiplicity that Geoffrey carefully trimmed, asserting that the Britons originated in Armorica. This dual genealogy reorients all future relations between Britain and Armorica to the benefit of the Britons as indigenous inhabitants.

The First Variant's account of the origin of Briton dominion thus proceeds nearly untroubled by signs of its end. Once Brutus arrives at the island, the redactors suppress his aesthetic *descriptio*. Moreover, they organize a linear chronology so that the Trojans destroy the giants (including Goemagog) before naming the land. The description of the wrestling match itself is devoid of Geoffrey's emotional epithets (as was the first presentation of Corineus, where Geoffrey's giant-lover turns into a "uir magne uirtutis et audacie" [a large man of strength and daring] [11]). The encounter proceeds, *breviter*, as an unambivalent description of matched strengths. The suppression of the name given to the site of Goemagog's demise further attenuates the encounter's commemorative value (16–17).

The redactors' divestment from the colonizer's cultural ambivalence surfaces again at Mont Saint-Michel with the repression of the giant's cannibalism (158). The Trojans thus establish their rule de facto, with little ambivalence about de jure interpretation or the effects of cultural memory. The redactors likewise overlook commemorative purposes when Brutus renames the land: *New Troy* appears in the present tense and without a prospective etymology: "Nouam Troiam uocat; que postmodum per corruptionem uocabuli Trinouantem dicta est" (He calls it *New Troy*; later, through corruption, the word is pronounced *Trinovantem*) (17). Here, *postmodum* (later) refers to a later Trojan time, not to the later London implied in Geoffrey's *Kaerlud* (92). From the beginning, then, redactors limit the narrative perspective to the Britons' dominion, exorcising the specters of their demise that haunt Geoffrey's *Historia*.

Redactors sustain Briton dominion by systematically displacing the cultural signification of a unified landscape. The island's division by Brutus's sons, for example, loses its impact as a sign of historiographical structure because the rivers are not named in the *descriptio*. In Wales, moreover, the partition of land resonates as one of several indigenous inheritance practices: J. Beverley Smith argues that while ordinary property was usually partitioned, dynastic inheritances were not—although multiple heirs often forced divisions (67–70). Smith concludes that while acrimonious conflicts over eligibility have created the impression that Welsh heirs expected partition, the principle of partible inheritance was in fact promoted by the English (74–75). In a Welsh context, then, the partition implies that a practice promoted by the Britons' conquerors is in fact indigenous. When the redactors subsequently maintain Geoffrey's attribution of customary primogeniture to the Trojans, the practice again appears indigenous. By appropriating both customs for ancient Britons, the First Variant ratifies the multiple consequences of conquest as if they all originated before colonial contact.

Most important, the unit of inheritance becomes the *realm* rather than the *island*: redactors systematically replace Geoffrey's *totius insulae* and *totam insulam* with nonterritorial measurements like *regnum* and *Britannia*.[17] Where *regnum* is already in place, it is sometimes fortified by a third term, so that Cassibellanus obtains "tocius regni *monarchia*" (49) and Vortiporius "monarchiam *totius* regni" (174). Redactors prefer *regnum* so thoroughly that it even displaces the seemingly flexible *patria* (145). The dismissal of *insula*, as word and cultural concept, pervades the narrative, generating a new kind of crown for Uther (129), a new route of retreat for the Saxons (142), a new perspective on Guenivere's beauty (145), and a new path of return for Ivor and Iny (192). At Arthur's crown wearing, redactors further dilute Insular identification by not naming the regions of the sword bearers (151). Finally, as Cadwallo struggles against the Angles, redactors rework the entire description to avoid mentioning the *fines* of the realm. Instead, the passage portrays the extension of the foreign *people*, "totum Saxonum Anglorum genus" (all the Saxon and Anglic people) (184). Through these kinds of revision, the Britons' *regnum* proceeds unbroken, although its geographic size fluctuates.

The *regnum*, a flexible concept of rulership that does not measure land, accords with the notions of power that Wendy Davies detects in the Welsh tradition prior to the twelfth century. Although the historical Welsh, like the historiographic Britons, were strongly identified with their region of origin, by the tenth century the notion of the *regnum* (*gwlad* in the vernacular) had a fluid spatial dimension: "*Gwlad* is not so much 'country,' 'territory,' 'political unit,' a piece of ground and its people; but rather the changeable, expandable, contractible sphere of any ruler's power" (17). The First Variant redactors obviously found the *regnum*'s flexibility preferable to the *insula*'s objective measurement: they could conceive a continuous Briton dominion despite obvious territorial losses. Moreover, as Welsh power expanded in the second quarter of the twelfth century, the restoration of the *regnum* did not require full Insular dominion.

This same fluid notion of rulership characterizes twelfth- and thirteenth-century Welsh expressions of dominion and explains the violence of Anglo-Welsh relations as the "mutual misunderstanding" of submission, which the Welsh took as an elastic notion of rule (prestige enhancing, even), and the Normans and English as a territorial concession.[18] Llywelyn expressed the Welsh perspective succinctly to Edward I in 1273, in terms that reverberate through the First Variant. Having received a letter instructing him not to build a particular castle, Llywelyn replies that his rights ("iura principatus nostri") are entirely separate from the king's ("omnino separata sunt a juribus regni vestri"), although he does hold his realm from the king ("quamvis nos sub regia vestra potestate teneamus nostrum principatum").[19] The First Variant's precise descriptions of Arthur's methods of subjugation seem to reflect similar conceptions of client service and submission (145–46). For the Welsh, then, hegemony did not necessarily mean territorial conquest or even direct territorial control.

The *regnum* reorders boundary concepts and strategies of spatial manipulation throughout the First Variant. Fundamentally, it weakens the importance of internal boundary markers, such as rivers, roads, and walls: they may divide the island, but they merely shift the contours of the realm. Belinus's roads lay out the clearest example of weakened boundary concerns. Whereas Geoffrey's Belinus creates clear limits in stones explicitly to counteract the ambiguity of the edges, the First Variant eliminates nearly all the references to *insula* in this passage devoted to Insular measurement and explains that the watery landscape itself intrudes on the roads' stability: "Erat enim terra lutosa et aquosa, utpote insula intra mare sita" (For the land was muddy and watery, since the island is situated within the sea) (34). The ubiquitous, nonnavigable water signifies a diffusion of boundaries, whereas Geoffrey's navigable waterways trace the paradox of permeable edges. Although this weakening of boundary concepts runs counter to some aspects of Welsh culture, where God can be called "Lord of all boundaries,"[20] flexible unities represent an equally strong current of Welsh cultural thought.

Architectural projects in general resonate very differently in the realm than on the island. Whereas Geoffrey's buildings separate dominion from the land and thus signify increased political stability (often to the Britons' detriment), architecture in the *regnum* evokes traditional Welsh defense strategies as well as Norman colonization techniques.[21] First Variant castles thus signify both the realm's defense and its domination: in Wales, the historical Britons appear powerful in the same architectural mode as contemporary Normans. Hengist, the arch-Saxon colonizer, exemplifies the complexity of architectural signification. He begins by explaining his need for a castle in Welsh defensive terms, conducting himself as a submissive sub-king rather than as an audacious colonizer. Addressing Vortigern as "My lord king" ("Domine mi rex"), he asks politely to speak rather than enumerating his services rendered (89). The redactors then omit his request for a title as well as Vortigern's rejection on ethnic and religious grounds. Instead, after recognizing Vortigern's previous gifts, Hengist explains that neither his life nor his possessions are safe because Vortigern's enemies hate him; he needs a castle in case they attack (90). Hengist goes on to underscore his defensive needs rather than his fidelity to Vortigern. From this perspective, Hengist's proposal sounds like the reasonable request of a devoted defender; his methods of land measurement seem innovative but not treacherous. At the same time, the Castle of the Thong clearly signifies the beginning of Saxon dominion. Hengist's defensive justification for the castle thus resembles Welsh uses of castellation, while his settlement technique and his actual fortification look Norman. This double perspective emerges from the complicity of Welsh and English perspectives in the First Variant: Hengist looks both "like us" and "like them" — as indeed the conquered English may have looked to the Welsh in the twelfth century. This same mixed perspective characterizes the conquest of the Giant's Ring, which first purveys Briton mastery of colonial history as in the *Historia* (122–26), and then its passage to Saxon possession in *Stanheng*, "Saxonica lingua" (175).

The dynamics of conquest are themselves reordered through the *regnum*. Maximianus, for example, conquers his neighbors without the excesses of emotion and desire that Geoffrey attributes to him (159). Instead of aestheticizing the Armorican landscape, he quantifies value objectively: he refers to the fertile "terra" instead of "patria," and replaces "nemora perpulchra, et saltus ubique amoeni" (beautiful woodlands and forests with pleasant places) with "nemora et saltus uenatibus apta" (woodlands and forests suited for hunting) (76). In Welsh tradition, in fact, Maximianus does not appear as a guilty usurper but as a noble Roman ancestor who legitimates Briton imperial ambition.[22] Conanus's subsequent settlement of Armorica legitimately returns the Britons to their origin, identified in the opening *descriptio*. Armorica's colonization thus reestablishes an anterior, already indigenous, dominion. Later, when Constantine of Armorica restores the "crown of the realm" ("dyadema regni") (82), he continues his ancestors' sovereignty rather than performing the first displacement of the *insula*.

From Gormund's conquest to the narrative's end, the redactors carve up Geoffrey's text extensively, attenuating the signification of dividing boundaries. They create this effect by redrawing the narrative's internal bounds. As the Britons flee to Wales and Armorica, for example, redactors excise the moralizing apostrophe that attributes their loss of dignity to internal division and discord. At the same time, redactors double the Briton perspective with an English view. This split takes the place of Geoffrey's fragmented partialities. As the Saxons take control of the entire region ("totam regionem") (significantly, not Geoffrey's "totam insulam" [282]), redactors limit their dominion by specifying (where Geoffrey did not) that the Saxons, who hold Loegria, are now called *Angles* and their land *Anglia* (177). Despite the loss of this particular region, then, the Britons remain sovereign in their *regnum*.

The political structure of the English realm, however, remains vague. Redactors pass over historical division to focus on Ethelbert's role in English conversion (a process Geoffrey barely develops) (178). The expanded, and positive, depiction of Ethelbert (probably drawn from Bede [72–78]) strengthens the narrative's dualism. The latter part of the First Variant thus oscillates between the Britons and the Angles. Indeed, redactors seem to establish English dominion with Ethelbert in the sixth century. Likewise, they seem to make Aethelstan a contemporary of Cadwallader, painting a laudable image of English honor and civil order as the Britons sail into exile (190). As Leckie and Wright have both observed, this account reconciles Geoffrey's *Historia* with Bede's at the same time that it seems to mistake Aethelstan as a seventh-century ruler.[23] Because the redactors go on to speak of Cadwallader and the Britons' future, the revision also maintains the integrity of the Briton realm after the coming of the Angles. Of course, the redactors may understand perfectly well that Aethelstan belongs to the tenth century: the effect of chronological conflation may arise from their separation of the folded strands of Geoffrey's chronology (similar revisions reorder the preparations for Arthur's Roman war [154–55]). In any case, the Briton realm clearly endures despite territorial losses.

By unraveling the *Historia*'s conclusion, the First Variant redactors repossess a portion of the English history appropriated by Geoffrey for the Britons. At the same time, they maintain the possibility of Briton continuity. They use the new structure to limit the Britons' loss of sovereignty, specifying that the Britons lost only Loegria (192) instead of Geoffrey's comprehensive "monarchy of the island" ("monarchiam insulae") (303). Despite subjugation, then, Kambria remains a recognizable *regnum* until the end. By foregrounding the *realm* instead of the *island*, the First Variant redactors grant the Britons continuous dominion.

Admirabile genus Britonum

The First Variant's *regnum* attenuates the *Historia*'s link between territory and genealogy significantly. Encounters that provoke genealogical arguments in Geoffrey's *Historia* often mobilize claims of inherent freedom in the First Variant. The redactors' genealogical maneuvers thus protect the Britons from the memory of colonial intermingling. The logic of freedom does not mean that genealogies hold no interest for the Welsh. In fact, they are famous for composing genealogical lists (examples of which preface three First Variant manuscripts).[24] Moreover, kinship ties form strong bonds of identity and obligation in Welsh culture, most prominently in relation to land title and kingship.[25] Redactors express ardent concern for ethnic integrity by accentuating the distinction that R. R. Davies identifies in Welsh law between *us* and *them*, *Cymro* and *alltud* (*alien*).[26] The details of the Britons' historic kinship relations thus matter less than their overall autonomy, itself bolstered by a heightened Christian tone that casts them as a chosen people.[27]

Brutus inaugurates the ethic of liberty by asking Pandrasus for permission to leave "cum pace liberi" (with peaceful liberty) instead of "cum diligentia tua" (with your approval).[28] And when the Romans first demand Briton submission, *libertate* replaces the *pater*: Caesar never mentions Priam, and Cassibellanus never refers to Aeneas. Moreover, Cassibellanus's letter and the Britons' discussion include references to liberty not found in Geoffrey's text (48–49). The account of Constantine's rise to imperial power pursues the ethic of liberty further by focusing on his liberation of the oppressed Romans rather than his global monarchy, and by not mentioning his family ties to Rome (71). Finally, when Cadwallo seeks assistance from the Armorican Britons, redactors suppress his lengthy oral history of the two groups' common ancestry (182). These notions of liberty, like the *regnum*, weaken the territorialization of identity.

Although the redactors do not change the *Historia*'s marriage patterns themselves, they do intervene sharply in marital discourses. They report Caradocus's recommendation that Octavius marry his daughter to Maximianus of Rome, for example, in indirect discourse and have him explain Maximianus's Briton heritage without cataloging the other marriage options; after a single sentence reporting the voyage to Rome and Maximianus's arrival in Britain, the redactors eliminate Caradocus's second speech promoting the endogamous strategy (73–74). Later, when Conanus requests Briton women for Armorica, redactors eliminate his warning against becoming *commixti* with the Armoricans (77). These revisions and excisions insulate identity and overlook differences whenever possible.

Whereas Geoffrey's speeches about identity patrol the boundaries of ethnic difference, the First Variant isolates the Britons from the differences that emerge in colonial contact. By weakening comparisons, redactors augment the Britons' autonomous glory. Most directly, the apostrophe "O admirabile genus Britonum" (O admirable Briton people) does not include Geoffrey's "tunc" (formerly) (56). Redactors thus excise retrospection and imply the Britons' enduring admirability. At the end of the apostrophe, redactors reject alien judgments (even when they are positive) by suppressing Geoffrey's citation of Lucan. And after the Roman withdrawal, they eliminate all references to the Britons' degeneracy, including the archbishop's speech to the plebes who must learn to be warriors, the narrator's lament of the Britons' former glory, and the archbishop's reminder to Aldroenus that Britain's warriors deserted the island to establish his realm in Armorica (79–81). Finally, the epilogue does not mention future Saxon history (192). In the First Variant, then, the Britons are simply overwhelmed by the multitudes of the enemy; they never lose their status as a prestigious ethnic group.

In fact, not even immense armies could overpower the admirable Britons without divine intervention. Although the redactors attenuate the Pagan/Christian dichotomy in the early encounters with Hengist in order to enhance Briton glory,[29] they construct an extensive Christian reasoning for Uther's defeat of Octa and Essa. Whereas Geoffrey simply explains a strategy for taking the Saxons by surprise, in the First Variant Gorlois adds that the strategy will succeed because the Saxons are idolaters ("ydolorum cultores"); since the Britons' sins have also offended God, they should confess before the battle (130–31). After recalling that the Britons fight for life and liberty ("pro uita et libertate"), Gorlois concludes: "nam si Deus pro nobis, quis contra nos?" (If God is for us, who can be against us?) (131). Subsequently, Octa and Essa are captured "per uirtutem Iesu Christi" (by virtue of Jesus Christ) (131). In preparation for the Britons' defeat, the redactors begin to thematize the Britons' sins and the efficacy of divine intervention. Gorlois's moving conclusion thus presages the consequences of having God as an enemy and explains already the Britons' eventual defeat as God's punishment.

The First Variant's representation of Christian identity ultimately profits the Britons' future sovereignty by divorcing their defeat from territorial losses or cultural inferiority. Their final departure from Britain firmly establishes their identity as a chosen, and punished, people. The narrator commiserates with their suffering by interjecting: "miserabile ac pauendum spectaculum!" (miserable and terrifying spectacle!) (188). Whereas Geoffrey focused on the Britons' prior greatness by listing all the people who had never conquered them, in the First Variant Cadwallader evokes only the Britons' shame before God. And while Geoffrey has Cadwallader recognize God's responsibility indirectly, in the First Variant he addresses his mourning ("lugubres uoces") directly to God ("ad Deum") (188). Geoffrey's ironic direct address to the enemies becomes indirect, as Cadwallader recognizes before God that He has given the island to the invaders (189).[30] Finally, the redactors make Cadwallader's own body the vehicle of memory by amending "reliquis eius" (their relics) to "reliquiis corporis sui" (the relics of his body). All of these revisions localize Briton glory in ethnic and corporeal integrity. The same maneuvers divorce legitimacy from territorial control. In the end, Cadwallader's durable body preserves the memory of Briton dominion as a nomadic and holy concept.

Briton identity in the First Variant thus turns on an almost immutable split between *us* and *them*, free and unfree, saint and sinner. These boundaries obscure direct ties to land or kin, and to historical precedent; they represent the most urgent and useful lines of difference for a conquered people. Irrespective of their territorial control, the Britons can remain inherently free. The boundary between the free and the unfree is a quintessentially colonial effect, turned here against colonial history—and in a period when the Welsh were in fact reversing colonial dominion.

De eorum lingua in nostram

Elsewhere, the First Variant overturns colonial subjugation through representations of language and etymology. Most of these imply a Briton-speaking reader who does not need to be told that *Habren* or *Kaerperis* are Briton names (20, 72). Thus if Geoffrey's claim to translate a Briton source suggests a colonial project, the First Variant suggests the beginnings of post-colonial translation—but only the beginnings. Since the text is still in Latin and since it preserves many of the *Historia*'s forms verbatim, it perpetuates their colonial effects in the midst of denials. These conflicts mark the First Variant as a border text.

The most telling example of colonial dissonance in linguistic identity is the closing etymology of the Welsh. Redactors reduce Geoffrey's three long sentences to two short ones by eliminating all references to the Saxons' achievements (the narration of their future has been moved back to Cadwallader's departure from the island). This structural revision removes one blatant reminder of colonial subjugation. Second, redactors suppress Geoffrey's opening reference to the strengthening "barbarians," temporarily forgetting the foreign origins of the English. Nonetheless, the passage preserves the possibility that the name *Welsh* derives from the people's barbarism (192): the English language and the Anglo-Saxon conquest still occupy the Welsh. In fact, all three of the etymological possibilities derive from foreign occupation, for the "Welsh" themselves preferred the term *Brytaniaid* through most of the twelfth century.[31] The etymology thus preserves the foreign origins of Briton history and identity, manifesting colonial subjugation alongside post-colonial resistance. The same doubleness surfaces in the epilogue, where redactors ventriloquize in Geoffrey's historiographical voice:

> Regum autem eorum acta qui ab illo tempore in Guualliis successerunt et fortunas successoribus meis scribendas dimitto ego, Galfridus Arthurus Monemutensis, qui hanc hystoriam Britonum de eorum lingua in nostram transferre curaui. (192)

> [But the acts of their kings who from that time in Wales succeeded and the fortunes of their successors I renounce in my writings — I, Geoffrey Arthur of Monmouth, who took pains to transfer this history of the Britons from their language into ours.]

The impersonation of authorship grants the text the authority of the original, while also identifying its alien origin. Imitation, in fact, identifies the narrator as a colonial subject, much like Vortigern speaking Saxon. "From their language" ("de eorum lingua") purveys the perspective of a stranger to Wales, a stranger who took on Welsh history but who renounces their future. The narrator's mimicry of Geoffrey's historiographical conquest thus claims indigenous ownership of a memory formed elsewhere. In this sense, mimicry disrupts colonial power on behalf of the colonized while also recognizing colonial subjugation. In these closing statements of origin, then, the ghosts of colonial ambivalence rise again.

Ex ordine

Meanwhile, however, the narration of an orderly, post-colonial chronology has proceeded apace. From the very beginning, the First Variant's redactors cast their *Historia* as an account of the Britons' continuous dominion. To Geoffrey's promise of a continuous account of all the Britons' acts, they add the claim that these acts have been "textualized" ("texuerunt") in order ("ex ordine"). The First Variant indeed presents an orderly text, one that performs the integrity of Briton sovereignty by repeatedly straightening out Geoffrey's folded chronologies (even at the sentence level). The resultant "smoother or more coherent narrative"[32] textualizes a mastery of historical memory that correlates with a vision of sustained cultural dominion. As the narrative moves from one point in the past to another with minimal references beyond the immediate horizon, redactors exorcise the ghosts of the Britons' defeated future. The (mostly) linear pattern implies a finite, knowable past; it ratifies Geoffrey's conquest of Saxon history while promising a return to power for the Britons. Although the specters of the text's foreign origins do occasionally haunt this view, the First Variant generally portrays paradoxes without recognizing them, that is, without observing the boundary itself.

The redactors excise the future in many small ways, too numerous to catalog. The description of Arthur's crown wearing at Caerleon, however, exemplifies the narrowing of temporal parameters. When Geoffrey names the kings participating in the procession, he identifies the twelfth-century names of their realms, so that we understand that *Albania* is now called *Scotia* (243). The First Variant's redactors, by contrast, suppress all of these prospections (except Demetia, "this is South Wales") and roll back the clock on Bedver's realm (making him duke of *Nuestria* instead of *Normandy*) (150). The narrator establishes a topography consistent with the historical moment by "forgetting" the colonial occupations that later imposed new names. The passage thus maintains an (almost) consistent focus on the historical moment of the procession.

In this historiographic environment, the *Historia's* synchronisms and annalistic dates no longer disrupt a genealogical measurement of time (itself weakened by the ethic of liberty). Instead, these temporal references anchor the narrative in objective linear time. The First Variant even extends annalistic measurement by specifying the date of Caesar's arrival in Britain: Roman year 693, sixty years before the birth of Christ (47). God's calendar guarantees a linear progress toward redemption, for the Britons and for humanity in general. Ultimately, the First Variant's deployment of temporal structures resists the time of colonization and imagines history from before conquest. The First Variant's reconquest of the Briton past thus subtly sustains the political conquest of Welsh sovereignty in the present. These post-colonial efforts hold out the promise of colonial reversal, in both narrative and politics.

Gladio nomine Caliburno

The First Variant's historiographical resistances converge on Arthur, the icon of popular Welsh resistance in the twelfth century. Redactors focus on Arthur as a physically powerful native hero who defends liberty, conquers oppressors, and lives beyond time. In the process, they substantially attenuate Geoffrey's ambivalences about the legitimacy of forceful conquest. Instead, Arthur performs the Britons' sovereign right unequivocally and with relatively little symbolic support.

From the moment of Arthur's conception, the narrator portrays him as sovereign of the world, "qui postquam adultus est probitate sua toto orbe enituit" (who after he is an adult brightens the whole world with his probity) (134). At his birth, redactors transform Geoffrey's factual statement of his name ("nomen filii Arturus") (225) into a laudatory "Arthurum famosum" (135). Arthur's fame rests on his superlative strength and his legendary immortality, both of which diminish his dependence on legal principles. Arthur of course does not accede to a territorially defined monarchy ("totius insulae monarchiam") (Geoffrey 229) but to the realm ("tocius regni"), like his predecessors and successors (138). And while Geoffrey goes on to emphasize that Arthur exercises authority by right of inheritance ("hereditario jure"), the First Variant immediately describes his preparations for a de facto demonstration in battle (137–38). The battle itself exacts revenge for damaged kin: Arthur attacks the Saxons "per quos et pater et patruus eius dolo perierant, per quos etiam tota terra turbata erat" (because they deceitfully betrayed his father and uncle, and because all the land was disturbed) (138). With the elimination of further speeches (which explain the battle's royal and Christian justifications in Geoffrey's *Historia*), family vengeance alone justifies the war. These revisions support the logic of counterconquest, wherein a subjugated people like the Welsh justifiably make war against those who steal their ancestral lands.

Revisions to the battle narrative itself emphasize Arthur's superlative strength while weakening the role of external legitimation. The arming portrait, for example, prepares him to succeed primarily on his own strength by reducing references to divine and magical presences: the shield represents Mary but not "Mary mother of God"; Caliburn is not *optimo*; fabrication in Avalon may be hearsay ("ut aiunt"); Arthur handles his lance ("muniuit") rather than being *decorated* by it (141). Each of these revisions locates the responsibility for superior performance in battle more in Arthur's hand than in his weapons or God's will. Finally, the lance's description may subtly contribute to a legitimation of forceful conquest: Wright argues that its phrasing echoes Virgil's *Aeneid*.[33] The echo not only retrenches the *Historia*'s relation to Trojan history, it ties Arthur's spear to both Aeneas (book 1) and Turnus, whose defeat founds Aeneas's dominion (book 12). Aeneas—like Brutus, Arthur, and the twelfth-century Welsh—forcefully overturns the jurisdictional claims of the land's current occupants. By restoring Virgil to the pattern of history (beginning, in fact, with Brutus's genealogy),[34] redactors once again alleviate the tendentious ambivalence of Geoffrey's historiography. Unabashedly, they reclaim the Britons' prestigious Trojan-Roman origins.

Arthur's arming represents a vision of sovereignty in which superior force legitimates rule. The idea that victory justifies authority, which only a demonstration of greater force can counter, accords with R. R. Davies's conclusion that Welsh royal power depends first and foremost on military might.[35] And indeed, the First Variant's Saxons never pose a significant threat to Arthur. Redactors not only abridge the battle narrative, they recast Arthur's motivation for and means of success. While Geoffrey's Arthur begins his attack in anger after watching his men fail, in the First Variant Arthur courageously climbs the hill immediately after the description of the Saxons' defensive position (141). He exhibits no emotion, and the narrator does not mention any prior skirmishes. Arthur then shouts general encouragement to his men without mentioning God or Mary, and achieves victory quickly through the strength of his right hand ("dextra") instead of with Caliburn. By substituting Arthur's body for the sword, redactors create a powerful giant-hero, equal in himself to an entire army.

The combat between Arthur and Frollo also underscores Arthur's efficacy over Caliburn's. Unlike Geoffrey, the narrator specifies that Caliburn is a sword ("ense Caliburno"): the name by itself does not represent the force of authority. Moreover, redactors imply a distance between the hero and the sword in the narrative's very syntax: describing the fatal stroke, they place *Caliburn* as far as possible from the verb *impressit*: "ense *Caliburno* totis uiribus per galeam in capud Frollonis *impressit*" (148). By contrast, forms of the sword completely surround the fatal verb in Geoffrey's text: "erecto totis uiribus *Caliburno impressit eum* per galeam infra caput Frollonis" (241). Where Geoffrey's syntax indicates the sword's closeness to the action, in the First Variant Arthur's strength comes between the sword and the strike. Typologically, Arthur's victory presents readers in Wales with an attractive image of counterconquest against the Normans. Arthur not only subjugates the French (from whom the Normans hold their continental lands), he installs Bedver and Kai as dukes of Normandy and Anjou (148–49). When these two Celtic heroes accede to power in the realms of Welsh oppressors, Arthur appears more strongly than ever as a figure for resurgent Briton sovereignty. His success here with Caliburn feeds a Welsh fantasy of reverse conquest, a fantasy that may have seemed quite realistic in the second quarter of the twelfth century.

Arthur's confrontation with the Romans culminates the extension of Briton cultural sovereignty. When the Romans arrive, they convoke Arthur in less legalistic terms than in Geoffrey's text: while Geoffrey has Lucius speak of *rectitudinem, sententiae,* and *justitia* (248), the First Variant redactors refer to "Roman dignity" and "satisfaction" ("Romanam dignitatem," "satisfacias") (152). At the same time, redactors augment the threat of forceful settlement with precise descriptions of the path of invasion and the threat of Arthur's forced removal to Rome as a hostage (152). Cador, moreover, does not laugh as the advisers retire; rather, he begins his speech amid an apparently heavy silence (153). Arthur's speech then displaces Geoffrey's condemnation of the Romans' "irrational case" with the ethic of liberty, riling the Britons by recalling the Romans' aggression: "Audistis Romanorum superbam legacionem, audistis quoque in eorum peticionibus nostram depressionem" (You heard the arrogant Roman legation, you heard also in their petition our disparagement) (153). Following several further revisions, Arthur concludes with a new, emphatic statement of the Romans' unjust desire to conquer ("subactus") free Britons ("liberis Britonibus") and drive them back into servitude ("in seruitutem redegerunt") (154). Redactors proceed to eliminate Hoel's reply and return the messengers directly to Rome. On the Briton scene, Auguselus makes a speech as he promises his service, in which redactors eliminate his rapturous praise of war while augmenting his praise of Arthur, the values of freedom, and the injustice of the Roman claim (156). The preparations for war thus express scant ambivalence or paradox: especially in the absence of Hoel's speech, the lesson seems simply that freedom must be defended when threatened.

Once the two sides meet in full-scale battle, redactors again make Arthur personally responsible for forceful victory. Not only do Arthur's men not achieve immediate success, they have in fact begun to retreat when he draws Caliburn to exhort them: redactors continue to avoid the superlative judgment *optimo* and pursue their Virgilian texture by using *ense* instead of the more common *gladio* to designate the sword (170). Redactors subsequently eliminate all of the rhythmic repetition from Arthur's speech. The retreat of the Arthurian army compels a drastic reworking of the opening sequence, which now reads: "Utquid fugitis? Quid pertimescitis? Ne abscedat ullus uestrum!" (Why are you fleeing? Why are you frightened? Don't let any get away from you!). Arthur proceeds to locate himself at the rhetorical center of the motivational powers of speech, referring to himself ("Ecce dux uester") instead of his ancestors (170). Without recourse to the anaphor of memory (*mementote*), Arthur proposes personal force rather than history as the basis of successful, justified action.

After brief mentions of strong right hands and liberty, Arthur himself springs into lethal action. Whereas Geoffrey uses this moment to narrate the sword at its most powerful, in the autonomous nominative case, First Variant redactors make no mention of the sword at all; instead, Arthur is compared to a famished lion (170). Arthur's heroism thus becomes naturalistically physical. From this point on, redactors eliminate all descriptions of the Romans' efforts. Geoffrey had suggested that the outcome remained in doubt for some time: "quandoque Britones quandoque Romani versa vice praevalebant" (at one moment the Britons prevailed, at another the Romans) (273). In the First Variant, however, Arthur intervenes decisively: "resistunt Romani quantum possunt" (the Romans resisted as long as they could) (170). Redactors thus considerably reduce the effect of equivocation, and move the Britons inexorably to victory once Arthur enters the fray.

Arthur's triumph of course does not last long. Redactors underscore the sexual treachery that occupies Britain's center by specifying that Mordred and Guenivere's transgression has taken place in the royal bedchamber ("thalamo") (172). They eliminate Geoffrey's reference to his patron as well as the passage alluding to truthful sources. Instead, they move directly to Arthur's reaction to the "fama, ymmo infamia" (the news, or rather, the infamy) (172). The absence of further comment during these final scenes diminishes the loss: Arthur's demise ends his reign, but not the Britons' honor. Likewise, the sword's absence from the final battle resonates less strongly as an anti-imperial judgment since the emphasis all along has been on Arthur's personal strength. Founded, defended, and extended by force, Arthur's dominion thus rests on the legitimate success of force, independent from legal and symbolic argument. Here, force legitimates de facto control and defends threats to liberty. Force in fact represents the most effective jurisdictional argument for a colonized people that does not control the law. Indeed, R. R. Davies argues that in thirteenth-century Wales territorial control gradually superseded legal principles.[36] In the First Variant, Arthur prosecutes this principle to its brilliant Briton conclusion, performing the recovery the Welsh themselves pursued. At Arthur's death, Constantine carries the *realm* forward seamlessly.

The First Variant and the *Historia* both leave Arthur's body in suspense in Avalon, where he goes to have his wound healed ("ad sananda [v]ulnera sua").[37] Arthur's implied personal recovery fueled fantasies that he would return to heal wounded Welsh sovereignty ("nos refovens"). Yet the most direct witness of the link between Arthur and Welsh recovery is not the *Historia*'s ambiguous account of his fate, but the nearly contemporary Anglo-French "Description of England":

> Apertement le vont disant
> Forment nus vont maneçant,
> Qu'a la parfin tute l'avrunt
> Par Artur la recoverunt,
> E cest païs tut ensement
> Toldrunt a la romaine gent,
> A la terre sun nun rendrunt,
> Bretaine la repelerunt.
> (Ll. 221–28)

[Openly they go around saying it, strongly they go around threatening us that in the end they'll have it all, by Arthur they'll recover it, and thus this country they'll take away from the Romanic people. To the land they'll give back its name: *Britain* they'll call it again.]

The First Variant actively vivifies these memories of origin and hopes of restoration. As the Welsh actually regained sovereignty in the second quarter of the twelfth century, the First Variant redactors extended sovereignty into the past by taking possession of the *Historia*. Their attenuation of paradoxes and ambivalences ultimately contests colonized subjectivity, providing an appropriately empowering historiography for a newly empowered Welsh polity.

Caletvulch

By the mid–thirteenth century, even Britons ignorant of Latin could read about their noble ancestors and nourish the ghosts of Trojan memory. During this new period of expanding Welsh sovereignty, translators took up the First Variant's suggestion of historiographic resistance and extended it into the vernacular. These Welsh *Brutieu* repossess Briton history by returning it to the language of Geoffrey's ostensible source. Since translation appropriates sources (in a colonial mode) while simultaneously preserving their authority (in a postcolonial mode), the vernacular translation of Briton history in Wales poses especially acute problems of cultural identification.

Although the Welsh were frequently dominated in the thirteenth century,[38] Welsh chronicles minimize these effects. Instead, they depict princes with sovereign powers surpassing the twelfth-century achievements of Owain and Cadwaladr. Llywelyn ap Iorworth, for example, married King John's daughter Joan, led the Welsh princes throughout the barons' revolt against John, and thwarted Henry III's realization of hegemonic rule in Wales; after Llywelyn's death, his son Dafydd successfully led the Welsh against Henry in 1245.[39] The achievements of Llywelyn ap Gruffydd, however, are unrivaled.[40] In terms resonant with conflicts narrated in the First Variant and the *Brutieu,* Welsh chronicles report that the princes appealed to Llywelyn in 1256 to lead them against the English, for they preferred death to the loss of liberty.[41] Llywelyn went on to reconquer many lands held by Anglo-Norman lords, and in alliance with the earl of Clare occupied London in 1267.[42] As a result of this bold success, Henry granted a formal treaty, brokered and sealed by the papal legate and later ratified by the pope: in return for an annual payment of thirty thousand marks, Henry recognized the title *Prince of Wales,* as well as Llywelyn's exclusive right to receive the homage of the Welsh princes.[43] After 1267, Llywelyn conducted himself as a fully independent sovereign, and withheld his homage from Edward in 1275.[44] Although they regained peaceful relations in 1277 and Llywelyn married Edward's cousin Eleanor in 1278, his insistence on sovereign control led to Welsh defeat in 1282. Tellingly, the Welsh chroniclers do not mention the much-cited relics that the Waverly chronicler says were transferred out of Wales to Westminster after Llywelyn's death.[45]

Welsh historians located Llywelyn himself firmly within the Trojan-Briton lineage. Versions of his lineage are associated with both Trojan and Briton genealogies, and in one case with a copy of a Welsh *Brut;* his connection to Wales is sometimes enhanced by tracing his lineage to Kamber instead of Locrinus.[46] Trojan memory in fact played a vital role in the thirteenth-century English conquest of Wales. On the one hand, the Welsh poet Bleddyn Fardd maintained Llywelyn's Trojan roots in an elegy that compares his wisdom to Priam's (165). On the other hand, the archbishop Peckham (active in mediating Llywelyn's relations with Edward)[47] attacked Trojan memory. When Peckham learned in 1284 that the members of the bishop of Saint Asaph's congregation (a bastion of Welsh resistance since Geoffrey's day) believed that they descended from Brutus, he ordered the bishop to exhort the Welsh to unite with the English as all men are united through Christ ("cor unum et anima una"). To achieve this unification, the bishop's people were to put their faith in evangelical visions "et non de Trojanis devictis et fugatis" (and not those of conquered and fugitive Trojans). Peckam went on to submerge Brutus's memory in colonial amnesia, asserting that the island was called *Albion* in the time of the first Germans (*Registrum* 2:741–42). This letter, along with the elegy, identify the Trojans as actively contested territory within English colonial ambition.

The *Brutieu* contributed directly to the circulation of Trojan memory in Wales. During the sovereign successes that preceded the 1282 defeat, several translations were made, often directly from the First Variant.[48] Indeed, Charlotte Ward's conclusions about the *Brut Dingestow*, one of the oldest witnesses to Welsh translation,[49] accord significantly with my interpretations of the First Variant: Ward finds that the translator presents Arthur as an invincible "culture hero" by suppressing details about the strengths of his opponents, eliminating depictions of emotional reactions, diminishing references to barbarians, and weakening the role of magic; the translator eliminates place-names outside of Wales and moralizes more than Geoffrey (384–88). Ward concludes: "[Arthur's] own fierce prowess admits little collaboration, either from contemporaries or from supernatural sources" (389)—or indeed, from his sword. Moreover, another translator enhances Arthur's value by interpolating a Latin poem to commemorate his death and adding details to Augustine's mission that may be indigenous to Wales.[50] This same translator domesticates native genealogy by making Guenivere the daughter of a giant named Ogvran.[51] These revisions, along with the translation project itself, assert Welsh ownership of Insular time and space. The *Brutieu* continued to play an important role in Welsh ethnocentrism into the fifteenth century, when the Welsh welcomed Henry Tudor to the throne as a fellow descendent of Brutus.[52]

At the same time, however, translation witnesses the history of Welsh subjugation. The rather confused dedicatory sentences that open the *Brut y Brenhinedd* demonstrate succinctly the dissonance of the Welsh conquest of Briton history. Whereas Geoffrey proudly proclaims that he has not used other men's words (71), the Welsh narrator has translated this book "although I was forced to gather strange words from other men's gardens" (3), thereby speaking the cultural dependence of Welsh historiography. Moreover, the translator writes in Welsh as if writing in Latin: "I took the trouble to turn and render this Welsh book into Latin" (3–4);

the conclusion reiterates that the book has been turned from Welsh into Latin (218). While the vernacular expression of these statements manifests history's return to its original linguistic form, their semantics attest to the colonial dismissal of Briton origins. Likewise, another translator's impersonation of Walter of Oxford (Geoffrey's reputed source for the Briton text) maintains the mediation of foreign domination: "I, Gwallter, Archdeacon of Rydychen, turned this book from kymraec [Welsh] into lladin [Latin]. And in my old age I have turned it the second time from ladin into kymraec."[53] While reclaiming Briton history's authentic origin, this conclusion recognizes the Latin intermediary and the permanent shadow of foreign origins.

Elsewhere, translators exorcise the ghosts of domination more successfully. In the *Brut y Brenhinedd*, for example, the translator measures nearly every reign from the Flood, including those that bear no time reference at all in the *Historia*.[54] After the birth of Christ, the translator systematically calibrates reigns with the Christian calendar. These regular temporal calculations present a structure of total memory, preserved from the origin of time itself. The translator thus eradicates historiographical uncertainty and asserts a complete, post-colonial possession of the past. As in the First Variant, the annalistic structure promises a linear progress toward redemption.

Similarly, the concluding etymology restores Welsh possession of history. The translator dismisses the *Historia*'s derogatory suggestion of barbarism and reasserts the Britons' prestigious Trojan ancestry: "those [who had survived] had been driven to Camber's part of the island. And they were not called Britons there but Cambrian" (217). Rather than identifying foreign judgment, the change from *Brytaniaid* to *Cymry* reflects a relatively recent change of indigenous practice: the Welsh gradually (and reluctantly) gave up their ancient attachment to Brutus in favor of Kamber in the course of the twelfth century.[55] The new form does refer to a more restricted territory, but it still derives from ancient Briton history. The translator thus effaces the memory of the foreign, English word that turns *Welsh* into *barbarian*, ratifying instead an indigenous nomenclature.

Since many aspects of the Welsh translations mirror the First Variant, and since this is the one area where I myself must rely on translations, I will focus here only on the translators' most notable innovation, the interpolation of Lud (Llud) and Llefelys. Lud appears in the *Historia*, but his brother Llefelys, king of France, is an entirely new figure. Most translations include their story;[56] it also appears as an independent tale in the *Mabinogi*. The story begins with Lud complaining to Llefelys that he is beset by three "oppressions." In the triad that probably inspired this story, the oppressions are called *gormes*, which refer in some cases to oppression by an alien race or conqueror.[57] Lud thus suffers from colonial troubles: each oppression allegorizes threats from would-be colonizers and successful defenses against subjugation. Together, the three oppressions express a cogent allegory of ethnic anxiety and postcolonial fantasies of pure freedom.

The first oppression expresses the fear of living among omnipotent strangers:

> One of [the oppressions] was a tribe called the Coranians, and so great was their knowledge that there was not a speech that the wind met with that they did not know when this wind got to them. And for this reason no one could harm them. (65)[58]

The Coranians are unique to Lud and Llefelys's story and its associated triad. Editors associate the word with fairies, dwarves, or Romans (*Cesaryeit*).[59] The tribe's name also suggests the word for the best-informed persons of Welsh society, the storytellers, *kyuarwyddyaid*.[60] In all of these incarnations, the Coranians master social knowledge. Here, it protects them from the Britons' efforts to defeat their colonizing desires, since they anticipate every strategy of resistance. Llefelys's solution (spoken through a special horn he builds to enable private conversation) promises to exterminate the foreigners without harming Lud's own people:

> And then Levelis said he would give him a kind of insect and asked him to crush them in water after he got home, and to bring together everybody in the kingdom and to throw this water over the people indiscriminately; and he assured him that the Coranians would die and the Britons would not be harmed. (67)

This genetically discriminating formula for genocide expresses the fantasy of an ethnically pure Insular hegemony. The destruction of an entire group enacts a postcolonial purification that returns the island to its original, "uncontaminated" state.

The second oppression also concerns conquering foreigners, allegorized as a destructive scream:

> The second was a scream that was uttered every May Eve over every hearth in the Isle of Britain; and this scream went through the hearts of all, so much that the men lost their color and their strength, and the women their unborn children, and the boys and girls their senses, and the animals and the trees it left barren. (65–66)

The scream, like foreign invasions, disrupts reproduction at all levels, from the biological to the agricultural. Llefelys's solution promises an infallible defense, so intricate it bears citation in full:

> The second oppression . . . is the dragon of your nation and another dragon of the foreign nation who fight every May Eve, and each of

them is trying to overcome the other. And when your dragon sees the other winning over her, then in anger she utters the horrible scream that you hear. And this is the way you can know that this is true. When you get home, have the island measured in length and breadth; and where you find the middle point, have a pool dug there, and put in this pool a cauldron full of the best mead that is to be found, and put a covering of brocaded silk over the mouth of the cauldron and watch over it yourself. And you will see them fighting fiercely in the air and casting flaming fire at each other. And after they come to the middle point of the island, neither one will flee from the other and there will be a frightful fight between them. And after they are exhausted they will fall in the form of two pigs on the top of the covering and will pull the covering down with them to the bottom of the cauldron. And then after they perceive it is wet about them, they will drink up the mead and become drunk and go to sleep. And then fold the covering around them, and in the strongest and most deserted place you can find in your kingdom, bury them deep in the earth in a stone tomb. While they remain there no oppression from another country shall land in the Isle of Britain. (67–68)

Llefelys's interpretation begins by allegorizing the Britons and the foreigners as two dragons: the scream signifies the agony of the island's subjugation. The solution traces the sources of colonial ambition to the attractive force of the sovereign center (identified as Oxford in some cases).[61] The measurement of the island in fact anticipates Hengist's colonial cartography: only by identifying the island's exact center can Lud capture and contain invasive conflict. Mathematical cartography thus promises to establish an impermeable Insular boundary. At the center, Lud contains the ethnic strife that results from invasion. The drunken pigs, entombed at Snowdon (69), protect the island from future invasions because they represent the pacification of competing claims to sovereign control of the political center. Yet even though Lud can control colonial invasions by guarding the sleeping pigs, he cannot kill them: the water will always conduct new invaders to the island's shores; no one knows how long the pigs will remain *quiet*.

If the first oppression represents foreigners (and their genocide) and the second represents invasions (and a magically effective border patrol), then the third represents the ghost of the indigenous inhabitants, returning to haunt the Britons' own royal halls:

The third oppression was that no matter how great were the preparation and provisions of food and drink made ready in royal courts, even though it were the provision of a year, nothing of it was ever had except what was used in the very first night. (66)

The solution, as Llefelys explains, requires Lud himself to reenact the primal scene of colonial contact:

> The third oppression is a mighty man of magic who takes away your food and your drink through magic and enchantment, and causes everyone to sleep so long as he is in it. You must therefore, in your own person, watch over your preparation and your supplies. And in order that you may not be overcome by sleep, have a cauldron of cold water beside you, and when sleep oppresses you go to the cauldron of water, and when you see your chance at the man avenge yourself on him if you want to. (68)

Lud can choose to engage the "mighty man," just as Corineus and Arthur overpower their giant adversaries. Or he can live with the ghosts of the colonial past. In the event, he exacts an oath of submission. Nonetheless, he cannot completely escape the history of coercive domination. Indeed, except for the extermination of the Coranians, the solutions to the oppressions leave the realm's security in the shadows of doubt. While the solutions appear to delineate a magical program for a Welsh utopia (an island inhabited by one group in "peaceful peace"), new oppressions always threaten to emerge: the pigs may sober up at any time and turn back into dragons. Welsh possession thus remains fragile in the *Brut y Brenhinedd,* just as it did in the thirteenth century. The *Brutieu* themselves possess history with confidence, but in the post-colonial border, possessions remain multiply partial.

CHAPTER 4

Here to Engelonde

Settling into the English Present

During the thirteenth century, a post-colonial Britain remained a furtive dream for the Welsh. Yet for the English, it gradually receded into the past. In this period, several writers shaped histories of English settlement out of the Briton past. To do so, they overlooked the boundaries etched in their local landscapes and books by colonial imaginations. Confident in their occupations, Laȝamon of Worcester and Robert of Gloucester pioneered Briton history in the English vernacular. Worcester and Gloucester, as it happens, sit on the bank of the Severn River, the navigable boundary between Wales and England. From the banks of England's most contentious edge, then, Laȝamon and Robert adapted the distant past to the regional culture of the present. Perhaps surprisingly, the Britons provided the historical foundation for post-colonial English imaginations.

The Severn sustained intense economic and political activity since it provided direct access to inland trade from the sea. Much of this activity concentrated in Gloucester and Worcester, where bridges enabled large-scale access to Wales and southern England for those not traveling by boat. What's more, historians in the area could easily perceive Insular affairs as local events, since kings and princes from both sides of the border met there in both peace and war. In the thirteenth century, as in the twelfth, the country's fate was often determined nearby. John and Henry III both fought battles against the barons in the fields around Worcester, Gloucester, Bristol, and Evesham, turning shire history into Insular history. Indeed, Rosamund Allen has already argued that in Laȝamon's English-speaking mind, Briton history became a form of local, ancestral history.[1] He certainly found plenty of local landmarks embedded in the Briton landscape.[2] The same holds for Robert some decades later, especially as he ventures beyond the *Historia*'s chronological bounds to address thirteenth-century events.[3]

The English vernacular also ties Laȝamon and Robert's histories to broader cultural developments. Indeed, much of what has been called the "Englishing" of the Insular monarchy in the thirteenth century took place along the Severn. John (former lord of Glamorgan), for example, adopted Wulfstan of Worcester as his patron saint and was eventually buried at his side.[4] His son Henry, crowned at Gloucester when his opponents blocked access to Westminster, revived the royal cult of Edward the Confessor, after whom he named his son.[5] According to Robert, Henry was the first in a hundred years to make offerings to the Anglo-Saxon Saint Frithewith (ll. 11324–27). *English* also took on greater clarity in opposition to the Poitevins and Savoyards brought to England by Henry and his queen, Eleanor of Provence.[6] Henry himself issued the first government document in the English language since before the Norman conquest when he confirmed the Provisions of Oxford in 1258.[7]

From the peripheral center (or the central periphery) of the Severn River Valley, English historians rewrote the island's history as a form of local history in order to establish and defend ownership of "our" English past. Here, where Anglo-Saxon culture survived the Norman Conquest more vigorously than anywhere else, the Britons, Angles, and Saxons all appear as the praiseworthy ancestors of the English. Laȝamon and Robert thus shape the past (from Brutus to Henry III, in Robert's case) according to the familiar contours of the present, settling Briton, Saxon, Danish, and Norman predecessors into a distinctly English post-colonial landscape.

Laȝamon at Ernleȝe

Around the turn of the thirteenth century, Laȝamon (modernized as *Layamon,* and often called *Lawman*) completed a history of the Britons in English, known as *Hystoria Brutonum* or simply *Brut*. A few decades later, a man downriver (called the "Otho redactor" after the manuscript that preserves the text) produced a second Briton history in English.[8] The Otho redactor may have revised Laȝamon's text or worked from an exemplar similar to the source of the extant text; it is remotely possible that one "ambitious" historian wrote both.[9] Whatever chain of events led to the two surviving texts, the Otho redactor clearly modulates the historical vision of "Laȝamon's text." Indeed, Elizabeth Bryan has shown that he sought to diminish Rome's role in Insular history.[10] I will therefore treat him as a distinct author. Although he has often been accused of "misunderstanding" or rejecting Laȝamon's purpose,[11] I find rather that he amplifies his source's cultural orientation, much like the First Variant redactors: he generally, although not rigorously, focuses more narrowly than Laȝamon on the present place and time.

The *Brut*'s first lines tell all that is known of Laȝamon's biography:

An preost wes on leoden. Laȝamon wes ihoten.
he wes Leouenaðes sone. liðe him beo Drihten.
He wonede at Ernleȝe. at æðelen are chirechen.
vppen Seuarne staþe. sel þar him þuhte.
on-fest Radestone. þer he bock radde.
(Ll. 1–5)

[A priest was of the *leoden*, Laȝamon he was called. He was Leove-nath's son (mercy on him, by God). He lived at Areley, at a noble church upon Severn's bank (he thought it was good there), right be-side Radstone; there he read books.]

Even before readers learn the author's name, *leoden* fuses his ethnicity with the landscape, for the multivalent term refers to both *land* and *peo-ple*. The geographical and genealogical fragments that follow trace the contours of Laȝamon's *leoden* in Worcestershire. The church at Areley Kings still sits just north of Worcester on the Severn's west bank, atop a prominent hill with a commanding view of the waterway. The church depended on the nearby priory at Martley, itself connected to Normandy. From Areley, then, Laȝamon could engage in a broad range of cultural con-tacts.[12] Indeed, the *Brut's* first lines state that he traveled far and wide collecting sources (l. 14); he may even have had contact with his Welsh neighbors.[13] Even in Worcester and the surrounding monastic libraries, he would have found a variety of historical and literary materials.[14]

Apart from reading books, Laȝamon probably performed devotional services. As a parish or household priest, his church may have been the site of the community meetings that Rodney Hilton describes as typical in the West Midlands (149 ff). Finally, according to the Otho redactor, Laȝamon wrote his own book, for a "gode cniþte" (good knight) (l. 3). Allen has suggested that this patron may have been William de Frise, who took over the manor at Martley in 1204.[15] Whatever its patronage, if any, the *Brut's* audience was clearly identified with the West Mid-lands and probably with the middle and lower social orders.[16] In all like-lihood, then, Laȝamon addressed people concerned with the local econ-omy and likely to fear and admire the powerful magnates represented in the *Brut*. Laȝamon includes, for example, many details of household and manorial concern.[17] Elsewhere, he laments treason, condemns fratricidal wars, and deeply regrets the human suffering caused by colonial aggres-sion.[18] Conversely, he admires common sense, and can even praise the traitorous Mordred when he sensibly tries to protect himself.[19] Funda-mentally, Laȝamon values a strong king, able to fight successfully against threats to his authority.[20] These are the values of a settled society, sub-ject to threat from within but stabilized by law, strong leadership, and economic generosity.

After locating himself on the local landscape, Laȝamon turns to a de-tailed historiographical *descriptio*. He presents the text as the product of a multilingual translation from three books he has conquered ("bi-won") on his travels: Saint Bede's English book, Saint Albin and Brother Austin's (Augustine) Latin book, and a book made by Wace, a French clerk (ll. 15–21). These books represent the cultural genealogy of Laȝa-mon's history, as well as a radical cultural reconquest written into book-skin ("boc-felle"). Looking over this historiographical "territory" (Otter

90), Laȝamon forcefully ("þrumde") sets together indigenous English, international Latin, and colonial French into English rhythmic verse. The *descriptio* implies a social convergence of native Anglophones, educated Latin clerks, and the ruling class of Francophones (invoked directly by the remark that a copy of Wace's book was given to Henry's Queen Eleanor [ll. 23–28]. These books reflect the multiethnic, multilingual society of post-Conquest Britain, increasingly unified toward the end of the twelfth century by the common use of English.[21] The textual composition itself, as Elizabeth Salter has amply demonstrated, manifests a formal hybridity shaped by English alliteration, French rhyme, and Latin rhetoric; the English itself mixes modern syntax with archaic vocabulary.[22] Within this hybrid heritage, English is so "common" for Laȝamon that he never offers the conventional apology for writing in the vernacular.[23] Laȝamon in fact draws almost exclusively on Wace's French book (which I discuss in chapter 5): he thus settles English directly and confidently in the place previously occupied by colonial ambition.

Tellingly, the Otho redactor redraws the boundaries of the *Brut's* conquest of history by altering its textual genealogy. The redactor casts Albin and Augustine as independent authors and eliminates reference to Wace, so that the *Brut* derives from one English book and two Latin books (ll. 16–19). These three saintly historians render Briton history always already English and Christian: from this perspective, the *Brut* does not repossess the past, it continues an established and sanctified English tradition. Indeed, working from Laȝamon's text, the Otho redactor received an already Englished Briton history:

Feþere he nom mid fingres. and wrot mid his honde.
and þe soþe word sette togedere.
and þane hilke boc tock us to bisne.
(Ll. 26–28)

[Feather he took with fingers, and wrote with his hand, and the true words set together, and the same book gave us for a model.]

The redactor explicitly presents the text as modeled on an already seamless English narrative, distinguishing *he* (Laȝamon) from *us* (the Otho redactor). The redactor completes the Englishing of Briton historiography by eliminating Laȝamon's reference to Henry's Queen Eleanor: for him, it may have evoked Henry III and his queen Eleanor of Provence, renowned and resented for bringing her French relatives to England. The redactor's revisions thus insulate Briton history from foreign influences.

Laȝamon concludes the prologue with a request that each worthy man ("alcne æðele mon") who reads the book and learns its runes ("leornia þeos runan") pray in the name of God for the souls of his family (his father, his mother, and himself) (ll. 29–35). The book's runes, its secret or hidden meanings, can only be "learned" through repeated reading and reflection. This kind of ethical reading leads to permanent memory, or literal incorporation.[24] Laȝamon thus asks male readers to repeat both prayers and history, thereby maintaining the memory of the Britons and of Laȝamon himself; for Bryan, these passages invite readers into an extended community of text-makers.[25] Within the *Brut*, Aethelstan (the first English king) models ethical runing when he renames the island's towns "on Sexisce runen" (with Saxon runes) (l. 15974). Prayer, reading, and translation all manifest English-owned history; they constitute the subjectivity of Christian Englishmen. In this way, Laȝamon proposes a pedagogy of history: by learning to repeat and create their own "Sexisce runen," readers perpetuate a refrain that marks out the territory of English culture. Their "runing," in the sense of private conversation, protects historical knowledge within the ever-increasing bounds of English speech. Although the Otho redactor eliminates the reference to the runes (and to Laȝamon's parents), his text itself responds to Laȝamon's plea for deep reading: the Otho *Brut* manifests an extended written "runing," proof that the redactor learned the lessons of Laȝamon's historiographical pedagogy.

The pedagogy of runes becomes concretely territorial when Laȝamon describes Marius's stone. Laȝamon characterizes Marius's decision to commemorate his victory over the Picts as "sællech" (remarkable, marvelous) and the stone itself as "sælcuð." The stone is inscribed with "sælcuðe run-stauen" (marvelous, unusual runes)[26] that ally the stone with the "boc-felle" that supports Laȝamon's own runes. The stone, which will stand until the end of the world ("ȝet he þer stoneð. / swa he deð al swa longe. swa þa woreld stondeð"), materializes the permanence of the historical memory created by readers who repeat the runes' refrain—as indeed, we continue to do. To read the *Brut* is in a sense to accept a partial identification with the Christian English masculine subject, an identification that disrupts the stability of historical, religious, ethnic, and gender differences.

Robert þat verst þis boc made

Some decades after Laȝamon completed his *Brut*, and probably around the time the Otho redactor completed his, Robert of Gloucester pioneered another kind of historical pedagogy. Robert has never been considered a pivotal figure of medieval historiography, when he has been considered at all. Literary critics and historians alike have passed over his twelve-thousand line metrical *Historia rythmis Anglicanis* as unremarkable verse and derivative historiography. Yet Robert succeeded where others before him had failed: he constructed a continuous vernacular account of Insular history, beginning with the Trojans and ending with events of his own day. When Wace (in the *Roman de Rou*) and Benoît de Sainte-Maure (in the *Chronique des ducs de Normandie*) attempted histories of similar scope for Henry II in the twelfth century, they barely brought their narratives out of the eleventh century. On one level, their historiographical failures witness the ongoing nature of the colonial project their narratives sustained. Even earlier, Gaimar seems to have conceived a similarly comprehensive history, from Jason and the Golden Fleece to William II. He forecloses connections to the present, however, by referring readers elsewhere for Henry I's reign.[27] Robert's post-colonial vision, by contrast, can close the book on colonial history while also addressing the present.

Even less is known of "Robert" than of "Geoffrey" or "Laȝamon." The narrator says only that Robert, who first made the book, had great fear during the battle of Evesham (ll. 11746–50). Robert was probably a clerk; in Gloucester, he could have served in one of several religious institutions. Indeed, it may not be pure fantasy to identify him with "Robert the clerk," bailiff for 1273 and 1274.[28] The text now known as Robert's may have been produced by more than one person; nonetheless, the result is ideologically consistent and clearly designed as a whole.[29] The narrator is very conscious of the dynamics of textual transmission, both oral and written, and often tells us what we will hear or what we have already read.[30]

The only direct suggestion of the chronicle's audience occurs when Robert declines to elaborate Merlin's prophecies because they are "derk" (dark) to "simplemen" unless they are well educated ("bot we were þe bet in lore") (ll. 2819–21). His concern for the poor and his frequent moralizations indicate a popular rather than learned piety. Robert observes, for example, that there would be less adultery if all "luþer holers" (evil whoremongers) were punished like Locrinus.[31] The assenting recipients of this lesson are broadly cast as lawful, Christian Englishmen. The fact that Robert translates Latin into English also suggests popular listeners. They may have been clerks, although the chronicle's language and politics invite the broadest possible reception. The lesson of Arviragus's "betrayal," for example, neatly justifies baronial revolt: mastery does not belong to a king but to the knights who shed their blood for him; a king should not be too stern with them.[32] While the chronicle's form invites a socially diverse audience, its geographical assumptions are more limited: the audience resides "here of þis souþ lond" (l. 4899), probably near Gloucester. Indeed, Robert narrates the earldom's creation at length and vividly describes the city's walls and gates during the battles between Henry III and the barons.[33]

From Gloucester, Robert takes possession of the Briton past as local English history. He conquers the past silently, never naming sources and never apologizing for writing in English. Robert did, however, work from several Latin sources, including Geoffrey of Monmouth, William of Malmesbury, and Henry of Huntingdon, precisely the sources of Saxon history that Geoffrey recommends.[34] Robert's English text dismisses these

Latin authorities, as well as the differences among them. He transforms the inherited shapes of English history by inserting anecdotes, moralistic conclusions, and legends throughout. His copy of the *Historia* probably contained elements from the First Variant, which links his narrative textually to Welsh post-colonialism.[35] Like the Welsh, he approaches Insular history as if his audience already owned it. He shares this proprietary vision with Wace (a predecessor who ratified colonial ambition), the Welsh translators of the *Brutieu* (probable contemporaries), and the Otho redactor (another probable contemporary).[36] The methodological similarities among these historians witness the intimate resemblances generated by colonial contacts, their differences the radical disruptions of those same contacts.

Unlike his contemporaries and predecessors, Robert makes explicit the analogy between distant and recent conquests implied in Geoffrey's *Historia* by extending the *Historia*'s territory into the thirteenth century. His chronicle creates a narrative *inquietatione* similar to Geoffrey's own expansion of Briton chronology. Here, the boundaries of the Briton past do not stand *stille* but take on an entirely new *Anglicanis* shape. By writing toward the present, and in English, Robert communicates both the measurable distance of historical events and their direct connection to the present. By comparing Robert of Gloucester with Laȝamon, rather than with his successor and northern compatriot Robert Manning, as Thorlac Turville-Petre has done, this English past acquires distinct regional contours — not the regionalism of "core values"[37] but an identity shaped in intimate contact with England's western edge.

Þis londe

The most striking sign of post-colonial settlement in English versions of Briton history is the pervasive use of deictic references to *this land* (*þis lond, þis kine-londe*) and *here*. Transitioning from Rome to Britain, for example, Laȝamon concludes: "þus hit ferde þære. wurs hit ferde here" (Thus it fared there, worse it fared here) (l. 5583); Robert remarks that the Trojans "come here to engelond" (l. 475). These practices imply an audience grounded on English soil, thoroughly identified with the topography and history surrounding the place of narration. *Here* thus refers to both the land and the book. The continuity of identification is strongest in Robert's case, since events in Brutus's time occur in the same places as those of the 1260s. Nonetheless, Laȝamon and Robert settle the Insular landscape for the English in two very different ways: where Laȝamon overlooks landscape (much like Wace), Robert devotes himself to its quantification.

Laȝamon reinforces the ambiance of English place by repeatedly pairing *lond* with *leod*, the term for *people* that collocates ethnicity, political association, land, and language; *lond* itself sometimes designates the people of the land.[38] Most important for patterns of boundary formation, Laȝamon reports that Brutus's three sons divide the "leod" (l. 1053) (tellingly, the Otho redactor substitutes "londes"). By conflating land and people, Laȝamon envisions a settled English countryside that overtly dismisses the colonial pairing of *gauster* and *gaainer* (*waste* and *win*) that he inherited from Wace. Meanwhile, however, Laȝamon follows Wace in overlooking the details of Insular jurisdiction. In Laȝamon's hands, the dismissal of the culturally charged border supports English (rather than Norman) settlement. Despite his proximity to the Severn, for example, he maintains Wace's description of Habren's death in the *Avon* River (ll. 1243–53). Laȝamon also follows Wace in dismissing Geoffrey's ambivalence toward the beautiful landscape. Diana's description of the island as "wunsum" (winsome, winable) (l. 618) comes closest to evaluative judgment; Brutus "beholds" the contents of the landscape but does not describe them (ll. 1003–8). And like Wace, Laȝamon does not have Cadwallader describe the land as he sails into exile (l. 15900). Laȝamon, however, turns Wace's colonial possessiveness to post-colonial ends. By repeatedly describing land as held in the *hond* (*hand*)[39] of successful rulers, Laȝamon dismisses Wace's feudal terminology (*honor* or *fief*), quantifying dominion (it fits in one man's hand) and enhancing the ruler's personal power (he holds, or beholds, the entire land).

Robert, for his part, takes post-colonial quantification literally, with an expanded *descriptio* of England (drawn from Geoffrey, Bede, and others). Over nearly two hundred lines, Robert seeks to prove the thesis of the first line, "Englond his a wel god lond" (England is a very good land), by naming and counting rivers, islands, towns, kingdoms, bishoprics, archbishoprics, shires, natural resources, marvels, and roads. The enumeration of the island's topographical and governmental structures performs a complete English settlement before the very first word of Trojans or Britons: *Englelonde* literally comes before *Bruteine* (which refers only to Brutus's era).[40] The very first events of Insular history thus take place on recognizably English land, and the first building projects create recognizably English architecture: the Trojans find the prologue's landscape (ll. 470–89); Lucius founds its episcopal sees (ll. 1659–73); ships move along a Severn that flows from the origins of Insular time (ll. 11610–16). Robert thus creates a pedagogy of history, not as a refrain of runes but as a counting of facts. Ultimately, the quantification of Insular space belongs to the domain of writing, for the *descriptio* concludes: "þat englelond is londe best. as his is iwrite" (England is the best land, as it is written) (l. 189). As *Englelond* becomes a text inseparable from the *Historia rythmis Anglicanis*, Insular history becomes post-colonial.

The wrestling match between Corineus and Goemagog offers a powerful early representation of post-colonial settlement. Laȝamon offers the most eroticized encounter in the tradition, as the two giants meet "breoste wið breoste" (breast against breast) (l. 939), and struggle so hard against each other that in their leaning, they seem about to lie down (l. 942). The critical blow comes when Goemagog pushes Corineus over backward with "his breoste" (l. 951). With the breast as weapon, the match begins and nearly ends in the erogenous zone. The encounter's heightened eroticism seems to recognize and admit the native's desirability. In the process, Goemagog ceases to embody the boundary between indigenous and colonizing desire. Robert likewise weakens the natives' difference by referring to them as "vorbriode men" (l. 490): although "disfigured," they are still more human than monster.

The absence of colonial boundary issues surfaces vividly as Corineus heaves the evil giant breast over the cliff. Whereas Wace maintains Geoffrey's portrayal of the bloodstained water (ll. 1165–66), Laȝamon's Goemagog never reaches the ground: "þat al þe feond to-barst. ær he to folde come. / & þus þe hæȝe scaðe. ferde to helle" (The fiend burst before he came to the ground, and thus the great miscreant went to hell) (ll. 962–63). For both Geoffrey and Wace, the native's destruction in the border between land and sea constitutes the Insular boundary as a site of colonial domination: the vanishing bones of Laȝamon's Goemagog, by contrast, signify the border's invisibility. Civilization here is not founded on the destruction of the almost-same, but on the elimination of the settler's own disruptive side. In Laȝamon's *Brut*, Goemagog's expulsion indeed goes right to the heart of the Trojan psyche, for his defeat makes Brutus's men all happy "on heora breost-þunke" (in their breasts) (l. 969). As the evil breast vanishes without a trace, the settlers' breasts fill with goodness; they become the *leod* of the *lond*. Robert likewise weakens Goemagog's relation to boundaries, as the body is only dismembered among the rocks without mention of stains (ll. 524–25): here, Goemagog becomes the disfigured man that he already was.

Following the wrestling match, Laȝamon adapts Wace's colonial vision with post-colonial confidence, displacing boundaries in numerous ways. Architecture, for example, does not represent the progression toward stability that it does in Geoffrey's *Historia* since Laȝamon does not invest in the thematics of navigable waterways. In the case of Belinus's roads, Geoffrey establishes a vivid image of stable jurisdiction independent from navigable water, and Wace (following the First Variant) describes a pragmatic solution to difficult travel across marshy land. Laȝamon, however, does not explain the motive: he has Belinus simply invent the law of peace for the roads, literally "laid on them" as a final surface ("þa leide þa king heom laȝen on") (l. 2415). The roads, then, do not solve legal or transit problems; rather, they create the possibility of legal use and easy travel (Laȝamon calls the one from Southhampton "swiðe hendi" [very handy] [l. 2412]). Robert weakens the roads' significance even further by merely noting in the *descriptio* that they are useful remnants of "þe olde kinges" that allow travel throughout the land (ll. 169–79). Not only does he not identify Belinus as their architect, he subsequently skips over his reign entirely (ll. 1015–18). Since he narrates both Leir and Gurguit reigns in expanded form, "abbreviation" alone cannot account for this radical revision of regnal chronology. Robert's post-colonial gaze purposefully overlooks one of the emblematic reigns of Briton colonialism, sidestepping the imperial theme and the boundary pressures that attend it.

The representations of Belinus's gate and Hengist's castle also elide relations between architecture and borders. For Geoffrey, both structures engage the dynamics of the edge, facilitating passages from shore to land; Wace attenuates but does not eliminate these engagements. Laȝamon, however, merely reports that the gate was made and named (ll. 3020–21); Robert never mentions it. Laȝamon's Hengist, moreover, looks for a "brædne fæld" (broad field) and builds his castle in a "fæire uelde" (fair plain).⁴¹ Distanced from the shore, the castle founds Hengist's settlement without reference to colonial processes. Likewise, Robert does not site Hengist's building at the shore; he notes the two current pronunciations, "þuongcaster" or "tangcaster," but offers no etymology (ll. 2497–502). From this perspective, nothing at all comes between this first Saxon building and the English present.

Stonehenge, finally, captures English settlement marvelously. Laȝamon's Merlin refers to the stones' medicinal properties in the present tense, without mentioning their history; when the Britons are in sight of the Giants' Ring ("Eotinde Ring"), Merlin incites their ardor by telling them that it came from Africa.⁴² Never, though, does Laȝamon refer to the giants themselves, their history or cultural practices. Africa, moreover, is Gormund's land, who gave England to the Saxons:⁴³ it thus suggests already an English alliance. With this geographic detail, Laȝamon thus severs the stones from one branch of colonial history (the giants') and attaches them vaguely to another (the English). Since the Otho redactor excises the reference to Africa, the Ring appears even more strongly always already *here*. When Merlin installs the stones, both redactors possess these ancient objects as English by naming them "Stanhenge" in the present tense (l. 8732). Later, when Aurelius is on the verge of death, he asks to be buried at "Stanhenge": pronounced by Arthur's uncle, *Stonehenge* moves English into Briton history. The monument's durability (frequently referenced) enshrines the durability of the English themselves.⁴⁴

In Robert's history, the stones also sign the permanence of English dominion. The "noble stones" are identified as "þe treche of geans" (the dance of giants), a crafty and artful structure ("quointe," "art") (ll. 3062–63). Since the men of Albion have not been called giants, the stones are not related to original settlement. Their *quointise*, moreover, associates them with laudable conquest and other crafty maneuvers. Merlin extends their marvelousness by practicing "ginnes," "quointise," and "enchanterie" to move them (ll. 3106, 3109, 3124). When they are set up in England (about 480 years after Christ [l. 3112]), Robert concludes: "þus was stonheng uerst ymad" (l. 3126). The absence of etymology blocks the memory of the stones' pre-English identity. Since their conquest completes the marvels mentioned in the prologue, they mark progress toward the familiar present.

In the *Brut*, Arthur's Round Table represents a portable version of the Giants' Ring's colonial English architecture.[45] In a sequence greatly altered from Wace, La3amon establishes the Table as a hegemonic force of peace and law. The episode begins at a celebratory dinner, where a bloody fight over social and political precedence breaks out among the international guests. The fight itself explicitly engages ethnic troubles, as does its resolution, effected by a foreign hostage (l. 11376). Arthur seals the peace by punishing all the kin of the man who started the fight and enumerating a detailed litany of threats against future disturbances; he seals the peace with a universal swearing on relics. Arthur thus effects a juridical solution to international discord, secured by both God and lethal force. The Table itself is crafted by one of Arthur's itinerant imperial subjects, a carpenter who heard about the fight while overseas. Meeting Arthur in Cornwall, the craftsman proposes a circular table for sixteen hundred knights, to be seated facing each other around the inside and outside of the structure. Moreover, Arthur can take the table with him when he travels; he thus need never fear competitive social strife, anywhere in the world (ll. 11425–43). This mobile architectural innovation forms a round boundary that encompasses social and ethnic differences; it encircles people of all origins within an English collectivity that can be taken anywhere. Arthur's Round Table thus signifies the moment when the violence of group boundary formation cedes to the peace of boundless hegemony.

Despite visions of an Insular landscape fully settled by the English, La3amon and Robert both maintain Briton legitimacy, even beyond the First Variant's aspirations. La3amon's Cadwallader grants his last possessions to Ivor and Iny, "inc Walisc lond. þat 3et stond a mire hond" (in Welshland, that yet stands in their hand) (l. 16056). Cadwallader claims to have maintained legal title to this land, and he asks his heirs to defend it as long as they can. According to La3amon, they succeed admirably:

Þæs Bruttes an ælc ende. foren to Walisce londe.
and heore la3en leofeden. & heore leodene þæuwen.
And 3et wunieð þære. swa heo doð auere-mære.
& Ænglisce kinges. walden þas londes.
& Bruttes hit loseden. þis lond and þas leoden.
þat næuere seoððen mære. kings neoren here.
Þa 3et ne com þæs ilke dæi. beo heonne-uorð alse hit mæi.
i-wurðe þet i-wurðe. i-wurðe Godes wille.
　　Amen.
(Ll. 16088–96)

[The Britons from every edge came to Welsh lands, and their laws they loved and their customs kept, and they still live there, as they will do for ever more. And English kings hold the land, and the Britons lost it, this land and those living in it, so that never since then have they been kings here. That hasn't come yet, that actual day. Be henceforth as it may; come what comes, come God's will. Amen.]

The Britons' immutable culture ensures that they can recover their dominion as prophesied, whenever that day might come. Their right to the land transcends their current territorial restriction. As Laȝamon returns to his initial Christian refrain, the potential for territorial recovery rests with God. This conclusion maintains the Britons outside of English settlement, while also overlooking the beginnings and ends of English dominion. This paradoxical vision, founded on postcolonial grounds, accommodates difference without assimilation and tacitly legitimates English settlement.

Robert expands the suggestion of Welsh recovery with a detailed measurement of the lands they will rule. After Cadwallader's withdrawal to Rome (and without mentioning Ivor and Iny), Robert reminds readers of the restoration prophecies:

Ac as þe angel sede er. & Merlin biuore.
Hii ssolleþ ȝut keuery moche lond. þat hii abbeþ y lore.
Al walis & al þe march. & al middel lond ywis.
Þat is al þat bituene temese. & humber is.
Al est toward londone. þis me ssal ȝut yse.
Ac vpe godes wille it is. Wanne it ssal be.
(Ll. 5132–37)

[But as the angel said once and Merlin before, they shall yet recover much land that they had previously — all Wales and all the March, and all the Midlands for sure (that is, all that is between the Thames and the Humber, all east toward London). This men shall yet see, but it is up to God's will when it shall be.]

Robert's precise measurement, laid across the lands of his prologue, clearly locates Welsh dominion within English territory. Just as in Laȝamon's *Brut*, God's judgment determines English dominion and Welsh expansion. As the narrative moves beyond the bounds of Geoffrey's *Historia*, the presence of Welsh princes testifies to their enduring cultural and territorial potential: "light and hardy" Welshmen fight alongside Robert earl of Gloucester at the battle of Lincoln; Llywelyn harries English lands and loses many footmen while assisting Simon of Montfort.[46] These interventions hold out the possibility of real territorial gain.

If Robert and Laȝamon both maintain the reality of Welsh territorial rights, they also present the island as always already unified—occasionally conquered but impossible to divide. Laȝamon adopts Wace's *regne* (the First Variant's *regnum*) as a general quantification of the whole island; Robert turns Geoffrey's *totam insulam a mari usque ad mare* into a two-hundred-line calculation, and never measures again. Post-colonial historians of a long colonial history, neither writer takes possession of the landscape, for it has always endured as English land.

Englisce kunde

Unified, unbounded land sustains the flexible boundaries that Laȝamon and Robert need to turn the Britons into English ancestors. In their chronicles, *this land*, belonging to *us*, legitimates the transition from Briton to Saxon dominion.[47] Moreover, they follow the First Variant redactors in claiming admirable predecessors as "ours" and casting the undesirables as "them." Constructing a continuous *leod* and *kunde* (kin-group), Laȝamon and Robert bind the Britons, Angles, and Saxons to the thirteenth-century English. As historians, they patrol the borders of English identity by manipulating representations of force, genealogy, and Christianity. In their hands, then, the boundaries of "English" expand like the thong that encompasses Hengist's first castle to include all of the island's legitimate inhabitants. These postcolonial strategies take history away from Norman colonizing desire. By conflating past and present, they telescope historical distance and keep the boundaries between groups on the move.

The English occupy these Briton histories from the very beginning. Laȝamon, for example, proposes to tell the story of "Engle. þa æðelæn" (the noble English) (1. 7). This Englishing of Briton history has created ethnic conflict for some modern critics, who prefer to transfer the nobility to "England."[48] *Engle*, however, deftly effaces the disparate origins of the island's peoples and blocks the perception of historical difference. The island itself provides the basis of continuity, a fact first recognized by the Otho redactor, who emended the controversial line to "Engelond þe ristnesse" (the richness of England). The change publicizes the identity of the people with the land implied throughout the *Brut*. Robert, for his part, begins with a lengthy portrait of English ethnic beauty ("veireste men in þe world") and purity (ll. 180–89). Brutus looks like the first of these fair men when he is introduced a few lines later as "þe verste man. þat louerd was in engelond. as ich ȝow telle can" (the first man who was lord in England, as I can tell you) (ll. 214–15). With these opening maneuvers, all three writers cast the Britons as the admirable predecessors of the English.

The depth of Laȝamon's vision of Insular unity can be measured in the waters of the island's marvels. Like Wace, Laȝamon insists on the

95

extreme marvel of the segregated fish (ll. 10978–84). The normality of ethnic mingling surfaces dramatically in Laȝamon's revision of the Severn's spraying water. Reversing all precedent, he turns the dangerous marvel into a salvific one:

ȝif þer cumeð æi mon. þat noht ne cunne þer-on.
þat seollic to iseonne. bi þere sæ-stronde.
ȝif he his neb wendeð. touwærd þan mære.
ne beo he noht swa loh iboren. ful wel he beoð iborȝen.
þat water him glit bisiden. and þe mon þer wuneð softe.
after his iwille. he wuneð þer uul stille.
þat no bið he for þan watere. naðing idracched.
(Ll. 10996–11002)

[If there come any man that knows nothing about it, that strangeness to see by the sea-strand, if he turns his face toward the mere, no matter how lowborn he is, he is very well preserved. That water will glide beside him, and the man will stay there softly, according to his will; he will stay there all still, so that in no way by the water will he be disturbed.]

For both Geoffrey and Wace, the local people must turn their backs to the spray to avoid harm. If the water rushing in represents the regular arrivals of foreign peoples, then Laȝamon's version promotes assimilation rather than separatism. By accepting foreigners, men of all social groups remain *stille* and unharmed. Laȝamon goes on to eliminate the dangerous counterpoint, not mentioning what happens if the people turn away.

The Otho redactor and Robert both excise this episode, testifying to the ultimate irrelevance of its message. Indeed, Robert replaces the *Mirabilia Britanniae* with three new *Mirabilia Anglie* (so called in one manuscript): Bath's hot waters, Stonehenge, and wind from underground (ll. 151–68).[49] Robert does elaborate a novel ethnic allegory, however, when describing the natural life cycle of the eagles found among the rocks where the Scots hide from Arthur:

Hii of scapede atte laste. bi norþe mony a myle.
Þet water geþ al aboute. & þer inne eke beþ.
Sixti grete roches. as men al day yseþ.
Þer inne nomon ne woneþ. ac in ech roche þer is.
In tyme of ȝere an ernes nest. þat hii bredeþ inne ywis.
Ech is in a roche him sulf. vor hii ne mowe noȝt ney be.
Vor hom by houeþ moche mete. & hii ne mowe noȝt wel fle.
Vor feblesse of hor brode. ac wanne hor briddes rype beþ.
Þer hii findeþ more mete. in londes aboute hii fleþ.
(Ll. 3666–74)

[They [the Scots] escaped off at last, by north many a mile. There, the water goes all about and therein also be sixty great rocks, as men say all day. Therein no man dwells, but in each rock there is, in season, an eagle's nest that they breed in, for sure. Each is on a rock by himself, for no more may there be. They store nearby much meat, and they may not fly very well on account of the feebleness of their brood, but when their young birds are ripe, then they find more meat, in lands nearby they fly.]

The eagles' care for their hungry broods presents the family as a model for peace and stability. While protecting their fragile eggs, the eagles never move a feather. Having used up their stores nourishing their young, they naturally fly off in search of more food. These eagles represent the social concerns of a unified *kunde*, rather than strife among different *kundes* (the Scottish birds are usually known for their screams that prophesy invasion). In place of Laȝamon's *stille*, Robert imagines a seasonal and peaceful circulation of parental nurturing. In both cases, the existence of a single group and the absence of violent themes signal allegories of postcolonial settlement.

In order to embed ethnic unification in the patterns of history and turn the line of Insular rulers into "our kings," Laȝamon and Robert mobilize several other intertwined strategies. First, as heirs to conquerors, they either neutralize or sacralize force as a means to dominion. Laȝamon's historical pedagogy, for example, teaches us that ethnic identity does not bear on the legitimacy of dominion. Historiographically, Laȝamon overlooks the forceful origins of settlement; he judges the maintenance, rather than the establishment, of rule. From this perspective, a usurper who maintains good laws is valued more highly than a legitimate but tyrannical heir. By dismissing the importance of origins, Laȝamon can treat all predecessors as potentially admirable *antecessors*. Laȝamon's relatively neutral attitudes toward force reflect the perspective of the ruled, the settled inhabitants who suffer from injustice no matter who holds the crown. The *Brut* in fact portrays the tradition's most overtly coercive Brutus: he exacts Anacletus's cooperation with a naked sword drawn across his neck (ll. 343–46). Rulers throughout the *Brut* enforce their will by threatening their enemies as well as their subjects with eye gouging, castration, and burning—all without a word of the narrator's disapproval. Nor does Laȝamon comment on Gormund's declaration that he will rule no land that he has not conquered himself through battle (l. 14420). Laȝamon's tacit legitimation of force facilitates the narrative acceptance of the English as rightful rulers, a perspective the English *Brut* brings to an Insular history designed to demonstrate Briton losses rather than English gains.

Robert also takes force for granted, noting that England has often been taken by strength (l. 1033) and that the weak are ever subjugated to the strong. Unlike Laȝamon, however, he pacifies some of the *Historia*'s more brutal representations. He eliminates Brutus's encounter with Anacletus and replaces the exiled Saxons' fear to disobey their elders with a gladness "for prowess" (l. 2319). More than strength, Robert values craft (*quointise*) as a conjunction of intellectual cunning and military prowess. Everyone from Brutus to Merlin to William the Bastard to the crusaders practices *quointise*.[50] Like *crafte* in Laȝamon's *Brut* and *engin* in Wace's *Roman de Brut* and the Arthurian prose cycle (see chapters 5 and 6), *quointise* turns easily from clever cunning to deceptive treason, from intelligence to siege engines. Like physical force, mental powers are neither inherently evil nor universally good.

The disruptive powers of force and cunning reorient colonial encounters so that differences between groups appear mobile instead of immutable. Laȝamon and Robert manipulate historic differences directly by revising genealogical discourses. They turn away from colonial anxieties about ethnic purity and the damages wrought by exogamy by eliminating existing genealogical arguments or, in Robert's case, creating new ones. Laȝamon inherits from Wace an already weakened pattern of ethnic genealogy, which he then revises more than any other aspect of his source.[51] Silvius, for example, emphasizes that the Trojan-Britons and the Trojan-Lombards are of the same strand ("strund"), and explains that the Trojans find the Lombard women undesirable ("laðe") (ll. 1367–68). Briton women are thus sent to Lombardy because Silvius rejects the local women, rather than the other way around, as in Geoffrey and Wace. More important, Laȝamon immediately remarks that the arrangement brought the Lombards misfortune: the brothers followed their sisters, raised an army, and conquered Germany (ll. 1371–80). Laȝamon recognizes the "grief" that Trojan endogamy brought to the local inhabitants. By presenting both native and settler perspectives, Laȝamon diffuses genealogical imperatives.

Robert eradicates exogamous anxiety most deliberating in his portrayal of Brutus's marriage to Innogen. First, Brutus is assimilated to the English, already described as the fairest men of all, when Pandrasus begins to love him for his good luck ("faire cheance"), fair body ("beste bodi"), noble genealogy ("noble kinne"), and prowess (ll. 271–79). Indeed, Pandrasus admires Brutus so much that he *offers* him his daughter, unsolicited, along with ships, land, and the right to leave if he prefers to conquer better land (ll. 280–87). Since Robert does not narrate the battle that leads to Pandrasus's imprisonment, the entire resolution of Trojan enslavement involves little coercion. Instead, the beautiful Brutus seduces Pandrasus, eradicating all discussion of ethnic intermingling.

With Armorica's colonization, Laȝamon stages his own direct dismissal of exogamous anxiety. He has already criticized the Britons for shamefully ("heokerliche") refusing to give women to the Picts (l. 5011); now, he excises Conan's speech about the necessity of endogamous marriage.

Instead, Conanus articulates the problem of maintaining proper social intercourse: he orders that each craft group be sent in its own ship (that is, not mixed together with other professions) and that no men accompany the women except the sailors (ll. 5902–5). Here, social segregation maintains differences among the Britons themselves, while the gender segregation suggests that men, of any ethnicity, cannot be trusted with virgins. Conanus's instructions thus identify the issues that threaten social order, not ethnic genealogy.[52] Moreover, the women's strident refusals to leave the island prompt brutal coercion: Athionard threatens to kill his own daughter, and to hang the others by their nipples, if they do not board the ships (ll. 5941–55). Laȝamon's graphic portrayal of their subsequent drownings, rapes, prostitutions, and heathendoms tacitly indicts the men who would force women to leave their homeland (ll. 6033–45). In Laȝamon's vision, compulsory exile from England engenders greater tragedy than intermarriage with foreigners. In this respect, Laȝamon's narrative of Armorican colonization purveys post-colonial judgment.

Robert takes the process a step further. He also excises Conanus's endogamous speech, but maintains the concern for the purity of the *kunde*: Conanus, "our prince" (l. 2081) sends for women, that the men "miȝte make hor kunde. al clene of hor blod" (might make their kin all pure of their own blood) (l. 2014). The account of the virgin drownings follows Geoffrey's text closely, except for the conclusion, which exposes the sexual secret of colonial compromise: "So þat to þe lasse brutaine. þer ne come aliue non" (so that to Brittany there came none alive) (l. 2020). Robert can speak of Briton intermarriage because he views the episode in post-colonial terms. As will become clear when Robert moves beyond Geoffrey's *Historia*, it takes only one parent to maintain the English *kunde*.

Helen's abduction by the giant of Mont Saint-Michel enacts virginal rape over Brittany again, this time as a violation that threatens family stability. In Laȝamon's *Brut*, the old woman describes the abduction itself as a home-invasion, and the messengers wonder if the giant has taken the girl "to wife" (ll. 12815, 12917–22). Although the giant clearly combines the monstrous assimilation of cannibalism with the intimate invasion of rape, Arthur treats him like any foreign knight once he has disabled him (ll. 12816, 12932–35). Wounded in his phallic thigh, the giant asks for mercy and to know who is fighting; Arthur identifies himself and asks the giant to do likewise, including his people ("cunne"), his father and mother, and his "londe" (ll. 13019–24). The fiend ("feond") agrees to tell all and obey if Arthur will grant mercy. Although the giant follows chivalric protocol perfectly and wisely seeks to confirm that mercy has been granted before identifying himself, Arthur angrily orders his beheading (ll. 13025–32). The scene thus mixes the desire to reintegrate the outlaw with the impulse for blood vengeance against family wrongs. The equivocation personalizes the dilemma as that of a knight and caring uncle (Laȝamon makes Helen Hoel's daughter [l. 12924]). The displacement of colonial concerns about sexual heritage is sealed in the conclusion, where Laȝamon excises Arthur's story about Ritho (ll. 13036–67). The scene thus inflects the threat of lawless neighbors. This threat recurs and in fact defines social intercourse, enacted in the giant's repeated, week-long rape of the old woman.[53] The episode performs the failure of traditional codes, settled society's worst nightmare. Robert domesticates the dangers of sexual compromise even more clearly. First, the "giant" is a deformed ("vorbroyde") man like the natives of Albion (ll. 4191, 4194). And in this account, unlike Geoffrey's history, Helen dies of rape, not fright: "Mid lecherye he hire slou" (with lechery he slew her) (l. 4198). In Robert's post-colonial history, as in Laȝamon's, rape can be spoken as a social violation without damage to the ethnic psyche.

These episodes, which for other historians engage colonial anxieties about ethnic integrity, expose Laȝamon's and Robert's perceptions of postcolonial identities. For them, differences recede to the edges rather than occupying the center of identity politics. Their revisions of the Britons' most difficult relatives, the Romans, illustrate this shift of focus dramatically. Laȝamon's Belinus and Brennius, for example, justify the first conquest of Rome as vengeance for their relative Romulus (ll. 2613–970). This argument, which Laȝamon seems to have invented, turns aggressive expansion into restoration. And when Caesar arrives at the island, he never claims genealogical precedence, even though he recognizes that the Romans and Britons are of one "kunne" (ll. 3620–25). Recounting what he knows of Briton history from books, he stops at Belinus's conquest to express sadness that his elders were shamed before his birth (ll. 3626–34): he resolves to conquer Britain in order to avenge his forefathers. This rhetoric, like Belinus and Brennius's, pursues expansion as the preservation of an anterior status quo. In fact, neither Caesar nor Cassibellanus ever mentions their common ancestors by name. Caesar identifies himself briefly in his letter, and claims tribute because he has imperial eyes: "for al hit is min aȝen. þat ic iseo mid min æȝen" (for it is all mine again, what I see with my eyes) (l. 3647). Cassibellanus, in turn, denounces the claim as greedy, and cites their common ancestry only to underscore their respective freedom and independence; he ends by threatening that Caesar should submit to him because of previous Briton victories over Rome (ll. 3653–77). Relations with Rome thus concern imperial precedence and are negotiated through force rather than genealogy. Britons do not speak of genealogy even when they marry Romans: no genealogical debate precedes Octavius's invitation to Maximianus; Caradocus later identifies Maximianus's nobility ("aðele cunne") rather than his parents (ll. 5699–724). By avoiding genealogical argument, Laȝamon dismisses ethnic difference.

Robert, by contrast, follows his inherited genealogies closely, including Caesar's speech, Constantine's conquest of Rome, and Caradocus's invitation to Maximianus.[54] All of these arguments turn on the integrity of the *kunde* and the *lond*, categories that Robert constructs through re-semblance rather than difference. Mothers, for example, repeatedly trans-mit the identity of the legitimate Insular *kunde* to their children, irre-spective of the fathers' origins. Robert thus mobilizes matrilineal descent against the *Historia*'s agnatic logic. In this way, he can integrate any ex-ogamous marriage into an ethnically pure genealogy. He articulates this principle most clearly in relation to the first Pict-Scot marriages, but it applies south of the Humber as well. The Scots, first of all, are actually Israelites, led out of Egypt by Moses (ll. 921–52). With this added detail, Robert establishes a firm ethnic boundary. Allowed to settle in Ireland, the Jewish-Scots agree to send women to the Picts on the condition that the children will take their name and inheritance from the mother when-ever the father's identity is in doubt, since the truth of the mother is more easily known than that of the father and family wealth must not fall "out of kunde" through misbegotten children: "In þis manere picars. mid scottes mengd hor blod" (in this manner the Picts mingled their blood with the Scots) (ll. 980–89). The Scots thus patrol their ethnic boundary through matrilineal inheritance; they even take their name from these Scot women from Ireland (the Picts' name is forgotten) (ll. 990–96). Robert appropriates this alien matrilineal principle in his analy-sis of the succession disputed between Henry I and his brother Robert Curthose: Robert concludes that although Curthose was older, Henry had the best right because he was married to Maud, the "kunde eir" (heir from the kin-group) (ll. 8754–57). In these and many other passages detailing marriage arrangements, Robert manipulates exogamy to keep England in the family.

As Laȝamon and Robert endeavor to graft the Britons onto the En-glish family tree, they face the significant challenge of recuperating the Britons' treacherous Saxon enemies into that same noble line. Both his-torians deploy the boundary between Christians and Heathens in order to disrupt the boundaries that lie among Britons, Angles, Saxons, and English. Christian alliances, as Lesley Johnson has shown, cut across both ethnic and family lines ("Reading" 151). The immutable difference between Christian and Heathen comes to coincide with the similarly intransigent opposition between *us* and *them: we Christians* can encom-pass any configuration of ethnic groups.

Robert sanctifies Briton history well before the Saxons arrive. The Britons, for example, defeat Caesar in the first battle "þoru godes grace" (l. 1146). When Christ is born, Robert praises the emperor who brought Pilate to justice for killing him (ll. 1412–19). Robert proceeds to give as much attention to the Roman emperors as he does to Briton kings, until imperial history takes over completely between Claudius and Marius (ll. 1538–635). Robert judges each emperor according to his treatment of Christianity. Trajan, for example, is so just that more than five hundred years later Saint Gregory brought his soul out of Hell, baptized him, and sent him to Heaven (ll. 1603–17); Robert commends Adrian for killing the Jews in Jerusalem (ll. 1618–24). On the opposite end of the spectrum, Nero goes completely insane ("pur gidy & wod") (ll. 1540–41) after slaying Saints Peter and Paul. He then kills his mother while trying to see the "fair chamber" of her womb where he lived before birth; he demands that his physicians make him pregnant, on pain of death (ll. 1542–53). As punishment for persecuting Christian apostles, then, Nero is compelled to pervert Christ's virgin birth. The physicians miraculously succeed, until Nero's womb is so large and sore that he threatens to hang them if they do not induce birth (ll. 1556–59). Again miraculously, the physicians succeed and Nero bears a "sori child," "a foul frogge": "ȝut þis gidie wrecche. louede þis foule best. / As wommon deþ hire child" (yet this giddy wretch loved this foul beast, as a woman does her child) (ll. 1560–65). Nero builds a court for the frog, called Lateran, which means *frog* in Roman; Robert notes that this "head church of all Christendom" has a better head now than the frog (ll. 1566–75). With Lateran, then, Nero inadvertently refounds Christiandom. The "giddy wretch" goes on to set fire to the city (in an effort to recover the joyous light of Troy in flames) before finally dying a vile death at the hands of the Roman citizens, "& þus him vel vrecche of god. vor he þe apostle slou" (and thus the wrath of God fell on him, for he slew the apostles) (l. 1585). Robert's Christian judgment of Roman history engenders this extended interpolation, whose grotesque performance of transgressive desire returns all the way to Troy.

During the reign of Marcus and Aurelius, Robert promises to tell how Pope Eleutherius brought Christianity to England for the first time (ll. 1629–32). He then follows Geoffrey's account in full, enumerating the episcopal sees that complete yet another portion of the opening *descriptio* (ll. 1640–74). Robert immediately refers to the "luþer emperour" Diocletian, who brought Heathenness back until Saint Augustine "unbound" it (ll. 1675–77). When Robert later comes to the Diocletian persecutions themselves, he treats the martyred saints as familiar names that "you can read in church" (l. 1822); he eliminates Geoffrey's criticism of Briton memory (where the martyrs have been forgotten because of the barbarians ["lugubri barbarorum divortio civibus adempta fuissent"] [150]). Suppressing the story of Albanus and adding references to Saints Christine, Foy, and Vincent (ll. 1806–27), Robert substitutes English memory for Briton amnesia.[55] These revisions populate Briton history with legendary English saints, whose reputations endure into the present.

The arrival of the Heathen Saxons throws Briton Christianity into heightened relief. From Vortigern's first palpitation for Ronwen, Laȝamon and Robert condemn the Saxons as Heathens instead of vilifying them as foreign settlers ("comelings"). During Vortimer's reign, all of the English are Heathens and all of the Britons are Christians; there are so many new settlers ("uncuðe leoden," "heaþene hundes," and "heþene-men") that it is impossible to distinguish between Christians and Heathens.[56] Robert repeats several times that marriages between Christians and Heathens are evil ("luþer"), and wonders what happens to the children when the fathers are Christian and the mothers Heathen.[57] Laʒamon portrays both the Romans and Mordred's supporters as Heathen hordes; Robert follows Geoffrey with a mix of Christians, Sarrasins, and Heathens.[58] Robert disperses ethnic identity directly when he owns the traitorous Saxons as ancestors ("vre faderes") while simultaneously claiming the Briton Vortigern (the "vnkunde ssrewe") as "vre feble king" (ll. 2696–98). Subsequently, Robert observes that the Saxons should learn better than to fight Christian men (ll. 3216–17). After Arthur's death, Robert immediately portrays the land's disintegration in Christian terms: the "luþer heathens" burn everything and drive out the "kundemen"; Christendom is beaten all to the ground, and the relics are taken into Wales (ll. 4619–53). Indeed, for Robert, Arthur's death ("Alas þe gode arþure") leads directly to "pur heþenesse" and the Saxons' "clene maystrie" (full mastery) (ll. 4652–56). Having thus established Christianity as the most relevant identity boundary, Laʒamon and Robert can easily represent these Saxons as noble ancestors and rightful rulers once they convert. After conversion, the English are more and more *our* heros, the Britons increasingly cast as *them*.

Although Laʒamon's Britons reject the English as recent converts (ll. 14844–64), the narrative pattern itself does not ratify this ethnocentric judgment. Laʒamon describes the contours of Edwin's realm, for example, in terms identical to Arthur's, inviting readers to transfer their admiration of Arthur to Edwin.[59] And when Cadwallo kills Edwin in battle, he becomes "king of the Angles" or "king of the English."[60] Laʒamon thus appropriates Briton history for the English by making one of the last Briton kings a sovereign of the English people. From this perspective, Laʒamon's sympathies are not reversed toward the end of the *Brut*, as Françoise Le Saux suggests;[61] rather, they are dispersed into multiple partial identifications with Britons, English, and Christians. Penda exemplifies this multiplication, for he is a traitorous Christian Englishman sworn to serve a Christian Briton king.[62] Cadwallader likewise embodies a border identity, for his mother is Penda's sister Helen (herself a figure of converging identities)[63] and he is an English king driven out by a Saxon king, Aethelstan.[64] The narrative thus invites the audience to admire the Britons, the Angles, and the Saxons as equally worthy ancestors of the contemporary English on the basis of their "common insularity."[65] Le Saux observes further that Laʒamon seems to be "trying to rub out the dividing line between Welsh and English." In the end, when Laʒamon says that Aethelstan was "þe formeste Englisce mon. þe al Ængle-lond biwon" (the first English man who won all England) (l. 15944), his achievement is to be admired as the first of *our* kings (the *Historia* and the *Brut y Brenhinedd* record his territorial consolidation with regret). Ultimately, Briton history ends as it began—in Christian prayer for the souls of generations of English ancestors ("Amen"). The repetition of prayers, and history, preserves English dominion as a Christian refrain that echoes across the land.

Robert takes a more radical approach to the passage of dominion. Right after Arthur's death, he excises all signs of Briton dominion—the reigns of Constantine, Aurelius Conanus, Vortiporius, and Malgo, as well as Geoffrey's apostrophe. Instead, on a page titled in one manuscript *Saxones plene Dominantes* (Saxons fully Dominant), Robert names the six Saxon kingdoms and fills in their history since Hengist, with an emphasis on Wessex: Cedric (whose origins Geoffrey does not mention) was the first king of Wessex; Kinrik was king after his father, and so on: "Ac þe kings of westsex. lengest gonne dure. / & alle þe oþere wonne to hom. as ȝe ssolle her after yhure" (But the kings of Wessex lasted longest, and won all the others to them, as you shall hear hereafter) (ll. 4655–714). While this enumeration takes place in Heathen time, it also fulfills the opening *descriptio* and thus a recognizably English landscape. Indeed, Robert reminds us that we can read about each kingdom's territory at the beginning of the book.

As the consolidation of Saxon dominion continues (with the enumeration of cities), Heathenness remains in all the land for about forty years until Saint Augustine's mission (ll. 4715–28). Where Geoffrey does not mention the Saxons' actual conversion, Robert specifically names the churches they founded and the bishoprics that fulfill the *descriptio* (ll. 4755–75). After adding a detailed account of Glastonbury's founding (ll. 4783–801), Robert maintains Christianity, rather than ethnicity, at the center of Insular identity with a savvy revision of Augustine's encounter with the Britons. In response to Dinoot's refusal to submit to the archbishop of Canterbury, Robert apparently invents a speech for Augustine, which prophesies the Britons' punishment for offending the Christian faith:

ȝif ȝe nolleþ quaþ seint austin. mid ȝoure breþeren in peys be.
þat beþ as ȝe witeþ wel. cristine as wel as ȝe.
& ȝif ȝe nolle englissemen. godes lawes teche.
& vorþ mid me among hom. cristendom preche.
ȝoure fon ssolle hor poer. among ow wide reche.
& bringe ȝou to deþe monion. & þat ssal be ȝoure wreche.
After seint austines day. to soþe come al þis.
(Ll. 4825–31)

["If you won't," said Saint Augustine, "be in peace with your brethren, who are as you well know Christian as well as you, and if you won't teach Englishmen good laws and go forth with me among them to preach Christendom, your enemies shall reach wide among you with their power and bring many of you to death and that shall be your punishment." After Saint Augustine's day all this came true.]

Casting the English as pastoral "brethren," Robert eradicates all ambiguity about Augustine's role in the monks' massacre: he merely predicts God's punishment. Robert notes that God does not neglect to punish the English king for the "luþer dede": the Britons defeat Ethelfrid and regain dominion south of the Humber (ll. 4860–74).

Subsequently, Briton success derives from English Heathenness. Cadwallo defeats Edwin and then Enfrid, as the English are all turned again to Heathenness (ll. 4942–45). The English themselves are soon divided along these same lines, as Penda the "heþene duc" (ll. 4986, 5012) martyrs Saint Oswy of the "cristinemen" (ll. 4975, 5011) (Robert does not mention Cadwallo's advisers' description of the value of intraethnic strife). Throughout these events, Robert barely mentions Cadwallo; his son Cadwallader recognizes God's punishment (ll. 5046–69) and dies a Christian death (ll. 5114–19). Robert then excises the episodes of famine, Saxon struggle, and Ivor and Iny's resistance. Instead, he unifies the English and Saxons at the very moment they build the prologue's towns: "Þe englisse þo & saxons. þat al one þo were. / Grete touns & castles. bigonne bulde & rere" (The English and the Saxons who were all one began to build and raise great towns and castles) (ll. 5120–21).

Despite their losses, however, the Britons maintain a legitimate claim to the land, on both ethnic and religious grounds:

Here we englisse men. mowe yse some.
Mod woche riʒte we beþ. to þis lond ycome.
Ac þe wrecche welissemen. beþ of þe olde more.
In woche manere ʒe abbeþ yhurd. hou hii it abbeþ ylore.
Ac þe feble is euere bineþe. vor hii þat abbeþ miʒte.
Mid strengþe bringeþ ofte. þat wowe to þe riʒte.
(Ll. 5138–43)

[Here we Englishmen may see in our own mind with what right we came to this land, for the punished Welshmen are more ancient. You have heard in what manner they lost it, but the feeble is ever beneath, for they who have might with strength often bring that woe to the right.]

Robert recognizes that force created English dominion without destroying Welsh rights; he seems to believe in the prophecy of Welsh restoration. Similarly, Robert notes that Maximianus took control of Brittany, "More þoru strengþe as ʒe seþ. þan þoru riʒt dom" (more through strength as you see than through justified right) (l. 2096). Robert's representation of warfare is in fact often fatalistic: although war causes much *wo* (which

Robert describes in gory detail for thirteenth-century events), a divine design always justifies the results that arrive *atte laste*.[66] God, while allowing defeat, does not deprive the weak defeated of their historical right: "The justice of God's vengeance...does not justify the actions of his agents."[67] Robert thus legitimates English dominion by attributing Welsh feebleness to divine judgment.

Laȝamon and Robert continue to manipulate ethnic boundaries as they struggle to maintain the *englisce kunde*'s historiographic integrity in the wake of Danish and Norman conquests. Although Laȝamon only witnesses these conquests in etymologies, his representations minimize their import. When Hengist builds his castle, for example, Laȝamon adds the castle's Danish name, noting that the Danes drove out the "Bruttes" (l. 7107). Blending ethnicities and centuries, Laȝamon overlooks the fact that the Saxons had already driven out the Britons when the Danes arrived. The Otho redactor is even less able or interested to designate groups, referring to those vanquished by the Danes as "cnihtes" (knights). By remembering the Danes at all, both writers return the narrative and the English to colonized experience, but only after declaring that the castle's English name stands "nu and auere-mare" (l. 7105). Danish conquest, then, fails to disrupt the continuity of English settlement.

The Normans, by contrast, change Insular nomenclature permanently. Summarizing how conquests have modified *New Troy*, Laȝamon concludes that no town anywhere in Britain has its original name (ll. 3549–55). The judgment is nostalgic yet not too regretful since Laȝamon's Englishing of Briton history has demanded relative neutrality on forceful changes of dominion. Laȝamon definitely deplores the suffering caused by the Normans (l. 3548), but he remarks elsewhere that the peasants always suffer in war, no matter who causes it. Moreover, Laȝamon tacitly assimilates *Normanitas* to English identity by translating from Wace and by outlining Saxon institutions in Norman terms.[68] As a descendent of English colonizers, Laȝamon thus easily appropriates Norman colonization for a post-colonial England.

Robert confronts Danish and Norman colonization directly when he narrates beyond the *Historia*, extending the strategies that encompassed Britons within English history — Christianity and genealogical manipulation — to the contemporary period. From the eighth century to the thirteenth, Christian progress mirrors English progress, and saintliness often leads directly to political power (whether the saint is a king like Edward or a bishop like Thomas).[69] Robert also incorporates extensive accounts of the Crusades and England's relations with the papacy.[70] Especially in the Norman period, Christian relations govern Robert's judgment. William the Red, for example, is a good king until Lanfranc dies.[71] And Robert Curthose's rejection of the kingship of the Holy Land elicits an extended apostrophe, beginning "Awey seli Robelin. seli courtehese" (Away silly Robert, silly Curthose!) and ending "Wat was þi strengþe

106

wurþ. & þi chiualerie. / Þo þou lore grace of god. ywis noʒt wurþ a flye" (What was your strength worth, and your chivalary? Without God's grace, surely not worth a flea!); Robert jokes that God understood Curthose's aversion to work, and so sent him to rest in prison.[72] Under John and Henry III, interdict and excommunication become tools of government, as those who hold against the king's Charter are repeatedly excommunicated.[73] Throughout, attacks on Insular Jews reinforce the boundary of English Christianity.[74] All of these representations maintain the continuity of the Christian English *kunde* by aggressively opposing it to foreigners, Heathens, excommunicants, and Jews.

Ethnic genealogies require more extensive labors. Robert begins by introducing the Danes as *them* almost as soon as the narrative crosses the borders of Geoffrey's narrative: the battles of Denmark were the worst "of alle oþer" because instead of holding the land, they robbed, injured, destroyed, burned, and slew the inhabitants.[75] Anyone who defeats them is thus a hero of the *kunde*. Summarizing Aethelwulf's victory a few years after the first invasions, Robert expresses the configuration of Christian English justice succinctly:

Ac vre suete louerd atte laste. ssewede is suete grace.
& sende þe cristine englisse men. þe maystrie in þe place.
& þe heþene men of denemarch. bineþe were echon.
Nou nas þer ʒut in denemarch. Cristinedom non.
(Ll. 5257–61)

[But our sweet Lord at last showed his sweet grace, and sent the Christian English men the mastery of the place, and the Heathen men of Denmark were beneath, each one. There was not yet in Denmark any Christendom.]

Just as with the Britons and Saxons, the rightful group of Insular rulers are all Christian and the invaders all Heathen. Moreover, the Christian definition of legitimate *kunde* leads to the clearest dismissal of ethnic identity yet, as Aethelwulf's son Alfred is crowned by the pope ("the crown is yet in this land") as "king of englelond. of all þat þer come" (king of England, of all who come there) (l. 5330); he is in fact the first "pur king" (l. 5333). Henceforth, no "comelings" can disrupt this sanctified English kingdom, for all Insular Christians are subsumed within Englishness: post-colonial dominion rules all who live in the territory, regardless of origin.

Only sin can disrupt English dominion: despite harrying the English throughout the century, the Danes only gain dominion through the sins of Saint Edward the Martyr's step-mother. She kills Edward to make her son Aelred king, and Saint Dunstan prophesies punishment for the crown unrightly won (ll. 5905–15). The Danes in fact come, but leave when Aelred acquires formidable allies by marrying Emma of Normandy after the death of his first wife. Defense against the Danes thus becomes explicitly intertwined with access for the Normans:

& here sprong lo þe uerste more as of hom of normandye.
Ware þoru hii come in to þis lond. & abbeþ þe maystrye.
Vor þe kynge adde bi þis emme. tuie sones ywis.
Alfred & seint edward. þat at westmunstre yssrined is.
& þoru þulke blode suþþe. william bastard com.
As ʒe ssolle her after ihure. & wan þis kinedom.
Þat poer muche of denemarch. in pes wiþoute strif.
Was hom ywent to denemarch. ar þe king weddede wif.
(Ll. 5966–73)

[And here sprang the first root from men of Normandy, through which they came to this land and have the mastery. For the king had by this Emma two sons certainly, Alfred and Saint Edward (who is enshrined at Westminster), and through that blood truthfully William the Bastard came, as you shall hear hereafter, and won this kingdom. That great power of Denmark, in peace without strife, went home to Denmark before the king wedded wife.]

The Danes may be intimidated by the Normans, but Robert does not let readers think for a moment that the English are safe. And indeed, the Danes harry the English throughout Aethelred's reign; at his death, Insular allegiance is divided between his son Edmund Ironside and the Dane Cnut.

During the Danes' extended disruption of legitimate English rule, Robert carefully traces out — with numerous prospective and retrospective references — the ethnic complexities generated by Aethelred's two wives (the first English, the second the Norman Emma), Emma's two husbands (the English Aethelred and the Danish Cnut), and Cnut's two wives (the first Danish, the second Emma). Throughout, the English line spawned by Edmund Ironside (Aethelred's son by his English wife) remains the legitimate one. As soon as Cnut takes power, Robert summarizes the fates of Edmund's sons, showing us immediately how "riʒt kunde" will return through Edmund's great-granddaughter Maud when she marries Henry I (ll. 6443–69). While the Danes do reign, Robert judges each king according to his Christian Englishness. Cnut, for example, makes amends not only by renouncing his illegitimate crown and making pilgrimage to Rome, but by honoring Edmund's grave at Glastonbury and confirming all of the charters issued to the abbey by English kings (ll. 6590–635). Cnut's veneration for both God and English tradition redeem his usurpation. His son Harold, by contrast, is an evil king because he is a pure Dane who hates the English and exiles Emma (ll. 6639–59); Cnut's son by Emma, Harthecnut, chosen by both Danes and English, is not such a bad king (ll. 6660–72).

After Harthecnut's death, Robert reminds us that Saint Dunstan's prophecy had come true: England had been "out of kunde," in pain and sorrow, for twenty-six years (ll. 6673–77). The Danish disruption is now definitively over with the accession of Saint Edward, Edmund's "riȝt eir of kunde" (l. 6680). Indeed, it is as if those twenty-six years had never happened, since dominion returns to the English line as it existed before Cnut...except for Edward's Norman uncles. As Turville-Petre points out, Robert absolves Edward himself of all responsibility for Norman oppression by casting him as a chaste saint (92–93): Edward defeats the Danes by prayer alone, and the disputed succession that leads to Norman dominion results from his chastity. All the blame falls instead on Harold son of Goodwin (Edward's wife's brother): Edward bequeaths England to his cousin William the Bastard, but Harold breaks his oath to William and usurps the crown (Edmund's grandson Edward Aetheling is the real "kunde eir"). This transition out of *kunde* is so complicated, the grafting of families so awkward for Robert, that his resolutely linear narrative progression dissolves, such that Edward dies three times (ll. 7030, 7175, 7259).

Just before his final death, Edward envisions the *kunde*'s restoration. On his deathbed, he describes a vision (well known from other sources)[76] of a tree struck down at its roots (ll. 7228–33). Robert says the allegory was well understood at the time: the tree signifies the noble kingdom of England and the "riȝt kunde" of Aelred, Edward's father. The family tree is struck down when Edward dies without heir; afterward, three kings of "vnkunde sede" hold the land (Harold the queen's brother, William the Bastard, and his son William the Red). *Kunde* returns when William the Bastard's other son Henry marries Maud, Edward's niece: "& normandie þoru þe king. & þoru þe quene englelond. / ioyned were þo kundeliche. as in one monnes hond" (and Normandy through the king, and through the queen England, were joined kinfully, as in one man's hand) (ll. 7240–57). Maud emerges as the most frequently and effusively praised individual of the entire narrative, the *kunde*'s real hero: no tongue can tell her goodness; she was well raised, and cared heroically for leprosy victims.[77] Through Maud, Robert presents Henry II's accession as a restoration of legitimate English *kunde* (ll. 7100–135).

Despite this skillful pruning of Norman identity from the stock of the English family tree, Robert insists rather tendentiously (for the later thirteenth century)[78] that the Normans are "yet among us." In the prologue, he says that the Normans won England "and shall evermore" (ll. 56–50); he concludes a summary of Insular conquest with the Normans: "Atte laste hii of normandie. þat maisters beþ ȝut here. / Wonne hit & holdeþ ȝut" (At last they of Normandy, who are yet masters here, won it and hold it yet) (ll. 7330–31). After the conquest, the English, like the Britons, await God's judgment:

& þus was in normannes hond. þat lond ibroȝt iwis.
Þat anaunter ȝif euermo. keueringe þer of is.
Of þe normans beþ heyemen. þat beþ of englelonde.
& þe lowemen of saxons. as ich vnderstonde.
So þat ȝe seþ in eiþer side. wat riȝte ȝe abbeþ þerto.
Ac ich vnderstonde þat it was. þoru godes wille ydo.
(Ll. 7495–503)

[And thus was that land brought into the Normans' hand, for sure,
so that one wonders if there is ever any recovering from it. The
Normans are the highmen of England, the lowmen the Saxons, as I
understand, so that you see on either side what right you have to
it. But I understand that it was done through God's will.]

Through the Saxons, Robert mobilizes the memory of English origins,
while distancing the narrator from their defeat by referring to "that
land" instead of his usual "this land." At the same time, he reminds his
English audience that they maintain a legitimate claim to the land,
even though God has punished them (through the Normans). The Normans' evilness (which Robert summarizes in detail) purveys just retribution for the sins of Aethelred's mother, "As þe gostes in auision. to
seint edward sede" (as the ghost said to Saint Edward in his vision) (ll.
7504–14). By maintaining the Normans as oppressors into the late thirteenth century, Robert draws attention to the continuity of English unity.

After the conquest, Robert maintains the English *kunde* by deploying
all of the boundary tools at his disposal. He telescopes historical distance by calling William "our king" (l. 7985) and draws attention to the
"kunde eirs" (Maud and her uncle Edward Aetheling).[79] Maud is in fact
responsible for all of Henry I's good laws; Robert refers repeatedly to the
kunde's restoration, already prophesied and narrated (ll. 8730–51). After
Henry's death, Stephen of Blois cannot be the real heir because he is not
related to Maud (ll. 7627–29). With the birth of Maud's grandson, Robert
shifts his judgment to religious issues, introducing the infant Henry as
Saint Thomas's martyrer (l. 9095) (not unlike the Heathen Roman emperors who persecuted the popes). By making Thomas Beckett a hero of
religious and legal principle, Robert overlooks his obvious identity as
one of the "Normans among us."[80] Although Henry embodies the *kunde*'s
restoration, Thomas becomes England's champion on religious grounds.
At John's accession, Robert judges Arthur of Brittany as a closer heir to
Richard since he is the son of Richard's older brother (John only keeps
the kingdom because he murders his rival, like so many of his Briton
and Saxon predecessors).[81]

With Henry III's accession, Robert defines the English in opposition
to the French, who plot to cast out "kunde englissemen" (ll. 10992–
1003). Yet the hero of the barons' wars against Henry is Simon of Mont-

fort, killed at the "murder of Evesham" where the "feebler" lost even though God remained on their side (ll. 11714–64). Robert draws Simon into the *kunde* because he fights to resurrect the saintly origins of English identity: he defends Saint Edward's charter of good laws, which "so ofte was igraunted er. & so ofte vndo" (so often was granted and so often undone) (l. 11019). Simon in fact exemplifies postcolonial ethnicity — a French nobleman, brother-in-law to the English king and distantly related to William the Conqueror, he galvanized English revolt against foreigners.[82] Although Turville-Petre calls Robert's sanctification of Simon "thoroughly tendentious" (100), J. R. Maddicott's depiction of Simon's shrine at Evesham evidences a broad popularity among English contemporaries discomfited by royal policy and foreign incursions (346–47, 367–68). Even though Simon reportedly considered English nobles untrustworthy,[83] the English in general (especially outside royal circles) considered him a hero of righteous reform. Although Robert appears to contradict himself when he vilifies the French "among us" and sanctifies a Frenchman like Simon, the representation is thoroughly consistent with a post-colonial identity politics: Robert defends the integrity of the English *kunde* at the cost even of ethnicity.

English identity ultimately rests on a set of converging ethnic and religious boundaries, strategically deployed in the service of the *kunde* so that continuity can flow even through partial disruptions. Laȝamon and Robert manipulate the representation of divine judgment in order to explain the defeat of the deserving and the successes of the undesirable. Legitimate English dominion thus derives from a sanctification of history that extends the borders of Christianity along with the repertoire of admirable ancestors. By shifting the borders around the center of English identity, Laȝamon and Robert disperse the colonized identifications they inherited; they develop postcolonial strategies of multiple partial identifications that work around colonial disruptions.

Hor owe speche

The *kunde*'s continuity also proceeds through language. English, like the narratives themselves, traverses the frontiers between ethnic groups and historical periods. Translation into English becomes yet another strategy for negotiating identity through colonial challenges. By the thirteenth century, in fact, English can function as an inclusive medium that addresses both monolingual Anglophones and bilingual Francophones.[84] Historiography in English thus expands both the audience and the meaning of colonial history. Although Ian Short may overestimate the Englishing of the Anglo-Normans when he affirms that the children of Wace's audience would have been a natural audience for Laȝamon (248), English certainly reached not only a different audience but a broader one as well. At the same time, however, English is exclusive because only the English use it.[85] Linguistic exclusion converges on the religious when Robert describes the traitor who poisons Aurelius as knowing "Langage of þis londe. / as he were a cristineman" (l. 3157). By expressing themselves in English, then, Laȝamon, the Otho redactor, and Robert draw their listeners, of whatever ethnic origin, into the Christian English kin-group.

The significance of English, however, differs with each writer. While Laȝamon poignantly settles a French text of Norman colonial power into an English landscape, the Otho redactor revises an already English text and may have been monolingual. Robert, for his part, takes a completely different tack, translating from multiple Latin sources that he never names. Effacing the boundaries that Geoffrey drew so clearly between himself and William of Malmesbury and Henry of Huntingdon, Robert turns Geoffrey's colonial ambivalence into a confident English occupation. Laȝamon and Robert thus dispossess French and Latin precedents and perform linguistic conquests of history. In a land imagined without borders, both proffer a history that appears always already English. The Otho redactor and Robert's revisers, who read and write only English, witness the success of this settlement.

In both the *Brut* and the English *Historia*, the representation of translation engages the historians' own linguistic practices. In the *Brut*, Alfred (England's "deorling") reflects Laȝamon's historiographic strategy in that he renders a text of ultimately Briton origin into English (ll. 3147–53). Since Laȝamon insists on the fact that Alfred's English laws were first made by the Briton Marcia, Briton origins and prestigious English translation coexist comfortably, as they do in the *Brut* itself. The juxtaposition of original and contemporary languages strategically bypasses all other interventions in the transmission process. Laȝamon advertises the Englishness of his own translation by mobilizing archaic forms, avoiding words of French derivation, and introducing Germanic patterns.[86] Moreover, he consistently rewrites his source's translations (unlike the Welsh translator of the *Brut y Brenhinedd*).[87] While the archaisms telescope historical distance by bringing the past into the present, these anachronistic translations bring the present into the past. Both strategies purvey a presentist historiography that renders the past familiar. Robert likewise speaks from the present by using *England* from the first line. He never even mentions that he translates and suppresses Geoffrey's paradigmatic figures of translation, Alfred and Gildas. Robert's pervasive presentism thus blocks the memory of translation, the technology that explicitly engages linguistic difference.

In these English-language narratives, historical Saxon speech ratifies the continuity of language, people, and dominion. Hengist's first naming of the days of the week, for example, resembles the audience's most recent experience of *Friday*.[88] Robert's rendering of Ronwen's toast implies an Anglophone audience most strongly, as he concludes obliquely that "[m]en þat knewe þe langage. sede wat was washail" (men who knew

112

the language said what was *washail*) (l. 2517). Robert makes the continuity explicit when the Saxons betray the Britons at Amesbury: since
the Saxon order to draw their knives would be perfectly understandable
to the Anglophone audience, Robert must explain: "Nou ne couþe þe
brutons. non engliss ywys. / Ac þe saxons speche it was. / & þoru hom
ycome it is" (Now the Britons didn't understand any English, for sure,
but it was the Saxons' speech and it is come through them) (ll. 2671–72).
At the same time, Robert uses linguistic anachronism to Anglicize the
Britons themselves: he says that Hamo was able to mimic the Britons
and kill "oure king" Guiderius because he had been raised in Rome with
Briton hostages and so "spac engliss" (spoke English) (ll. 1444–53).
These and other representations provide Britons and Saxons with English tongues, assimilating their speech to "ours."

Etymologies bring the past into direct linguistic contact with the present and thereby further the settlement of English culture on historically Briton grounds. Since etymologies prove the durability of recognizable English forms, Laȝamon and Robert rarely use language to judge
the relative legitimacy of past dominions. Laȝamon, for example, portrays language as a reflection of inevitable change, most succinctly in
explaining that the Angles changed *Brutaine* to *Ængle-lond*, "for hit wes
al on heore honde" (for it was all in their hand) (l. 14675). Laȝamon's
neutrality is most evident when he explains that names occasionally
have frivolous origins:

Nu þu iherest of wuche gomen. aras þer þe to-nome.
swa doð a feole wise. to-nome ariseð.
& ofte of lutle þinge. þe longe ilaste[ð].
for nis nauere non oðer gomen. þat cleouieð alswa ueste.
(Ll. 4679–82)

[Now you have heard from what game arose there the name; so
many times do names arise, and often from a little thing, which
lasts long, for there is no other game that cleaves so fast.]

The repetition of *gomen* emphasizes the arbitrariness of naming Hampton
after Hamo, dismissing potential moral or political meanings. In this
light, Laȝamon's most frequently cited judgment—against the Normans for the renaming of London—does not seem to purvey such a
strongly negative connotation. The first account portrays the changes
quite neutrally: *Lundin* comes from "oþer tir. & neowe tidinde" (another dominion and new customs) (l. 1027); the French change the name
to *Lundres*, "þa mid fehte heo bi-wonnen" (who with fighting won it) (l.
1030–33). Since Laȝamon portrays many forceful victories without condemnation, the passage can be read as a report of inevitable change.

The second passage reflects a less neutral version, where the customs
are not simply "new" but brought by "vncuð folc" (foreign folk) (l. 3543);

the *French* become specifically *Normans* who change all the names of "þissere Bruttene" "mid heore niŏ-craften" (this here Britain, with their tricky craft) (ll. 3554, 3547). Although *niŏ-craften* is often understood to indicate evil malice,[89] Le Saux suggests that the animosity is more political than ethnic, the judgment more factual than hateful.[90] And Kenneth Tiller associates the term with the "craft of translation" (210), again returning the judgment to neutral ground. Read against the first description, Laȝamon's approach does seem relatively calm. After all, Lud, an admired ruler, changed the city's name even before the Normans. For Laȝamon, then, renaming is a constant process, as inevitable and unregrettable as conquest itself. Whether purposefully imposed or the result of accident, linguistic change renders the topography familiar, making it difficult for an Anglophone audience to condemn the process. Thus when the English formally call the land *England* (ll. 14672–82), the change marks the beginning of the familiar present rather than the regretful end of the distant past (as it does in the *Brut y Brenhinedd*).

Laȝamon's Englishing of Briton history concludes with his addition of a flattering etymology for the English and the attenuation of the negative one found in Wace's text. Drawing from Bede, Laȝamon reports how Pope Gregory exclaimed that the "Ænglisce" are so fair they resemble "englen" (angels) (ll. 14713–15). This addition counterbalances, and seems designed to overshadow, the English reputation for having tails. Laȝamon carefully explains that this deformity only afflicts those of Dorchester, who were punished by God for mocking Augustine; unfortunately, foreigners ignorant of the true facts mock good Englishmen who had nothing to do with the guilty persecutors (ll. 14762–72). Finally, Laȝamon honors the Britons as admirable predecessors by not recording their change of name or anything suggesting barbarism. Since the vilification of the Welsh grew with English imperialist ideology,[91] Laȝamon's neutrality represents another way in which he turns Briton history away from colonial ambition and toward English settlement.

Robert's linguistic revisions are more drastic in that he eliminates most of Geoffrey's etymologies. Those retained usually record only the original and present names without delineating processes of change. When London is named for the first time, for example, Robert begins with the familiar present name and then identifies the first name as *New Troy,* leaving out the intervening forms (ll. 533–34). In the second account of the naming, Robert does explain the changes, but as phonetic rather than colonial events:

Þe toun me clupeþ ludestoun. þat is wide couþ.
& now me clupeþ it londone. þat is liȝtore in þe mouþ.
& niwe troye hit het er. & nou it is so ago.
Þat londone it is now icluped. & worþ euere mo.
(Ll. 1029–32)

[The town was called *Ludstown,* that is widely known, and now it is called *London,* which is lighter in the mouth. And *New Troy* it was called before, and now it is so long ago that it is now called *London,* and worth ever more.]

Each line contains a different name and represents a different historical moment, but two of these four are *Londone* in the present. Furthermore, *Ludston* becomes *Londone* simply because it is easier to pronounce. Robert treats the change from *Habren* to *Severn* the same way: Gwendolen called the river "auerne," but through "diuerse tonge" we call it "seuerne," and add one letter to it "& namore iwis" (and no more, for sure) (ll. 636–38). With this etymological approach, Robert divorces the ethics of conquest from the aesthetics of language: change reflects mechanical rather than cultural processes. When dominion passes from the Britons, Robert excises Geoffrey's colonial ambivalence by noting (twice) that the land was no longer called "bruteyne" but "englelond" (ll. 5125, 5144–45) and stating unequivocally that the Welsh took their name from their duke Wallo (ll. 5126–28). Laȝamon and Robert are thus both comfortable with English occupation of the past and present. Even though they worked from very different sources, they arrive at similarly neutral portrayals of the relationship between language and conquest.

From this postcolonial perspective, bilingualism becomes a valuable advantage rather than a cultural threat. Laȝamon in fact reflects the cultural skills most admired in the thirteenth century when he casts himself as a trilingual narrator in the prologue.[92] Within the narrative, Vortigern receives wise counsel from a man who "cuðe tellen of ælche leod-spelle" (could speak the language of every land) (l. 7863). Gawain also performs admiral multilingualism. Arthur chooses him to meet Lucius because he understands both Roman and Briton;[93] when Gawain's diplomacy fails, the ensuing battle enforces bilingualism at sword point: Gawain mocks the headless Marcel, saying that he would have done better to have stayed in Rome, "for þus we eou scullen techen. ure Bruttisce speche" (for thus we shall teach you our Briton speech) (l. 13248). Arthur later challenges Petreius with the same promise: "Nu ic þe wulle teche. Bruttisce spæche" (now I will teach you Briton speech) (l. 13393). In both cases, the Romans ironically lose their heads at the very moment they are invited to speak.

Robert also values bilingualism. He praises William the Bastard as a noble prince, and describes the advent of Insular bilingualism as a strength and honor:

þus com lo englelond. in to normandies hond.
& þe normans ne couþe spek þo. bote hor owe speche.
& speke french as hii dude atom. & hor children dude also teche.
So þat heieman of þis lond. þat of hor blod come.

Holdeþ alle þulke speche. þat hii of home nome.
Vor bote a man conne frenss. me telþ of him lute.
Ac lowe men holdeþ to engliss. & to hor owe speche ӡute.
Ich wene þere ne beþ in al þe world. contreyes none.
Þat ne holdeþ to hor owe speche. bote englelond one.
Ac wel me wot uor to conne. boþe wel it is.
Vor þe more þat a mon can. þe more wurþe he is.
(Ll. 7537–47)

[Thus came England into Normandy's hand. And the Normans could
speak nothing but their own speech, and spoke French as they did
at home, and their children they did also teach, so that the high
men of this land who came of their blood all hold that speech that
they name after themselves. And unless a man knows French, one
tells of him little. But low men hold to English, and to their own
speech yet. I think there are no countries in all the world that don't
hold to their own speech, but one, England. But it is good to know
both very well, for the more that a man knows, the more worthy
he is.]

Robert finds the preservation of French natural and its acquisition a sign
of worth. As an English clerk of moderate status, he values learning for
its social advantages. Indeed, he seems to presume a certain familiarity
with French among his audience, for he does not translate the bishop of
Hereford's accusation to the rebel who attacks him: "Par crist he sede
sir tomas. tu es Mauveis. / Meint ben te ay fet. vor he adde muche god. /
þer biuore him ido" (*By Christ, he said, sir Thomas, you are bad. I have
done many good things for you, for he had done much good for him before*) (ll. 11119–21). Robert's attitude reflects the prevailing social cli-
mate of the thirteenth century, when the ability to speak French had
come to signify social value more than ethnic origin.[94] His conclusion,
moreover, distantly echoes the explanation imagined by Alfred, England's
revered figure of nationalist translation, for the absence of translation
among early Insular Christians: "woldon ðæt her ðy mara wisdom on
londe wære ðy we ma geðeoda cuðon" (they would have it that more
wisdom would be in the land the more languages we knew) (1:5). Robert's
comments thus assimilate the linguistic innovations wrought by recent
colonization to traditional English values.

If multilingualism has its advantages, monolingualism can be fatal.
Laӡamon's Ronwen successfully deceives and poisons Vortimer because
he cannot fathom her foreign speech: "Fortimer spæc Bruttisc. & Rou-
uenne Saxisc. / þan king þuhte gomen inoh. for hire spæche he loh" (Vortimer spoke Briton, and Ronwen Saxon. The king thought [it] game
enough; for her speech, he laughed) (ll. 7473–74). The Otho redactor emphasizes the point by adding that he laughed heartily ("smere"). The

Britons, moreover, are massacred because they cannot understand the Saxon signal to draw knives. These deaths testify to monolingualism's fatal consequences—not a *gomen* at all, but a deadly handicap, characteristic of unsuccessful colonial subjects. La3amon and Robert's sources purvey colonial anxieties about traitorous linguistic mimicry where they themselves underscore the advantages of language acquisition. From postcolonial perspectives, safety and success both require proficiency in more than one language.

Nu and auere-mare

The English occupation of Briton history reorients temporal as well as linguistic patterns. La3amon and Robert both pursue a presentist historiography that occludes the perception of non-English history. Through verbal patterns, anachronism, and annalistic references, they collapse temporal differences. As a result, their chronicles lay claim to a timeless English dominion, secured by a Christian telos.

La3amon and Robert mingle the past with the present in a number of ways. For example, they often use present-tense verbs to indicate the continuing presence of historical artifacts: La3amon remarks that Tenvantius's body "liþ" (lies) in London, and that Cymbeline's "liþ" still in York; Robert multiplies these kinds of references and frequently notes the practices that endure "3ut to þis day."[95] The present also continues seamlessly into the future on La3amon's repeated promises of "nu and auere-mare" (now and evermore).[96] The Otho redactor extends this process by using modern vocabulary. Robert, for his part, calls attention to history's creation in the present by qualifying information as personal understanding ("as ich vnder stonde") and by referring to eyewitness experience.[97] He also adds anachronistic explanations that evoke thirteenth-century social contexts, such as the fact that Hengist feared Aurelius because he had won many tournaments in France (ll. 2893–901). Finally, both historians often write as if they had seen distant events with their own eyes. Robert, for example, makes himself the subject of distant rulers by referring to them as "our king." These and other anachronisms draw the past closer to the present, creating what Le Saux calls a principle of narrative implication that effaces historical and emotional distances.[98] Presentism also draws attention to the unfinished nature of history and casts England's current situation as an explicit consequence of the past.[99] The narrators thus imply that any thirteenth-century Englishman can see what historical persons saw, that any reader can experience the continuing presence of the past.

La3amon and Robert couple this presentism with a restoration of the traditional Anglo-Saxon chronology of dominion. La3amon not only anticipates the arrival of the Angles as soon as Brutus sets foot on the island (l. 991), he writes as if dominion passes to them with Ronwen's toast, the first given "in Ænglene londe" (l. 7140). Moreover, as Leckie has shown, Laȝamon (following Wace, who follows the First Variant) restores English dominion to the seventh century by making Aethelstan Cadwallader's contemporary (118). Although this chronology is as "confused" as the First Variant's, since Aethelstan lived in the tenth century, it nonetheless stages a significant counterconquest against Geoffrey's Briton chronology. Robert's account of Saxon settlement, by contrast, leaves no room for confusion. When Hengist builds his castle, Robert identifies the year as 449 (l. 2539). Later, less than one hundred lines after Arthur's death in 542, Robert enumerates the six Saxon kingdoms and fills in their history since Hengist: Kent was founded fifty-eight years after Hengist, Wessex began a little before King Arthur, and the first king of Northumberland came after Arthur in 547 (ll. 4655–90). With retrospective precision, Robert enumerates the chronology of Saxon settlement such that their dominion clearly coincides with their first castle.

As Laȝamon and Robert claim Briton history for the English, they recalculate the temporal patterns inherited from their sources. Laȝamon eliminates almost all synchronic references, and facilitates the extension of Saxon dominion by eliminating the years of Arthur and Cadwallader's deaths. He retains only the reference to Romulus and Remus (ll. 1934–35) and to Lucius's death in 160 (l. 5114). Both of these references anchor time in Rome: Romulus and Remus identify Rome's origin (and the origin of Briton dominion there), while Lucius received the Roman evangelists who brought Christianity to Britain. Laȝamon bolsters the relation between time and Rome in his lengthy praise of Caesar, which includes the remark that Caesar made the calendar that appoints the months and the year (ll. 3599–601). Here, the very possibility of temporal calculation originates with imperial ambition. Laȝamon's restricted system of temporal references thus enhances English dominion by locating it vaguely within a recognizably imperial timeline.

Robert, by contrast, extends Geoffrey's system of calculation. In a maneuver similar to the Welsh translators who calculate years from the Flood, Robert assembles the temporal references found in various sources into a single edifice of retrospective and prospective calculation. The ability to count becomes a measure of possession: kings possess their kingdoms because their reigns can be counted (by year, duration, and ruler's age), and the English possess history because Robert can count out the years. Quantification begins in the prologue, with the numbering of towns. Brutus's arrival mobilizes the origin of time itself: he reaches England's shore in the third age since the world's beginning, in the time of Abraham and Moses—that is, 3,083 years after the world's creation and 1,130 years before Christ's birth.[100] When Robert subsequently preserves Geoffrey's synchronisms, he usually reinforces them with Christian annals, even before Christ's birth.[101] Robert dates major dynastic and religious changes with particular care. Caesar, for example, arrives exactly

118

60 years before Christ's birth and 493 years after Rome's foundation; the Saxons convert in 582 after there have been fifty emperors in Rome (since God's birth), 150 years after they first came to England, and about 40 years after King Arthur's death; the Battle of Hastings takes place on a Saturday in 1066 when William is 39 years old, in the 31st year of his dukedom.[102] Robert's annalistic method leads him to add numerous synchronic references, including the founding of churches, the deaths and marriages of local figures, weather, crops, and supernatural signs. All of these retrospective calculations seem to be the results of Robert's own mathematical labors. They combine imperial and religious time, encompassing international and local events within the English timeline.

Imperial and English dominion permeate time at the level of the yearly calendar as well. After the naming of the weekdays, for example, every reference to a specific day recalls Saxon origins. And once Julius Caesar and Augustus name months after themselves,[103] every subsequent reference to July and August recalls imperial origins. Imperial counting even structures the narration of Christ's birth: Robert explains Augustus's census and taxation effort, juxtaposing the beginning of the numbering in Jerusalem with Christ's birth in Bethlehem (ll. 1386–404). The description, which includes a counting of shires, sounds almost exactly like Robert's description of Domesday, William the Conqueror's census of Insular wealth (ll. 7674–85). In each case, the ability to count signifies political power.

Throughout the narrative, Robert controls historiographical time by telling us what is too long to tell, what we shall hear, and what we have already heard.[104] He also clearly identifies the moment when prophecies come true, be they Merlin's, Dunstan's, or his own predictions.[105] Saints and magicians thus know the future, and Robert knows their history with retrospective precision. When he admits that quantities, like Maud's goodness, escape quantification (l. 270–74), he underscores the ordinary countability of everything else. Always measuring time in several different ways, Robert calibrates historical dominion to accurate enumeration. An accountant of history, Robert extends English dominion through the years of good weather and bad. In two very different ways, then, the one representational and the other presentational, Laȝamon and Robert lay claim to the imperial, Christian origins of English time.

Calibeorne his sweord

Laȝamon's Englishing of Briton history extends to his account of Arthur, as does his divestment from the ethics of force. Unlike the heroic tradition represented by *Beowulf*, Laȝamon diminishes as far as possible the semiotics of power inherent in the representation of armor.[106] In fact, compared with other Arthurian historians, Laȝamon barely engages the semiotics of swords. Although he offers the greatest number of arming descriptions (including Morvidus [ll. 3215ff.] and Bedver [ll. 12880ff.]), the portraits serve relatively narrow functions. When, for example, Corineus's sword breaks, the fractured blade signifies not a fractured soul but a negligent smith (l. 780). Laȝamon's pragmatic approach to armor emerges from his general approach to force as a tool, not a sign of legitimacy. His striking revision of Caliburn, which reduces Wace's four namings to two, bypasses the sword in order to emphasize Arthur's personal role as a valiant English hero in God's service.

Laȝamon uses the first arming description to insinuate Arthur's Englishness and establish his personal heroism. The portrait begins with a cuirass apparently invented by Laȝamon, either named Wygar or made by a crafty smith named Wygar (the reference is ambiguous).[107] In either case, *Wygar* identifies Arthur as an heir to Anglo-Saxon culture:[108] the cuirass literally covers Arthur's body with English history. Having set an Anglo-Saxon tone, Laȝamon revises the rest of the portrait he inherited from Wace to enhance Arthur's physical power. After enclosing his legs in steel armor, Arthur girds on Caliburn, wrought with marvelous craft ("wiȝelefulle craften") in Avalon (ll. 10547–48). The repetition of *craft* links the sword to the cuirass, made with noble craft ("aðelen crafte"). Reinforcing this emerging image of indigenous ingenuity, Laȝamon gives Arthur's helmet an English name, Goswhit (l. 10552). He also specifies that the helmet belonged to Uther, "þas aðelen kinges" (l. 10551), an epithet that assimilates him to Arthur's English armor and the noble Englishmen evoked in the prologue. Although the shield's Briton name, Pridwen, disrupts this English portrait (l. 10554), Laȝamon concludes with a laudable image of Arthur's strength: spear in hand, he leaps on his horse fully armed (rather than midway through the arming process, as in Wace); Laȝamon ends with a four-line meditation on Arthur's superlative qualities (ll. 10546–62). The Otho redactor subtly enhances the Englishing of Arthur's arms by modernizing the vocabulary and excising the line that ascribes the helmet to Uther. In the absence of this reminder of Arthur's Briton genealogy, his reputation can float more freely toward the English. Despite the elaborate presentation of Arthur's arms and Caliburn's great *crafte*, Laȝamon does not name the sword in the ensuing battle. Indeed, the lance Ron delivers the critical first blow, which Arthur celebrates with a cry to the Lord and His Mother (ll. 10591–98). A greater share of heroic power thus goes to Arthur himself and to God, transcendent legitimator of the war against the Heathens.

By enhancing Arthur's Christian identity, Laȝamon assimilates him to the noble history of the Christian English. In the confrontation with Frollo, Laȝamon continues to develop Arthur's portrait as a servant of God. Arthur accepts Frollo's challenge with an elaborate prayer; his men pray to both God and His Mother during the duel (ll. 11842–54, 11923). Just prior to the confrontation, Laȝamon adds a second arming description, unique to his narrative (ll. 11856–76). With the exception of Cal

iburn, every element of Arthur's regalia is different; the generic article
ænne introduces each anonymous object. Although the spear once belonged to Uther (and was made in Caermarthen by a smith named Grif-
fin), the generic weaponry renders the armor a tool of force rather than a
sign of imperial value. Although Le Saux suggests that the substitute armor signs Laʒamon's criticism of Arthur's expansionism,[109] it seems
rather to evade symbolic force. Indeed, Uther's spear (which is Laʒamon's
invention) associates the duel with Cheldric's defeat, in which Arthur
wore Uther's helmet. Moreover, Laʒamon concludes the portrait with
an even lengthier encomium to Arthur's virtues. Once again, the Otho
redactor generalizes Arthur's reputation by modernizing vocabulary and
excising Uther. During the duel, Laʒamon names the sword in action
for the first and only time as Arthur delivers the fatal blow (l. 11965). In
the end, Laʒamon seems more interested in Arthur's Continental legal
practices than in the legitimacy of his territorial claim or its imperial
consequences.

Nine years later, back in England, the Romans demand both France's
return and England's submission. Their arrival touches off an extensive
discussion of legitimate jurisdictions. First, they claim Britain because
Caesar conquered the island in battle (l. 12374). In response, Arthur focuses on self-defense, dismissing both Cador's blood-lust and Gawain's
reasonable description of the advantages of peace. Rejecting Caesar's claim
as "unrihte," Arthur proceeds to show how the Britons could make the
same claim against the Romans (ll. 12480–516). He leaps from this hy-
pothetical reversal to proclaim his own desire to possess Rome; he concludes by attributing victory to divine judgment:

> He wilneð al. and ich wilni al. þaet wit beiene aʒæð.
> habben hit nu and aʒe. þe hit æð mæʒen iwinne.
> for nu we scullen cunne. wham hit Godd unne.
> (Ll. 12531–33)

> [He wants all, and I want all, that which each has. Have it now and
> forever, whoever can win it! For now we shall know to whom God
> gives it.]

Arthur's stark declaration of forceful jurisdiction (strengthened by the
Otho redactor, who excises God's role) leaves no room for equivocation
or ambivalence. Accordingly, Hoel and Auguselus ratify Arthur's decision without extending the discussion of legitimation. With no possible
judicial conclusion to the competing vengeance claims, armed conflict
becomes unavoidable. Victory, moreover, proves legitimacy because it
derives from God.

The ensuing battle takes on the same dimensions as the earlier Saxon
conflict, since Laʒamon presents the Romans as Heathens rather than
as Trojan cousins (ll. 13635–70). Yet during the battle, Arthur does not

carry Caliburn and barely participates in the fight; he delivers more speeches than blows. Moreover, Laȝamon reduces even the speeches to a minimum and ends the battle quite suddenly (l. 13880). Like the rest of Arthur's equipment, the sword falls into anonymity and ceases to occupy a privileged place in the narrative structure. A comparative reader expects to find the sword in action here; an Anglophone audience knowing no other version may well expect another chivalric portrait. In the absence of both, Laȝamon shifts attention away from the imperial value of force and toward its use as a tool for resolving impossible judicial dilemmas. This shift legitimates the victor's dominion as an expression of divine will, or at least of proven superior strength.

In Laȝamon's text, as elsewhere, Caliburn does not engage Arthur's defeat. As with Helen and the giant of Mont Saint-Michel, Laȝamon sexualizes the concluding episode and amplifies its brutality. Guenivere's active betrayal is presaged in the dream Laȝamon invents for Arthur: while Mordred hacks at Arthur's hall, Guenivere pulls down the roof with her own hands (ll. 13992–94). In the dream, her punishment also equals Mordred's: Arthur beheads Mordred and hacks up the queen "mid deore mine sweorede" (with my dear sword) (ll. 13998–4001). Although the sword is unnamed, the phrasing suggests that Arthur punishes the realm's destruction with the emblem of its defense. The severity of the treachery forces him to exact this punishment with his left hand (his right arm broke when the hall collapsed) (ll. 13995, 13998). Once Arthur learns of the dream's prescience, Laȝamon amplifies discussion of betrayal: the Britons clamor for Mordred and Guenievere's death, Arthur proclaims that he will kill them both, and Gawain declares he will have Mordred hung and Guenivere torn apart by horses.[110] As Arthur prepares to march on Mordred, Laȝamon deepens Guenivere's betrayal: she goes personally to warn Mordred, "þat wæs hire leofuest monnes" (who was the dearest man to her) (l. 14101). As the battles wage on, she escapes to the convent at Caerleon, and no one hears from her again: "þa heo hire-seolf weore. isunken in þe watere" (as if she had sunk into the water) (l. 14216). This idiomatic expression for "disappearance without a trace"[111] submerges Guenivere in the aquatic origins of Britain's misfortunes. Like a Habren or a Hamo, she drowns at the edge of legitimacy.

In the wake of Guenivere's disappearance, Arthur also takes to the water—in a boat governed by fairies and headed for Avalon (ll. 14277–80). Arthur's death completes Laȝamon's Englishing of the Briton hero. He repeats the prophecy of Arthur's return no fewer than four times—twice by Merlin, once by Arthur himself, and once by the narrator.[112] It may seem paradoxical, ironic, or even ambivalent of Laȝamon to champion Arthur's possible survival, since Arthur would seem to represent a Welsh threat to the English. Laȝamon, however, does not disparage contemporary Briton beliefs in Arthur's return because he assimilates him to English history. As Le Saux has argued, for Laȝamon the English have as much claim to Arthur as the Welsh.[113] In the final version of the prophecy, the narrator even hopes that "an" Arthur will yet come to help the "Angles" (l. 14297). The phrasing clearly claims Arthur's return as a boon to the English, that is, the *Brut*'s audience, settled into the English landscape and suffering from the effects of weak monarchies. The instability that reigned in varying degrees from the 1190s through Henry III's reign could contribute to the desire for the return of strong government. By claiming Arthur for both the Britons and the English, Laȝamon extends the promise of restoration across the entire island[114] (although it seems unlikely that he envisions an English revolt against Normans, as James Noble suggests [178–79]). The Otho redactor, by contrast, retrenches Arthur's historic ethnicity by replacing "Anglen" with "Bruttes." Rather than exposing the redactor's ignorance of Laȝamon's true purpose,[115] the substitution indicates that he understood the *runes* all too well and chose to distance the narrative from the Englishing of Arthur. With this slight resistance to Laȝamon's historiographical conquest, the redactor limits the future of Arthur's death.

The absence of a systematic alignment of *Caliburn* with Arthur's imperial progress ultimately maintains a focus on tools, not theories, of force. Arthur himself resembles the giant-hero of the First Variant and the *Brut y Brenhinedd* more than he does Wace's colonial lord. The absence of a clear grouping of imperial battles also suggests the random nature of history. While Geoffrey and Wace's repeated namings give history a cyclical structure and a sense of predictability outside of a Christian telos, for Laȝamon the patterns of history and the future lie beyond human perception. He cannot judge the legitimacy of any individual conquest in terms of ethnicity or ideological value; he can only lament the inevitable destruction caused by force and admire its use as a tool of justice. Insular history thus does not legitimate the land's present or past ownership; it only affords examples of relative strength and weakness, justice and tyranny.

Sire Calibourne

Robert, unlike the Otho redactor, uses Arthur to expand English jurisdiction over the Insular past. Robert frames Arthur's reign with Caliburn's edge by introducing the sword into Arthur's duel with the giant of Mont Saint-Michel and the final battle with Mordred. This pattern represents either a remarkable innovation (since the Latin sources never mention the sword at these moments) or a remarkable synthesis of French narrative (since Wace includes the giant and the *Mort le roi Artu* Mordred). Whatever its origin, the new pattern disperses the semiotics of the sword, very much like the French prose cycle (see chapter 6). Robert's approach entrenches swords' semiotic relation to boundary issues, tempering them with chivalry and drawing out their moral implications.

Robert moralizes sword blades throughout the narrative, suggesting historiographical affinities with the French prose *Estoire del saint graal.* Aethelstan, for example, carries a relic sword granted by God, which remains in the royal treasury; over Antioch, a flaming sword of justice appears in the sky to inspire the crusaders. The usurper Stephen of Blois has two swords, which evoke the semiotics of spiritual and temporal jurisdictions: when both swords have broken—that is, when Stephen has lost all grounds of legitimacy—he is captured. And when Thomas Beckett is murdered, the point of the sword breaks, signaling the murderers' immorality in the blade's fracture; the sword point is still honored at Canterbury.[116]

Robert conjoins gladial morality to authorial control when he introduces a metaphor peculiar to literature in English: narrating Arthur's crown wearing, he avers that he could not describe the feast "þey my tonge were of stel" (l. 3956). The most striking example of the metaphor's Englishness surfaces in a lament for the death of Edward I, translated from a French elegy. Where the French version asserts the difficulty that Aristotle or Virgil would have in enumerating Edward's worth, the English translator says that he could not capture Edward's goodness "þah mi tonge were mad of stel."[117] The elegy's chronological proximity to Robert's chronicle suggests that the steel of the English tongue was mined from the real struggles of vernacular expression that followed colonial conquest. Just as the translator reclaims Edward from the French, so Robert reclaims Insular history from Anglo-Norman historians. In his hands, this metaphor for poetic strength associates territorial control with narrative control: just as the kings of Robert's *Historia* establish dominion over the land with the sword, Robert claims historical terrain by writing. Kings and historians both acquire their subjects forcefully.

When Robert applies his steel tongue to Arthur, he establishes the famous king's service to Christian morality. As in Geoffrey's *Historia*, the saintly Dubricius sets the Christian tone of the battle against Cheldric by inciting the men to fight for their "kunde," the "lond folc," and the "londes riȝt" (ll. 3597–607). Several revisions to the arming scene enhance Arthur's ties to divine authority (ll. 3609–19). Robert diminishes the sword's magical associations by not mentioning Avalon and by describing it as simply strong, unique only in Robert's personal judgment ("nas nour no such ich wene"). At the same time, he increases the presence of the divine by adding a reference to Christ to the existing image of Mary. Robert subordinates Arthur's success to God's will more strongly when he describes him on the battlefield giving himself to God before drawing Caliburn. After the slaughter, Robert concludes: "& þerto nadde he oþer help. bote god & seinte marie. / & calibourne is gode suerd. to do such maistrie" (and thereto he had no other help but God and Saint Mary and Caliburn his good sword, to do such mastery) (ll. 3637–38). In the end, greater credit for success accrues to Mary and Christ than to magical weapons or human strength. For Robert, Caliburn captures force as an act of God.

After Arthur establishes Christian peace on the island, Robert sends him off on his overseas conquests with an exact measurement of Europe and the lands he aims to dominate (ll. 3758–64). Arriving in France, Arthur fights Frollo, slicing through his head with "sire calibourne" (l. 3841). In what is always Caliburn's most aggressive engagement, Robert here implies that territorial expansion ennobles. The effects of the epithet "Sir" are strengthened by the fact that Robert almost always refers to Arthur as "King Arthur." Casting Caliburn as a loyal knight, Robert joins the sword to the legitimate interests of chivalric values and ratifies a providential interpretation of knightly aggression. The valuation of chivalric force endures throughout the narrative, as Edmund Ironside meets Cnut for a duel in the midst of the Severn (ll. 6266–99) and Henry III's son Edward becomes a champion of tournaments in France (much like his ancestor Hengist) (ll. 11040–45).

Arthur himself celebrates victory back in England with a "round table" in the thirteenth-century style, replete with chivalric games.[118] The list of lords attending reproduces the outlines of the opening *descriptio* (ll. 3890–911), making Arthur's dominion contiguous with contemporary England. Robert goes on to enhance the gathering's imperial dimension by referring to Bedver and Kai as "kings" of Normandy and Anjou (ll. 3948, 3951). When the Roman messengers disrupt the celebration, Robert manifests his mastery of historical time by noting that the only tribute Arthur ever sent was Lucius's body (ll. 4011–14). The ensuing speeches by Cador, Arthur, Hoel, and Auguselus follow Geoffrey's *Historia* closely, reproducing its paradoxes of justified force and counterconquest. The paradoxes pose little ideological trouble in Robert's narrative, however, since he has already dispersed the ethics of force. Moreover, he assimilates war to chivalry (ll. 4132), and thus to the normal, legitimate activities of King Arthur, Sir Caliburn, Prince Edward, and all other knights.

On the way to Rome, Arthur meets the giant of Mont Saint-Michel, and defeats him with "Calebourne is gode suerd" (l. 4237); his men trust him all the more for his achievement (l. 4246). With this third naming, Robert creates the expectation that the sword will accompany Arthur's every aggressive, divinely sanctioned act. This third naming also draws the implications of Helen's rape directly into the theme of imperial progress. For Robert, both are domestic affairs that play out in an always already post-colonial England. He makes the domestication explicitly gendered when Arthur exhorts his troops before the Roman war by reminding them of the lands of which they have made Britain "leuedy" (lady) (l. 4365). World dominion thus becomes a domestic affair played out between fair lords and ladies.

The battle itself against Lucius serves, as it does in Geoffrey's *Historia*, to establish who has "betere riȝt" ("maius jus") to France. The rhetoric of battle downplays the enemy's otherness by referring to them as "half-men" (like the giants who are "deformed men") instead of women ("muliebres").[119] Immediately after concluding his customary speech, much shortened from Geoffrey's *Historia*, Arthur enters the fray, chivalric sword in hand:

> Sire calibourne is suerd. he bi gan to ssake anon.
> & slou to grounde her & þer. ac he ne smot noȝt on.
> Þat he ne slou him oþer his hors. & among hom echon.
> Þe king of lybye. & of bytynie. him sulf gan to quelle.
> Mid calibourne & send. hor heþene soule to helle.
> (Ll. 4458–62)

[Sir Caliburn his sword he soon began to shake, and slew to the ground here and there, but he never smote a man that he did not slay either him or his horse, and among them both the king of Libya and of Bithynia he himself went to kill with Caliburn and send their heathen souls to hell.]

Robert begins with the chivalric sword, but ends with the destruction of Heathen souls, conjoining knightly and moral justifications. He proceeds to eliminate Geoffrey's representation of the Romans' successful resistance: perhaps following the First Variant, he passes directly to Morvidus of Gloucester's definitive offensive and the Britons' mastery of the field (ll. 4463–74). Arthur's own action thus leads more directly to the final victory than in Geoffrey's text, augmenting his chivalric prowess as well as the decisiveness of divine judgment. In the end, Robert judges that there has been no greater battle except the Trojan one, as Arthur reigns supreme from the west side of the world to the east (ll. 4491–95). The Trojan comparison strategically recalls the Britons' prestigious origins at the height of Arthurian dominion.

Robert carries Arthurian prestige into the final battle against Mordred by having Arthur continue to fight with Caliburn. Prior to the battle itself, Robert suggests that Guenivere initiated the treachery by advising Mordred to crown himself king (ll. 4503–4). Able to imagine a usurping queen, Robert exhibits little anxiety over the consequences of irregular intercourse. Guenivere herself, the "luþer quene" (l. 4537), flees in fear when she hears of Arthur's arrival. Throughout the passage, Robert maintains a political focus that disengages the treachery from fundamental identity issues. In the course of the battle itself, political and religious legitimacy reinforce each other, as Robert (like Laȝamon) depicts Mordred's allies as Heathens (l. 4528). The outcome, however, does not establish who has "betere riȝt": Mordred simply has more men (l. 4563). By insisting on the practical limits of force, Robert divorces the victory from moral or legal legitimacy:

He drou calibourne is suerd. & in eyþer side slou.
& vorte he to þe traytour com. made him wey god ynou.
He hente verst of is helm. & suþþe mid wille god.
Anne stroc he ȝef him. mid wel stourdy mod.
& þoru hauberc & þoru is coler. þat nere noþing souple.
He smot of is heued as liȝtliche. as it were a scouple.
Þat was is laste chiualerye. þat vaire endede ynou.
Vor þat folc so þikke com. þe wule he hor louerd slou.
Aboute him in eche half. þat among so many fon.
He aueng deþes wounde. & wonder nas it non.
(Ll. 4573–82)

[He drew Caliburn his sword and he slew on either side, and he
made his way well enough until he came to the traitor. First he
caught his helmet and then with great will he gave him one stroke
with a very sturdy mind right through his hauberk and through his
collar, which was not at all supple. That was his [Arthur's] last
chivalry, that ended fairly enough, for that folk came on so thickly
about him on each side because he had slain their lord, that among
so many foes he had death's wound, it was no wonder.]

Robert's realistic reasoning for Arthur's defeat makes clear that his foes
enjoy no legitimacy; the reference to chivalric values excludes providential or imperial interpretations. Set against the sword's first naming, this
final inscription carves a frame around Arthurian conquest, an imperial
project that begins and ends at home. The faithful sword takes the place
of Avalon (which Robert never mentions) as both origin and destination.
In this pattern of events, Sir Caliburn serves as a faithful knight, attending Arthur's role in the drama of dominion but powerless to change the
course of divinely ordered events.

After the battle, Robert leaves no doubt that Arthur deserves his superlative reputation. Like every other king, however, he must take his
place in the sum of historical calculation. Whereas Laȝamon affirms
Arthur's return and Geoffrey and Wace record doubts about his death,
Robert is almost alone among the early Arthurian historians in recording the death with absolute certainty:

& he let hime lede in to an yle. vor to hele is wounde.
& deide as þe beste kniȝt. þat me wuste euere yfounde.
& naþeles þe brutons. & þe cornwalisse of is kunde.
Weneþ he be aliue ȝut. & abbeþ him in munde.
Þat he be to comene ȝut. to winne aȝen þis lond.
& naþeles at glastinbury. his bones suþþe me fond.
& þere at uore þe heye weued. amydde þe quer ywis.
As is bones liggeþ. is toumbe wel vair is.

In þe vif hundred ȝer of grace. & vourty & tuo.
In þis manere in cornwaile. to deþe he was ydo.
(Ll. 4587–96)

[And he let himself be led to an isle, for to heal his wounds, and died as the best knight that was ever found to defend. And nonetheless the Britons and the Cornish of his kin think he is alive yet, and have in their mind that he will come yet to win again this land. And nonetheless at Glastonbury men have since found his bones, and there before the high altar in the midst of the choir surely his bones lie; his tomb is very fair. In the five hundredth year of grace, and forty-two, in this manner in Cornwall, to death was he done.]

This anonymous island imparts no magical healing, just a fine burial place. Like his probable contemporary the Otho redactor, then, Robert maintains Arthur's identity as a Briton—a dead Briton with a very rich tomb at Glastonbury, the land's oldest religious foundation. Robert thus separates the belief in Arthur's resurrection from the restoration of ancient Welsh rights: these rights are transcendent, and do not depend on the life of one man, no matter how superlative his qualities. Since Robert goes on to narrate Glastonbury's foundation at the appropriate historical moment two hundred lines later, as well as the great fire of 1184 after which Arthur's bones were discovered (l. 9852), Arthur stands out as a great king for the same reasons as Constantine and Edward the Confessor, not for any additional supernatural reason. Of course, the death does bring much sorrow to Christendom (l. 4653). Moreover, it is literally epoch-making, as Robert measures time from Arthur's death more than once:[120] these references fix the moment in time and place and communicate the true historicity of Arthur's demise. They also give the impression, like the London French *Brut*, that "[c]ontemporary England... is understood as the aftermath of Arthurian England."[121] The strength of this understanding contributed to King John's desire to murder Arthur of Brittany in 1203, lest Arthur in fact come again (ll. 10112–22). The fear of resurrection, however, afflicts only those who fail to dominate Insular space or its historical equations.

As much as a hundred years apart, the *Historia Brutonum* and *Historia rythmis Anglicanis* conquer Briton history for the English. Laȝamon, the Otho redactor, and Robert all proffer perspectives on *simplemen*'s culture, defining legitimacy from the perspective of the ruled. Comfortably settled into an English landscape shaped by the course of the Severn River, they pursue paradigms of continuity and invisible origins. While literally overlooking the Severn, they figuratively overlook many contested historiographical boundaries. By constructing linguistic, ethnic, and religious resemblances across conventional historical differences, they invite admiration for English successes. They figure the land itself as the material basis of these continuities. Their perspectives on how force, ethnicity, and religion affect the land inform their semiotic relation to the Arthurian period, and to instruments of war generally. Shaped by post-colonial perspectives, their narratives ultimately dismiss inherited colonial paradigms. The modern impulse to see irony or ambivalence in these English ennoblements of Briton history must thus confront the transient modes of postcolonial subjectivity. For in these narratives, we can recognize fragmented, partial, or temporary identifications that nonetheless assume the immutability of the *kunde londe.* To identify the "Englishness" of this land is not to discover the ancient origins of "nationalism" but rather the perennial novelty of narrative engagements with legacies of coercive contact.

Trans marinis

CHAPTER 5

L'enor d'Engleterre
Taking over the Past from Normandy

Each of the previous three chapters addresses Briton history from the Severn River Valley. Together, they demonstrate that Arthurian border writing thrived on the edge between Wales and England throughout the twelfth and thirteenth centuries. This local engagement is paralleled by a more distant reception on the Continent. In this chapter and the next two, then, I address Briton history from the eastern side of the Channel. Continental border writing also spans the twelfth and thirteenth centuries, and here I return to the *Historia*'s early reception in Normandy. This chronological disruption, produced by my geographical focus, underscores the pliability of border writing and colonial relations. Wace's colonialist vision, which I develop in this chapter, follows Welsh post-colonial resistance (chapter 3) while providing a source for English post-colonial settlement (chapter 4). Postcolonial moves thus do not necessarily follow colonial ones: both arise from local discursive practices that can emerge at any time.

As Continental families and regional groups attended to the boundaries of their identities, some historiographers turned to the Briton past, keeping Arthur on the edge of history. Geoffrey's *Historia* may have traveled to the Continent as early as 1138; at least portions of the First Variant had arrived by the early 1150s when Wace began translating the *Historia* into French. These textual immigrants retrace the voyage of the earliest Britons, reversing the beginning of their own narratives. And like later Britons, these narratives settled into the French landscape. Here, amid struggles over regional power (often in relation to Insular rulers), Arthurian border writing took root.

Perhaps not surprisingly, Normandy proved fertile ground for a stridently imperial version of Briton history. In the regional origin of Geoffrey's colonial ambivalence, itself founded by forceful settlement, the *Historia*'s patterns of conquest evoke the epic feats of local ancestors. The Norman Conquest of Britain in 1066 cast these ancestors directly into the line of spectacular Insular accomplishment. Attachment to the Briton empire thus inflects a nascent regional imperialism. In the 1140s, in fact, a Norman poet presented the Norman capital of Rouen as an ancient city ("urbs antiqua") adorned with imperial honor ("Imperialis honoriticentia te super ornat") comparable to that of Rome ("Tu Rome similis"). Indeed, according to the poet, "Rothoma" (Rouen) derives directly from

133

"Roma"; the poem's conclusion summarizes the tributes received in Rouen from Brittany, England, Scotland, and Wales.[1] From this perspective, Rouen resembles the *Historia*'s Rome while directly subjugating its London to Norman imperial hegemony. In Normandy, then, Briton colonial expansion becomes a prelude to successful Norman efforts in the same direction.

While Rouen's panegyrist imagines the region through its metropolitan center, Normandy also occupies a border periphery. Caught between the Insular and the Parisian monarchies, the Norman frontier remained contested territory until Philip II forcefully imposed a royal French border along the shore in 1204. After Henry I died in 1135, for example, Normandy nearly joined Champagne when the Continental Normans invited Thibaut of Champagne to rule as duke before learning that the Insular Normans had recognized his brother Stephen. In the ensuing war between Stephen and Matilda, Matilda's husband Geoffrey of Anjou captured the undefended duchy in 1144. Throughout the subsequent reigns of Henry II and his sons, Normandy remained a site of equivocation as a tenancy held by a duke who was also a king.[2] Finally, even though twelfth-century Normans may not have felt the ambivalent pull of Frankish and Scandinavian identities that Cassandra Potts has identified in the eleventh century, *Normanitas* remained an effect of several partial identities; indeed, powerful Franco-Norman families frequently shifted their allegiances between the Insular and the French kings.[3] All of these dynamics shape a Continental identity distinct from Insular Anglo-Normans.[4] Within a central geopolitical edge, then, Continental *Normanitas* rests on shifting patterns of domination.

The simultaneity of metropolitan and border identifications in Normandy opens the possibility of a colonial ambivalence analogous to Geoffrey's—that is, the possibility of imperial fantasies haunted by nightmares of domination. Yet Norman ideology, like Welsh, expresses little ambivalence about forceful conquest. In both regions, Arthurian historiography sustains fantasies of dominion while blocking out the nightmares of subjugation. This ideological and historiographical resemblance exposes the intimate relations between colonialism and post-colonial resistance. Perhaps not surprisingly, expansion and resistance both forget founding traumas and remember only timeless dominion. Like the reception *ultra Sabrinam*, the view *trans marinis* attenuates and even eradicates paradoxes. Ultimately, the Norman reception of Briton history sustains an expansionist ideology wherein conquest legitimately increases prestige as well as territorial control.

Antenor et alii profugi

Geoffrey's *Historia* probably began its Continental expansion at Bec, where in 1139 Henry of Huntingdon declared himself stupefied ("stupens") to have discovered an account of the Briton kings that had been unknown to him (558). Writing to Warin the Briton, Henry refers to the Britons as "parentes tui" (your relatives) and concludes by recommending that Warin ask for "librum grandem Galfridi Arturi" (the great book of Geoffrey Arthur) if he would like to read a comprehensive account (580–82). For Henry, then, the *Historia* represents a family history of personal interest to the Britons' contemporary descendents. Yet in Normandy, and perhaps especially at Bec, the *Historia* also represents Norman family history: the Britons become the Normans' cousins through Antenor, Corineus's ancestor in the *Historia* and the Danes' in the *Gesta Normannorum ducum*. Moreover, the explicit reference to the Danes' Trojan origins was inserted into the *Gesta Normannorum ducum* by Robert of Torigni (14–16), Henry of Huntingdon's host at Bec and later abbot of Mont Saint-Michel under Henry II's patronage. Together, the *Historia regum Britanniae* and *Gesta Normannorum ducum* provide a full account of a Trojan diaspora. Indeed, of the eight surviving *Historia* manuscripts that probably originated in Normandy, three contain parts of the *Gesta* and two include separate accounts of Antenor.[5] These collocations cast Norman dominion in Britain as a restoration of the Trojan line usurped by the Angles and Saxons.

The *Historia*'s Continental *Normanitas* can be ascertained in some detail thanks to Wright's edition of Bern, Burgerbibliothek MS 568, a text written at Fécamp that probably circulated only in Normandy.[6] Wright's summary of the differences between the Bern text and Faral's critical edition demonstrate how the Norman reception distances the text from an Insular perspective.[7] Several revisions, for example, attenuate the Saxons' treachery and seem to present their conquest as bloody but not illegitimate. The Normans' forceful conquests can thus also appear legitimate. The Bern redactor also advertises a neutrality, or even complicity, with the Britons' subjection by recording Arthur's death unequivocally: "Anima eius in pace quiescat" (His soul rests in peace) (132). Since the Bern text is probably contemporary with the First Variant, this negation of immortal hope may respond to the real threats posed to Norman landholdings by Welsh expansion in the 1130s. As if to counteract history in historiography, the redactor later affirms that the Britons lost their dominion permanently: "numquam postea monarchiam insulae recuperauerunt" (never again did they recover the monarchy of the island) (147). This sentence does not occur in all manuscripts, and certainly not in the First Variant. All of these revisions draw the text closer to the Norman historiographical patterns that Ingledew identifies in the *Historia* in general (681–88). Ultimately, they purvey colonial confidence in the justifiability of forceful expansion.

Even without direct textual *correctione*, the *Historia* resonates in unique ways in Normandy. In general, every time Britons sail from the island toward the Continent, they move closer rather than retreating

into the distance. Gaul likewise becomes a nearby site of historical conflicts. And when Arthur defeats Frollo, he subjugates the Normans' royal
rivals: Arthur's dominion over Anjou and Normandy, as Knight notes
(55), appeals directly to the political fantasy of a twelfth-century Normandy ruled by a Norman-Angevin king. Arthur himself becomes the
Cornish heir of the Trojan Danes thanks to Antenor, an important genealogical detail for any argument that could make Arthur central to
Norman identity. Finally, Briton rule of Scandinavian territories alludes
to further entanglements with ancient Norman lineages. When Wace
translates the *Historia*, he amplifies these continental orientations by
calling Gaul *France*, detailing Caesar's conquests there, and repeatedly
enumerating the Continental contours of Arthur's dominion.[8]

The *Historia*'s representation of Brittany provides a further site of Continental contact. The very ambiguity of the term *Briton* alludes repeatedly
to Norman neighbors, making the Bretons familiar cousins. Maximianus's
conquest of Armorica in fact establishes Brittany's Insular origin and affirms its ancient independence from both France and Normandy. Wace reinforces these latent patterns under the First Variant's influence: he adds
Brittany to the Trojans' early Continental itinerary and seems to distinguish between Continental and Insular Britons (*Bretun* and *Gualeis*).[9] In
Arthur's reign, he enhances Brittany's prestige by making Hoel king rather
than duke and noting that Arthur's best kin live in the realm (ll. 9142–44).

Finally, in Normandy the imperative to augment one's family ("familiam suam augmentare") sustains a familiar practice of kinship expansion. Searle argues that the Norman aristocracy made kinship the basis
of ducal power and social cohesion, and so a form of predation coextensive with territorial gains (10–11). The practice of kinship as *linkage*
(rather than *lineage*) expanded the line of legitimate heirs and so facili-
tated territorial expansion (165–77, 246–47). Searle concludes that when
William invaded England, "*all* could call him brother or cousin" (177).
Ingledew in fact diagnoses the *Historia* as a "symptom" of the Norman
territorial enterprise (669). In Normandy, the fulfillment of Trojan patterns that Ingledew observes (688) can proceed unambivalently as a defining component in an established collective identity. These effects are
latent in Geoffrey's project as an attractive ideal that he nonetheless re-
gards ambivalently. The Continental Norman reception, by contrast, ratifies the attraction while attenuating ambivalences. Here, *Normanitas*
takes a more clear and less troubled form. The strength of Norman reception should not, however, overshadow the *Historia*'s contentious genesis. Although the *Historia* may be read as an idealized political allegory
or as a continuation of Dudo of Saint-Quentin's Norman history *De
moribus et actis primorum Normanniae ducum*,[10] these singularizing
visions belie the multiple partialities of the colonial dynamic that generated the *Historia* in the first place.

Maistre Wace

Just as the *Brutieu* amplify the First Variant's Welsh orientation, Wace's *Roman de Brut* accentuates the *Historia*'s Norman perspectives on Insular history. Part of this Norman ideology actually derives from the First Variant, which provides significant portions of the French text.[11] In all likelihood, then, Wace translated from a hybrid text that included both vulgate and variant material (like the one edited by Jacob Hammer). The hybrid Latin *Historia* itself witnesses postcolonial accommodations to ambivalence while also denying them. When translated into French, this hybridity performs the attraction of native cultures for colonizing minds. The translated text also captures the ideological complicity of colonial subjects on both sides of the struggle for power. The close relation between Welsh and Norman historical visions thus goes well beyond the accidents of textual transmission. Each profits in its own way from the legitimation of violent territorial expansion; each draws ideological force from the presentation of history itself as an object of conquest. Wace's *Roman de Brut* thus places tools of resistance in the service of domination during what was actually a period of violent jurisdictional negotiation in the Norman duchy (between 1144 and 1155).

Wace himself (like Geoffrey, the Welsh redactors, Laȝamon, the Otho redactor, and Robert) wrote from a border culture. In the midst of the *Roman de Rou* (translated from the *Gesta Normannorum ducum*), Wace identifies himself as a Channel Islander from Jersey, "qui est en mer vers occident, / al fieu de Normendie apent" (which is in the sea toward the west, dependent on the fief of Normandy) (ll. 5303–4). From upper Normandy, Jersey indeed lies to the west, just south of the larger island Guernsey; in the twelfth century both were tenurially attached to Normandy. A Continental perspective on the Channel Islands surfaces clearly in the *Roman de Brut* when Wace describes Guernsey as "[u]n isle vers soleil culchant" (an island toward the setting sun) (l. 14189), even though Cadwallo is sailing east from Britain at the time. Wace thus views his insular origin from the Continental shore, casting the islands as both near and far. The Channel Islands in fact constitute an insular border that touches all of the aquatic passages between Brittany, Normandy, Cornwall, and southern England. Wace himself manifests an acute awareness of the precarious transit between shores with sea-faring metaphors and vivid descriptions of stormy seas.[12] John Le Patourel, also a native of the Channel Islands, has presented the islands' border perspective in some detail while tracing the confluence of Briton, Norman, English, and Angevin influences (3–38, 435–61). Wace likewise suggests the simultaneous insularity and permeability of life along these navigable borders.

Although Wace's perspective remains slightly offshore, he writes from the Continental side of the border, describing an early move to Caen, a period of study in France, and a return to Caen to write.[13] This itinerary, somewhat like Geoffrey's, passes through metropolitan centers of academic and political power (either Chartres or Paris).[14] While Wace's stay in France evokes French royal dominion, Caen itself is closely associated with the Insular monarchy through the burial of William the Conqueror, the birth of Robert earl of Gloucester (Geoffrey's patron), and the abbeys' Insular landholdings.[15] The coastal location in fact placed Caen at the center of ducal and royal itineraries. On the Norman coast, then, Wace lived between domination and the dominated, in a region disputed by neighboring kings and conquered in his lifetime by an Angevin count.

Despite this apparent formula for multiple partialities, Wace banishes ambivalence by affirming an immutable barrier between the known and the unknown. He frequently repeats the formula "ne sai" (I don't know) in order to explain the absence of descriptive or explanatory information, most spectacularly in the triple anaphora "ne jo n'ai mie" (I don't have any idea at all).[16] Throughout his account of Arthur's reign, Wace takes special care to circumscribe the limits of the knowable by excluding doubtful fables, difficult prophecy, and conjectural biography.[17] By repeatedly exposing the boundary between truth and *fables*, Wace mobilizes a discourse of objectivity that ratifies each ruler's legitimacy. In one sense, the difference between the known and the unknown coincides with the difference between what one possesses and what one does not. Thus by representing the bounds of historical knowledge, Wace identifies a colonizing vision that denies partialities and ambiguities: historiography dominates information. Indeed, Wace describes his written achievements as conquest in the *Roman de Rou* when he notes that the difficult work of translation becomes easy if his "enging" revives and "quant je cuit conquester" (when I believe I conquer) (1:60, ll. 1357–59).[18] These are the same values — craft and force — that Wace ascribes to successful rulers in the *Roman de Brut*. The hero and the historian thus both seek the material *gain* of *conquester*.[19] Moreover, as Hanning points out, *engin* collocates chivalric and poetic craft.[20] Even though Wace ultimately loses his battle with history in the *Roman de Rou*,[21] the symmetry between historical conquerors and the historiography of conquest effaces the difference between deeds and their textualization. Wace thereby legitimates domination as a cultural activity that eradicates doubt and ambiguity. Successful narration thus redounds to the honor of the hero, and his historian.

The *Roman de Brut*'s prologue announces an already triumphant possession of Briton territory by eliminating the *descriptio* of Britain. Instead, Wace offers comprehensive knowledge of Insular succession to anyone who understands French:

Ki vult oïr e vult saveir
De rei en rei e d'eir en eir
Ki cil furent e dunt il vindrent
Ki Engleterre primes tindrent,
Quels reis i ad en ordre eü,
Ki anceis e ki puis i fu,
Maistre Wace l'ad translaté
Ki en conte la verité. (ll. 1–8)

[Whoever wants to hear and wants to know, from king to king and from heir to heir, who they were and from where they came, those who first held England, which kings there have been in order, who was first and who next, Master Wace has translated it, who recounts the truth of it.]

Presenting a past that seems to have no history, this introduction outlines a genealogy of generic kings, never identifying their ethnic or geographic origins. The narrative thus records the succession of royal tenants who have "held" England rather than the history of a particular kinship group. Wace promises to follow the line of inheritance from heir to heir, in proper order, but does not refer to any particular time period. Although the kings and heirs remain anonymous and achronic, the name of their land (England) and their historian (Wace) orient the orderly succession toward the present: from this perspective, the narrative could easily encompass the twelfth century. Historiographically, then, the Insular landscape always already belongs to the Francophones who desire its history. Wace captures the permanence of historiography by linking Marius's stone, sign of military triumph, to his own triumphant control of historical knowledge through the vocabulary of witness ("testemonie").[22] Wace and the stone both convey immovable history; they each testify reliably to historical truth. The *Roman de Brut*, like this stone called *Vestinaire*, offers an absolute memory, unaffected by time or language.

Many critics have held that Wace staked out this territory of true history specifically for Henry II; Beate Schmolke-Hasselmann even calls "King Arthur" a "literary name" for Henry II.[23] Henry did spend his formative youth at the court of his uncle, Geoffrey's patron Robert of Gloucester, and Wace was definitely writing the *Roman de Rou* for Henry between 1160 and 1174. And the *Roman de Brut* does support royal allegory: Henry made the Britons' jurisdictional challenges his own; he could see himself in every Briton who successfully conquered the monarchy from a rival relative, and Stephen of Blois in every usurping cousin. Yet Wace probably began work on the *Roman de Brut* in 1150 or 1151,[24] when Henry's kingship was far from assured. Whether or not Henry had anything to do with the *Roman de Brut* (and nothing links him directly to the text),[25] his political, military, and literary activities in the 1150s provide a compelling context for Wace's legitimations of force. After inheriting Normandy from his father Geoffrey of Anjou in 1149, Henry focused his attention on conquering the kingship. He forced Stephen to sign a treaty recognizing him as heir in 1153, but his succession remained precarious right up to Stephen's death (which was unexpected).[26] After Henry acceded to the throne in December 1154, he continued to consolidate his territorial control. He immediately asserted firm lordship over Norman magnates; he was planning to conquer Ireland by the end of 1155; he sought to subdue Brittany in 1156; he campaigned in Wales in 1157 and 1158.[27] This aggressive itinerary justifies Rita Lejeune's judgment that Henry was too busy with battle to bother with literature, and perhaps even M. Dominica Legge's more categorical judgment that "Henry II never had much use for vernacular literature of any kind."[28] Yet while Wace wrote, Henry pursued an almost continuous program of conquest: the *Roman de Brut* legitimates and glorifies similar efforts by Briton kings.

Henry passed through Caen in 1154, and at least twice more between 1156 and 1161,[29] all occasions on which Wace may have caught his attention. The nature of Henry's interest, if indeed there was any, is partly revealed in the other works dedicated to him between 1153 and 1155 — Osbert of Clare's panegyrical poem, Henry of Huntingdon's *Historia Anglorum*, and Aelred of Rievaulx's genealogy of English kings.[30] While Osbert praised Henry himself and Henry of Huntingdon provided an English history initially completed around 1130, Aelred set out specifically to prove Henry's place in English history.[31] After addressing Henry as lord of Normandy, Aquitaine, and Anjou (711), Aelred follows praise of Henry with admiration for David of Scotland, reminding Henry that he received knighthood from the Scottish king. Aelred proceeds to use the history of the English kings to demonstrate Henry's ties to Scotland, making the key figure Henry's great-grandmother Maud (716), just as Robert of Gloucester will make her the hero of the English *kunde* more than a century later. Following the matrilineal line to Edward and then all the way to Adam, Aelred extends the network of Henry's family obligations through customary Norman "linkage." Aelred's genealogy, just like Robert of Gloucester's, exploits the full range of available kinship to argue a specific point of identity. In this sense, the matrilineal line does not embarrass or signify loss;[32] instead, it provides Aelred with a compelling argument in favor of Henry's obligations to his recently orphaned Scottish cousins, Malcolm and William.[33]

Henry himself incarnates a matrix of ethnic identities (all implicated in the *Historia*); he is identified at least partially with each of them at one time or another. As Wace embarked on the *Roman de Rou* in the 1160s, for example, Aelred dedicated his "Vita et miracula Edwardi regis" to Henry, pointing out that he descends from Edward and forms the cornerstone ("lapidum angularem") where English and Norman histories meet (738). With John of Marmoutier's dedication of an abbreviated Angevin history,[34] Henry's historiographic associations cover nearly all of his genealogical shadows. Finally, perhaps by chance, Benoît de Sainte-Maure's *Chronique des ducs de Normandie* culminates with a genealogy of Angevin counts, tracing their royal history *d'eir en eir* in order to explain the great honor that Geoffrey Plantagenêt brought to Henry's mother Matilda (ll. 41837–936). Together, these narratives portray Henry as triply royal (from English, Norman, and Angevin heritage), and as cousin to the Scottish and French royal families. From this perspective, the *Roman de Brut* grafts together several genealogical branches, all redounding to the greater glory of Henry's territorial expansion.

The *Roman de Brut* has been associated with Eleanor as often as Henry, largely on the basis of Laȝamon's declaration that she received a copy of the text. Eleanor was indeed in Normandy frequently between 1154 and 1160, although not before.[35] It seems unlikely, however, that Eleanor commissioned the work from its inception, as Lejeune suggests,[36] even if it later caught her attention. Wace's own statements in the *Roman de Rou* indicate an independent motivation, in which he took it upon himself to write *romanz*; he also emphasizes service to God instead of praising his royal benefactors.[37] Whatever the *Roman de Brut*'s path to royal readers (if it had any), its initial audience could easily have been the lesser nobility ("honorial barons" without Insular holdings)[38] or the lesser clergy (not trained in Latin and not otherwise likely to learn history).[39]

A broad, mixed audience accords well with the prologue's address to all who wish to listen and learn. Wace reinforces this inclusive pedagogy with frequent first- and second-person plurals (*apelons, oez*). These references open history's lessons to an ever-expanding community, from twelfth-century royals to twentieth-century critics. Royal legitimation, then, only accounts for part of the work's appeal.[40] The *Roman de Brut* also touches broader Norman ideologies. As both regional and imperial historiography, the *Roman de Brut* possesses land, kinship, and time by force. It proffers a record of conquest legitimated by its own success. Ultimately, the reading community is not limited by class, ethnicity, or even chronology — only by language.

Terre bone a gaainer

For royal, aristocratic, and clerical audiences alike, Wace focuses on patterns of admirable domination with a colonizing gaze colored by the First Variant's indigenous possession of Insular landscape. In an especially tricky historiographical and ideological maneuver, Wace's translation of the hybrid *Historia* uses the First Variant's paradigms of resistance to sustain unencumbered domination. Wace thus turns a blind eye to the *Historia*'s aestheticized landscapes, extending the First Variant's logic of the realm (*regne*) to the feudal logic of the fief (*enor, fieu*). The land it-self becomes a generic place, legally but not culturally meaningful; it acquires value only when possessable and agriculturally productive. As a result, territorial expansion articulates waste and gain (*guaster, gaainer*) as military and economic activities. Otter refers to this collocation of desirable and arable land as a central motif of twelfth-century historiog-raphy (although without discussing the *Roman de Brut*) (59–60); Leckie explicitly correlates military and cultural dominion in Wace's text (115). Wace's complicity with the Welsh is thus not merely textual: the un-measurable *regne* sustains expansionism brilliantly.

Where the First Variant redactors attenuate the ambivalence associ-ated with the imperial landscape gaze by removing aesthetic elements from the opening *descriptio,* Wace excises the entire passage. And when the Trojans meet the giants, in a colonial encounter often fraught with ambivalence toward the desirable native, Wace approaches the giants as he would any other civilized society: he explains that the giants of Albion made Goemagog lord ("seinnur") because he was the strongest, and apologizes for not knowing the names of the others (ll. 1067–72). And in startling contrast to the *Historia,* Wace dresses both lords for the match: Corineus ties up his shirttails ("Des pans de sa cote se ceinst, / Parmi les flancs alques s'estreinst") while Goemagog equips himself ("Goë-magog se racesma / E de lutier s'apareilla") (ll. 1113–16). The wrestling match itself progresses in a series of bilateral descriptions that fuse the two wrestlers into a single entity (ll. 1117–68). This singularizing vision serves the aesthetic pleasure of two colonizing audiences, the Trojans and the Normans. Because both have already claimed their foreign inher-itance by force (Wace follows the First Variant's revisions), the match becomes a sport for those already in possession rather than a trope of new dominion.

When Wace does finally proffer a *descriptio,* he envisions monoto-nously generic space:

> Brutus esguarda les montainnes,
> Vit les valees, vit les plainnes,
> Vit les mores, vit les boscages,
> Vit les eues, vit les rivages,
> Vit les champes, vit les praeries,
> Vit les porz, vit les pescheries,
> Vit sun pople multepleier,
> Vit les terres bien guaainier...
> (Ll. 1209–16)

[Brutus looked at the mountains, he saw the valleys, he saw the plains, he saw the moors, he saw the bushes, he saw the waters, he saw the rivers, he saw the fields, he saw the prairies, he saw the ports, he saw the fisheries, he saw his people multiplying, he saw the lands producing well . . .]

This landscape described in dramatic anaphoric excess is visually empty: no adjectives color the scene; only the motionless *bien* rustles in the distance. Since audiences cannot visualize the scene that Brutus beholds, seeing becomes a metaphor rather than an action (underscored by Wace's claim that Brutus "sees" his people multiplying). In this passage, Brutus does not take possession with an imperial gaze, but rather quantifies his holdings with a lordly view.

Wace distances the narrative further from the island's symbolic cartography by substituting the Avon for the Severn (ll. 1435–40). Moreover, he follows the First Variant in systematically dismissing the island in favor of the *realm*. This *regne* weakens the significance of boundary formations, so that Belinus's roads merely mitigate the difficulties of travel across the marshy landscape (ll. 2605–10). In Wace's expansionist historiography, the realm's flexible measurement legitimizes new conquests and becomes synonymous with the fief. Indeed, Wace uses *regne* and *enor* interchangeably during the reigns of Leir and Belinus, and textual variants during Archgallo's reign include *regne, enor,* and *terre.*[41] The land, then, sustains crops rather than collective identity. When productive, the land becomes a valuable fief. It actually coincides with cultural value, since tenurial terminology connotes social attributes — honor (*enor*) and faith (*fieu*). From this ideological perspective, the *Historia*'s aestheticized landscapes give way to the colonizing pair *guaster* and *gaainer.* Each term has both military and agricultural connotations, and either can lead to new dominion: expansionist kings can lay waste (*guaster*) to desirable land and so gain control (*gaainer*); alternatively, uncultivated land (*guaster*) can be possessed through cultivation (*gaainer*). The value of arable land, then, makes conquest the admirable achievement of ambitious lords.

The description of Loegicia establishes the effects of *guaste* in preparation for Brutus's *gain*. While the *Historia*'s Loegecia mirrors Britain's beautiful landscape, Wace portrays agricultural devastation:

Home ne feme n'i troverent;
Tut unt trové le païs guast
Ke n'i aveit ki gaainast.
Utlage l'orent tut guasté,
Chacied la gent, l'aveir porté.
Tute esteit la terre guastine. . . .
Guaste unt trovee une cité
E un temple d'antiquité.
(Ll. 622–34)

[They didn't find man or woman there, they found the whole country wasted because there was no one to gain from it. Pirates had
completely wasted it, chased away the people, carried off the goods.
The land was completely wasted.... They found a wasted city and
a temple of antiquity.]

With four different forms of *guast*, this landscape bears the marks of
conquest as a scar. With the contrasting rhyme *guast/gaainast*, Wace introduces the conquering pair; soon after, Brutus celebrates victory over
the Poitevins, happy with his "gaain" and with "[t]utes les terres...guas-
tees" (l. 933). As in the *Historia*, Loegecia presages future destructions of
Britain, but for Wace devastations are periodic, not permanent—periods
between crops rather than devastating ethnic judgments. The promised
island, unlike Loegecia, is "abitable," "delitable," and "bone...a cul-
tiver" (ll. 681–85), and so looks like the desirable fief it will become.

Throughout the rest of the *Roman de Brut*, the colonial and agricultural values of *gaainer* shape a succession of admirable territorial expansions. The Spaniards' settlement in Ireland, for example, evinces a description of agricultural opportunity; they come explicitly looking for a
"lieu" (place) to hold as a "fieu."[42] Wace also describes the Pict settlement in positive terms because they have "aré e guaainied" a land that
had been "en guastine" and "laissiee a salvagine" (left in a savage state)
(ll. 5185–92); later they are again given fields "desertee" to cultivate (ll.
7941–45).[43] Maximianus's description of Armorica also presents the
land as "gaainable" and "delitable." The rest of the description recalls
Brutus's generic topographic catalog; Maximianus concludes by describing the enfeoffment and gain he proposes for the conquered land (ll. 5918–
25). Here and elsewhere, successful cultivation coincides with successful dominion. Indeed, when Vortigern engages Hengist, he pointedly withholds arable land and promises to give only money and goods ("livreisuns,"
"soldees," and "duns") (ll. 6811–12): the Saxons have not yet *gaainie*
anything.

Wace's conception of the *enor* supported by *terre bone a gaainer* reorients the end of the Britons' dominion significantly. After Gormund's
conquest, Wace does not lament the disinherited Britons so much as the
impoverished land:

Dunc pristrent la terre a destruire;
Deus, quel dolur e quel injuire
De bone terre e de gentil,
Que turné est a tel issil!
(Ll. 13473–76)

[Then they took the land to destroy it. God, what pain and what injury, that good and gentle land is turned to such ruin.]

144

In the end, agricultural disaster rather than foreign conquest or divine retribution forces the Britons to abandon the land:

En sun tens fud falte de blé
E de la falte vint chierté,
E de la chierté vint famine. . . .
Ovoc cele mesaventure
Revint une altre altresi dure;
Mortalité fud grant de gent
Par air corrompu e par vent. . . .
Cil ki porent fuïr fuïrent,
Lur fieus e lur meisuns guerpirent,
Tant pur la grant chierté de ble,
Tant pur la grant mortalité.
(Ll. 14661–96)

[In his [Cadwallo's] time there was a failure of wheat and from the failure came shortage, and from the shortage came famine. . . . With this misfortune came another just as hard: mortality was great among the people because of corrupted air and wind. . . . Those who could flee fled, their fiefs and their houses they abandoned, as much for the great shortage of wheat as for the great mortality.]

Angles and Britons alike are evicted by bad air and bad crops. The empty "terre guast" (ll. 14707–12), however, soon looks like "terre. . .bone guaainier" (l. 14727) to the Angles' overseas relatives. Their labor cultivates and conquers the land as legitimately as Brutus's or Arthur's. The Welsh themselves are disinherited ("forsligni") and lose their lands ("enor") (ll. 14849–54). Meanwhile, English agricultural success maintains the land as available and desirable for whoever can overpower them and establish a new "eritage" for their own "lignage" (as the Normans did). By grounding identity in the control of the regne as fief and focusing on agricultural productivity, Wace feudalizes the First Variant's regnum, making it legitimately available to the strongest hand. He thereby legitimates any conquest (gaain) that sustains cultivation (gaain). And while Geoffrey's Britons derive their identity from Britain, even when in exile, Wace's Britons derive theirs from the possession of land in general: once disinherited, they exist no more. Each successive passage of dominion takes place in a novels lieus that effaces prior claims. The new place redounds to the honor of the conquering group—and the memory of the old only to the historian.

Eirs bien conqueranz

With the fief at the center of history, the quality of the heirs becomes the most important aspect of identity—quality defined as the ability to enforce and expand inheritance claims. Wace thus emphasizes the difference between the strong and the weak at the expense of ethnic dynamics, turning the First Variant's ideological pair *us/them* into *winner/loser*. And as in the First Variant, de facto demonstrations reign over de jure legitimations: possession is the greater part of valor. The value of the *enor* itself transcends the mechanisms of its transmission, so that force, craft (*engin*), and genealogy all legitimize inheritance equally. Marriages also facilitate territorial expansion, and subsume the problem of ethnic intermingling. Ultimately, *eritage* foregrounds immediate kinship relations (*parenté*), so that the narrative tells the history of the land's tenants ("ki tindrent") with little ethnic partiality. From the perspective of Britain's Norman owners, then, the *Roman de Brut* recounts how the stronger legitimately overpowered the weaker.

Norman historiography in general often justifies force and chronicles the laudable achievement of territorial expansion.[44] Like Brennius, for example, Rollo and William the Bastard had to "cunquere sun heritage" (l. 2653); like Uther, the fathers of men who defended their lands during Stephen's reign rejoiced to have "eirs bien conqueranz" (l. 8396); like Loth in Norway, Henry II had to conquer his "dreit...par force" (ll. 9831–32). Force thus dominates the discourse of legitimacy in Wace's narrative: degenerate men fail to seize their inherited lands; weak men honor their betters by submitting; sons who lose their fathers' lands bring shame to their family.[45] Gormund embodies the admirable extreme of this ideology by renouncing his inheritance in favor of his younger brother and vowing to rule only what he himself has conquered (ll. 13391–400). The prestige of territorial success sustains colonial visions by establishing relative cultural worth according to military achievement. This triumphant vision of colonial expansion dismisses ethnic legitimation and shapes mimicry into flattery: Wace praises Marius because he honors the Romans by learning their culture, Coilus because he imitates Roman law and custom perfectly, and Gawain for his Roman upbringing; conversely, he criticizes the Britons who defy the conquering Romans as "fiers e orguillus" (proud and prideful).[46] The praiseworthy mimic men perform an idealized colonial subjectivity because they successfully assimilate the value of the dominating power.

In Normandy, the nesting eagles of Loch Lomond readily capture the value of force in creating collective unity. The image of the eagles as sembling to fight whenever invasion threatens the island (ll. 9435–40) resonates with Dudo of Saint-Quentin's aviary allegory. There, Rollo dreams that birds of many different kinds nest together without contention ("sine discretione generum et specierum"), each with one red wing. A Christian interpreter informs Rollo that the red wings represen warriors' shields, the different species the different origins of those wh will serve ("homines diversarum"), and the nests the cities they wil build (146–47). Searle comments that this founding scene of *Not*

146

manitas captures the essence of the Norman polity, made of different groups united by choice in common aggressive cause (65, 244). Wace's eagles, birds of a single species, displace the multiple origins signified in Dudo's allegory; they portray the unifying effects of collective domination. Indeed, Wace turns the *Historia*'s acquatic marvels of ethnic separation into extreme "merveille" (ll. 9537–86), diffusing their allegorical force by conjuring strangeness. Like La3amon and Robert of Gloucester, then, Wace assumes collective unity while overlooking ethnic difference.

The logic of unifying force reorients all significant conflicts over dominion in the *Roman de Brut*, displacing ethnic legitimation and giving freedom a feudal turn. Caesar, for example, recognizes that Belinus and Brennius won dominion over Rome, but since Rome is now stronger, the tenancy must change (l. 3880). Cassibellanus in turn defends the freedom ("franchise") of the fief, claiming that no ancestor has ever done homage for Britain (ll. 3943–60). Roman strength subsequently establishes their legitimate dominion over the island, which Wace ratifies by remarking after the Britons' rebellion that Rome recovered "sa dreiture" (its right) (l. 5044). In conflicts over jurisdiction, then, strength matters more than any other quality, and everyone eventually meets their match: those who win one day lose the next (ll. 8867–68). Indeed, Wace's battle descriptions model generic conflict, most dramatically in an anaphor of indefinite pronouns during the war between Arthur and Lucius: "Les uns ferir, les uns buter, / Les uns venir, les uns turner, / Les uns chaeir, les uns ester" (Some strike, some pillage, some arrive, some turn, some fall, some remain) (ll. 12566–68). Wace catalogs here ordinary acts of war, without attributing them to anyone in particular. The description mirrors his overall approach to force as an autonomous value, independent of legal or social identity.

Wace complicates the role of force by also valuing *engin,* a term of quintessentially ambivalent success in twelfth-century heroic discourse.[47] Whereas courtly ideology denigrates *engin* as unheroic and dishonorable, Wace admires crafty rulers. In his hands, all the meanings of *engin* contribute directly to conquest: *engin* is a fabricated instrument of war, an intellectual perspicuity, and a deceitful manipulation. Together with *force, engin* counters the First Variant's *libertate;* it prepares the ground for Robert of Gloucester's post-colonial *quointise*. Wace's admiration of effective *engin* surfaces from the very beginning of the *Roman de Brut.* As soon as Brutus has conquered his reputation ("los conquesté") (l. 162), the Trojans begin to fight the Greeks: they defend a castle with mangonels built by "engigneors" (ll. 329–31); when Brutus plans to trick the Greeks in their sleep, the narrator interjects approvingly: "Boisdie e engin deit l'en faire / Pur destrure sun adversaire" (Tricks and craftiness one must do to destroy one's adversary) (ll. 363–64).[48] The aphorism presents an exemplary truth about the imperative to dominate through all available means. Wace later admires Dunvallo's ingenious ("enginnus") use of trick-ery to consolidate his dominion (l. 2245) and Cador's use of "grant veis-die" against the Saxons (ll. 9374). Clever cunning can also accomplish treachery, as when Brennius plots to attack Belinus; Belinus, however, knows how to answer with equal trickery: "Veisdie fist contre veisdie."[49] A similar contest of wits is played out between Hamo and Arviragus (ll. 4931–84). Numerous pairings of *force* and *engin* activate all of *engin*'s senses simultaneously: Vortigern's diviners advise him to build a tower that will not be taken "par force" or "par engin" (ll. 7321–22); Gormund sends burning sparrows flying into Cirencester (ll. 13579–606); Arthur kills Dinabuc ingeniously with his sword ("engiegnus") (l. 11530). All of these crafty strategies evince the narrator's admiration rather than condemnation.

Conquest and craft come together in Belinus's gate, erected with "merveillus engin" (l. 3212) to commemorate his successful expansion of the *regne*. The association of *engin*, architecture, and conquest is strongest, however, in the importation of the Giants' Ring. When Aure-lius asks how the stones could possibly be moved, Merlin's reply ex-pands on the aphorism Wace used with Brutus:

Reis, dist Merlin, dunc ne sez tu
Que engin surmunte vertu.
Bone est force e engin mielz valt;
La valt engin u force falt.
Engin e art funt mainte chose
Que force comencer nen ose.
Engin puet les pieres muveir
E par engin les poez aveir.
(Ll. 8057–64)

["King," said Merlin, "don't you know that *engin* surmounts *vertu*? Force is good and *engin* worth more; *engin* works there where force fails. *Engin* and art do many things that force doesn't dare begin. *Engin* can move the stones and by *engin* you can have them."]

The expedition to remove the stones from Ireland underscores the rela-tionship between force and clever manipulation, as Aurelius fights the Irish and Merlin crafts the stones ("les piere enginnereit") (ll. 8088–92). Wace, however, does not make Merlin master of superior "machina-ciones," but, following the First Variant, a master of magic spells as he utters some kind of "oreisun" (incantation) that Wace does not know.[50] Stonehenge thus stands for the collocation of brilliant architectural achievement and superlative military strategy. Credit for this achieve-ment passes easily from the Britons to the Normans as Wace identifies the stones' various names:

Bretun les suelent en bretanz
Apeler carole as gaianz,
Stanhenges unt nun en engleis,
Pieres pendues en franceis.
(Ll. 8175–78)

[The Britons used to call them *Giants' Ring* in Briton, they have
the name *Stonehenge* in English, *Hung Stones* in French.]

The succession of names and languages traces the history of Britain's
tenants, heirs to the stones' own colonial origins. As a monument to
clever force, then, Stonehenge commemorates the achievements of
whoever currently dominates the land.

Force and *engin* both facilitate expansionism. In the process, they side-
line ethnic concerns by establishing a colonial boundary between winners and losers. Wace reinforces this boundary by turning the earliest
Trojan scenes away from ethnicity and toward family structures. Exploiting the ambiguity of the Latin "prosapia" (*race* or *family*),[51] Wace
implies that Brutus finds several Trojan families ("lignages") in Greece:

De cels de Troie iluenc trove
Tute la lignee Eleni,
Un des fiz al rei Priami,
A d'altres lignages asez
Ke l'on aveit enchaitivez;
E mult i out de sun lignage,
Mais tenu erent en servage.
Brutus trova sun parenté.
(Ll. 150–57)

[Of those of Troy he found there the whole line of Helenus (one of
the sons of king Priam) and several other lineages who had been
enslaved, and many of his own lineage, but they were held in servitude. Brutus had found his family.]

Enumerating at least two specific families (Helenus's and Brutus's), this
description presents the ethnic group as a linkage between family lines.
The final "parenté" can refer equally to Brutus's own family ("sun lignage") or to all the Trojans as a whole ("cels de Troie"). Wace soon introduces a third term, *gent*, which also refers both to ethnicity (Assaracus
helps the Trojans because he is of their "gent" [l. 206]) and available family members ("gent" describes the Trojans who gather to fight the Greeks
[l. 405, 493]). Indeed, in Latin, *gens* refers as much to a common descent
group as to a race.[52] *Gent* and *parenté* thus work as synonyms that con-
flate ethnic genealogy with kinship so that history becomes a family affair.

Once the Trojans reach the island, they celebrate their acquisition of a "novels lieus" as an "eritage" for their "lignage" (ll. 1080–84). Their identity thus depends on the acquisition of inheritable land. The subsequent division of this "eritage" establishes a model of peaceful family transmission, as Wace underscores the perfect fraternal amity that reigns among Brutus's three sons (ll. 1289–92). Perhaps surprisingly, Wace does not mention primogeniture as a Trojan custom, even though both the Bern *Historia* and the First Variant preserve the reference. Although Wace does repeatedly explain that older brothers rule before younger ones because they are wiser, the choice always depends on individual qualities rather than a legal principle. In the twelfth century, partition in fact remained a normal Norman practice, recognized as such in contemporary customals.[53] Searle argues that unigeniture of any kind created too great a strain on family resources, since it required continual expansion if families were not to grow progressively poorer. The *Roman de Brut*'s flexible *eritage* is thus deeply compatible with Norman cultural expectations, where family wealth outweighed principles of unity.

Numerous other episodes throughout the *Roman de Brut* enumerate family relations in place of ethnic arguments. Membritius, for example, lists all the Greeks' relatives who will remember their slaughter: "Lur parenz, lur uncles, lur peres, / Lur cosins, lur nevuz, lur freres, /...lur altres amis precains" (Their relatives, their uncles, their fathers, their cousins, their nephews, their brothers,...their other close friends) (ll. 531–33). Later, Arviragus underscores his responsibilities as nephew in order to dissuade Caesar from annihilating the Britons (ll. 4796–803). Even Constantine's imperial achievement is cast as a family affair, for he is very much attached to his relatives and goes to Rome to help his mother's uncles (ll. 5696–711). And when Arthur returns to the island after nine years on the Continent, Wace describes the homecoming as a family reunion, with daughters embracing fathers and aunts kissing nephews (ll. 10176–96). These and many other passages envision significant historical interactions through immediate family relations.

The most valuable family relations, in the *Roman de Brut* as in Normandy, are those formed by marriage. Marriages enhance family value because they lead directly to expanded inheritances. Wace specifies, for example, that for four years Aeneas held "La feme e l'onur" (the woman and the honor) (l. 73). Likewise, Claudius makes Arviragus "his man" by giving his daughter to him (ll. 5045–48), and Maximianus inherits England by marrying Octavius's daughter (ll. 5871–72). Both of these marriages involve Roman inheritance, but Wace is more concerned with the fief's integrity than with Roman dominion. Linking marriage to land acquisition, Wace has little concern for the ethnic repercussions of sexual heritage and says nothing of the value of endogamy. This approach reflects the dominant strategy of Norman kinship, whereby women brought new warriors into the family (enabling forceful expansion), drew potential rivals into the web of kinship obligation, and expanded family terri-tory.[54] Wace in fact marvels at resistance to exogamy, claiming that he does not know "par quel felonie" (by what felony) the Lombard women refused to marry the Trojans (ll. 1576–80) and saying nothing about the Britons' refusal to send their women to the Picts (ll. 5192–94). Most re-vealingly, Conanus's antiexogamy speech turns emphatically on the tenurial rather than the ethnic problems of intermarriage:

Pur sa terre mielz guaanier,
Pur pupler e pur herbergier,
E pur sa gent asseürer,
Volt as humes femes duner.
Ne lur vult pas doner Franceises,
Ne pur force, ne pur richeises,
Ne lur lignage entremeller
Ne lur terres acomuner.
(Ll. 6005–12)

[To better gain his land, populate it and cultivate it, and to reassure his people, he wanted to give women to the men. He did not want to give them French women, not for force nor for riches, so as not to intermingle their lineage or encumber their lands.]

The marriages that Conanus envisions map out the sexual ground of healthy agriculture since they will facilitate both conquest and cultiva-tion ("guaanier," "peupler," "herbergier"). Yet even though Conanus's men stand to gain both a larger fighting contingent ("force") and greater riches by marrying local women, Wace emphasizes that they would also incur the danger of disputed inheritance by complicating their lineage. The value of endogamy thus turns here on the fief's integrity, not the ethnic group's. Indeed, in Normandy marriages with "the French" posed acute problems to the regional defense of autonomy. Contrary to the *His-toria*, then, where exogamy weakens valuable ethnic integrity, the *Ro-man de Brut* uses marriage to extend landholdings. In most cases, the advantages of predatory kinship outweigh the potential for complicated inheritance.

By identifying the native Armoricans as French, Wace exposes his blindness to the finer points of Insular ethnicity. In the *Roman de Brut*, the integrity of the *enor*, like the First Variant's *libertate*, often over-rides ethnic genealogy: Wace sometimes distinguishes Saxons from An-gles, sometimes not; he declares that he does not know why Constan-tin's Pict assassin hated him (l. 6462). This ethnic vagueness derives from, or creates, the honor of the individual strong enough to maintain and expand his landholdings. Since family leaders acquire prestige along with their conquests, successful aggression attracts admiration no matter who pursues it. Wace thus offers a superlative portrait of Caesar—"Li forz, li pruz, li conqueranz"—because he conquered more territory than anyone else, not unlike William the "bon conquereur."[55] And Wace admires the Saxons' beautiful physical appearance—not once but twice (ll. 6078, 6724)—and praises Hengist for looking after his personal interest: "D'avancier sei s'entremeteit / Cume chescuns fere devreit" (he set about advancing himself, as everyone should do) (ll. 6847–48). Rightful inheritance thus proceeds from strength, not from immutable law or ethnic heritage; even Arthur succeeds through strength rather than through morality or ethnicity.[56] The French equivalent of Geoffrey's *quietatione*, in fact, occurs only once in the *Roman de Brut* (l. 3359): "quieté" represents an aberration in the inexorable project of tenurial expansion.

The structure of Insular history thus takes shape through inheritance. When land goes unclaimed, chaos reigns. Geoffrey, for example, communicates the disorder that follows the deaths of Ferrex and Porrex by describing the land's multiple divisions; Wace, in contrast, explains that no one of their "lignage" could hold the "eritage."[57] Similarly, when Lucius dies without heirs, Wace claims that no one of his "parenté" holds his "erité" (ll. 5271–72); Wace especially regrets Arthur's lack of children (ll. 9657–58, 13294). Meanwhile, relations between groups turn on fee-holding arrangements.[58] The inherited fief, sometimes taken by force, thus dominates collective identity, displacing ethnic genealogy and even legal argument.

Even Christian identity is bound to the fief. Faith and fealty coexist in the term *fieu*, which indicates the faithful holding of land from a lord as well as faith in the Lord.[59] When Uther rejoices at his victory over Octa and refers to the Saxons, "Ki mun fieu e les voz destruient" (who destroy my faith and yours) (l. 8938), he refers indistinguishably to the Christian faith destroyed by their Pagan presence and to the fertile lands destroyed by the war. The currency of this conceptual confluence is explicit in the speech Aelred of Rievaulx attributes to Walter Espec in "De bello Standardii": "Cur enim de victoria desperemus, cum victoria generi nostro quasi in feudam data sit ab Altissimo?" (Why then should we despair of victory, when victory has been given to our people, as if in fee by the Highest?) (705). In the *Roman de Brut*, the collocation of territorial and spiritual services identifies the law of the *regne* with religious law, such that Pagans and Christians alike recognize that those of one law should have one king.[60] The Christian *fieu* implies a dramatic extension of the *regne*, which can expand to encompass the territorial extent of Christian populations. While Christianity attenuates ethnic difference in the service of hegemony (just as in other accounts of Briton history), it also legitimates expansionism.

As the strong legitimately overpower the weak (and the unimaginitive) dominion passes from *lignage* to *lignage* until the end of Brutus's line and the *Roman de Brut* itself:

Ci falt la geste des Bretuns
E la lignee des baruns
Ki del lignage Bruti vindrent,
Ki Engleterre lunges tindrent.
(Ll. 14859–62)

[Here end the deeds of the Britons and the line of the barons who came from Brutus's lineage, who long held England.]

Whereas Geoffrey's conclusion demonstrates the Britons' failure as a race, Wace has told the story of Brutus's family. The family's "gestes" shape history; when the last of the "lignee" loses the "demeine terre," the story belongs to another family. Eventually, Britain falls into the strong hands of the Normans, the currant tenants of England, and the absent center of the inherited narrative pattern.

Li nom une chose senefient

With each passage of dominion, new tenants bring new names while the land itself remains the same productive fief it has always been. As part of this spirit of timeless possession, Wace never names sources and so overlooks the origins of the *Roman de Brut* itself. He does, however, claim to translate, thereby eliding antecedents in order to more easily transfer the Britons' history to their conquerors. His unambivalently colonial translation assumes and subsumes the Normans' conquest of the island. From the confident colonial perspective of the Francophone lords of the *enor* of "Engleterre," proper names and etymologies record the succession of ownership while dismissing signs of ancient, violated legitimacies. Wace thus manages to weaken the shadows of resistance and the paradoxes of linguistic border crossing that are displayed so dramatically in the Latin *Historia*, the Welsh *Brutieu*, and Laʒamon's *Brut*. Robert of Gloucester will go further by not even presenting himself as a translator. Robert and Wace in fact approach language in similarly technical terms, suggesting yet another way in which the colonized and the colonizing share postcolonial tools.

Wace brings more emphatic attention to his own translation process than any other historian. Outside of the well-known opening and closing passages, he often refers to himself as translator in relation to details about names and places that he has found "written" or "while reading" and that have been said or recorded in "l'estorie."[61] Wace, like Robert of Gloucester, reinforces his authority by citing personal experience (l. 7608) and oral reports (ll. 9595, 10209). All of these anonymous references alienate historical information from the means of its transmission, with translation as the last step in a neutral process.[62] This silent dismissal of meaning from the transmission process collapses the differences between languages and sources from an implied position of superiority. Wace locates himself dramatically at the origin of knowledge when he presents the narrative as a record of his own historical testimony: "Mais puis i sorst une discorde, / Ço testimonie e ço recorde / Ki cest romanz fist, Maistre Wace" (But then there began a disagreement, this witnesses and records the one who made this *romanz* [French translation], Master Wace) (ll. 3821–23). By manipulating the display of translated knowledge, Wace establishes his name as the sign of historiographic mastery, possessing history as conquerors do the land. This historiographical stance replicates the dynamics of a colonial gaze: it overlooks origins that might challenge the legitimacy of the present. The imposed strength of this gaze patrols the limits of memory and eradicates the faint ghosts of past differences.

If Wace himself dominates through linguistic mastery, so do many of his historical characters. Multilingualism in particular dramatically facilitates colonial domination in several instances. Wace portrays second-language proficiency as an admired tool of expansion, not as a threat to group integrity like some other historians. Hamo and Uther's assassins, for example, are multilingual rather than merely bilingual (ll. 4946, 8970). Their linguistic skills thus do not target the Britons specifically, but can attack a range of enemies. Wace's admiration for such skills shows clearly in his extended description of Vortigern's personal translator, named and known as the first Briton to learn the Saxon language (ll. 6957–80). Wace's positive rather than menacing portrayal of multilingualism resonates with the linguistic values that Searle adduces in Norman culture in general, where Norse and French bilingualism contributed to cultural cohesion rather than fragmentation (242–43). Wace's application of linguistic prowess ultimately reflects his own linguistic capacities, frequently displayed in the trilingual presentation of Briton, English, and French names. The *Roman de Brut* thus manifests a colonial linguistics, where translation constitutes an expansionist technology. Since superlative learning of all kinds repeatedly derives from Rome, multilingualism functions as a specifically imperial technology.

Wace's deployment of proper names and etymologies reflects this confident possession of colonial dominion. Whereas Geoffrey's names nourish the ghosts of Briton sovereignty, Wace takes possession for the Normans almost nonchalantly. Emptied of most of its cultural significance, language designates place transparently and neutrally. Wace expresses this principle most succinctly after giving the Briton and English names for Walbrook: "Li nom del son diversefient / Mais une chose senefient" (The names diversify in their sounds but they signify one thing) (ll. 5567–68). Names thus only reflect changes of ownership (usually after forceful conquest); their history records the succession of tenure without judging legitimacy and without ambivalence. Wace's etymologies thus confirm the narrative's historiographical arguments rather than introducing troubling alternative chronologies. In other words, Wace transfers history to the present more than he recuperates the past. The strength of Wace's presentist perspective leads him to refer almost interchangeably to *Bretaine* and *Engleterre*, a practice that invites audiences to identify with the Insular past and regard it as their own.[63] To strengthen this identification, Wace regularly concludes etymologies with an inclusive *apelum* (we name), assuming collective and contemporary Francophone usage.

The perspective of present Norman dominion directly shapes the island's etymology. Like Geoffrey, Wace combines retrospection and prospection in these extended passages of linguistic description. Wace, however, moves the narrative confidently to the present as he traces tenurial history: Brutus displaces "Albion" with "Bretaine" (ll. 1175–78), and the Angles install "Engletere" (ll. 1192–98). *Engletere*, however, already implies the passage of dominion from the English to the Normans.[64] The second, lengthier etymology makes clear that new names reflect legitimate new dominion, without lamenting or condemning the old:

Pur un lignage dunt cil furent
Ki la terre primes reçurent
Se firent Engleis apeler
Pur lur orine remenbrer,
E Englelande unt apelee
La terre ki lur ert dunee.
Tant dit Engleterre en franceis
Cum dit Englelande en engleis;
Terre a Engleis, ço dit li nuns,
Ço en est l'espositiuns.
(Ll. 13643–52)

[Because of a lineage of which they were who first received the land, they called themselves *English* to remember their origins, and *England* they called the land that was given to them. *Angleterre* says the same thing in French as *England* does in English, "land of the English" says the name, that's the explanation of it.]

Like Brutus, these English have found a "novels lieu" for their "lignage." As the French "Engleterre" attests, the Normans have subsequently acted just like the English and kept their preferred customs and language in a new place (ll. 13653–62). Wace might have noted, as he did in the evolution of *Cornwall* (ll. 1187–88), that the first part of the French name remains the same (*Englelande* is only partly translated in *Engleterre*), but he passes over in silence this trace of cultural and tenurial accommodation. Instead, he presents the new inhabitants as colonial lords who refuse assimilation. English possession is secured with a further lengthy translation lesson from "gualeis" (Welsh) to "engleis"—mediated of course by French. The conflation of temporal orders in the whole passage identifies the perspective of present French usage, where the difference between *Bruteine* and *Englelonde* can only be seen retrospectively in relation to *Engletere*. Once again, French remains the unnamed authority.

London's etymology follows the same historiographic path as England. Wace proceeds from Brutus's naming ("Troie Nove") (l. 1224) to Lud's ("Kaerlu") (l. 1231) to the English and French: "Londenë en engleis dist l'um / E nus or Lundres l'apelum" (*London* in English one says, and we now call it *Londres*) (ll. 1237–38). Brutus's intention "ses anceisors remembrer" (to remember his ancestors) (l. 1223) looks altogether quaint as Wace narrates the multiple erasures of historic forms. Wace concludes by summarizing, rather dispassionately, the coercive processes that led to present French practice:

Par plusurs granz destruiemenz
Que unt fait alienes genz
Ki la terre une sovent eüe,
Sovent prise, sovent perdue,
Sunt viles e les contrees
Tutes or altrement nomees
Qui le anceisor nes nomerent
Ki premierement les fondrent.
(Ll. 1239–46)

[By several great destructions that alien peoples have done who have often had, often taken, often lost, the land, are towns and countries all now differently named than the ancestors named them who first founded them.]

Wace does not judge this succession of foreign conquests or the onomastic interventions that coincide with the arrival of new conquerors. Since the land does not signify an immutable cultural identity, names identify ownership and dominion neutrally. Like the prologue, this summary remains silent on the cultural identities of the successive winners and losers. Two lines added after line 1230 in several manuscripts heighten the impression that translation does not affect ontology: "Urbs est latins citez romanz, / Cestre est angleis, Kaer bretanz" (*Urbs* is Latin, *cité* romance, *city* is English, *kaer* Briton). Although the original Briton names have been lost through several linguistic dismissals, Wace's etymologies do not recuperate defeated legitimacies: they remember old forms only in order to complete history's linear progression and thereby the historian's conquest of the past.

When Lud makes the change already announced, Wace reviews London's etymology again, making explicit the role of foreign languages in the linguistic evolution: "Londoïn" arises because "sunt estrange hom venud, / Ki le language ne saveient" (foreign men had come who didn't know the language) (ll. 3762–63); English and Saxons "recorumperent le nun" (corrupted the name again) to produce "Lundene" (ll. 3765–67); Normans and French produce "Londres" because they did not know English, "Ainz distrent si com dire pourent" (and so they said it the way they could) (l. 3772). In each case, the linguistic changes result from the pronunciation difficulties created by colonial contact. This process preserves traces of several languages for the astute multilingual observer, but Wace consistently abstains from judging relative legitimacy:

> Par remuemenz e par changes
> Des languages as gens estanges,
> Ki la terre unt sovent prise,
> Sunt li nun des viles changied,
> U acreü u acurcied;
> Mult en purreit l'on trover poi,
> Si come jo entent e oi,
> Qui ait tenu entierement
> Le nun qu'ele out premierement.
> (Ll. 3775–84)

[By movements and changes of the languages of foreign peoples who have often taken the land are the names of the towns changed, either lengthened or shortened. Very few can be found, so I understand and hear, that have entirely kept the name they first had.]

Wace emphasizes the names' form (either longer or shorter) rather than their cultural content. He recognizes force as the origin of change and identifies the partial remnants of older forms. Nonetheless, the words' practical functions override cultural memory. The foreigners, the legitimacy of whose presence is never questioned, simply pronounce the unfamiliar sounds as best they can.

Elsewhere, Wace focuses almost entirely on phonetic calculation. Describing the evolution of *Caerleon*, for example, he instructs his audience on phonetic erosion:

> Pur Kaerusc fud Karlion,
> Li dreiz fust Kaerlegion,
> Mais genz estranges unt le nom
> Abregied par subtractiun:
> De Legion Liun unt fait
> E de Kaer unt e retrait
> E pur tut unt Karlion dit
> Si unt fait le nun plus petit.
> (Ll. 3195–204)

[For *Kaerusc* was *Karlion*; the proper name was *Kaerlegion*, but foreign people abridged the name by subtraction: from *legion* they made *leon* and from *kaer* they took away *e* and altogether they said *Karlion*. Thus they made the name smaller.]

Wace draws no moral lesson from these changes, nor does he judge the results in cultural terms: *Karlion* is simply smaller than *Kaerlegion* (a term not used in the *Historia*). Wace gives similarly precise and neutral accounts of Bade (ll. 1633–36) and Cernel (ll. 13791–803).[65] In each case, "corruption" seems used neutrally, the way modern linguists use "erosion": it accounts for phonetic change in the absence of conquest or direct intervention. Thus when Wace says that *Trinovent, Kaerlu,* and *Eborac* have been "corrupted," he describes rather than judges.[66] Wace states his etymological neutrality succinctly when he apostrophizes (after the naming of Hampton for Hamo) that sometimes a very minor event gives rise to a name that endures a long time (ll. 5001–4). Nowhere does Wace lament the loss of original forms.

The functional relation between names and ownership figures prominently in Wace's representations of Brittany and Wales. While Wace records the loss of the name *Armorica,* he avers that the land will never lose its current name (ll. 5949–52). In a text where names record dominion, this observation insinuates that the Bretons will not lose their ownership. The naming of Wales also foregrounds territorial possession. When Wace refers to "Guales" at the beginning and end of the narrative, he clearly identifies the queen and duke who may have given their name to the land (ll. 1276–82, 14855–58). The land thus takes its name from the rulers, and the people from the land (just like Brutus and Kamber originally). In the Latin *Historia,* however, the etymology addresses the people, not the land. In Wace's version, then, the name remains rooted in the land; no judgment shadows the people. Moreover, Wace does not mention the "barbarian" option, despite its presence in the First Variant.

Whether names change through phonetic subtraction, foreigners' mispronunciations, or new rulers' forceful interventions, change inevitably comes. For Wace, all names are equally legitimate, since they identify true locations and current owners, not historical memory. Language in fact facilitates forgetting, a force the English manipulate when they change the form of "Sexes" (Saxon knives) to forget the dishonorable treason committed by their ancestors (ll. 7297–308). This deliberate intervention manipulates linguistic commemoration by displaying the disjuncture between language and memory. As a result, changes merely reflect successive usage *de rei en rei,* fulfilling the prologue's promise to tell truthfully who was *ainz* and who *puis.* The *Roman de Brut* thus represents language as a mirror of conquest, not its tool. Wace imports present forms into the past, eliding origins and infusing language with established colonial authority.

D'eir en eir

Wace's pervasive linguistic anachronism establishes a presentist relation to historical time. This universalizing presentism surfaces with the first line when Wace appeals to anyone who wants to hear and know. Throughout the narrative, aphorisms and proverbs weaken historical and cultural differences while strengthening resemblances across time.[67] The figure of Fortune also universalizes historical experience by disrupting temporal specificity. Wace's simultaneous insistence on brevity, the clarity of succession, and annalistic references constructs a teleological progress toward the present. Moreover, his refusal of prophecy keeps the present in focus by denying the future. This combination of presentist teleology with historical timelessness sustains a vision of colonial hegemony: possession looks timeless; neither origins nor conclusions come into clear focus.

Wace refers repeatedly to the present, whereas his First Variant source minimizes references beyond the immediate historical horizon. In addition to implying the present through anachronistic names, inclusive plural verbs, and the present tense, Wace appeals directly to personal experiences. When Aurelius wants to be healed from his sickness, for example, Wace comments, "Cume chascuns de nus vuldreit" (as each of us would want) (l. 8268). And aphorisms implicate these individual experiences in patterns of universal truth, such as when Wace concludes historical episodes with comments like "Fol est qui trop en sei se fie" (Crazy is the one who trusts too much in himself) (l. 3440) or "Ne deit pas huem a buen chief traire / De faire ço qu'il ne deit faire" (A man shouldn't apply himself to doing what he shouldn't do) (ll. 6539–40). These affirmations declare timeless truths about human conduct rather than culturally or historically specific judgments. By implication, events from different places and times do not differ fundamentally.

Wace uses the figure of Fortune to underscore the repetitive, cyclic pattern of history, in which events from different times do in fact repeat each other. Leir is the first to lament the vagaries of Fortune:

> Fortune, tant par es muable,
> Tu ne puez estre une ure estable;
> Nuls ne se deit en tei fier,
> Tant faiz ta roe tost turner.
> Mult as tost ta colur muee,
> Tost iés chaete e tost levee.
> (Ll. 1917–22)

[Fortune, you are so changeable, you can't be stable for one hour. No one should have faith in you, so soon do you make your wheel turn, so soon is your color changed, soon cast down and soon raised up.]

Leir continues for twelve more lines on the changeability of Fortune. Later, Caesar appeals to Fortune as an explanation for the changed relationship between the Britons and Romans: in the past, the Britons legitimately conquered the Romans, but now "Fortune ad sa roe tornee" (Fortune has turned her wheel) (l. 3883) and Rome is the stronger; Wace repeats the image in indirect discourse as Caesar encourages his army (ll. 4665–68). Both of these passages overlook legal or historical legitimation; instead, they account for power through arbitrary patterns. As a cyclic figure, Fortune's wheel is bound to multiple, overlapping temporal references. As a result, history on the wheel confounds stable judgments of legitimacy: as Jean Blacker has noted, defeat becomes not moral but inevitable.[68] Indeed, Wace uses the same expression of alternation to describe dice gaming as he does war: "Li un perdent, li un guaainnent" (Some lose, some gain) (l. 10562).

Alongside this temporally indeterminate past, Wace organizes a clear teleology and an ordered succession of events. Indeed, this is the paradox of presentism: while moving the present into the past, it also makes a direct line from the past to the present. In the structure of narrative time, for example, Wace seems to propel events toward the present as rapidly as possible. Ultimately, the process of battle concerns him less than its outcome. He thus skips over moments of indecision and uncertainty in order to arrive quickly at the next stable conclusion. After introducing the war between the Trojans and Poitevins, for example, Wace concludes decisively: "Briefment vus en dirrai la fin, / Vencu furent li Peitevin" (Briefly I'll tell you the end, the Poitevins were vanquished) (ll. 919–20). Elsewhere, he queries rhetorically why he should give a long account and then announces the result. Wace's principle of *brief* elides the narration of uncertainty, just like the First Variant's *breviter*. These overt manipulations of historical scale, as in Robert of Gloucester's narrative, purveys a mastery of time itself.

The results of these rapid conflicts often establish the land's next heir. History thus proceeds decisively from heir to heir, just as the prologue promises. Moreover, Wace ratifies the First Variant's chronology by declaring at the very moment of Brutus's settlement that Gormund's conquest began English dominion.[69] Leckie argues further that Wace also modifies the depiction of Aethelstan to clarify the First Variant's chronological ambiguities (115). Leckie's exposition of Wace's reconciliation of the *Historia* with traditional English chronology astutely points out that Wace uses territorial control, rather than the establishment of government, to determine relations between peoples (113). In other words, Wace resolves the *Historia*'s obvious temporal dissonances by foregrounding de facto jurisdiction at the expense of de jure judgments. The result envisions continuous Anglo-Saxon unity, rather than a progression from fragmentation to unification (114–15). The clarity of the passage to English dominion suggests a parallel with the subsequent passage to Norman rule: once a new group controls the land, its leader becomes the legitimate heir. As a result of this territorial understanding of tenure, the chronological gaps and synchronisms inherited from the Latin *Historia* do not trouble the legitimacy of successive rulers.

The *Historia*'s annalistic references take on a new relation to the present when Wace declares that he completed the narrative in 1155 (l. 14865). The *Historia* already implies a teleological progress, since the reader can calculate the time between the present year and the deaths of Lucius, Arthur, and Cadwallader. By dating his own narrative practice, Wace fixes the point toward which all events lead and from which they are seen. Subsequent readers can calculate the distance between these events and Wace's translation, and between the translation and the moment of reading. The closing date of 1155 thus underscores the linear movement to the present and the powerful effects of calculating time retrospectively. Moreover, it enrolls narrative itself in the annals of history.

Wace's refusal to translate Merlin's prophecies also keeps the focus on the present. Wace does refer to prophecies when they relate to events told within his narrative, such as Arthur's fate and the Britons' exile. But he reports these as things said about past events, not predictions of future events. When it comes to Geoffrey's book of prophecies itself, Wace states:

Ne vuil sun livre translater
Quant jo nel sai interpreter;
Nule rien dire ne vuldreie
Que si ne fust cum jo dirreie.
(Ll. 7539–42)

[I don't want to translate his book when I don't know how to interpret it. I would not want to say anything at all unless it were as I would say.]

Wace seems most concerned to maintain the boundary that he has asserted from the beginning between the known and the unknown. Since he cannot verify the truth of the prophetic statements (precisely because they pertain to the future), they fall outside of his historiographical bounds. Moreover, should Merlin have been wrong, Wace would be responsible for disseminating false information. Just as he has noted elsewhere his ignorance about certain details, so here he excludes material that he does not know. He could, of course, report them as something he found written, as he does elsewhere with unverified material. Their ontological unverifiability, however, puts them in a different class of information, excluded by Wace's historiographic principles as well as by his temporal perspective.

The *Roman de Brut* ultimately imparts an impression of timelessness within a clearly defined historiographical frame that closes in 1155.

As Wace patrols the boundary between the known and the unknown, his pervasive authorial presence weakens the bounds of time. Confusion about these two related processes has fueled much of the debate about the boundary between truth and fiction in Wace's historiographic discourse. Attention to these issues as boundary differences clarifies the firmness of knowledge bounds in relation to the weakness of temporal bounds. Both strategies propel a discourse of timeless hegemony, congenial to expansionist ideologies.

Caliburne

Arthur's reign represents the high point of the family history of expansionism as well as its timeless, exemplary qualities. After Arthur recovers his inherited land from the Saxons, he enlarges his inheritance through extensive conquests, until finally losing his *demeine terre* to Mordred. As Shichtman has observed in his analysis of Gawain, conquest appears as the "beautiful and rightful activity of those with romantic vision" (113). This aestheticization of domination ultimately legitimates colonialist exploitation. Arthur's sword encodes this ideology of expansion and laudable conquest, as well as the inevitability of defeat. Arthur himself, as in the First Variant, wields Caliburn as a sign of his own superlative strength.

Beginning with Arthur's arming, Wace portrays a king of exceptional physical force. By adding references to Arthur's clothing and horse, Wace provides a complete pragmatic account of battle preparation: Arthur dresses, covers himself with protective gear (including Caliburn), mounts his horse, and arranges his heavier gear (the shield and the lance). The sword itself, although made in Avalon, has no extraordinary qualities: "bien fu lunge e bien fu lee" ([it] was quite long and quite broad) (l. 9280). Wace then adds to the *Historia*'s description of the helmet that it had belonged to Uther (l. 9288). Alongside this genealogical reminder, Wace adds the comment that when armed with the shield Pridwen, Arthur "ne sembla pas cuart ne fol" (didn't seem cowardly or crazy) (l. 9292). When Arthur finally takes up his lance, Wace repeats the qualities of an effective weapon: "Alques fu luncs e alques leez" ([it] was pretty long and pretty broad) (l. 9299). Altogether, these descriptions identify the ordinary strength of Arthur and his weapons, along with their genealogical and divine authorizations. Wace thus concentrates responsibility for Arthur's success in his religious faith and physical strength. Caliburn's absence from the actual battle reinforces this portrait of heroic power (as in the First Variant). After reminding his men to remember how the Saxons have destroyed their families ("parenz," "cusins," "amis," "veisins") (ll. 9319–30), Arthur himself calls on both Mary and God and claims the first blow (l. 9342). The battle ends very quickly, however, after only four lines of general description and eight of Arthur's own prowess (ll.

9349–56). By not describing the press of battle, Wace focuses attention on Arthur's strength and establishes him as a giant-hero equal to an entire army.

Having established peace by expelling the Saxons, Arthur pursues conquests across the water, not to restore rights but because winter has passed: "E od le chaut revint estez, / E mer fu bele a navïer" (And with the heat summer returned, and the sea was beautiful for sailing) (ll. 9660–61). After conquering Ireland and other nearby islands, Arthur returns to Britain. As part of his efforts to establish order at home, he constructs the Round Table. This architectural innovation, which first appears in the *Roman de Brut*, enforces equality among Arthur's imperial subjects. He orders the table himself in order to avoid excessive rivalries among his men, whose various regional origins are immediately identified at length (ll. 9747–74). As Schmolke-Hasselmann makes clear, equality among the knights does not serve egalitarian or democratic purposes; rather, it enhances Arthur's control.[70] The Round Table thus forcefully domesticates the multiple and conflicting influences brought home from abroad. Constructed in the aftermath of overseas expansion, the Round Table materializes Arthur's imperial ambitions.

After twelve years of peace, Arthur again embarks on conquest, this time to Norway and France (ll. 9799–806). Again, rather than claiming any particular ancestral rights, Arthur seeks to enlarge the family inheritance and honor those who depend on him: he seems to deserve whatever authority he can successfully assert. After his success in Norway, he proceeds with good weather and wind ("bel tens," "bon vent") to Denmark (ll. 9870–71). Finally, he arrives in France (whose tenurial status Wace describes with precision [ll. 9905–13]). As in the *Historia*, Arthur triumphs over Frollo with Caliburn. Wace describes the sword in Arthur's hand before the blow, echoing the previous description of the lance Ron: "Caliburne out, s'espee, el puin, / Qu'il out eüe en maint besuin" (Caliburn he had, his sword, in hand, which he had had in many times of need) (ll. 10083–84, 9300). Separating the name from the fatal action, Wace subtly foregrounds Arthur's own strength in the accomplishment.

Arthur's conquest of Paris, as well as of western France from Anjou to Lorraine (ll. 10109–12), reflects positively Henry II's efforts to establish control over the western continent before and after his accession to the throne late in 1154. Indeed, in the *Roman de Rou*, Wace identifies the Norman-French border as a specific source of anxiety for the Normans when he laments the "boisdies de France" (tricks of France) designed to disinherit the Normans.[71] Contrary to the jurisdictional disputes that dominated Insular politics during the early years of Henry's reign,[72] the *Roman de Brut* elides the troubling memories of historical dominion and establishes new ones unproblematically. Wace thus emphasizes the legal aspect of land redistribution by having Arthur enfeoff ("enfeufer") Anjou and Normandy, along with Flanders and three other regions (ll. 10151–71, 10591). The Frollo episode thus defends Norman-Angevin territorial claims, at the direct expense of the French.

In a more extreme defense of Norman-Angevin boundaries, one "André" (possibly from Mont Saint-Michel) composed a short satirical account of the Frollo episode sometime between 1150 and 1200. André has an imaginary English king (and commander of drinking) named Arflet issue a charter refuting a French "fable" that apparently claims that a giant cat killed Arthur and wore the crown of England (ll. 17–36). Arflet defends his sovereignty from French ridicule by enumerating the English conquerors of France—Arthur, Brennius, Belinus, Maximianus, and Constantine (ll. 37–44). He goes on to catalog the places that Arthur conquered in France "o ses Engleis" (with his English) (ll. 61–64), including a battle with a degenerate and cowardly Frollo. In the end, Arthur places the French in his servitude, "[ou] encore est tot lor lignage" (where all their lineage is still) (l. 206). After more than a hundred lines of satiric commentary on the poverty of French culinary habits, Arflet concludes his charter by drawing a circle of challenge around Paris: he enumerates the groups (from Flanders to Gascony) that have signed the charter against the French (ll. 385–96). In the period that culminated in Philip's conquest of Normandy in 1204, the French claim to sovereignty over "English" lands was not idle. André's mordant exposé of French degeneracy represents an extreme version of a Norman appropriation of Briton history in response to threatened boundaries.

In the *Roman de Brut*, after Arthur settles his men in France, he returns to the island and celebrates his second major peace at Caerleon. When the Romans arrive to demand tribute, Wace represents the defense of Insular rights by dismissing legal principles (like the First Variant) and adopting force (rather than freedom) as the foundation of legitimacy. Lucius opens the debate with reproach for Arthur's infringement on the powers of Rome (ll. 10651–74); he then refers to Caesar "nostre ancestre" as conqueror of Britain and to Frollo's wrongful death (ll. 10675–86). As Arthur retires with his barons to consider a response, Cador laughs (as in the *Historia*) and discourses on the dangers of peace, which he says produces laziness and weakness (ll. 10737–64). Wace has Gawain reply by invoking the pleasures of peace (ll. 10763–72), first among them (even before the "drueries" of women) that "[p]lus bele e mieldre en est la terre" (the land is prettier and better for it) (l. 10768). Arthur, however, praises his barons for enabling his conquests and ridicules the Romans' prideful claims (ll. 10779–810). He does recognize that Caesar conquered Britain, but concludes: "Mais force n'est mie dreiture / Ainz est orguil e desmesure. / L'um ne tient mie ço a dreit / Que l'um ad a force toleit" (But force is not right, rather it is pride and excess. One does not hold by right what one took by force) (ll. 10829–32). This statement combines the conclusions of Arthur and Hoel in the *Historia*. Arthur points out that by the same reasoning, the Britons can demand tribute from Rome because of the conquests of Belinus, Constantine, and Maximianus (ll. 10851–80). Arthur does not make this counterargument to legitimate Briton right; rather, the comparison ridicules the reasoning that tenure derives from historical precedent:

Il cleiment Bretaine, e jo Rome!
De mun cunseil est ço la sume
Que cil ait la rente e la terre
Ki purra sur l'altre conquerre.
(Ll. 10881–84)

[They claim Britain, and I Rome! This is the conclusion of my counsel: that he have the rents and the land who can conquer the other.]

The right to rents in the present depends on the demonstration of greater force in the present: arguments through precedent prove nothing. Arthur repeats the principle succinctly a few lines later: "Or ait tut ki aver le puet; / Altre dreiture n'i estuet" (Let him have all who can have it; there is no other justice) (ll. 10893–94), and again at the end: "Quant jo chalenz e il chalenge, / Ki tut purra prendre, si prenge!" (Once I challenge and he challenges, whoever can take everything, let him take it!) (ll. 10903–4). Hoel's speech ratifies this forceful logic (ll. 10910–26), while Auguselus's underscores the service owed by those who hold their fees and lands from Arthur, as well as the beauty of war and the need for vengeance (ll. 10958–104). Auguselus encourages further conquest after Rome, and ends with the strongest statement yet of legitimizing force: "Tut prendrum a dreit e a tort" (We'll take everything, by right or by wrong) (l. 11035). Avoiding references to courts or history, the Arthurian response to Roman imperialism argues that claims will be defended and prosecuted solely through force.

Having landed on the Continent on his way to protect and expand the limits of his territory, Arthur hears that a giant has stolen Hoel of Brittany's niece and carried her off to Mont Saint-Michel. As a responsible overlord, Arthur sets off to kill the giant, thereby protecting the lands of the man he had enfeoffed in Brittany. Wace turns this giant into a civilized neighbor by giving him a name, Dinabuc (l. 11317), just as he domesticated the giants of Albion by naming their lord. Moreover, the giant is not a cannibal but eats roasted pork, staining his beard and lap with the charred meat like any messy dinner guest (ll. 11482–86). Wace thus dismisses the trope of problematic assimilation, instead portraying the similarities among powerful men in general. Indeed, for a fleeting moment, Arthur appears almost cannibalistic as he asks his "buteillier" (sommelier) to cut off the giant's head (ll. 11556–57). And when Arthur recounts his earlier fight with Ritho, Wace specifies that Arthur himself completed the coat of beards after his victory (ll. 11585–92). Wace thus breaks down the differences between Arthur, Dinabuc, and Ritho, establishing them all as legitimately ambitious lords.

Wace also domesticates the encounter by dramatizing its sexual violence. Helen has in fact been raped, and has died from the weight of the giant (ll. 11408–12), whereas she dies of fright before violation in the *Historia*. The nurse defends herself against the suspicion of sexual pleasure by swearing to God that she has been forced to remain; she survives the rapes because she is older, stronger, bigger, harder, hardier, and surer than Helen (ll. 11433–37). Civilizing the giant and sexualizing Helen, Wace exposes the danger of neighborly aggression against valuable daughters. These domestic threats can be spoken without damage to dominion itself. Wace is apparently the first to turn the episode toward rape; he is also alone (along with the redactor of the prose *Merlin* [428–31]) in overlooking cannibalism. The combination suggests a forceful dismissal of founding anxiety, consonant with a stridently colonialist discourse: sexual violence remains a threat from outlaw neighbors even after settlement, but the violence of assimilation cannot be spoken by colonial ambition.[73] Laȝamon, Robert, and the author of the *Gesta regum Britanniae* subsequently return to cannibalism while perpetuating the scene of rape on postcolonial grounds.

In the press of the combat, Wace expands the *Historia*'s pattern of naming by having Arthur defeat Dinabuc with Caliburn (ll. 11545–48). The name draws the giant and the Mont into the sword's logic of conquest. Unlike the *Historia*, where the episode iterates founding ambivalence toward the native, the *Roman de Brut* civilizes the giant and makes the Mont the site of a border dispute among rival lords. The Mont itself occupies the border between land and sea and between Brittany and Normandy. It presents the paradigmatic boundary problem of the shore, as it fluctuates with the tides between insular and continental topography. The stroke of the sword thus draws the boundary between civilized Brittany and the untamed sea on the far side of the Mont. Previously, the boundary lay between the Mont and the shore, and Hoel's men could not cross it to rescue Helen: their boats were destroyed on the rocks and many drowned in the water (ll. 11305–8). *Caliburn* thus forcefully asserts that the Mont belongs to Arthur's land, and implies that the resolution of this border dispute has imperial consequences. Moreover, the chapel Hoel founds to commemorate Helen's death attributes the Mont's religious origins to Bretons, a vision consonant with eleventh-century patronage patterns.[74] In Wace's time, the Mont itself remained contested territory: after Henry I's death, its inhabitants sided with Matilda and those of nearby Avranches with Stephen.[75] The appointment of Robert de Torigni as abbot in 1154 significantly strengthened the abbey's orientation toward Normandy and ended a lengthy period of instability.[76] Several years later Guillaume de Saint-Pair affirmed the Mont's *Normanitas* in his *Ro-*

man du Mont Saint-Michel: identifying the local rivers, Guillaume notes that some are in Brittany and "[l]e[s] autres sunt en Normendie; / Si est le mont, je n'en dout mie" (the others are in Normandy, as is the Mont, I don't have any doubt) (ll. 455–56). By adding the Mont to the group of victories signed by Caliburn, Wace similarly claims the island for the Normans as the most recent heirs of Arthur's *enor*.

Having established his jurisdiction over the Mont, Arthur moves on to the larger contest over France. As always, "grainur dreit" (greater right) (l. 11664) rests on superior force. The repetitive rhythm of Gawain's speech to the Romans, as well as its content, calls for forceful resolutions:

Ço te mande que rien n'i prenges
E si tu sur lui la chalenges,
Par bataille seit chalengee
E par bataille deraisnee.
Romain par bataille la pristrent
E par bataille la cunquistrent,
E il l'a par bataille eüe
E par bataille l'ad tenue;
Par bataille reseit pruvé
Kin deit aver la poësté.[77]
(Ll. 11719–28)

[He orders you to take nothing, and if you challenge him for it, let it be challenged by battle and by battle defended. Romans took it by battle, and by battle conquered it. And he had it by battle and by battle held it. By battle let it be proven again who should have the dominion.]

Gawain completes his aggressive speech with aggressive action, beheading Lucius's nephew when he suggests that the Britons speak more bravely than they act (ll. 11745–56). Whereas in the *Historia* Arthur remains ignorant of the ensuing battle until it is over, here he personally sends Ider to help Gawain (ll. 11928–32). When the battle begins in earnest, Arthur addresses himself "a ses nurriz, / A sus baruns e a lur fiz" (to his dependents [and] to his barons and their sons) (ll. 12395–96). He encourages his family members with a rhythmic pendant to Gawain's *bataille* speech:

Vus avez vencu les Norreis,
Vus avez vencu les Daneys,
Vus avez vencu les Franceis
E tenez France sur lur peis.
Bien devez veintre les pieurs
Quant vencu avez les meillors.
(Ll. 12417–22)

[You have vanquished the Norwegians, you have vanquished the Danes, you have vanquished the French, and you hold France under their pennant. Of course you should vanquish the worst when you have vanquished the best.]

Arthur mobilizes here the memory of domination in order to inspire new imperial expansion: the *vencu* speech declares the *bataille*'s desirable outcome.

As in the First Variant, however, the Britons do not vanquish the Romans immediately and are on the verge of retreat when Arthur intervenes with a second speech. Naming himself, Arthur casts himself as the rhetorical and conceptual center of the Britons' success: "Jo sui Arthur ki vus cundui" (I am Arthur who leads you) (ll. 12876–86). Wace makes the relation explicit when he says that Britons attacked the Romans anew "[a]s cops Arthur e as ses diz" (because of Arthur's blows and his words) (l. 12919). And as in the *Historia*, Arthur himself answers his speech with the sword's lethal action:

Calibuerne tint, mult sanglente;
Cui il ateint, mort le gravente.
Ne puis ses cops mettre en escrit;
A chascun cop un hume ocit.
(Ll. 12891–94)

[Caliburn he held, very bloody; whoever it reached, death claimed him. I can't put his blows in writing: with each blow he killed a man.]

Wace continues to emphasize Arthur's control rather than the sword's autonomy: Arthur manipulates the bloody Caliburn, exerting such power that his blows cannot be written (ll. 12895–904). Reinforcing this characterization, Wace names the sword again in Arthur's mocking speech to the decapitated king of Libya:

Puis li ad dit: "Mal aies tu
Ki ci venis armes porter
Pur Calibuerne ensanglanter."
Cil ne dit mot, ki mort se jut.
(Ll. 12908–11)

[Then he said to him: "May you have misfortune, you who came here bearing arms to bloody Caliburn." He said nothing, he who lay dead.]

The *Historia* does not name the sword here, nor in the final description of Arthur's offensive: "De Calibuerne granz cops meist" (with Caliburn he gave great blows) (ll. 12926). These additions emphasize the sword's bloody effects: for Wace, successful force guarantees its own legitimacy. Especially when Arthur speaks the sword's name, taking Caliburn between his own teeth, he dominates coercive performance. Whereas the First Variant wrote Caliburn out of the decisive Roman battle, Wace expands the sword's presence as he expands the legitimation of force.

Arthur now faces the final challenge of recovering his *fieu* and *demeine terre* from Mordred. At the first news of betrayal, Wace keeps dominion between the virile lords: he does not name the queen and attributes all of the active treachery to Mordred:

> Fist Mordred altre vilainie,
> Kar cuntre cristïene lei
> Prist a un lit femme lu rei,
> Femme sun uncle e sun seignur
> Prist a guise de traïtur.
> Arthur oï e de veir sot
> Que Mordred fei ne li portot;
> Sa terre tint, sa femme ot prise.
> (Ll. 13026–33)

[Mordred did another villainy, for against Christian law he took to bed the king's wife; the wife of his uncle and his lord he took like a traitor. Arthur heard and knew for true that Mordred did not hold faith toward him: he held his land, he had taken his wife.]

Mordred's theft of the queen resembles the Dinabuc's theft of Helen: both attack the family and its lands through irregular intercourse. As Arthur again overturns sexual challenge with physical force, the queen flees. Still unnamed, Wace identifies her own erotic desire as the source of betrayal:

> Membra lui de la vilainie
> Que pur Modred s'esteit hunie,
> Lu bon rei aveit vergundé
> E sun nuvou Modred amé;
> Cuntre lei l'aveit espusee.
> (Ll. 13207–11)

[She remembered the villainy with which she had shamed herself for Mordred: she had dishonored the good king and loved his nephew Mordred; she had married him against the law.]

Irregular intercourse dishonors the king as lord of the land, but its transgressions can be fully repaired if the lord overpowers the usurper. Adultery, then, and even bigamy, cannot permanently damage the family or the land so long as the lord is strong.

While the queen disappears into the confines of a convent (ll. 13215–22), the battle rages toward an uncertain end amid anaphoric negativity:

Ne sai dire ki mielz le fist
Ne qui perdi ne qui cunquist
Ne qui chaï ne qui estut
Ne qui ocist ne qui murut.
(Ll. 13259–62)

[I don't know how to say who did better, nor who lost nor who conquered nor who fell nor who remained nor who killed nor who died.]

Here, even force loses its decisiveness. Everyone seems to have been destroyed but no one has won. In the end, the sword does not function as a sign of authority, but only as an instrument of war. It signifies great strength, not transcendent right. The success of that strength against multiple enemies establishes Arthur's rightful, admirable control over vast territories. Yet when he meets a stronger force, he loses all he has gained. The most troubling aspect of this final encounter is perhaps not that Arthur loses but that no one wins. If force cannot reliably clarify rights on the battlefield, then legitimate dominion cannot in fact be established. The absence of a winner signals the depth of the cultural breakdown at the end of the Arthurian era.

In Wace's resolutely expansionist view, coercive boundary formation leads to peace and greater wealth. Arthur's defeat may be troubled by uncertainty, but his heir does accede to the *demeine terre*. In place of Geoffrey's ambivalent equivocations on the value of force, then, Wace presents the arbitrary patterns of fate dispassionately: superior force explains and legitimizes victory; the inevitable turn of Fortune explains defeat. Ultimately, many of Wace's historiographical strategies derive (directly or indirectly) from innovations introduced by the First Variant redactors. Wace follows the First Variant in strengthening flexible categories like the realm, but in the *Roman de Brut* they facilitate expansion rather than ancient legitimacy. Likewise, Wace adopts the First Variant's legitimation of force: just as de facto arguments sustain the legal claims of those who do not control the law, they effectively create new laws for those who do. Whereas the First Variant's pervasive valuation of force derives primarily from the ideology of liberty, in the *Roman de Brut* force sustains colonialist domination. Finally, where the First Variant sidelines Caliburn, Wace expands the sword's conquering presence. The First Variant (along with the *Brutieu*) and the *Roman de Brut* thus wield similar historiographical tools as they absorb the historical effects of conquest and work toward strategic post-colonialism. Their resemblances suggest the complicity of domination with resistance, and vice versa.

CHAPTER 6

En la marche de Gaule
Messages from the Edge of France

As Arthurian historiography spread across the Continent, it eventually returned to Geoffrey of Monmouth's founding ambivalence. Seemingly far from Geoffrey's colonial border, the story of Arthur and Lancelot took root in "la marche de Gaule," that is, in the borders of Brittany and France ("Gaule qui or est apelee France").[1] This extended French prose narrative of Arthurian history thus presents itself as a form of border writing, well within the *Historia*'s cultural tradition. Indeed, like the *Historia*, the thirteenth-century prose cycle invents the Arthurian past in the interstices of established history.[2] This story that begins in the border of Gaul ultimately includes five parts and vast territories, from the *Estoire del saint graal* through the *Estoire de Merlin*, the *Livre de Lancelot*, the *Queste del saint graal*, and the *Mort le roi Artu*. Spanning the ages from the Old Testament to the eighth century and the lands from Jerusalem to Camelot, the cycle intertwines the history of Arthurian Britain with the very beginnings and ends of time. It purveys monumental ambivalence toward authority at a time when political centralization had already eroded aristocratic autonomy.

Although Lancelot's story clearly begins in France's western borders, the prose cycle's own origins are more difficult to locate. Compositionally, scholars have long considered that the earliest parts of the cycle were written last, although Jean-Paul Ponceau has recently revived doubts about this interpretation. Given this uncertainty, as well as the testimony of some early compilations that include the *Estoire del saint graal* and the *Merlin*, I will follow the cycle's fictional chronology in my analyses.[3] As for regional origins, the narrative's internal geography makes Champagne seem a reasonable possibility, although Berry has also been proposed (and Bloch calls the author "Anglo-Norman").[4] Champagne does seem to provide the most fertile ground for a monumental Arthurian project. Here, the countess Marie supported Chrétien de Troyes in the late twelfth century; in this period clerical and chivalric mentalities mingled in ways that suggest a receptive audience for the prose cycle's visions of pious chivalry.[5] In the next generation, the countess Blanche may have commissioned the Guiot manuscript, which displays Champenois attachments to Arthurian narrative spectacularly while also manifesting a style distinctly resistant to Parisian influences.[6] The prose cycle itself draws on many of the Guiot texts, including Chrétien's *Chevalier de la Charrette*, Benoît de Sainte-Maure's *Roman de Troie*, and Geoffrey's *Historia*; indeed, one of the earliest *Lancelot* manuscripts originated in Champagne.[7] Moreover, the comital court, in conjunction with local Cistercian libraries, harbored the Continent's second largest collection of *Historia* manuscripts.[8] In the twelfth and thirteenth centuries, the Cistercians and the secular aristocracy alike struggled against political centralization; both seem to have been attracted to histories of Briton resistance.

The tangled genealogies of the Champenois counts also drew the region into the Arthurian orbit. Since the eleventh century, when William the Conqueror's daughter Adela married into the house of Blois, the Champenois identified closely with the Normans.[9] The Norman lords even declared Thibaut of Champagne duke of Normandy at Henry I's death, before learning that his brother Stephen of Blois had seized the English throne. From the Champenois perspective, Stephen usurped the rights of his elder brother, and Henry II those of Stephen's Champenois heirs.[10] Nonetheless, through Stephen's kingship, the Champenois could claim royal status. Anglo-Norman affinities seem to have been strongest in the area of Meaux,[11] precisely where the prose cycle locates Arthur's final battle. Since Norman historiography links the Britons and the Normans through Antenor, the latent *Normanitas* of Champenois culture provides imaginative access to Arthurian history. Indeed, late in the twelfth century, Marie de Champagne seems to have strategically oriented local genealogical imaginations toward the Britons.[12] All of these circumstances suggest that the Champenois development of Briton historiography would exploit a broad genealogical inheritance, deployed within genealogical anxiety.

Champagne's unique relations with the Capetian family make it a particularly rich site for narratives portraying ambivalence toward royal authority. From Adèle of Champagne's marriage to Louis VII to Jeanne's to Philip IV, the comital and royal lines braid together. Although Adèle engendered prestige for her Champenois family along with her son Philip II, she also gave her Champenois nephews a dangerous uncle.[13] And like other counties, Champagne came under increased pressure to submit to his royal authority. Unlike Normandy and Flanders, however, the county maintained a fragile autonomy throughout Philip's reign and into the later decades of the thirteenth century. Overall, however, the royal blood that flowed in Champenois veins weakened comital power.[14] While the Arthurian prose cycle was being shaped, Champenois power reached a low point. Although the Champenois did safeguard certain privileges by exploiting their many border areas as sites of homage, Philip took advantage of the premature death of Thibaut III in 1201 and the threat of rival claims to the succession to impose significant limits on the autonomy of Blanche's regency.[15]

As the Champenois imagined resistance to royal authority, they did not turn to genealogical history. While they did preserve their inheritances fairly successfully, they ignored the "fabulous genealogies" cultivated by their Flemish cousins who claimed royal Carolingian lineage.[16] The absence of Carolingian genealogy in Champagne opens imaginative space for universal historiography in an Arthurian frame. In Champagne, the Arthurian prose cycle can function similarly to the French prose translations of ancient history commissioned in Flanders. These translations offered the Flemish what Gabrielle Spiegel, in *Romancing the Past*, calls a "historiography of resistance to royal centralization" (97, 317), a "site for a contest over the past that is the textual analogue of the political contest for power and authority in contemporary society" (225). Spiegel's conclusions echo Bloch's argument that the prose cycle expresses aristocratic trepidation about the extension of royal jurisdiction; Erich Köhler and Schmolke-Hasselmann posit that contemporary verse romances also express the fears and fantasies of aristocracies suffering crises of legitimacy.[17] Like the verse romances and the prose histories, the Arthurian cycle manifests ambivalence toward royal authority, imperial history, and genealogical legitimation. The cycle turns historical sites of resistance into fantasies of a world geography that transcends imperial domination through pious chivalry.

The prose cycle has numerous affinities with contemporary French prose historiography, including ancient histories and crusade chronicles. On a formal level, the narratives share similar sources, methods of reporting, and the prose medium; resemblances between the prose cycle and the narratives of Champenois crusaders are especially strong.[18] On a social level, all of these narratives engage problems of aristocratic status. And ideologically, the Arthurian prose cycle's redactors, like the Flemish translators, depart from imperial conventions: the *Estoire del saint graal* opens in Jerusalem (not Troy), and the *Mort* ends in an indeterminate place of prayer (not Rome). While the cycle's overall structure evades the ideological irony of claiming autonomy through shared relatives, individual episodes do incorporate ancient genealogies, most notably in the *Merlin*. These episodes establish the cycle's vital links to the topos of imperial *translatio*. The troubled dynamics of ancient family histories ultimately unsettle the Arthurian monarchy's authority in ways that appeal to aristocratic audiences under pressure to defend their own claims to autonomy.

Like conventional historiographical narratives, the Arthurian cycle patrols the boundaries of truth incessantly. In the late twelfth century, prose itself became increasingly associated with reliable discourse. Indeed, the prose form, more than shared sources or politics, sustains the Arthurian cycle's ideological conjunction with prose historiography. Prose, like the imperial histories it purveys, confronts limits and then passes over them.

A self-referential mode that encompasses irreconcilable differences, prose offers rich terrain for imaginative modes of possession. Expansionist ideologies are thus uniquely at home in prose. Indeed, Jeffrey Kittay and Wlad Godzich argue that prose took shape in direct opposition to consolidations of royal power at the turn of the thirteenth century (179). That is, they link the medium itself to the social goals Spiegel discerns in the earliest prose translations. Although Kittay and Godzich paint with some broad and even superficial strokes, their essay provocatively (if not definitively) suggests the possibility that *prosaics* can be theorized as legitimately as poetics. Prosaics, moreover, purvey border dynamics with special force.

The ability of prose to constitute a self-referential textual domain derives from two characteristic strategies: the decentering of narrative voice and the use of conjunctive syntax. For Kittay and Godzich, the absence of the jongleur's voice, which marks the site of oral performance, decenters prose narration (17–18); Michèle Perret explains prose narration in similar terms. In the absence of this stabilizing voice, reference remains enclosed within the narrative space rather than opening onto the exterior world of performance. In the prose cycle, narrative subjectivity is so dispersed that controversies endure over authorship (which was probably multiple to some degree); even the chronology of composition is still being revised.[19] The fact that these uncertainties have not hindered literary criticism attests to the powerful enclosure of narrative voice within the bounds of the narrative itself.

Conjunctions likewise shape the discursive terrain of prose narration. *Et, puis, apres,* and *tandis que* extend the narrative without imposing hierarchical epistemologies. Cultural differences break down as conjunctions forcefully reconcile conflicting histories in extended narrative.[20] Conjunctions thus replicate the order of border knowledge, facilitating contact and suggesting resemblances while impeding resolutions. Following an analysis of *tandis que*, Kittay and Godzich conclude, "Conjunction and disjunction work formally together: they are both seams" (124). The seam, which joins while separating, is a border structure that flows through the narrative like a boundary river. In the seam, or border, all references point to the narrative space itself, foreclosing external interventions. The prose cycle's dominant seam, "Se test ore atant li contes de...; Or dit li contes que..." (The *conte* now at this point stops talking about...; Now the *conte* says that...), encloses reference grammatically in the reflexive verb ("se test"), whose active subject is the narrative itself ("li contes"). In the seam, all time converges on the "here and now" ("ore atant") of narration.

Conjunctions and the destabilization of narrative subjectivity both contribute to a totalizing effect, that is, to the ways in which prose seems to possess time and space absolutely while occluding the autonomous existence of alternate narratives.[21] Prose thus furnishes the desirable landscape of expansionist imagination by remapping boundaries of identification within its own referential space: "the preexisting opposition between what is *our* territory (the inside, the true) and what is not (the foreign, the untrue) is remapped to allow what is ours to be either historical or fictional."[22] In the context of the analyses I have been pursuing, this is a properly colonial effect. Kittay and Godzich go so far as to cast prose as hegemonically borderless: "[Prose] can contain all margins and manipulate them but is itself untouched by them" (137); "[i]t works more by occupying the interstices between existing entities, which it then redefines and realigns within its own domain" (205). Prose can thus unmoor history from the political structures it sustains, opening up the spaces of imperial fantasy. Arthurian prose specifically remaps the boundaries of royal authority in relation to Christian dominion and aristocratic autonomy. The prose medium's totalizing effects enable aristocratic patrons and audiences to cast themselves within an ever expanding universe, at the very moment when their real territorial identities are shrinking.

Encounters with the totalizing border of prose demand a new kind of literacy. Prose's ability to cross cultural borders links the medium to expansionist ideologies, since each border crossing provides the reader with new territorial possessions: "With the emergence of prose, virgin territory becomes that which can be explored. The unseen can be seen if the reader is willing to venture onto uninhabited ground, ground that prose shows to be habitable but only by a reader."[23] Prose thus furnishes the desirable landscape of colonial settlement, a discursive space akin to the Insular *locus amoenus*. Kittay and Godzich describe the reader of this landscape in terms that resonate with the transience of border subjectivity: "the reader is to unmoor himself or herself from a single or singular perspectives and travel the road of positionality" (124). This road follows the seam of the border, where no "master subject" can impose permanent limits. To travel along the border road, readers must adopt a transient subjectivity, a "fragmentary discursive perspective both furnished and implied in the text" (130). In the prose cycle, the voices of loquacious damsels pave the way for this perspective: "The *demoiselle's* voice... provides a narrative locus where one can meander at length without being forced to choose between opposites."[24] The voice that traces the *conte's* path purveys border subjectivity, touching multiple sites without belonging to any. Strikingly, Kittay and Godzich refer to a reader "armed" with this kind of literacy (126), as if reading in the border aggressively defied hegemonic authorities. Following the damsel's path, the prose-literate reader forcefully occupies multiple disconnected positions, performing multiple partial identifications.

The potentially endless chain of substitutions afforded by prose literacy disrupts hegemonic discourse;[25] hence the medium's initial attractiveness as a mode of aristocratic resistance. Yet this same endless chain can also subsume resistance itself: no boundary is off limits. Indeed,

Kittay and Godzich conclude that the prose literacy that enjoins border subjectivity also serves the demands of centralized authority (202). The prose medium thus contributes to the ironies that Spiegel and Bloch both identify in prose patronage: aristocratic readers helped refine a form that served the ideological goals of the monarchy that ultimately disempowered them. The defense of chivalric ideals (such as individualism), for example, ultimately proved their impossibility; the monarchy itself eventually adopted prose for its own chronicles.[26] The verse prologue of a lost prose history of Philip II inflects royal appropriation directly: the author explains that he will not write in rhyme, "Por mielz dire la verité... Si com li livres Lancelot / Ou il n'a de rime un seul mot" (in order to better tell the truth, like the book of Lancelot, where there is not a single word of rhyme).[27] This historian apparently takes the *Lancelot* as an example of prose truth, in order to justify a royal genealogy in prose. The formal and narrative ironies are palpable; they derive from border paradoxes. Thus, like other tools of resistance, such as translation and swords, prose and prose literacy easily cross the boundary to domination. As a border medium, prose belongs to all sides of the struggle for authority and true history.

The Arthurian cycle abounds with emblems of prose borders and equivocal relations to domination. The Grail, for example, encompasses infinite limits without containing an edge. Yet this "unlimited source" of nourishment and knowledge also defines absolute limits between the chosen and the unchosen.[28] The Grail thus signifies paradox, performed by Galahad when he constructs a box to enclose the uncontainable container (*Queste* 277). The heterodox Grail becomes the quintessential boundary object and a synecdoche of border writing. Its quest represents not just a "quête du récit" (quest for narrative) or even a "quête du récit par lui-même" (quest for narrative by itself),[29] but a quest to write borders, the limit of limits. The Arthurian cycle's named swords also signify border struggles. As the cycle exalts the social and spiritual merits of the chivalric class against those of kings,[30] it encodes this social tension in the named swords, synecdoches of the chivalric function. The swords enforce absolute political and spiritual differences, while mobilizing troubling resemblances in their genealogies and etymologies. Escalibor (Caliburn) appears frequently, along with two other monumental blades: the Sword of the Extra-Ordinary Baldric ("Espee as estranges renges") and Marmiadoise. These three swords define the limits of service bonds, jurisdictions, and ancestral identities that reverberate through an intricate story line that spans millennia.

The cycle's fictional chronology structures a coherent and complex relationship between Escalibor and the Sword of the Extra-Ordinary Baldric. Both swords surface in the narrative with their literal functions impaired: the Sword of the Extra-Ordinary Baldric cannot be drawn from its sheath and Escalibor cannot be drawn from the stone. Once in action, each represents a political theory: the Sword of the Extra-Ordinary Baldric identifies Galahad's celestial chivalry while Escalibor signs Arthur's earthly chivalry. The swords' intertwined biographies trace the conflict between these theories through the narrative. Each sword's fate frames a judgment of its version of legitimacy: the Sword of the Extra-Ordinary Baldric moves from the *Estoire del saint graal* through the *Queste* until the Grail ascends to God; Escalibor travels from the *Merlin* to the *Mort*, where Arthur has it thrown in a lake. Within these frames, the *Lancelot* mediates between the forces of the two swords. The Sword of the Extra-Ordinary Baldric ultimately incarnates and subsumes history: it coincides with the cycle's longest continuous lineage while sharing in the Grail's transcendent theology. In the end, the Sword of the Extra-Ordinary Baldric remains at Sarras, Escalibor rests in the lake, and Marmiadoise presumably lies somewhere else in Britain, each a sign of a struggle lost by all sides.

In the broadest terms, the Arthurian cycle is informed by an ideology of preservation, mined by the paradox of its own impossibility. Continental families could not really hope to expand their territories in the thirteenth century, as the Welsh and Normans had in the eleventh and twelfth. They could only try to hold their own against royal expansion. By 1215, when Normandy and Flanders had both fallen to Philip through forceful conquest (and the Arthurian cycle was probably under way), Champagne was locked in an earnest struggle to preserve what autonomy remained, a struggle partly lost by 1230 (when the Arthurian cycle was mostly complete). Wherever the cycle originated, it developed as a historiography of resistance and in resistance to conventional historiography. The redactors' innovative approach to genealogical legitimation enables a critique of the foundations of royal power that does not undermine aristocratic authority. In Champagne, the struggle against royal dominion ended quietly in 1284 when the king of France married the Champenois heiress, assuming the countship in a bloodless conquest through genealogical assimilation. The cycle's ambivalence arises from the attractiveness this royal power obviously held for the dominated and from the fragility of genealogical differences.

Li nons de chelui qui cheste estoire met en escrit

The tenuousness of difference in general permeates the cycle through the *conte*'s meandering voice. Throughout, the dynamics of narration and authorship unsettle truth claims and keep the narrative on the edge of ambivalence. At different moments, the *conte* ascribes the text we read to three mortal authors: a hermit named Nascien, Robert de Boron, and Walter Map. Numerous other figures also intervene in the process. The *Estoire del saint graal* (hereafter *Estoire*) actually presents Christ as its ultimate author, while the *Merlin* substitutes Merlin and his stenographer Blaise. The *Lancelot* diffuses authorial identity further as knights become the narrators of their own stories; the *Mort* amplifies this effect almost exponentially with a cadre of anonymous court historians. The cycle thus constructs an elaborate image of authorship and translation that displays the bounds of truth while also ensuring that their limits can never be measured. Like Geoffrey's claim to translate a Briton source, the prose cycle's representations of translators enhance narrative authority and authenticates their inaccessible sources. Yet the circularity of the translation claims also deconstructs the possibility of authoritative narration.[31] Thus while the prose medium and its succession of authors guarantee the *conte*'s truth, the multiplicity of the guarantees keeps truth elusive.

The hermit who writes (at least) the *Estoire* opens the cycle under divine authorization: he writes the *estoire*'s nobility ("hauteche") and dominion ("signourie") on the Lord's orders ("par le commandement du grant Maistre") (1). This claim combines feudal discourse (evident in Wace's history) with the pious discourse of prayer (evident in Laȝamon's history). The combination identifies an audience of believers, capable of extending dominion throughout Christendom through attentive reading. Indeed, the narrator sends greetings and salvation ("mande...salus") to a Christian audience of men and women ("a tous cheus e a toutes cheles ki ont lor creanche en la sainte, glorieuse Trinité"). The gendering of the audience identifies its (at least) dual subjectivity, anticipating and enclosing divergent receptions (nonetheless unified under Christianity). The narrator's imagination of female readers is unique in the tradition: Wace does not foreclose the possibility when he addresses whoever wants to hear ("ki"), but neither does he directly address women; Geoffrey, Laȝamon, Robert, and the author of the *Gesta regum Britanniae* (see chapter 7) all address specifically male readers. From the first lines, then, the narrative mirrors the implications of prose by embracing differences within resemblances.

The narrator goes on to express the dangers of translation when he explains why the author's name is withheld: in addition to fearing the envious and incredulous, he wants to avoid blame if anything evil is introduced into the book "par effacement ou par le vice des escrivens qu apriés le translataissent d'un lieu en autre" (by erasure or by the vice o writers who translate it later from one place to another) (1). Christ contradicts this fear when he explains to the hermit in a vision: "nule oevre ne puet estre maufaite qui par moi soit commenchie" (no work can be done badly which is begun by me) (21). Later, the narrator again warns that lies should not enter the divinely inspired book:

> car chil seroit de trop foursené hardement plains qui oseroit ajouster mençoingne en si haute chose com est la sainte estoire que li vrais Cruchefis escrist de la soie propre main. (257)

[For he would be really far out of his mind who would dare add lies to such a noble thing as the holy *estoire* that the true Crucified wrote with his own hand.]

This legitimation itself is rather outrageous ("forsené"), since Christological writing has no orthodox basis.[32] To incorporate this heterodoxy within the bounds of truth, the narrator explains that Christ also wrote two other texts: the Pater Nostre and the judgment of a woman caught in adultery (258). The rarity of Christological writing, he reasons, enhances the *Estoire*'s value; anyone who claims that Christ wrote anything else has no divine authority and is a liar (258–59). These statements assert an absolute boundary between truth and lies, dismissing the contingencies of the hermit's own translation. Yet, as Rupert Pickens points out, the hermit identifies himself as a sinner with a limited understanding of divine communication (99–103). Through the hermit's own admissions, then, doubt shadows the transmission of Christ's truth from the beginning.

Later, it becomes clear that Christ's book has been translated into Latin, and then into French by Robert de Boron (391, 478) (who actually was responsible for grail romances in the early thirteenth century). As the hermit's own writing fades into oblivion, the narrator (who seems to be neither the hermit nor Robert) lends Robert credibility by saying that he translated on orders from the Church (478). The narrator goes on to note agreements between Robert's French translation and his own source (of what origin?). The most important corroboration arises from the lineage of King Loth and his ancestor Perron: the narrator reports that Robert also tells the true story of Perron's Christian conversion, but that the "Estoire del Brut" says nothing of him (546). Supposing that this is because the "Estoire del Brut"'s translator did not know the "Estoire del Seint Graal," the narrator concludes that the translator acquitted himself by either lying or equivocating with the phrase "Einsint le dient alcunes genz" (so say some people) (546). The narrator seems to refer here to a version of the *Roman de Brut*, by Wace or someone else, while clearly positing the *Estoire*'s superior historicity. Elsewhere, the narrator declares his "Estoire des estoires" completely free of mere hearsay (unlike the *contes* of lesser narrators) (249). These kinds of cross-references control against translators' "vices" and assert the reliability of the narrator's historical knowledge.

In the *Merlin*, the narrator names the hermit *Nascien*, identifying him as an Arthurian knight who later became a priest and received divine vision (222). Nascien became a saintly hermit indeed, living from the *Merlin*'s events in the fifth century until receiving his vision in the eighth (as reported in the *Estoire*). The faithfulness of Nascien's transmission becomes immediately suspect, as both chronologically improb-

able and tainted by Arthurian interests. Tellingly, the narrator identifie
Nascien as the *Estoire*'s hermit just as he loses his horse to Rion; h
only survives the battle through Merlin's enchantments (223). Autobiog
raphy—nearly cut short—quite literally threatens historiography, bot
of which are rescued by the equivocal value of Merlin's magic.

Nascien and Robert de Boron both lend doubtful authority to the *Es
toire* and the *Merlin*. Similarly, in the *Queste* and the *Mort* the name o
Walter Map patrols the shifting borders of dubious truth. At the end o
the *Queste*, Walter appears (like Robert) as the translator of a Latin sourc
(280). By the beginning of the *Mort*, Walter has put the "Aventures de
Seint Graal" in writing "assez soufisanment si com li sembloit" (fairl
sufficiently as it seemed to him) (1). King Henry, however, disagrees an
asks for the story of the death of the knights already mentioned. Havin
narrated those events to their conclusion, the narrator defines the fina
limit of truth and narration:

> Si se test ore atant mestre Gautiers Map de l'*Estoire de Lancelot*,
> car bien a tout mené a fin selonc les choses qui en avindrent, et
> fenist ci son livre si outreement que aprés ce n'en porroit nus riens
> conter qui n'en mentist de toutes choses. (263)

> [Now here Master Walter Map stops talking about the *Estoire de
> Lancelot*, for he has surely brought everything to the end according
> to the things that happened there, and he finishes here his book
> categorically, so that after this no one could recount anything about
> it who didn't lie about every bit of it.]

Like the hermit who withholds his name to preserve his reputation from
lying translators, this narrator secures a similar immunity by defining
continuation as a lie: the narrative presents itself as immutably bounded
Map's discourse in the *Mort* thus establishes the limits of narrative as
coextensive with the truth of the events.[33] As a boundary mechanism,
the assertion of terminal authorship puts the narrator "out of bounds,"
in the mobile subjectivity of the syntactic seam ("si se test ore atant").

The use of Map as a figure for immutable truth, however, ensures instability. The attribution itself must be spurious because Map and Henry
II both died well before the cycle's composition. Map, moreover, earned
a reputation as an expert liar, according to Hue de Rotelande (380). The
Mort thus appeals ironically to a notorious liar as guarantor of narrative
truth.[34] The attribution of the apparently pro-Cistercian *Queste* to Map
is especially ironic, since Map inveighed against both the Cistercians
and the Templars in his *De nugis curialium*.[35] In a final irony, the text
whose continuation Map's narrative voice forecloses extends a story that
had already been told sufficiently ("soufisanment") in Map's own judgment. Subsequent redactors manipulate the fiction further by recasting

ap as one of Arthur's court historiographers.[36] The vision of Map as a
urt stenographer also lends itself to ironic play, since he is most fa-
ous for comparing courtly life to Hell itself. Finally, Map's name casts
e pall of Anglo-Welsh ambivalence across the French cycle, for he iden-
ies himself as a son of the Welsh March, and he enjoyed a prebend on
e Severn.[37]

While the use of Map's name and reputation may be properly facetious
cetus), as he himself may have appreciated, it is not entirely gratu-
us. Map's reputation was probably well known in Champagne, where
had visited the comital court in the late twelfth century.[38] Moreover,
was also known for progressive views of vernacular writing: Gerald
Wales cites a letter from the eloquent Map ("eloquio clarus") as he
presses the hope that someone will translate his *Expugnatio Hiber-
ca* into French, noting that Walter is more widely known than Gerald
cause he has spoken in the common language ("communi idiomate")
410–11). As his translator, Map would bring Gerald a deservedly broader
putation. Gerald seeks, in other words, someone to enact precisely the
le attributed to Map in the prose cycle. Gerald and Map, like Geoffrey
Monmouth, are sons of border culture, practiced in the various arts of
anslation and bound to transient subjectivities. Their itineraries mir-
r in some ways the social dilemma of a French aristocracy caught be-
veen the prestige of the royal court and submission to it. Map's author-
ip thus casts the cycle into a familiar indeterminacy, identifying it as
e textual product of ambivalent desires.

De la terre de Babiloine en la terre d'Escoche

he mobility and multiplicity of authority in the prose cycle sustains
e vast geographical itineraries of its characters. The overall conception
space in the cycle foregrounds border concepts, from the frequency of
e verb *marchir* to the many realms that are in fact *marches* to the
ver Marcoise.[39] Even the Trinity is presented as a boundary mystery.[40]
n omnipresent limitation and invitation, the border orders morality as
ell as topography, as supernatural islands and wild forests provide the
oving grounds of spiritual faith.[41] The *Estoire* itself begins in one of
e most barren ("sauvage") places in Britain (2). Throughout the cycle,
nchanted architectural spaces (like ships and castles) replicate the mor-
lized topography of barren islands, endless seas, and deserted forests.
Vhile the cycle amplifies the *Historia*'s boundary dynamics, it departs
gnificantly from its geographical itineraries. In place of the Trojans'
oyage from Greece to Britain to exile in Wales and Brittany, the prose
ycle follows the Hebrews from Jerusalem to Camelot and east again to
arras. Across continents and millennia, then, the cycle superimposes
e absolute value of spiritual space over the equivocal value of coloniz-
g settlement.

The episodes prior to Britain's settlement, like those in the *Histori* establish the relationships that govern the future of history. This pr Insular landscape represents an urban, eastern geography as Joseph fo lows the course of the Euphrates from Arimathea to Jerusalem and the Sarras.[42] In the thirteenth century, Jerusalem harbored not only sacre religious origins but also Champenois royalty: Henry of Champagne o cupied Jerusalem's throne from 1192 to 1197, and his daughters posed rival claim to the county (forcefully prosecuted after 1213 by Erard c Brienne).[43] The redactors double this contentious site with one remove from the literal map (like Troy): Sarras. With the *Estoire*, Sarras is als under Champenois authority: the city's lord Evelach learns that he wa born in Meaux (where Arthur fights his last battle, "entre Champaigr et Borgoigne").[44] The Euphrates, navigable path from Jerusalem to Sarra thus provides an aquatic conduit from Hebrew origins to the Arthuria future. The fulfillment of this journey resides symbolically in the Swor of the Extra-Ordinary Baldric: half of the handle is made from the bon of a "cortenaus," a fish found only in the Euphrates (*Queste* 202–3). Whe Galahad journeys to Sarras, "cortenaus" at his side, he returns the na rative to its sacred origins. From the shadows of both Jerusalem and Sa ras, then, the redactors dismiss Troy for a sacralized version of expar sionist settlement that never in fact leaves home.

Joseph, like Brutus, leaves his native city and receives propheti promises about a future insular dominion, "la terre qui pramise est a lc oirs" (the land that is promised to [his] heirs) (*Estoire* 402). The miracu lous navigation of Joseph's followers across the Channel judges thei moral standing as heirs: the chaste (that is, those who have suspende genealogical continuity for God) transcend the natural laws of aquati boundaries (416–17):

> Josephés passa le lignaige Joseph, son pere, outre mer jusqu'en la Bloie Bretaigne, qui ore a a non Engletere, et si les passa sans aviron et sans gouvernal, et onques n'i ot voile ke le geron de sa chemise sans plus. (23)

> [Josephé went with the lineage of Joseph, his father, across the sea to Blue Britain, which now has the name England, and they crossed without oar and without rudder and there was never any sail except the flap of his shirt, nothing more.]

In accordance with this moralized navigation, the Insular *descriptio* tha greets them at the shore allegorizes the landscape:

> [T]ot autresi come mescreance et malvese loi i est fermement tenue, autresi covient il qe la lois Jesucrist, qui est buene et droite et seinte a la vie perdurable, i soit plantee et enracinee et cele autre loi de sertee et ostee qui ore i est coutivee et tenue. (418–19)

[Just as disbelief and bad law are firmly held there, so it is appropriate that the law of Jesus Christ, which is good and right and holy to eternal life, be planted there and rooted and that other law deserted and removed which is now cultivated and held.]

his myth of Insular conversion describes the passage of religious dominion in agricultural terms. The land is not empty (of people, crops, or religion), but badly cultivated; with proper care, its sterile crops can be uprooted in favor of spiritual fruits. Joseph, first guardian of the Grail, thus takes Brutus's place as the founder of Britain's civilization.[45] The land's conversion, however, is no less a colonization than Brutus's. The conquering vocabulary that describes Sarras's earlier conversion, for example, could have been lifted from Wace: "En tel maniere com vous avés i fu li regnes de Sarras conquis et gaaigniés au serviche del glorieus non lesucrist" [In such a way as you have heard was the realm of Sarras conquered and gained to the service of the glorious name of Jesus Christ] (63). In Britain, Joseph and his clan occupy all of the island's regions through systematic conversion: North Wales, Wales, Land of the Giants, Scotland, Orcanie, and Ireland; these events penetrate the *Lancelot*, anchoring all origins to Insular conversion.[46] Colonizing settlement thus proceeds morally, claiming Insular soil for Christian dominion.

Like the major regions, the island's cities convert to the Christian empire. Camelot noticeably displaces London (perceptively described in the "short" *Lancelot* as "en la marche de toutes les terres" [in the border of all lands] [3:114]). Originally a center of Sarrasin strength (*Estoire* 479), Camelot becomes the symbolic and political center of a Christianized Logria. Once converted, knights continuously arrive and depart from Camelot's court, and Josephé builds Saint Stephen's church there (484). And when Lancelot goes into exile, he sends his shield there (*Mort* 162): the local people treat it like a relic; it contains the last vestiges of the sacred Hebraic lineage at the center of the realm. Moreover, although Galahad completes the Grail quest in Sarras, Bohort returns to Camelot (*Mort* 1), the East's Arthurian double. Both cities in fact begin as powerful Sarrasin capitals, later claimed by forceful Christian expansionism.

The converted cities and regions map a spiritual hierarchy that endures until Arthur. Every region is ruled by descendants of Joseph's original Hebraic clan, and the narrative frequently traces their dominion to the Arthurian era. Scotland and Land Out of Bounds ("Terre Forraine") occupy the top of the spiritual order. Both Joseph and Josephé are buried in Scotland; God honors Josephé's corpse by ending a famine, "et fu veritez provee et les estoires meesmes d'Escoce le tesmoignent" [and it was a proven truth and the *estoires* of Scotland themselves witness it] (555–57). Land Out of Bounds joins the spiritual order when Alain (Helein), keeper of the Grail, leaves Galefort to settle some "terre gaste" with his "lingnage" (558). When they arrive in Land Out of Bounds, they find it

well populated: "il avoit plenté de nice gent qui pou savoient, fors seul
ment de terres coutiver" (there were plenty of ignorant people who kne
little, except only the cultivation of land) (559). Given this agricultur
knowledge, "gaste" clearly refers to the unconverted rather than to th
agriculturally barren. Here, Alain builds the castle of Corbenic and esta
lishes the Grail's domain and honor ("anor") as territory Out of Bound
The redactors strategically sanctify feudal vocabulary here, turning col
nial settlement into a divine adventure (later, Arthur dreams of pio
souls who have "conquestee" the house of God [*Mort* 225]). When Varl
subsequently strikes Lambor with Sword of the Extra-Ordinary Baldr
Land Out of Bounds becomes "gaste" in both the spiritual and agricu
tural senses: God turns it and Wales into Wasted Land ("Terre Gaste
where nothing is gained ("gaaigniees"):

> qe de grant tens les terres as laboreors ne furent gaaigniees, ne n'i
> croissoit ne blé ne autre chose, ne li arbre n'i portoient fruit, ne es
> eves ne troivoit l'en poison se molt petit non. (566)

> [so that for a long time the lands were not cultivated [*gaaigniees*]
> by laborers: neither wheat nor any other thing grew, nor did the trees
> bear fruit, nor did one find fish in the waters, except very small
> ones.]

Lancelot links this desolate Land Out of Bounds with Galehot's Sorelo
in Arthurian opposition when he calls upon both for help against Arthu
knights of Wasted Land and Sorelois also fight on the same side of a tou
nament (*Mort* 111, 137). Direct challenges to Arthur's authority thus ori
inate repeatedly from the most sacred sites of original settlement, Sco
land and Wasted Land.

Sorelois harbors resistance to the Arthurian order not only throug
its association with Land Out of Bounds, but through its rival imperi
ambitions. Not far from Arthur's land—between Wales and the Foreig
Islands, along the borders of a French realm and the Humber, closed o
by the impassable Assurne River[47]—Sorelois comprises a colonial *locu
amoenus*:

> la plus delitable terre qui fust sor les illes de mer de Bertaigne et la
> plus aaisie de boines rivieres et de boines forés et de plentiveuses
> terres. (*Lancelot* 8:128)

> [the most delightful land that was on the sea-islands of Britain, and
> the most replete with good rivers and good forests and plentiful
> lands.]

Just as Sorelois fulfills the role of desirable ("delitable") land, Galeho
echoes Brutus in that he does not receive it in inheritance but gains i
("gaaignie") by force (8:128). Although no indigenous peoples disrupt hi

confident settlement, Galehot comes to exemplify colonial ambivalence. Not only does he give up his conquered territory for love of Lancelot (submitting to Arthur even though he has the force to conquer him), he is a giant and is vividly remembered as "Son of the Giantess" on his tombstone (8:1, 2:212). As a giant possessed by extreme homosocial desire, Galehot embodies the force of ambivalence generated by colonial ambition. In one sense, he represents the native's seductive return to the scene of colonization. His territorial losses and death presage the consequences of even the most insulated conquests — and the fate of Arthurians who fail to inhabit the spiritual landscape.

As Sorelois's Assurne suggests, Britain's rivers reinforce the regional divisions of Insular order. The Severn traces the limit of the Saxons during Arthur's early wars, and he fights Rion along the Thames.[48] More dramatically, the regions north of the Humber all challenge both Christian and Arthurian authority. Like Hamo in the *Historia,* a group of drowning Heathens first put the northern river on the map (*Estoire* 443). The aquatic border thus again contains resistance, marking a place of coercive contact. Later, the river traces a new line of resistance when Lancelot takes control of Dolorous Guard (renamed Joyous Guard) on the Humber's banks (*Lancelot* 7:312–419); he later takes Guenivere there after rescuing her from the stake (*Mort* 126).[49] Since Lancelot holds this land from no one,[50] it occupies an autonomous base of counterhegemony like Sorelois. Lancelot himself mirrors Galehot's ambivalence, in his love of Guenivere and Galehot as well as in his refusal to assume any kingship (most pointedly when he casts off the crown that appears on his head during the enchanted dance and leaps out of the chair "por ce que signe de roi senefioit" [because it signified the sign of a king] [*Lancelot* 4:287]). The conflicts engendered by Lancelot's equivocations ultimately lead to his exile from Loegria (in terms that recall Cadwallader in the *Historia*) (*Mort* 163–64). The navigable Channel, which begins as a moral boundary (dividing the chaste from the sinful), ends here as an ethical one (dividing the loyal from the traitorous).

Architectural monuments often replicate these equivocal topographical relationships. The Tower of Marvels, for example, also commemorates the death of the Heathens who drown in the Humber. Simultaneously, the tower stands for the marvels to come in Arthur's time (initiated by the stroke of the Sword of the Extra-Ordinary Baldric) (*Estoire* 444). Moreover, the narrator prophesies that Lancelot will destroy the tower in his pursuit of Mordred's sons after Arthur's death (445). The tower thus immures a complete history of border events, directly bound to Christian and Arthurian coercion. And as in the *Historia,* the ashes of Vortigern's tower signify the frailty of dominion (*Merlin* 23–36); the narrator in fact excises Hengist's castle, the one monument of durable dominion ("ie ne vous doi mie retraire daugis ne de ses afaires" [I need not tell you anything about Hengist or his affairs]) (*Merlin* 22–23). In the *Lancelot,*

Galehot's castle performs a full cycle of failed dominion: designed for his imperial coronation (1:9), it represents the architecture of domination; when it crumbles in his dreams (1:11), colonial desire tumbles to a fragmented death. The tower and the castle thus both progress toward postcolonial rubble. For aristocratic castle builders, their demise depicts the desirable fall of royal dominion, along with the frightening failure of dominion per se: the prose cycle provides no assurances that do not undo themselves.

Against these fragile structures stand the great stones of Ireland. The *Merlin* narrator extracts them from history by never naming them, never mentioning giants or their history, and forgetting the Irish entirely. Instead, the stones sign the completion of Merlin's dominion over Uther, just before he explains his absolute mastery of historical knowledge (derived from the Devil) and future prophecy (derived from God). In fact, bringing the stones to Britain is entirely Merlin's idea, and he moves them without help from anyone; no one even sees them arrive (52–53). Once in Salisbury, Merlin suggests raising the stones because "eles seroient plus beles droites que gisans" (they would be prettier upright than lying down) (53). The aesthetics of romance judgment thus evacuate history from the monument. The narrator mentions twice that the stones still stand at Salisbury, suggesting Merlin's enduring dominion. Indeed, at Salisbury, the site of Arthur's battle with Mordred, Merlin has also left stone inscriptions that proscribe the imperial disaster long before its inception (*Mort* 228–29). All of Salisbury's stones thus purvey Merlin's divine and diabolical dominion over Insular knowledge.

Immediately after setting up the stones, Merlin once again performs his mastery of both Uther and Britain with the project of the Round Table. Unlike Wace's and Laʒamon's tables, this architectural innovation encompasses an overtly spiritual authority. Merlin alone conceives the idea of the table, its exegesis, its construction, and the election of its fifty knights (*Merlin* 53–55). According to him, it completes a trinity that includes the Table of the Last Supper and Joseph's Grail Table. It thus occupies a spiritual order that coincides with political dominion. The object itself is never described: "merlins sen ala & fist faire la table & ce quil sot quil y couenoit" (Merlin left and had the table made and what he knew was appropriate for it) (55). Thus, just as the stones arrive unseen, the table takes shape without witnesses. Merlin concludes the episode by instructing Uther to hold feasts three times per year (56) and to keep them as honorably as he can "por lonor de ceste table" (for the honor of this table) (58). The table, then, constitutes a whole realm of signification, the seated knights merely decorative place holders who make visible its one empty seat. Indeed, throughout the cycle, narrators and characters repeatedly describe the Round Table as owning knights, suffering losses when they die, and increasing its prestige when they triumph. During the final battle between Arthur and Mordred, for example, Yvain exclaims: "Ha! Table Reonde, tant abessera hui vostre hautesce!" (Ha! Round Table, so far will your nobility fall today) (*Mort* 235).

The Round Table's principal design feature is not physical but emotional: Merlin promises that once the knights are seated they will never wish to return to their own lands (*Merlin* 55). Indeed, at the end of eight days, they declare that they have no wish to leave, and instead will have their wives and children brought to the court (55). They explain further that they feel too close to each other to be separated: "nous entramons tant ou plus comme fiex doit amer son pere" (we love each other as much as or more than a son must love his father) (55). The Round Table thus substitutes filial love for ethnic and regional attachments, all for the greater glory of the king and God. In this sense, the table exerts a centripetal force, reversing what Bloch has called the "geographic dispersion characteristic of the Wasteland."[51] This reversal is, of course, ideologically advantageous only from the perspective of the imperial center. From any other perspective, the Round Table usurps local authority. Thus, while it stabilizes the Arthurian community by purging violent tendencies and weakening both lineage and vassalage,[52] it threatens the stability of all other communities. It serves imperial interests by effacing ethnic, genealogical, and geographic differences.

When a recluse explains the Round Table's origins to Perceval in the *Queste,* she conjoins its spiritual and imperialist dimensions even more overtly than Merlin:

Car en ce qu'ele est apelee Table Reonde est entendue la reondece del monde et la circonstance des planetes et des elemenz el firmament; et es circonstances dou firmament voit len les estoiles et mainte autre chose; dont len puet dire que en la Table Reonde est li mondes senefiez a droit. Car vos poez veoir que de toutes terres ou chevalerie repere, soit de crestienté ou de paiennie, viennent a la Table Reonde li chevalier. (76)

[For in that it is called *Round Table* is understood the roundness of the world and the circumference of the planets and the elements of the firmament, and in the circumference of the firmament one sees the stars and many other things, therefore one can rightfully say that in the Round Table is signified the world. For you can see that from all the lands where chivalry resides, either of Christendom or of Pagandom, the knights come to the Round Table.]

The recluse here casts the table as a symbol of the entire cosmos, capable of dismissing even the seemingly immutable difference between Christians and Pagans. Moreover, she goes on to equate membership at the Round Table with superlative territorial conquest:

[I]l s'en tienent a plus boneuré que s'il avoient tout le monde gaang-
nié, et bien voit len que il en lessent lor peres et lor meres et lor
fames et lor enfanz. (77)

[They [the knights] hold themselves more happy than if they had
gained the whole world, and one can well see that for it they leave
their fathers and their mothers and their wives and their children.]

Unlike the familial in-gathering described in the *Merlin*, in this more
aggressive vision the Round Table incarnates an antifamily policy (the
recluse goes on to criticize Perceval for abandoning his mother). Membership strengthens the Arthurian empire through an idealized chivalric fra-
ternity, but leaves all other lines sterile. The Round Table, then, affirms
the success of a centripetal ideology that threatens aristocratic autonomy,
while the cycle as a whole (somewhat) reassuringly demonstrates its ultimate failure.

Secure dominion in the prose cycle is thus fundamentally spiritual:
Britain is settled by conversion, not giant wrestling. As in contemporary
Welsh and English histories, then, religious identity rather than political
dominion forms the most important geographical boundaries. Alongside
the hegemony of the island's original Christian settlement, the narrative cycle also maintains exemplary spaces of colonial counterhegemony
(like Sorelois and Joyous Guard). The heroes of this colonial landscape,
Galehot and Lancelot, challenge the Arthurian order—which also attracts
them. Meanwhile, the Arthurian realm itself, *Logres* (the only Insular
designation to appear consistently throughout all parts of the cycle) fuses
with its capital city, *Logres*, displacing the origins of both *Bretaigne* and
Engleterre. Aristocratic readers, then, encounter an Insular geography
fraught with paradox, providing no grounds for stable political dominion (royal or otherwise). This vision unsettles the idea of dominion per
se, sustaining aristocratic fantasies as well as nightmares. In a world
where the most durable monuments have no history, anything is possible.

Crestiens ebrieus

In turning from Troy to Jerusalem, the Arthurian cycle also turns from
Trojans to Hebrews. Indeed, the blood of Joseph's Hebraic clan flows in
the veins of every major hero except Arthur himself. This ambitious new
family tree overrides ethnic and regional origins as it fulfills desires for
transcendent genealogy. Simultaneously, the cycle exposes the weaknesses
of genealogical legitimation by portraying the many forces that threaten
filiation: incest, adultery, fratricide, infertility, chastity, castration, and
so on. These disruptions, which lurk around the *Historia*'s edges, become
here the very vehicles of history. In one way or another, each engages

the dynamics of resemblance and difference that structure border identity. By exposing these processes, the cycle deconstructs genealogical legitimation, once again obviating stable grounds of identification.

The *Estoire* establishes desires for absolute genealogical memory by coyly referring to, but not describing, the hermit-narrator's family history. When the hermit quotes the first line of the book he receives from God, "Chi est le commenchemens de ton lignaige" (Here is the beginning of your lineage) (6), we do not read over his shoulder as he learns his ancestors' exploits. When he then expresses his elation at this unexpected history, the one thing he most wanted to know (6), the narrative introduces a knowledge gap that exposes readers' desires to know. While the divine book fulfills the hermit's dream of absolute genealogical knowledge, the *Estoire* itself points out that most people lack this knowledge. Subsequently, however, the *Estoire* satisfies readers' frustrated genealogical desire by prophesying the future of the Hebrew lineage. After learning Evelach's family history along with him (98–100), readers discover the full Hebrew history (from the biblical David to the Arthurian Galahad) when Nascien receives a letter during a vision (402). Oriented toward the future, the "brief" fulfills the deepest genealogical desire (expressed by Solomon in the *Queste* when he wants to know the end of this same family line). Unlike the hermit, however, this Nascien quotes the "branche" in full; he then performs his own fertile relation to genealogy by holding the "brief" to his chest, like a mother with a child (403–4). Indeed, the *brief* itself never mentions the mothers: the genealogy proceeds through the same agnatic reasoning that structures Geoffrey's *Historia*. Yet Galahad must trace his link to David through his paternal grandmother Helen (just as Henry II must go through Maud to reach the English). The Hebrew line thus maintains its identity by overlooking gender differences to focus solely on the continuity of male resemblance.

The memory of these Hebrew origins also structures the *Lancelot* and the *Queste*, as Lancelot and Galahad are repeatedly related to David and allegories of the nine generations between Joseph and Galahad abound. The *Lancelot*, as Emmanuèle Baumgartner notes, establishes Lancelot's origin in Perceval's territory by pointing out that the first Galahad converted Wales.[53] The *Estoire* itself specifies some of the intervening marriages, so that Lancelot's heritage also includes Irish and Gaulish blood (572). The branches of Lancelot's lineage thus cover the island as well as the Continent (casting him further into the border). Lancelot's tenuous relation to Arthurian service intimates that the spreading limbs of Hebrew lineage harbor Arthurian animosity: he holds no lands from Arthur, he betrays the king with his love for Guenivere, and he outmaneuvers Arthur militarily.[54] Meanwhile, Galahad's very existence condemns the Arthurian court's spiritual poverty, and his success in the Grail quest occurs at the expense of the mass of Arthurian knights. The family tree that sprouts from the Hebrews thus nourishes everything that contributes to Arthur's destruction.

The lateral branches of the Hebrew tree also disrupt the security of Arthurian dominion by promulgating superlative chivalry. The powerful family of Orcanie, for example, descends from Galahad of the Faraway Islands ("Lointaignes Illes") (*Estoire* 412–13). Following the pattern set by Perron of Jerusalem, who converts Orcanie and marries the indigenous daughter (546), each successive son marries a woman from a different ethnic group. Gawain and his brothers thus have Hebrew, Irish, Saxon, Welsh, and Briton blood (547). The descendants of this exogamous strategy erase ethnic differences, while silently preserving the shadows of genealogical and religious contamination. The narrator reminds readers, however, that only the origin counts:

> Einsi poez veoir que par droite generacion oissi cil Gauveins, que l'en tint a si buen chevalier, del lingnage Joseph de Abarimacie; et si ne le cuidierent mie moutes genz. (548)

> [Thus you can see that by direct generation this Gawain, whom people held as such a good knight, issued from the lineage of Joseph of Arimathea—even if many people didn't believe it.]

By noting the incredible nature of this genealogical claim, the narrator exposes the labor of grafting all the greatest Arthurian knights onto the Hebrew family tree. Even the Welsh descend from Galahad, the first Christian king of Wales (*Lancelot* 2:33), whose marriage to the indigenous daughter eventually produces Yvain:

> celui meesmes Yvein qui puis fist mainte proece au tens lo roi Artur et fu compainz de la Table Reonde et morut es plaignes de Salesbieres, en la grant bataille qui fu entre Mordret et lo roi Artur, la ou Mordret fu ocis et li rois Artus navrez a mort. (*Estoire* 552)

> [this same Yvain who later did much prowess in the time of Arthur and was a companion of the Round Table and died at the plain of Salisbury in the great battle that was between Mordred and King Arthur, there where Mordred was killed and King Arthur wounded to death.]

By summarizing Arthur's ruin within Yvain's sacralized genealogy, the redactor underscores once again that all good chivalry returns to Joseph and to Jerusalem.

The Hebrew line thus combines superlative chivalry, exemplary Christianity, and divinely guarded ethnicity. This collocation ensures durable and sanctified genealogical memory, materialized in the Grail. Since the Grail-keepers cultivate chastity, the object itself conveys vital spiritual continuity. This continuity, paradoxically, depends on genealogical discontinuity: no biological relation legitimates the Grail's transmission from Josephé to Alain, since Josephé devotes himself to chastity (*Estoire* 559). Since spiritual perfection forecloses genealogical production, the products of spiritual insemination (*semence*) do not proceed linearly: they pose a basic challenge to genealogical time.[55] The knights who later seek the Grail must precisely evade a genealogical relation with time by refusing to engage the sexual drama of difference and near-resemblance.

Within the Grail line, castration also disrupts filiation. Several generations after Alain, Pellehan guards the Grail, "qui fu mehaigniez des dous cuisses en une bataille de Rome" (who was maimed in both thighs in a Roman battle) (*Estoire* 566). The description suggests that the Maimed King has lost his reproductive abilities while pursuing imperial ambitions. The *Queste* offers an alternate explanation of the Maimed King's wound, linking it to spiritual transgression: a lance strikes him between the thighs when he tries to draw the Sword of the Extra-Ordinary Baldric (209). The Sword of the Extra-Ordinary Baldric and the Grail both symbolize fertile transmission in the place of biological reproduction;[56] at the same time, both disrupt reproduction through castration and chastity. This paradox engenders ambivalence toward both spiritual and imperial dominion.

Where the Grail line maintains itself by refusing sexual encounters, the Arthurian line disintegrates through failed or illicit sexual reproduction—infertility, adultery, incest, and sodomy. Arthur himself is born in enchanted adultery, raised as an orphan (in a dramatic departure from the *Historia*, where questions of paternity never arise), fails to produce an heir with Guenivere, and generates Mordred incestuously with his sister. Arthur touches irregular intercourse again when he adopts the sword Marmiadoise, heir to a Greek history that includes Tydeus, a fratricide from Calidonia who befriends Oedipus's son and brother Etiocles (*Merlin* 230). The bone of the Calidonian serpent that forms half the hilt of the Sword of the Extra-Ordinary Baldric keeps this Greek history moving through the cycle and against Arthur. Incest also shadows the adulterous Lancelot, along with his Grail relatives.[57] Gender difference itself equivocates in Lancelot's feminization and the homosocial erotics of his relationship with Galehot; "de ceste chose ne covient pas tesmoing avoir" (of this thing, it is not fitting to have witness).[58] Arthur and Lancelot thus ominously perform genealogical anxiety: their every action subverts linear filiation.

Throughout the cycle, genealogy remains anxiously unstable, as "fictions of difference" displace scandalous semblances.[59] By mobilizing failed and tangled lineages in the midst of linear genealogical fantasies, the prose cycle occupies an edge of ambivalence. In the edge, the cycle draws ideological power from Christian Hebrews while undermining temporality. Specifically, in Champagne, where families did not generally develop genealogical histories, this "roman familial"[60] can be read as a vast meditation on the powers and dangers of genealogical legitimation because it offers a vision of authority that does not ultimately depend on filiation. In place of Wace's confident assertions of kinship and Welsh visions of inherent liberty, the prose cycle installs a transcendent moral lineage while exploring the violent consequences of everything that threatens ordinary filiation. Paul Rockwell argues in fact that the cycle's critique of semblance is inimical to the Plantagenet practice of genealogical legitimation, concluding that the ideological benefits accrue to the Capetian monarchy (182–84). Yet such a critique, like the ideology of individualism (another challenge to semblance) and the prose form, disrupts royal authority as easily as any other. Readers of all sorts thus find proof of the dangers of genealogical desire, alongside a moral lineage that bypasses imperial filiation. The combination can inspire admiration without inciting imitation; it withholds durable legitimacy from all earthly efforts.

Un non ebrieu

Like Hebrew genealogy, Hebrew etymology poses a complex challenge to authority. The cycle claims numerous Semitic etymologies, referring to both Hebrew and Chaldean. (Tellingly, the Insular landscape's traditional etymologies, *Britain* and *London*, are entirely absent, and *Logres* refers interchangeably to both.) The Semitic languages write sacred authority into Arthurian history and surface at moments of conversion or divine intervention: the angels at Josephé's consecration have white Hebrew letters on their foreheads, Evelach and Mordrain receive Chaldean baptismal names, God writes on Solomon's ship in Chaldean, and *Corbenic* is written in Chaldean letters; "en celui langage vaut autretant conme en françois 'liu a seintisme vessel'" (in that language it means the same in French as "place of the most holy vessel").[61] The status of Hebrew in the thirteenth century, however, undermines its transcendent authority for contemporary readers: Hebrew learning and the Jews themselves posed direct challenges to hegemony. In Champagne, where Rashi's rabbinical school had flourished in Troyes since the eleventh century and the count was deeply indebted to Jews "belonging" to the king, the challenges of Hebrew are particularly acute.

Problems of language and authority converge in Escalibor, which receives an extended Hebrew etymology as Arthur engages the Saxons in battle:

> & ce fu cele espee quil ot prinse el perron. Et les lettres qui estoient escrites en lespee disoient quele auoit non escalibor & cest .j. non ebrieu qui dist en franchois trenche fer & achier & fust si disent les lettres voir si comme vous orres el conte cha en arriere. (*Merlin* 94)

[And this was the sword that he had taken from the stone. And the letters that were written on the sword said that it had the name *Escalibor*. And this is a Hebrew name that means in French "cuts iron and steel and wood," and the letters tell the truth, as the *conte* will show you hereafter.]

Just like the *Estoire*'s Semitic references, Hebrew here signals divine intervention, for the sword appears in the stone as a sign of Christ's election of the rightful king (91–92). The entire narrative demonstrates the truth of this divine writing, like the text of a proven prophecy. Narrated in the pitch of battle, the Hebrew letters sanction Arthur's military success as a defense of sacred royal legitimacy. The etymology thus sheaths the sword between biblical history and the Arthurian future, thrusting the blade into the border between legitimacy and transgression. The strategy is probably deliberate, since the etymology has no known source and a Champenois redactor could have encountered suggestive words like *chereb* (Hebrew for *sword, dagger,* or *knife*) and *calibs* (Latin for *steel*) in local Hebrew texts with French glosses.[62] Curt Leviant has in fact suggested that the *Merlin* redactor had some knowledge of Hebrew because of the proximity of monastic libraries housing Hebrew texts (79). By overlooking the apparently obvious Latin roots of *calibs* (fully exploited by William of Malmesbury),[63] the redactor strategically deploys Arthur's sword as a sign of ambivalent authority.

In the thirteenth century, the "non ebrieu" places an instrument of culture disruption in the hands of the royal arbiter of culture. While Hebrew connotes divine presence in Christian culture,[64] Christians also associated Hebrew with evil. Many treated documents written with Hebrew characters with great suspicion, associating the mysterious forms with Jewish black magic and Satan.[65] Hebrew thus threatens malevolent attacks on the sacred. The sword in fact manifests this demonic potential soon after Arthur gives it to Gawain. With Escalibor in hand, Gawain slaughters his fellows on the steps of Saint Stephen's; eventually, the knights flee, crying out that a devil has been loosed from hell (*Merlin* 330). Contaminated by demons, Gawain not only destroys the foundation of social order by killing other Arthurian knights, he blasphemes by murdering them in front of the sacred portals of Camelot's first church, founded by Josephé himself (*Estoire* 484). Escalibor's Hebrew etymology thus demonizes the sword at the same time that it sanctifies it.

Practical knowledge of this powerful language also engenders ambivalence because it both disrupts and extends Christian dominion. Jerome's translation of the Bible from Hebrew to Latin brought Christian teachings to the Roman world. His Latin text was then taken as the immutable foundation of divine truth in the Western Church, so that later translators and philologists were considered heterodox. In the eleventh century, Gilbert Crispin registered the threat of Hebrew philology by representing a debate about the relative authority of the Hebrew and Latin Bibles (1026–28). Reacting against Christian Hebraists like Hugh of Saint Victor, Rufinus and other canonists later asserted that the Hebrew Bible was useless for understanding Scriptures.[66] Ecclesiastical decrees against Christian Hebraism in the late twelfth and early thirteenth centuries also register the disturbing potential of biblical correction.[67] Yet by the second quarter of the thirteenth century, the friars (especially the Dominicans) actively cultivated Hebrew language skills and debated Jewish exegesis in order to convert Jews and extend the Church's authority.[68] Since Escalibor's Hebrew etymology implies Christian Hebraism, it conjures these contradictory effects: Hebraism supported the extension of Christian hegemony at the same time that it dispersed central doctrinal authority. The etymology conjoins the sword to these broader movements, suggesting that it can also extend hegemony (by contributing to military victory) while destabilizing authority (by killing indiscriminately).

Like the Hebrew language, the Jewish people are cast into "existential ambivalence" by the Christian Church.[69] On the one hand, the medieval Church followed Augustine of Hippo in considering the Jews a protected social group because they had witnessed Christ.[70] At the same time, however, the Jews were considered dangerous outsiders, and their persecution increased after 1200. The Church sought greater social control with several decrees at the Fourth Lateran Council of 1215, including the requirement that Jews wear distinguishing clothing.[71] Theological ambivalence gave way to clear social displacement in the course of the thirteenth century, especially as expanding urbanism reduced or eliminated traditional Jewish economic roles.[72] Finally, Christian Hebraism exposed the gap between current Jewish practices and those described in the ancient sources,[73] thus depriving the Jews of their authenticity as historical witnesses to Christian truth. For all of these reasons, Augustinian tolerance gave way to persecution.

For a Champenois audience, the Jews' changing social and economic status directly engaged local relations with the monarchy. In the thirteenth century, Philip II, Louis VIII, and Louis IX consolidated their political authority in part by legislating Jewish activity.[74] Philip began his centralizing efforts early in his reign and expressed his control of the counties most directly and most bloodily against Champagne in the 1191 massacre of the Jews of Bray-sur-Seine. Nonetheless, Champenois rulers maintained their sovereignty with respect to the Jews well into the thirteenth century.[75] Indeed, the Jews are the subject of the royal decrees that grant the county the greatest autonomy.[76] When Philip sought stricter control over Jews in 1222, Thibaut IV rejected his policy and issued a decree allowing Champenois Jews to purchase their liberation.[77] In 1223, Thibaut again refused to sign onto royal Jewish policy.[78] The wealthy Jews of nearby Dampierre, where Louis VIII's *stabilimentum* was in effect, recognized the fiscal and social advantages of Thibaut's resistance and sought to relocate to Champagne.[79] Thibaut himself was deeply in debt to the king's Jews, and in 1224 Louis ordered him to pay under the terms of the *stabilimentum*.[80] Forced to accept the payment schedule, Thibaut lost a measure of his autonomy: in 1230 he joined all the other lords in signing Louis IX's general order concerning the Jews.[81]

The *Merlin* was written in the midst of these dramatic changes in royal authority, and its Hebrew Escalibor transfers their dynamics to Arthur. On the one hand, the Jews represent the successful preservation of aristocratic autonomy. On the other hand, they show the count indebted and subjugated to the king, his autonomy eroded much like that of the Jews themselves. In the *Merlin*, the Hebrew sword is placed in Arthur's hand just as he begins to consolidate his royal power: Escalibor can create that power (as the Jews did for Philip) or resist it (as the Jews did for the counts). Striking through this paradox, Escalibor works for and against Arthur's royal authority, conjuring linguistic, social, and political ambivalence. The "Judaized" Escalibor also engages the cycle's own ambivalent Hebrew history. The Hebrew etymology thus associates Escalibor with Old Testament error, exposed in the *Estoire* and *Queste*. Yet in these same narratives, Galahad redeems the Old Testament, in opposition to the Arthurian future: accomplishing the Grail quest with the Sword of the Extra-Ordinary Baldric at his side, Galahad establishes a celestial order in opposition to the earthly, Arthurian order. The Hebrew etymology draws Escalibor into this matrix of opposition to the Arthurian monarchy. "Judaized," Escalibor inaugurates a reign of ambivalence; it represents the fragility of the Arthurian order that it defends. The sword guarantees Arthur's rule while condemning him; it stands unreliably for both legitimacy and transgression, truth and error. These ambivalent equivocations take us straight back to Geoffrey of Monmouth, where the attraction to prestige is haunted by the fear of domination.

Tens des aventures

From within this border of domination, the prose cycle pursues two fantasies of liberation, both recognizably postcolonial. On the one hand, redactors construct a fiction of total memory that exceeds even Robert of Gloucester's wildest dreams. On the other, they undermine temporality per se. This paradox structures a historiography that surpasses history for eschatology and romance, yet always returns to historical limits. Time is always already a fixed place (*liu et tens*, place and time, as narrators say frequently), but on a map without borders.

The prose cycle mobilizes many of the same strategies as Geoffrey, Wace, and Robert to purvey the mastery of time, from annalistic dates to synchronisms. The narrative action itself spans all of human history, from Adam to Henry II (just like Aelred's Henrician genealogy). Throughout the cycle, numerous prospections and cross-references to emperors, eastern kings, and biblical characters bolster a totalizing historical memory.[82] The only annal given refers to Galahad's arrival at the Arthurian court 454 years after Christ's Passion (*Queste* 4), realistically within the traditional time of Arthur's reign, whose end Geoffrey dates as 542 A.D. Like Wace, the *Estoire*'s hermit dates his own writing—717 years after the Passion (2). In relation to the *Historia*'s chronology, the hermit lives about a generation after Cadwallader's exile and in the early years of Saxon dominion. On the other end of the scale, the translation of the *Queste* and *Mort* takes place in the twelfth century.[83] The writing of millennial history thus takes almost five centuries. It culminates in the present, when the island is "now" called *England* and its capital *London*.[84] This monumental temporal edifice covers all imaginable space, neatly captured in one narrator's comment that the Island of the Giant is five days long and two days wide ("qui duroit cinc jornees de lonc et dous de lé") (*Estoire* 364). This edifice is founded on Merlin's divinely diabolical genealogy, which grants him dominion of time per se through absolute knowledge of both past and future.[85]

This elaborate temporal structure masks, however, the dissolution of time. As in the *Historia*, the mingling of prospection and retrospection destabilizes the linear progress of memory. References to weekdays without years, such as the Monday on which the *Estoire*'s hermit begins translating (21) or the tenth day before May when Lancelot dies (*Mort* 261), further the temporal disruption by evoking recurring cycles independent of linear processes. The *conte*, moreover, is constantly propelled into the future by prophetic objects, inscriptions, and the bodies of the undead. Although it puts itself back on the "droite voie" (straight path), it frequently steps out of its own bounds. These detours into narrative borders contain both truthful explanations and hints of deception.[86] The *Lancelot*'s extensive system of *rappels* and *annonces*[87] mines the entire cycle with marginal spaces (islands of true doubt) outside the boundaries of the *conte*'s "voie." Likewise, the ubiquitous "or" (now) discontinues narrative lines rather than building linear progressions.[88] As the narrative contorts temporal difference, linear chronology dissolves.

Strategies like typology, analogy, and allegory also break down temporal differences. They propel the narrative to atemporality by obscuring or even effacing differences between characters, episodes, and historical periods. The cycle's three identifiable historical periods (biblical, Josephan, and Arthurian), for example, mirror each other analogically and so lose their temporal grounding.[89] And Galahad, figure of Christ, embodies ahistoricity as he abolishes customs, mends swords, and closes the gaps between the Arthurian and the biblical.[90] Allegory confounds temporal differences by traveling across the boundaries of discontinuous signifying fields. The substitution allegories that dominate the *Estoire* and the *Queste* erase temporal specificity by transmuting events to an anagogical level. Through *semblance*, the cycle eventually collapses differences

196

of all kinds, installing a "perpetual present" that simultaneously performs the past and future.[91] Burns likewise concludes: "One goal of these tales is to erase time so that the past can be made present, so that King Arthur can live on."[92] As in Geoffrey's *Historia*, then, the weakness of temporal boundaries casts the narrative into historical equivocation.

The Wheel of Fortune (introduced to Arthurian history by Wace) materializes all of the cycle's temporal gambits:[93] a literal circle, it can rotate forward and backward, move in a nonlinear line, and travel without moving forward. It spins history into timeless romance. Although the wheel can contain complete memory, its periodic repetition disconnects memory from history. The memory, moreover, directly envisions imperial possession in spatial and genealogical terms. When Arthur dreams himself atop Fortune's wheel, he sees the "circuitude" (circumference) of "tout le monde" (the whole world) (*Mort* 227). Once Mordred has gouged out these imperial eyes, Arthur recognizes Fortune herself as his mother: "Fortune qui m'a esté mere jusque ci . . . or m'est devenue marrastre" (Fortune who has been mother to me until this point now has become s-mothering) (247). *Marrastre* implies both a denatured, malevolent mother and a stepmother: in either case, Fortune turns infanticidal, disrupting the genealogical norms that sustain dynastic success. Through Fortune, then, the cycle's temporality surpasses the dominion of history, proffering a timeless yet twisted present to those suffering from losing battles with the future.

Je sui mervelle a veoir

Throughout the cycle, swords bear complex relations to time. They trace the bounds of history and historiography by identifying relationships among the hands that hold them. These relations directly engage the cycle's geographies, genealogies, and etymologies, rendering the swords fundamental actors in the cycle's historiographical vision. The *Estoire* begins by introducing many anonymous swords, as well as the blade that will become the Sword of the Extra-Ordinary Baldric. All of these blades patrol the borders of the divine as an absolute boundary of faith and truth; most of them travel through time and across great distances to reach Arthurian Britain. The most vital of these swords, originally wielded by King David, travels from the Old Testament to the Arthurian court as the sign of Galahad's Hebrew lineage and divine sanction. In the process, the Sword of the Extra-Ordinary Baldric performs a monumental lesson in historiography.

The links between Hebrew history and the Arthurian future are forged when Josephé is first consecrated bishop. As Christ anoints him with holy oil, the narrator explains that the same oil was used to anoint all the kings of Britain until Uther and promises that the *estoire* will tell how unction was lost at that time (*Estoire* 80). Uther thus breaks the sacral link to Josephé, the founding bishop-king; before Arthur is even born, the cycle excludes him from the continuous line of Insular Hebrew kings. From the beginning, then, the cycle refuses to sanction Arthur's role in salvation history—a judgment iterated by the Grail and the divinely inspired swords that defect from Loegria to Sarras with the three chosen knights.

Galahad makes the journey to Sarras carrying the Sword of the Extra-Ordinary Baldric. The sword (not yet named) arrives in the *Estoire* even before Josephé arrives in Britain. Nascien (Galahad's ancestor) meets the ship that carries the sword on his own circuitous journey to Britain. Exploring the mysterious vessel, Nascien discovers a sword bearing inscriptions on the hilt, blade, and scabbard that prophesy the sword's attachment to a unique future hero. The hilt and blade both declare their ability to discern the rightful hero from all other seekers:

> Je sui mervelle a veoir et graindre mervelle a counoistre, car on-ques nus ne me puet empoignier, tant eüst grande la main; ne ja nus ne m'enpoignera ke uns tous seus, et chil passera de son mestier tous chiaus qui devant lui aront esté et qui aprés lui venront. (263)

> [I am marvelous to see and more marvelous to know, for never can anyone handle me, no matter how large the hand. Never will anyone handle me except for one only, and he will surpass in his skill all those who will have been before him and who after him will come.]

The scabbard, after reiterating the intended knight's superiority, speaks of the woman who will replace the sword's ragged baldric:

> Et chele feme apielera cheste espee par son droit non et moi par le mien, ne ja devant dont ne sera qui par nos drois nons nous sache apieler. (265)

> [And this woman will call this sword by its rightful name and me by mine; never before will there be anyone who by our rightful name knows how to call us.]

The events between here and the *Queste*, when this naming takes place, are cast as a quest for the identities of the knight, the scabbard, and the sword. For the time being, however, readers can only marvel along with Nascien at the objects' loquacity.

Nascien continues his explorations, and learns from the other side of the blade that the sword will betray the one who praises it most (265). The *conte* interrupts his exploration to warn readers that this is neither the place nor the time to divulge the histories of these objects (266), but the *conte* is soon forced to leave its "droite voie" in order to dispel all doubts about the colored spindles Nascien discovers (267). This history in the margins (on the edge) returns to the beginning of time with Adam and Eve (268–74) and Cain and Abel (274–77); it continues "d'oir en oir" (from heir to heir) until the Flood (277–80). Finally, the story arrives at the time of Solomon, son of David, who faces a historiographical predicament of monumental proportions: he discovers that both Christ and a knight surpassing all others will descend from his lineage, and he wishes to communicate his foreknowledge to the knight, who will not be born for over two thousand years (282–83). Solomon, for all of his "science," cannot find a solution to the temporal problem until he confides in his wife.

With her "grant engin" (intelligence, deception, and engineering skills), Solomon's wife guides the construction of the historiographical signs that will convey Solomon's foreknowledge into the future. First, she has Solomon construct a ship designed to withstand rot for four thousand years; then she recommends that he place his father David's sword in the ship, since it surpasses all other swords just as the knight will surpass all other knights (284). She does not merely offer the sword as an antique artifact, she directs Solomon to dismantle it: he must remove the pommel and the hilt, and leave the blade "tote nue tornee a une part" (all bare, returned to a solitary state) (285). By stripping the sword to its bare essence — the blade — Solomon removes the genealogical and ethnic signs of his Hebrew father. The blade "tornee a une part" becomes an empty signifier. In salvation terms, it returns to an original state prior to time; the refurbishment extracts it from the processes of history initiated by the Fall. The blade can now enter into a monumental relation with the redemptive future.

Solomon's wife gives detailed instructions on how to prepare the blade for this future:

[V]os, qui conoissiez la vertu des pierres et la force des herbes et la matire de totes les choses terrienes, faites un pont de pierres precieuses jointes soutilment si qu'il n'ait aprés vos regart terrien qui puisse deviser l'une pierre de l'autre, ainz cuit chascuns qui la verra que ce soit une meesmes pierre; aprés, si i faites une enheudeüre si merveilleuse que nule ne soit si vertuouse ne si riche; aprés i faites un foerre si merveilleus en son endroit come l'espee sera el suen. Et qant vos avroiz tot ce fait, g'i metrai les renges teles come il me plaira. (285)

[You, who know the strength of stones and the force of herbs and the matter of all things earthly, make a pommel of precious stones joined subtly so that after you there will be no earthly gaze that can distinguish one from the other, rather each person who will see

it will believe that it is one stone; then, make a hilt so marvelous
that there be none in the world so strong or so rich; then make a
scabbard just as marvelous in its own way as the sword is in its.
And when you have done this, I will put on a baldric such as will
please me.]

These instructions demonstrate the limits of Solomon's wife's access to
the truth, limits signified by the artifact they aim to create. First, her
knowledge (along with Solomon's) is grounded in the "terrien": within
these limits it is superlative, but it will never comprehend the "celestien." Second, her knowledge is restricted to the world of romance,
where the height of achievement is "merveilleus" rather than "spirituel." Finally, her assertion of individual will ("come il me plaira") presents the new baldric as a product of romance desire rather than of "de-
vocion" to a divine will. The reconstructed artifact materializes this gap
between the Old Testament world and Galahad's spiritual destiny, where
the *terrien,* the *merveilleus,* and the *moi* will all give way to the *spirituel.*
   Solomon accepts his wife's instructions, except where they require il-
lusion:

[S]i en fist tot ensi come ele li ot devisé, fors que del pont ou il n'ot
c'une seule pierre, mais cele estoit de totes les colors que l'en por-
roit trover ne deviser. (285)

[He did everything as she had described to him, except with the pommel where there was only a single stone, but it was of all the colors
that one could find or describe.]

Defying his wife for the first and only time, Solomon here refuses the
deception that she practices by "grant engin," thereby reclaiming a portion of his authority. Substituting the single stone for the fabricated
one, Solomon presents a pommel whose surface transparently reflects its
ontological reality. Solomon's refusal of craft, or *engineering,* rejects evil
and tacitly accepts divine authority: the "engineor," after all, practices
deceit as a devilish activity explicitly opposed to divine will.[94] The pommel must ultimately satisfy this "regart celestien." Its true wholeness
signifies Galahad's spiritual completion, as the narrator of the *Queste*
insinuates when he later says that each color has its own "vertu" (202).
Galahad's various qualities, like the stone's colors, form his singular devotion to God and are inseparable from each other. By contrast, Solomon's
wife's fabricated stone cobbles together un-Christian deception. Its fragmentary art represents fatal disbelief, tellingly realized in the Sarrasin
tomb that eventually covers Galehot and Lancelot (*Mort* 261–63) and
that is "[faite] de pieres precioses jointes si soltielment l'une a l'autre
qu'il ne sambloit pas que hom terriens peust avoir fete tel oevre" ([made]

of precious stones joined so subtly the one to the other that it didn't seem that an earthly man could have made such a work) (*Lancelot* 2:254). Dead or alive, Lancelot and Galehot lack Galahad's ontological integration: they are men of the border, men covered with seams.

To complete the sword, Solomon inscribes the blade with the prophecy promised by the divine voice: no one except the destined hero will draw the sword without repenting (285–86). The inscription textualizes the blade's latent historiographical function and limits its proper reception to one person. Finally, Solomon's wife brings a baldric "si laides et si povres come de chamvre et si foibles par semblant que eles ne peüssent mie l'espee sostenir" (so ugly and so poor like hemp and seemingly so weak that it couldn't possibly sustain the sword) (286). She explains to a surprised Solomon that a future damsel will replace what she has done wrong ("meffait"), just as the Virgin will redeem Eve (286). The historiographical sword thus remains *a faire*, its conclusion still unwritten. Solomon completes the preparations for this future by writing the history of these "faits" in a "brief" addressed directly to his heir, "chevaliers beneüreus qui sera fin de mon lingnage" (happy knight who will be the end of my lineage) (288). This "brief" and the ship's artifacts ferry a complete history into the future, encompassing Adam, Christ, David, and Galahad. The narrator immediately conjoins this history to the Arthurian future by reminding readers that this "happy knight" will end the Grail's adventures in Loegria (288).

As readers absorb this lengthy explanation, Nascien wonders whether these marvels contain any falsehood: his doubt provokes the ship to dump him unceremoniously in the water (291). The narrative thereby purports to prove its own truth. Nascien, however, needs more than an unexpected swim to engender his faith in divine will. When a giant later threatens him, he reaches for the forbidden sword, which promptly breaks (as promised) (333). He then prays to God for help, and finds a sword that had been left on the ground "par aventure" (by chance) (333). In his next moment of dire need, he repeats the same prayer—and his enemy immediately falls down dead (397). Nascien learns to trust solely in God, as does Lancelot when he tries to draw his sword against the lions who guard Corbenic (*Queste* 253–54). The cycle's historical pedagogy thus teaches that mortal combat must yield to immortal faith.

In the Sword of the Extra-Ordinary Baldric's final adventure in the *Estoire*, Lambor receives the Dolorous Stroke that pierces through time to Galahad. While Lambor rules Land Out of Bounds from Corbenic, his Sarrasin neighbor Varlan wounds him with the Sword of the Extra-Ordinary Baldric: to punish this mishandling, God creates the "terre gaste" (Wasted Land) and the adventures that only the Grail hero can end (566). The narrator reminds readers of this Dolorous Stroke when Galahad is conceived in the *Lancelot* (4:210), linking the reversal of *gaste* directly

201

to reproduction. Varlan's stroke, however, casts a shadow of doubt over divine agency: how can Varlan, an infidel, even enter the ship without being struck dead, let alone lift the sword that self-destructed immediately in Nascien's hand? If Varlan can handle the sword just like the chosen hero and holy oil can be inexplicably lost, the foundations of prophetic faith crack. Within these seams, absolute principles equivocate and differences turn to resemblance. At the *Estoire*'s end, the partially complete Sword of the Extra-Ordinary Baldric contains similar seams, which are the very principles of historiography.

L'espee qui estoit une des boines del monde

The Sword of the Extra-Ordinary Baldric expresses divine prophecy and, ultimately, spiritual perfection. The ambivalence signed by Varlan's hand on the sacred hilt, however, soon permeates Arthurian action. Not only does Escalibor purvey ambivalence through its Hebrew etymology, Arthur trades this sign of divine election for a foreign sword named Marmiadoise.[95] In these episodes, the *Merlin* redactors insinuate an anti-Arthurian and antiroyal perspective through ancient genealogies, imperial history, and gladial ceremony.

Escalibor begins, like the Sword of the Extra-Ordinary Baldric, with a unique and divinely ordained destiny. In answer to the barons' prayers for a king after Uther dies, a sword lodged in an anvil appears in a stone, inscribed with God's intention: "cil qui osteroit ceste espee seroit rois de la terre par lelection ihesu crist" (the one who would withdraw this sword would be king of the land by the election of Jesus Christ) (81). This divinely authorized sword guarantees the legitimacy of royal genealogy in the place of the absent paternal phallus. The bishop immediately expounds the doctrine of the Two Swords, identifying the sword in the anvil as a sign of earthly justice (82). This explanation subordinates the gladial sign to divine will, so that (according to the archbishop) the king wields justice on God's behalf and with the archbishop's approval. The archbishop clarifies this doctrine when he sends Arthur to draw the sword after his dubbing, and again when Arthur lays the sword on the altar during the coronation (88). Arthur thus occupies the throne under divine approbation, promising to obey God and the Church.

Episcopal control and divine sanction do not, however, protect Arthur from serious challenges to his authority. The barons delay his crowning three times before finally accepting the archbishop's interpretation of the sword. Immediately after the coronation, neighboring kings refuse to recognize Arthur's rule because they doubt his royal birth. Genealogical uncertainty plagues Arthur here in ways that never trouble the *Historia*. As Arthur fights the native rebels (not foreign Saxons, as in other histories), the narrator conjures Escalibor's Hebrew etymology, a further challenge to stable authority. Finally, pagan antiquity invades the *Merlin* as the battles drag on and Arthur confronts Rion: the narrator sketches a Greek genealogy for Rion and his sword Marmiadoise that confronts Arthur's own Trojan origins. Rion both attracts and repels Arthur, implying once again that the ghosts of subjugation frequently haunt fantasies of domination. Like Escalibor's Hebrew etymology, Marmiadoise's Greek genealogy challenges the authority of the Arthurian hand that grasps the hilt. The repercussions of this challenge extend to the legitimacy of genealogical authorizations of power in general.

Arthur has already won several battles with Escalibor when he meets Rion, the twenty-four-foot-tall king of Ireland. After an extended skirmish, Arthur pursues the wounded giant into the woods. As Rion reaches for his sword, the narrator interrupts the confrontation with the genealogy:

> Lors met main a lespee qui estoit vne des boines del monde. Car cestoit ce dist li contes des estoires lespee hercules qui mena iason en lile de colco par querre le toison qui estoit toute dor. & de cele espee ochist hercules maint iaiant en la terre ou iason amena medea qui tant lama. mais puis li fali il la ou hercules li aida par sa grant deboinairete car pitie len prinst. (230)

> [Then [Rion] put his hand on the sword, which was one of the best in the world. For it was, so says the *conte* of the *estoires,* the sword of Hercules who brought Jason to the island of Colcos in quest of the fleece that was all gold. And with this sword Hercules killed many giants in the land where Jason brought Medea, who loved him so much. But then he failed her, there where Hercules helped her in his great goodness because pity seized him.]

This summary of how Jason captured the Golden Fleece (with Medea's help) alludes to the beginning of Benoît de Sainte-Maure's *Roman de Troie* (although this "conte des estoires" says nothing about a Marmiadoise). The "land of giants" where Jason brought Medea also recalls the *Estoire*: Hippocrates visits Island of the Giant, so named for the world's largest giant, killed there by Hercules (364). If we imagine, then, that Hercules carried Marmiadoise throughout his career, Rion's sword commemorates a superlative Greek knighthood that threatens giants and Trojans and succors women. This Greek knighthood also overpowers royal authority. Before Jason and Hercules arrive at Colcos in the *Roman de Troie,* they land at the port of Troy and pillage the surrounding countryside.[96] When King Laomedon accuses them of occupying the land without permission, Jason partly apologizes but Hercules promises to avenge the dishonor of their expulsion (ll. 1074–1106). Like Rion and the *Merlin*'s other rebel kings, Hercules refuses to recognize the legitimacy of royal jurisdiction. Unlike the rebellious kings, however, Hercules successfully enforces his autonomy when he later destroys Troy (ll. 2079–756). Hercules's sword thus illustrates the relativity of legal legitimacy by forcefully denying a claim of royal jurisdiction. This relativity troubles Rion's own relation to his Herculean ancestry because he—a giant—carries the sword of a renowned giant-killer.

The *Merlin*'s allusion to events from the beginning of the *Roman de Troie* conjure the rest of the story as well—the second siege of Troy and the Trojans' flight. The confrontation between Rion and Arthur reproduces this historical rivalry, so that Rion attacks Arthur with a sword whose history has already defeated Arthur's. Several *Merlin* manuscripts in fact remind readers pointedly of Arthur's Trojan ancestry amid his struggles with the rebels. Two redactors insert a brief explanation of Britain's origins as Merlin sails to Brittany to gather more knights:

> Il est uoirs que apres la destrusion de troies. auint que doi baron sen partirent et fuirent hors dou pays et de la terre pour la doutacee des greigois que il ne les occeissent. Li vns des .ij. barons qui sen afui a tout grant partie de sa gent si ot non brutus. . . . li autres princes qui de troies issi si ot non cormeus. (*Merlin* 110 n. 3)

> [It is true that after the destruction of Troy it happened that two barons left there and fled out of the country and out of the land for fear that the Greeks would kill them. One of the two barons who fled with a great part of his people had the name Brutus. . . . the other prince who issued from Troy had the name Corineus.]

This summary of the beginning of the *Roman de Brut* hints at Trojan cowardice while reminding audiences of the historical foundations of Arthur's rule. A third redactor interpolates a complete prose adaptation of the *Roman de Troie* between Arthur's coronation and the beginning of the rebellion.[97] Merlin narrates this Trojan plot to Blaise as a continuation of the coronation; Blaise willingly transcribes it "car aussi avoie ge grant desirrier de savoir en la verité" (because I also had great desire to know the truth about it).[98] The truth, however, exposes Arthur's defeated history at the very moment when defiant kings challenge his inheritance. Both of these interpolations thus expand the Trojans' narrative presence in ways that weaken rather than strengthen the efficacy of genealogical legitimation.

Having raised the ghosts of Trojan defeat, the *Merlin* follows the genealogy of Rion's sword back in time to the siege of Thebes:

> & li contes dist que vulcans forga lespee qui regna au tans adrastus qui fu rois de grece qui maint ior lot en son tresor. cele espee ot tideus li fiex le roy de calcidoine le iour quil fist le message al roy

ethiocles de tebes. qui por pollicenes son serorge ot puis mainte paine. (230)

[And the *conte* says that Vulcan forged the sword, who reigned at the time of Adrastus who was king of Greece, who for many days had it in his treasure. Tydeus the son of the king of Calidonia had this sword the day that he brought the message to King Etiocles of Thebes, [Tydeus] who for Polynikes his brother-in-law had great pain.]

This passage refers to the early events of the *Roman de Thèbes* (another *conte* that does not mention a Marmiadoise). When Polynikes and Etiocles inherit Thebes from their father and brother Oedipus, they agree to each rule the city in alternating years. While waiting for his turn, Polynikes meets Tydeus on a rainy evening in Argos. They fight almost to the death over Adrastus's dry porch; having thus proved their worth, they marry his daughters (ll. 944–1205). Etiocles soon refuses to give up Thebes, and Tydeus travels there to inform him that Polynikes intends to claim his rightful inheritance (ll. 1288–463). As Tydeus returns to Argos, fifty of Etiocles's barons attack him (ll. 1558–671). Through Tydeus, then, Polynikes challenges royal authority, just like Hercules and Rion. Unlike Hercules, however, Polynikes fails to enforce his interpretation of legitimate law. Etiocles also fails to maintain his authority, and is killed during the siege. The fratricidal conflicts that permeate the *Roman de Thèbes* expose once again the relative dangers of Greek history. Not only do Polynikes and Etiocles wage war to their respective deaths, but Tydeus only arrives in Argos because the Calidonians have exiled him for fratricide (ll. 750–55). His sword, a gift from his father (ll. 1672–75), signifies the principle of filiation he has violated with this murder. Indeed, the entire history of Thebes, which Marmiadoise inherits, turns on families who cannot keep their differences in order: patricide and fratricide extinguish filial lines, while incest ties genealogical linearity in circular knots.

The very origin of Tydeus's sword activates relative power. As Tydeus defends himself against Etiocles's barons, the narrator describes (but does not name) the sword itself:

Galanz li fevres la forgea
et dans Vulcans le trejeta;
treis deuesses ot al temprer
et treis fees al tregetter.
Ja por nul cop ne pliera,
ne ja roille ne coildra;
ne ja nuls homme n'en iert naufrez
qui de la plaie seit sanez.
(Ll. 1676–83)

[Galant the smith forged it and Sir Vulcan carved it; there were three goddesses to temper it and three fairies to carve it. Never on account of any blow will it bend, nor will it ever be burned by rust, nor will there ever be a man hurt by it who will heal from the wound.]

The sword's mythological team of fabricators design the blade for absolute efficacy, but Vulcan binds it to genealogical relativity because he also fabricates Aeneas's armor in the *Roman d'Enéas*. Vulcan agrees to forge the armor in exchange for a night of reconciliation with his estranged wife Venus (ll. 4297–522); the sword (described at length) (ll. 4469–506) and the other pieces of armor are, like Aeneas himself, the fruits of Venus's sexual labors. Vulcan's steel progeny are all implicated in heterosexual intercourse; the swords in particular signify the productivity of the paternal phallus. Escalibor's Latin root *calibs* could thus identify it as Marmiadoise's cousin, since Chalybs is the name of Vulcan's island in Virgil's *Aeneid*. Having given Escalibor a Hebrew etymology, however, redactors have severed the sword from Vulcan's potential paternity. Willfully forgetting the sword's Latin history, the redactors establish Escalibor as a sign of legitimacy independent from genealogy. Escalibor does signify absent fathers (Uther, God), but does not itself enter into a line of filiation. Marmiadoise, in the other hand, captures a threefold association with ancient genealogy through the *romans* of *Thèbes*, *Troie*, and *Enéas*. Within this trilogy, Vulcan engenders the tools that create and destroy filial relations (Theban, Greek, Trojan, and Roman alike).

The multiple magic powers of Tydeus's sword ensure a perfect durability that contrasts sharply with Tydeus himself, killed by the Thebans during the siege (force is indeed relative) (ll. 7269–316). The consequences of Tydeus's death lead the narrator straight to Troy: as Adrastus induces the Calidonians to continue fighting by promising to let them take Tydeus's son back to rule Calidonia after the war, the narrator intervenes to explain that this infant Diomedes will distinguish himself in the Trojan War and that he would have defeated Aeneas himself if Aeneas had not received help (ll. 7821–32). After the bodies have been sorted on the Theban fields, Adrastus apparently keeps the sword in lieu of the departed father and son, an emblem of Greek power later passed on to the Greek victors of the Trojan war. Tydeus's survivors (Marmiadoise and Diomedes) could not oppose the Trojan line (Aeneas and Arthur) more directly.

These allusions to Benoît's *Roman de Troie* and the *Roman de Thèbes* recall the beginning of each narrative; they also propel our memory forward to the *romans'* respective conclusions. The last three thousand lines of the *Roman de Troie*, for example, recount the deaths of the major Greek leaders and several family murders. In these encounters, genealogical ties turn to menace rather than legitimizing strength. The siege of

Thebes ends even more disastrously in the last five hundred lines: with all but three of the Greeks killed, the duke of Athens and twenty thousand Greek widows (led by Adrastus's daughters) dismantle the walls of Thebes. The Greek women return to Argos (now subjugated to Athens) with their family lines extinguished; Etiocles and Polynikes enact genealogical annihilation in perpetuity, as their cinders attack each other in their common tomb (ll. 12020–29). The troubled fates of the Greek victors in both of these *romans* tinge Marmiadoise with the destructive forces of relatives.

The *Merlin* narrator concludes Marmiadoise's genealogy by extending the chronology continuously from Hercules to Rion: "& puis ala lespee tant de main en main & doir en oir que ore est au roy rion qui fu dou lignage hercules qui tant fu preus & hardis" (And then the sword went so much from hand to hand and from heir to heir that now it belongs to King Rion, who was of the lineage of Hercules who was so brave and strong) (230). When we remember the often violent relations between these Greek hands (joined in combat as often as solidarity), this claim to continuity clearly overlooks many broken lines. Indeed, the synecdochic expression of continuity (through *hands* and *heirs*) mobilizes a rhetorical form of discontinuity that silently obscures the actual filiation of fathers, mothers, and children. The durable sword itself engenders only certain death.

These paradoxes and ironies derive from the fundamental instability of genealogical differences, which collapse into ambivalence when a rival bears a more prestigious (and thus more desirable) history. The *Merlin*'s readers encounter the force of this ambivalence when the narrator finally names Rion's sword and establishes Arthur's covetous desire:

Quant li rois rions vit que sa mache fu colpee si traist lespee qui tant fu de grant bonte. & si tost quil lot ietee hors du fuere si rendi si grant clarte quil sambla que tous li pais en fust enluminees . & si auoit non marmiadoise . Et quant li rois artus voit lespee que si reflamboie se le prise moult & se trait .j. poi ensus por regarder le si le couuoite moult durement & dist que bur seroit nes qui le poroit conquerre. (231)

[When King Rion saw that his club had been cut he drew the sword that was of very great goodness. And as soon as he had thrown it out of the scabbard it made such a great brightness that it seemed as if the whole country was illuminated by it. And it had the name Marmiadoise. And when King Arthur saw the sword that flamed so, he prized it much and pulled back a little further to watch; he coveted it very much and said that blessed would be the birth of the one who could conquer it.]

As Escalibor meets Marmiadoise, the emblem of absolute legitimacy crosses the force of relativity. The contact reveals the relative weakness of Arthur's power: although the narrator has said that Escalibor "ieta si grant clarte comme se ce fust vns brandons de feu" (threw out a great brightness, as if it were a torch of fire) (230), one torch seems a minor achievement compared with Marmiadoise's pyrotechnics. When Arthur realizes that Escalibor literally cannot hold a candle to Marmiadoise, he covets the origin of his adversary's power. Arthur's desire expresses the ambivalent attraction that a conquering culture holds for the heirs of the conquered. Oblivious to the dangerous implications of comparisons, which contaminate differences with the shadows of resemblances, Arthur judges himself happy if he can touch the ancient hilt. His success will pull him into the genealogy defined by the history of the hands that have held the sword. In such intimate contact, difference fades into resemblance: in order to avenge his Trojan ancestors, Arthur must join their Greek conquerors.

The conclusion of Arthur and Rion's fight inaugurates a new valuation of the imperial filiation that originates in Greece. After Arthur and Rion identify themselves and defy each other openly (posing the clash of swords overtly as a clash of histories), Arthur finally blesses his birth by conquering Marmiadoise. He forces Rion to relinquish the sword, which has stuck in Arthur's shield, by striking his arm. Their duel, however, descends into a wrestling match as Rion grabs Arthur by the shoulders and Arthur grabs the neck of his own horse with both arms. They remain locked in this double embrace until Ban uses his own sword, Angry ("Courechouse"), to force Rion to release Arthur (235). After rescuing Arthur from Rion (just as the Trojans rescued Aeneas from Diomedes), Ban inquires after Escalibor's fate:

& il li dist quil le ieta a terre si tost comme li iaians le courut enbrachier. & si vous di que iou ai hui fait le plus riche gaaig & que ie miex aim que iou ne feisse toute le millor cite qui soit en tout le monde. (235)

[And he [Arthur] said to him that had thrown it to the ground as soon as the giant ran to embrace him, "And I tell you that I have made today the richest gain and the one I love better than the best city that there is in the whole world."]

Giving only brief and dismissive attention to the instrument that initially legitimated his authority, Arthur forces a comparison—a relation of almost-sameness—between the Greek sword and cities. As a constructed sovereign space (like Thebes, Troy, Rome, or Camelot), a city is the architectural sign of centralized authority and domination over lands near and far. A sword, however, incarnates the mobile force that can deroy this space without destroying itself (Marmiadoise, for example, has ıtably outlasted both Thebes and Troy). Arthur's fetishization of the ɾreek object takes the place of cities and the empires for which they ınd. Arthur thus implies that he loves Marmiadoise more than Rome, ıd trades imperial desire for individual heroic history. This desire ɔliterates Escalibor's Christian origins: Arthur soon judges it worthless ɔmpared with Marmiadoise, which follows his desires ("talent") per-ctly (240).

The rebellion's resolution dismisses Rome more overtly. As the battle ɔntinues after dusk, Arthur kills many rebels with Marmiadoise, and ɔpes that the battle will continue all night so that he can adequately test la boine espee quil auoit conquise" (the good sword that he had con-uered) (239). After many more battles, Arthur reaches a truce with the ɛbels—except Rion, who challenges Arthur to a duel where he finally ıeets his death (409–19). Immediately after Arthur receives homage for ıe lands he gains along with Marmiadoise, Merlin goes to Jerusalem ınd prophesies the Sarrasin king's Christian conversion (420–21). The ıarrator then takes up Arthur's war with Rome (as recounted in Wace's *oman de Brut*), including the reminder of the previous conquests of ome by Belinus and Constantine (424–27). After killing the rapist gi-ıt of Mont Saint-Michel (with the sword he conquered from Rion) (428–1), Arthur defeats the Romans. At this point, the redactors abandon ɾthur's imperial progress: instead of claiming Rome or returning to ɾitain, Arthur fights a giant cat from Lausanne (441) (legends of Arthur's ɛline troubles thus extend well beyond André's satiric poem). After more ɫrange adventures, including Jerusalem's Christian conversion and Ga-ɾain's transformation into a dwarf, the Romans retake Gaul (465). The ɔoman episodes thus lead to marvels and Jerusalem rather than to im-ɛrial dominion. The genealogical telos dissipates into sterile *merveilles*, ɹhile the eschatalogical time of Christian conversion subsumes history.

Meanwhile, Arthur's acquisition of Marmiadoise has led directly to ɛscalibor's alienation. During a temporary peace, Arthur dubs a number ɟf new knights. On Merlin's advice, Arthur gives Gawain "sa boine es-ɛe quil osta del perron" (his good sword he had lifted from the stone) ʔ53). Describing Arthur's extraction but not God's insertion, the pas-ɑge displaces divine legitimation with Merlin's counsel. Escalibor now ɛsembles the twelve nameless swords that Arthur distributes to Gawain's ɔmpanions the same day—swords also acquired according to Merlin's ıstructions (251).[99] Arthur grants his kingdom to Gawain along with ɦe sword, justifying his action with only "car ie le uoel" (because I want ɫ) (253). Arthur's "ie uoel" expresses the same romance desire as Solo-ɱon's wife's "come il me plaira;" Bohort concludes the *Mort* with the ɑme expression ("comme il voudroient") (263). In each instance, auton-ɔmous desire dismisses genealogical constraint, ecclesiastical dominion, ɳd the logic of history. The dangers of rogue autonomy surface in Gawain's growing *demesure* as he turns a friendly tournament into a deadl massacre on the steps of Saint Stephen's (*Merlin* 330–35).

Escalibor and Marmiadoise each challenge royal authority in diffe ent ways. The peripatetic *Merlin* traces their troubled histories, intertwir ing them with the foundation, defense, and expansion of the Arthuria realm. The narrative keeps these histories in motion, fictionalizing lir ear romance desire in order to escape the demands of linear history. Fc aristocratic readers, the cycle offers a fantasy of royal weakness by ex posing the forces of relativity that inhere in genealogical legitimatior The *Merlin*'s Greek histories resonate with particular strength in Chan pagne, where many knights and lords (including the historian-knighr Geoffroi de Villehardouin and Robert de Clari) had participated in th sack of Constantinople in 1204. At that time, they abandoned a crusac ing tradition of Greek identification and avenged the Trojans' ancier defeat by installing Baldwin IX of Flanders as emperor of the Greek en pire.[100] Indeed, Robert de Clari identifies the site of Troy near Constar tinople with precision, and makes vengeance a major motive for the cru sade (159, 216). Like Arthur's conquest of Marmiadoise (valued *more* tha any city, and thus more than the Greek imperial capital), the Trojar Flemish rule of Constantinople overturns an ancient order of domina tion. The dynamics of Arthur's Greek fetish demonstrate, however, tha the new order causes as much ideological trouble as it resolves.

Espee de toutes armes la plus honoree

Together, the *Estoire* and the *Merlin* establish a hierarchy of swords tha enforces a hierarchy of values. The Sword of the Extra-Ordinary Baldri (sign of divine transcendence) subordinates Escalibor (sign of politica justice). Arthur, however, willfully subverts this semiology by exchang ing Escalibor for Marmaidoise's imperial genealogy. This transfer turn the hierarchy into an opposition, as the artifacts aligned with God (th Sword of the Extra-Ordinary Baldric, the Grail) threaten those aligne with the monarchy (Escalibor, Marmiadoise). The *Lancelot* plays or this tension while introducing a complex of multiple allegiances that de fies all linear solutions. Lancelot himself occupies the guilty center c these conflicts.

Lancelot (a disinherited orphan) receives his first sword from th Lady of the Lake (7:258), who presents the blade as an instrument c Christian justice. The Lady articulates a complete theocratic hierarchy citing the testimony of Scripture as she explains that knights were cre ated to protect the weak from the strong and to guard the Holy Churcl (7:249–50). Drawing from Saint Paul's letter to the Ephesians (Eph. 6:14 17), the Lady allegorizes the instruments of knighthood. Each stage o her hermeneutic exercise connects chivalry to ecclesiastical obligation and casts the knight as a servant of divine justice. She elaborates th vord's significance in the greatest detail, since it is the most honored the arms ("de toutes armes la plus honeree") because it can wound in ree ways—striking with each edge and thrusting with the point (7:252). ach mode signifies a specific authority: one edge avenges transgressions ;ainst Christianity; the other punishes earthly crimes; the point signi- es strict obedience ("moult a droit obedience") to both domains of au- iority "[c]ar ele pointe" (because it pierces) (7:252). This rigorous alle- >ry of the sword defines the place of all blades in a divinely ordered :onomy of force.

Armed with this knowledge, Lancelot sets out for the Arthurian court, itent on receiving knighthood from Arthur. The Lady, however, en- eavors to protect him from Arthurian allegiance by stipulating that her word be used in the ceremony. Crossing the Channel from France to Loe- ria, Lancelot enters the court already bound to the other side of the bor- er: he cannot help but enter into conflict as he carries unsettling mul- .plicity into the Arthurian center. He does actually evade direct service > Arthur in the knighting ceremony: in the excitement over Lancelot's idacious offer to remove the weapons from the body of a wounded night, Arthur forgets to gird Lancelot's sword (7:278). Although Yvain iter remembers and informs Lancelot that he is not yet a knight since ie king did not gird the sword, Lancelot leaves the court anyway. He does ot desire ("n'a talent") to receive knighthood from the king, "mais 'un autre dont il quide plus amender" (but from another who he thinks e'll help more) (7:286). Until Lancelot receives this sword, he never uses ne in combat. Eventually, he sends two damsels he has won from an rrant knight to the court with a message for the queen:

[E]t li dites que je li mant que por moi gaaignier a tous jors, que ele me fache chevalier et qu'ele m'envoieche une espee com a chelui qui ses chevaliers sera, car mes sires li rois ne me chainst point d'espee, quant il me fist chevalier. (7:298)

[And tell her that I ask her that in order to gain me forever that she make me a knight, and that she send me a sword as for the one who will be her knight, because the king did not gird any sword on me when he made me a knight.]

ust as Arthur conquered Marmiadoise (a "riche gaaig"), Guenivere can >ossess Lancelot: he offers himself as a conquest ("gaaignier") that the |ueen can cultivate for her own enrichment. Once he girds on her mag- iificent sword, he is truly a knight and belongs to Guenivere (7:298, ;:106). By maneuvering to hold the queen's sword, Lancelot keeps him- .elf outside the bounds of the Arthurian and the ecclesiastical[101]—in the eminized border between Guenivere and the Lady of the Lake.

Lancelot does, however, circulate within the court as well as against t. Eventually, he encompasses Arthur within his divided identity. In battles against the Saxons, for example, Lancelot and Lionel identify the Arthurian allegiance by shouting "Clarence," the city of one of Arthur ancestors (8:468). Moreover, Lancelot fights with a sword belonging t Arthur:

> [E]t quant ses glaives li brisa, si sot bien mettre le main a l'espee trenchant qui avoit non Seure, c'estoit une espee que li rois ne portoit s'en bataille mortel non. (8:468)
>
> [And when his lance broke he knew well to put his hand on the slicing sword that had the name Sure. This was a sword that the king did not carry except in mortal combat.]

Since Lancelot is not a king, the description clearly attributes Sure t Arthur. Like Gawain with Escalibor, then, Lancelot defends the king's ir terests with the king's sword. Through his three swords, he identifies a least partially with Arthur, Guenivere, and the Lady of the Lake. He hin self perceives that he only exists as the sum of these parts: "je sui plus autrui qu'a moi" (I belong more to others than to myself) (2:248). Lancelc recognizes here the split subjectivity of the border. In his homoerotic re lationship with Galehot, he becomes the quintessential border-crosse, partially identified with an ever multiplying range of subject positions.

The instability of Lancelot's border subjectivity contaminates th Arthurian center dramatically during the crisis over the False Gueni vere (an exemplary situation of troubling resemblance). As Lancelot de fends Guenivere against the charges of the False Guenivere (whose cas Arthur embraces), some manuscripts report that he carries Escalibor fo love of Gawain (1:134–35). Gawain, who carries Escalibor as his own an is elected king when the barons think Arthur is dead,[102] purveys roya and chivalric authority. Lancelot's hand on his hilt draws the Arthuria center (already split by the two Gueniveres) into the fragmented edge of identification. Even if, as other manuscripts report, Lancelot carrie Galehot's sword for love of him (1:134–35), Lancelot's multiple partial ity thrusts his defense into irony: he challenges Arthur with either th king's own sword or that of a rival king who nearly defeated Arthur. Dur ing the battle, Lancelot addresses specific praise to the sword, remark ing that he who carries it "doit avoir cuer de preudome" (must have th heart of a worthy man) (1:140). If he speaks to Escalibor, the sword touche three heroes (Gawain, Arthur, and Lancelot) who in fact fail to prov themselves truly worthy. If he addresses this praise to Galehot's sword he conjures the shadows of a homosocial desire equally "unworthy" o witness.

The *Lancelot* contests the linear basis of hierarchical authority b representing these multiple and fragmented allegiances. Lancelot an Galehot, heroes of the border, disrupt the Arthurian center with thei boundary-crossing identifications. Lancelot's multiple partialities in par ticular disperse hierarchical order, and bring dispersal right to the center of the court. There, his exemplary position (best of all knights) exposes the center's dependence on the transient subjectivity of the edge. For aristocratic readers, then, Lancelot offers a fantasy of effective peripheral power, capable of realigning royal identities. At the same time, of course, he performs the fatal risks of guilty and fragmented subjectivities.

L'espee as estranges renges

When Galahad arrives at the court in the *Queste,* he displaces Lancelot as its most exalted member. The substitution exiles the play of fragmentation, stabilizing value through inimitable spiritual perfection. This new center, however, disrupts the court more violently than Lancelot's border effects because it excludes the spiritually unworthy, which is to say most of the royal court. Following the *Lancelot,* the *Queste* illustrates a model of chivalric behavior (already theorized by the Lady of the Lake) that exposes Arthur's spiritual failure—that is, the breaking of promises made when he received Escalibor. Galahad completes the Round Table by occupying its empty seat, only to empty out thirty-two others (*Mort* 2). When the Grail and the Ship of Faith (carrying the Sword of the Extra-Ordinary Baldric) finally land on Britain's shores, they depopulate the land like spiritual invaders and then retreat to their original domain.

Galahad's resemblances to his father only underscore their differences. Like Lancelot, for example, Galahad handles three different swords. In Galahad's case, however, they successively close off the potential for multiple allegiances. Galahad receives his first sword (at the abbey where he has been raised) from Lancelot (*Queste* 2), suggesting engagement with Lancelot's own multiple identifications—the ultimate father David, the surrogate mother Lady of the Lake, the adulterous lover Guenivere, the homoerotic lover Galehot, the dependent lord Arthur. Yet Galahad not only refuses to return to the court with Lancelot, he arrives there the next day with neither sword nor shield (7). Galahad thus refuses the Arthurian allegiance implied in Lancelot's gift[103] and seems to have summoned his father only in order to reject him and his fragmented identifications.

Galahad's second sword directly displaces Lancelot's position at court. It arrives lodged in a stone that floats in the river, bearing an inscription that identifies the one person who can lift it as the best knight in the world (5). Galahad's successful extraction proves that Lancelot is no longer the best knight in the world (11–12). This supernatural blade thus signifies Lancelot's exclusion from the center of meaning, exiling his border subjectivity to the edges of relevance. Galahad himself carries the sword unencumbered by earthly allegiance, for he girds it on himself (12). As soon as he encounters the accompanying shield, given to Mordrain by Josephé (*Estoire* 556), he abandons his Arthurian companion Yvain (31). Now fully endowed with divine armor, Galahad has passed through

Arthur's court only to demonstrate his distance from it. His movements redraw the boundaries of value, consigning the court itself to sin.

The Grail manifests the new boundary dramatically. Like a hostile foreign knight, it "attacks"[104] the court and proclaims dominion. Although Arthur at first expresses happiness at this sign of the Lord's benevolence ("debonereté," "amor") (16), he rages in anger when he realizes the Grail's destructive effects. Since Gawain swears first to the quest to find the Grail, Arthur formally accuses him of treason (21). Gawain did indeed divide his loyalties between Arthur and a rival Lord when he pledged allegiance to the quest. Since all the knights have made the same pledge, the Insular landscape will now be divided between Arthur's earthly knights ("terrien") and Galahad's celestial knights ("celestien").

Each knight's experiences on the quest reveal his place along this new boundary. While most of the knights, like Gawain, reside firmly on the side of the *terrien*, Lancelot once again lives in the border itself. Before he leaves, Guenivere accuses him of treason, just as Arthur accused Gawain (24). Guenivere recognizes that Lancelot has adopted an allegiance that excludes all others. If he succeeds in the quest, he will trade his multiple partialities for a single, unified, spiritual wholeness. And he does succeed—partially. His transformation begins when a knight, recently healed by the Grail, steals his sword while he sleeps (60). Divested of the sign of his earthly allegiance to the queen, Lancelot finally confesses his sin with Guenivere (in part) to a hermit (64–66). This hermit, with little ceremony, gives Lancelot a new sword before he proceeds on his repentant path (117). These new arms signify Lancelot's new spiritual service. For the time being, his loyalties are secure enough for him to reject his former sword when he vanquishes the knight who stole it (132). Lancelot eventually achieves sufficient purity to (partly) glimpse the Grail (253–55), but in the end he returns to Arthur's court like all the other sinful knights. Lancelot's relation to both chivalries remains equivocal, and at the beginning of the *Mort*, he has returned to his adulterous love more audaciously than ever before (3).

Meanwhile, Perceval, Bohort, and Galahad inhabit the *celestien* unequivocally. They meet together for the first time at the Ship of Faith which has sailed to Britain from the Old Testament. Here, Galahad receives his third and final sword, the Sword of the Extra-Ordinary Baldric sign of perfect divine identification. Like Galahad, the sword comes from David's high lineage. Both, however, lose this genealogical history as they are re-signed beyond time. The *Queste* narrates much of the sword's history as the knights explore the ship and read the same inscription that Nascien did in the *Estoire*. The baldric, however, is emphatically aligned with the transfer from Old Testament errors to divine completion. Whereas in the *Estoire* Solomon's wife surprises him with a baldric as poor as hemp (286), in the *Queste* she angers him with "renges d'estoupe" (a baldric of crude fiber) (223). Such fibers form impenetrable bound aries, and the verb *estouper* refers to blocked passages: a devil promises to leave a body "si me destoupe la voie" (if you unblock the path for me) (*Estoire* 18), and Lancelot awakes from an enchantment to find the windows "estoupees" (blocked up) (*Lancelot* 4:211). *Estoupe* thus refers figuratively to a blockage of truth. For Solomon, the crude baldric indeed belies the sword's richness. Yet Solomon's wife's inability to *engineer* an appropriate baldric communicates truthfully the limits of her knowledge, as she herself explains (*Queste* 223). She cannot sustain ("sostenir") the sword because it signifies a Christian purity whose advent lies in the future and that will displace romance desire ("come il me plaira"). Thus while Solomon condemns the baldric as a product of deceptive *engin*, it derives not from artifice but from honest partial understanding.

Solomon's wife prophesies that the sword will be completed (that is, redeemed to true understanding) by a superlative virgin, who turns out to be Perceval's sister. She recounts the ship's entire history to the three knights; they accept it as true once they have read Solomon's "brief" (226). As they are about to leave to seek the noble virgin who can complete the sword, she shows them "unes renges ouvrees d'or et de soie et de cheveux mout richement" (a baldric worked in gold and silk and hair very richly) (227). She attaches this baldric to the sword, "si bien com se ele l'eust fet toz les jorz de sa vie" (as well as if she had done it every day of her life) (227). This is of course the first and only time she performs this engineering feat—but she has no need to learn it, since her spiritual devotion inspires her movements. Her unique work is perfect from inception, just like the hero it will adorn.

Perceval's sister completes the sword's translation from history by christening it "l'Espee as estranges renges" (227). "Estranges" refers ambiguously, for it can designate either Solomon's wife's surprisingly poor baldric or Perceval's sister's inconceivably rich one. This ambiguity thematizes the object's distance from the familiar while effacing the memory of its association with David and Solomon. In place of this genealogy, the name locates the baldric—and Galahad—beyond all limits, across the boundary of known history. The baldric of virgin hair integrates the feminine into the phallic symbol,[105] crossing yet another identity boundary. When Perceval's sister chastely girds the Sword of the Extra-Ordinary Baldric on Galahad, he attains true knighthood for the first time (228); he is reborn as the son of a genealogy that undoes time rather than performing it. The sword from "beyond" ("estranges") signifies the borderless, hegemonic dominion of perfected spirituality.

Before Galahad can leave Britain and ascend with the Grail, he must mend the sword that broke in Joseph's thigh (266). At the end of the quest, Bohort carries this ancient sign of Insular Christianity (in place of the sword given by Lancelot)[106] and Perceval carries the one that Galahad drew from the floating stone: each sword reflects the hero's place in the *Queste*'s moral economy.[107] The celestial order thus assimilates the logic of chivalric allegiance to Christian hegemony. This new dominion disinherits Arthurian dominion, as the three knights sail from Britain along with the Grail:

> Et en la maniere que je vos ai devisee perdirent cil del roiaume de Logres par lor pechié le Saint Graal....Et tot autresi come Nostre Sires l'avoit envoié a Galaad et a Joseph et aus autres oirs qui d'ax estoient descenduz, par lor bonté, tot autresi en desvesti il les malvés oirs par lor malvestié. (274–75)

> [And in the manner that I have described to you, those of the realm of Loegria lost the Holy Grail on account of their sins....And just as Our Lord had sent it to Galahad and to Joseph and to the other heirs who were descended from them because of their goodness, so He divested the bad heirs because of their badness.]

The Grail's departure punishes those who failed to achieve celestial chivalry as much as it rewards those who succeeded. The narrator's lament echoes Cadwallader's exile speech, except that in this spiritualized landscape, dominion itself leaves the island (with no desire to return) while the Britons remain.

Galahad's voyage to Sarras reverses Joseph's voyage to Britain with the Grail in the *Estoire*. Galahad returns the sacred vessel to its native land, so that it can return to God. Its sojourn on the island is thus an interlude of mobility between these two poles of fixed truth. When the Grail casts the light of this truth across the Insular landscape, it catches only a few reflections. The Grail's immutable, timeless identity also opposes Arthurian lineage, except where the Arthurian crosses the Hebrew. Ultimately, the adventures that define Arthurian activity result from the fissures opened in the Insular landscape by historical transgressions. Once Galahad closes these gaps, Arthurian dominion has no future. The *Queste* thus attempts to dispel the ambivalences mobilized in the *Merlin* and the *Lancelot* in favor of stable divine limits. These limits dominate royal power and prove as disruptive to political authority as Lancelot's equivocations. From a rather different direction, then, the cycle once again proffers a fantasy of royal loss.

Escalibor, bone espee et riche

Escalibor, born within the frame of ambivalence, survives beyond the limits set by the *Queste*. From its inception in the *Merlin*, it moves away from the divine allegiance contained in the Sword of the Extra-Ordinary Baldric. Unmoored from its origins when Arthur transfers it to Gawain, it moves through the *Lancelot* and the *Mort* as a sign of transient service. At the same time, the *Lancelot* bolsters the *Merlin*'s dismissal of genealogical legitimation by presenting images of Troy in relation to frutrated eros (genealogies never generated) rather than deriving lessons of imperial heritage.[108] By the time the *Mort* opens, the fragmentation of imperial identifications, in conjunction with the consolidation of spiritual transcendence, has mined the Arthurian landscape with fatal conflicts.

From the *Mort*'s beginning, Arthur divorces his authority from the *Queste*'s celestial order. He rejects the Christian ideology embodied in the Sword of the Extra-Ordinary Baldric (now presumably lying in Sarras) by avoiding the logic of swords altogether. As the conflicts multiply, Arthur repeatedly defines his kingship through his crown and his genealogy: confronted with Lancelot and Guenivere's infidelity, he swears by his *crown* to bring them to justice (65); debating whether to pursue Lancelot (who has taken the queen to Joyous Guard), Arthur reminds his knights that he has not lost a war since he was *crowned* (135); he swears by Uther's soul that he will pursue Mordred (228). Forgetting his royal sword (sign of justice), Arthur overlooks his bonds of obligation to both the Church (where he received the sword from the altar) and his knights.

As Arthur dismisses his obligations to others, his reactions become increasingly violent, recalling Gawain's rogue autonomy in the *Merlin*. Pressing his nephews to disclose their thoughts about Lancelot and Guenivere, for example, he grabs a sword that happens to lie nearby and threatens to kill Agravain (109). This murderous impulse borders on infanticide, and threatens to destroy family and vassal at the same time. The encounter exemplifies Arthur's defiance of the control of violence usually achieved through fealty bonds (signified in the giving and receiving of swords). Arthur rejects the political system per se, wherein the logic of sword relations distributes blows justly within a closed network of lateral and hierarchical allegiances to knights, kings, and archbishops. The dismantling of this system sets allegiances in motion, touching off a fatal chain of warfare—Arthur lays siege to Joyous Guard, Gawain attacks Lancelot, the Roman emperor challenges Arthur, and Mordred usurps the throne. By breaking vassalic bonds, Arthur engenders a cultural disaster that eventually destroys him and returns the land to its original barren state ("les terres gastes et essilliees") (232). This landscape bears no traces of history as the postcolonial nightmare converges on the precolonial myth of empty land. In this Insular desert, memory withers on the vine as if dominion had never taken root.

Although the causes of the disaster are multiple (as has long been noted),[109] Mordred and Guenivere demand close attention in relation to the dynamics of Arthurian betrayal established in the *Historia*. The queen's adultery in this case obviously concerns Lancelot, not Mordred. Although the irregular intercourse began in the *Lancelot,* only in the *Mort* does it disrupt the social order as Lancelot's political rivals strive to reveal it to the king.[110] Unlike other Arthurian histories, the queen is in fact convicted of adultery and judged to die at the stake (121), yet she avoids intercourse with Mordred once he seizes the throne (166–78). Her conviction, however, leads directly to the possibility of this unnatural marriage, because Arthur leaves Mordred in charge of the kingdom in order to pursue Lancelot on the Continent: while rescuing Guenivere from the stake, he accidentally killed Gawain's brother, and Gawain insists on blood vengeance (165). Adultery and political usurpation thus remain intimately intertwined. Mordred himself plots the elaborate betrayal because he loves the queen uncontrollably, in terms identical to Lancelot (171). Romance desire thus directly undermines stable dominion.

The process of betrayal serves, in part, to expose a whole set of irregular intercourses. If adultery forms one root of disaster, incest forms another. In the midst of the letter that Mordred crafts to convince everyone that Arthur is dead, he himself (or the narrator?) insinuates an irregular origin when he has Arthur ask the barons to make Mordred king, "qe ge tenoie a neveu—mes il ne l'est pas" (who I held as nephew, but he isn't) (172). Guenivere publicizes the irregularity when she denounces Mordred as a traitor and "filz le roi Artu" (son of King Arthur) (176). Mordred's origins are thus incestuous, since his mother (Loth's wife) is Arthur's half sister (*Merlin* 73, 96, 128–29). Arthur himself declares the incest as he swears vengeance: "Mes onques pere ne fist autretant de fill comme ge ferai de toi, car ge t'ocirrai a mes deus meins" (But never did a father do to a son what I will do to you, for I will kill you with my two hands) (211). The narrator concludes the battle with a final reminder: "Einsi ocist li peres le fill, et li filz navra le pere a mort" (Thus the father killed the son, and the son wounded the father to death) (245). Multiple genealogical disruptions thus converge on the final disaster: adultery, incest, infanticide, and patricide. The Roman war becomes almost incidental (the emperor is never named) (207–9), utterly overshadowed by the extended conflicts among Gawain, Lancelot, Arthur, and Mordred.

Escalibor reemerges in the narrative at a critical juncture in the disaster, as Gawain and Lancelot meet in single combat to resolve their protracted war. Their meeting distills the conflict between the Arthurian center (delegated to Gawain) and the disruptions of the border (embodied in Lancelot). Gawain engages Lancelot with the emblem of (tainted) royal authority, "Escalibor, la bone espee le roi Artu" (Escalibor, the good sword of King Arthur) (195). This coercive encounter harks back to Lancelot's first arrival at court, where he pointedly refused Arthur's sword. The duel replays the crisis of allegiance engendered by this refusal, as well as the crisis of authority provoked by Arthur's substitution of Escalibor for Marmiadoise in the *Merlin*. Having received Escalibor, and carried it throughout the *Lancelot*, Gawain speaks for Arthur yet deforms royal justice by pursuing vengeance beyond the constraint of law and chivalric virtue; the Roman emperor and Arthur himself later pursue the same deformed logic of force (207, 225–27). Accordingly, toward the end of the combat, Gawain's grip on royal justice begins to fail: he is so tired "qu'a peinne puet il tenir s'espee" (that he can hardly hold his sword

(201). Forced to relinquish the offensive and take cover, Gawain's defeat signals his misunderstanding of the sword, a misprision he inherits from Arthur's own efforts to sever authority from the limitations of political allegiances. In the end, Escalibor no longer conjures triumphant, singular loyalty but the losses of divided allegiance.[111] The inconclusive duel, in which the determination of justice eludes everyone, performs the final dispersal of authority.

Arthur manages to collect these fragments together briefly, but only in order to remove the sword from circulation altogether. Arthur himself never touches the sword until his last moments. Previously, he struck the Roman emperor with an anonymous sword "clere et trenchant" (bright and sharp) (209) and killed Mordred with a lance "gros et fort" (large and strong) (245). The Roman battle in fact departs dramatically from the *Historia* tradition by reducing the battle narrative to a minimum,[112] not naming Escalibor, and having Arthur himself kill the emperor. The cycle thus once again evacuates the imperial theme, shifting focus to the dissolution of dominion per se. Just before the ultimate dissolution, Arthur resurrects Escalibor's relation to the divine order of justice:

> Ha! Escalibor, bone espee et riche, la meilleur de ceste siecle, fors cele as Estranges Renges, or perdras tu ton mestre. (247)

> Ha! Escalibor, good sword and rich, the best in this world except the one with the Extra-Ordinary Baldric, now you will lose your master.

Arthur places Escalibor in the same relation to the Sword of the Extra-Ordinary Baldric as Lancelot to Galahad—superlative only on the terrestrial plane and subordinate to spiritual authority. Moreover, governed by a "master," the blade obeys the logic of vassalic service (just like Robert of Gloucester's Sir Caliburn). On the verge of death, then, Arthur draws Escalibor back into the system of constraint he had dismantled at the beginning of the *Mort*, or perhaps as early as the *Merlin*.

Arthur goes on to deplore the absence of Lancelot, Escalibor's only imaginable heir. The irony of the impulse is palpable, for Lancelot would compound (not control) the sword's tainted ideological history. To invest his border subjectivity with the emblem of royal justice would shatter the stable differences on which centralized authority depends. Lancelot is suitably absent from the scene, and since Arthur fears the "malvès oir" (bad heirs) who remain (that is, Mordred's sons), he orders Girflet to throw the sword in a nearby lake (248). Girflet covets Escalibor just as Arthur did Marmiadoise, but Arthur—unlike Rion—maintains his mastery to the end: Girflet's substitutions (first of his own sword and then of the scabbard) fail, and Arthur does not rest until he hears that a hand has risen from the lake to claim the sword (249). Gasping his last breath, Arthur recovers the authority he lost when Lancelot's affair was publicized, or perhaps back when the Grail first attacked, or perhaps even as early as the conquest of Marmiadoise. Ironically, he can only use this authority to oversee his own demise. The aquatic hand withdraws the (tainted) sign of legitimation and aborts future filiation: there will be no passage from this hand to another heir. Having spanned the entirety of Arthur's political life, Escalibor drowns in "useless immobility";[113] its fate signs the "evacuation" of the imperial myth that Dominique Boutet reads in the *Mort* as a whole.[114]

Appropriately, the *Mort* concludes with an abnegation of genealogy's dynastic purpose. Once Lancelot has killed Mordred's sons (253–57), he wanders into the forest and becomes a hermit rather than proceeding by *droite voie* to the capital city (257–59). Bohort, meanwhile, leaves Loegria to rule his own lands (260) but returns the day of Lancelot's burial (263). Retiring to pray, King Bohort orders his men to make "tel roi comme il voudroient" (whatever king they would like) (263). No principle other than individual desire governs this final passage of dominion (which concerns Gaunes, not Loegria), just as only Arthur's desire ("talent") governed Marmiadoise. Arthur's tombstone in fact bears no witness to genealogy or history, only conquering force: "Ci gist le rois Artus qui par sa valeur mist en sa subjection .XII. roiaumes" (Here lies King Arthur, who by his valor put twelve kingdoms in his subjection) (*Mort* 251). The memory of dominion fades in this deserted realm. History dissolves in romance desire, discrediting genealogical filiation. The dissolution sustains aristocratic ideologies that value royal dependence over vassalic submission and that reject the concentration of authority in exclusionary genealogies.

The prose cycle's named swords enact an extended conflict between competing authorities. The *Estoire* launches durable signs of spiritual perfection, while the *Merlin* traces the dangerous consequences of political judgment divorced from this divine order and the *Lancelot* explores the complexity of political equivocation. The *Queste* finally condemns terrestrial politics altogether, while the *Mort* explores the bloody details of their failure. Dismissing imperial ambitions, the cycle turns the very idea of dominion into a romance fantasy. The prose medium itself insinuates the illegitimacy of autonomous action: every conjunctive seam connects to another and no part of the narrative can function alone. The possibility, or even the inevitability, of continuation[115] ratifies desires for a world of borders (of endless seams) — and, paradoxically, a borderless world. The cycle thus chronicles a history of absolute boundaries that converges on the impossibility of boundary formation. Subverting the very mechanisms that usually determine limits, the cycle sustains aristocratic fantasy while also conjuring imperial nightmares.

Specifically in Champagne or more generally elsewhere, the Arthurian prose cycle delegitimizes royal authority that refuses lateral service bonds

It also challenges the potency of Trojan origins (favored by the French monarchy), exposing the ideological dangers of genealogical legitimation in general: relatives, no matter how prestigious, cannot sustain absolute principles. Arthur himself becomes the active emblem of genealogical paradox (enchanted bastard, incestuous philanderer, infertile king, and so on). While the cycle's plot glorifies his achievements, the consequences of his victories unsettle his history. Once he trades Escalibor for Marmiadoise, every coercive encounter recalibrates his authority. An aristocratic audience (especially one with royal pretensions of its own) could identify with Arthur as well as with the critique of his power. Generating ambivalence about the Arthurian past, the prose cycle ingeniously resists history with spiritualized genealogies. As the heroes of history return to their sacred origin in Sarras, the victims pray in the deserted Insular forest.

CHAPTER 7

In Armoricam
Bloody Borders of Brittany

B rittany occupies a unique place among Arthurian border histories since it borders every region discussed so far: the Channel ties it to England and Wales, its northern edge touches Normandy, and several political alliances draw it into the Champenois orbit.[1] Fittingly, the *Historia*'s Continental itinerary includes this land of Briton exile. In the 1230s, a Breton monk returned Brutus to his epic origins with a Latin hexameter poem, the *Gesta regum Britanniae* ("Historia Britonum uersificata" [2]). Dedicated to Cadioc (bishop of Vannes from 1235 to 1254), this *Gesta* moralizes cultural contacts in order to justify the Britons' exile and motivate contemporary readers to resist English and French domination. The *Gesta* thus conveys an anticolonial approach to Briton history that overturns Geoffrey's ambivalence, sidelines Wace's colonial confidence, and cripples the post-colonial strategies of various other writers. Paradoxical as any border, the *Gesta* poet accomplishes this anticolonial history in epic form, and by deploying many of the same strategies as other Arthurian historians (one manuscript even includes a copy of the *Historia* itself).[2] The poet (sometimes identified as William of Rennes), for example, engages force through landscape metaphors, an ethic of liberty, etymologies, figures of universal time, and apostrophe. In the *Gesta*, where violent conquest cannot found legitimate dominion, Caliburn contains all that is wrong with Arthur's expansionist vision. Ultimately, the *Gesta* directs the imperial Briton past against the very concept of conquest.

The poet's strident historical judgment addresses the losses of a colonized people, in a region dominated by neighboring authorities. Within the fissures of multiple resistances (to neighbors, lords, and foreign kings) and along multiple borders, regional identity rallied around legendary and real Arthurs. Not only did Bretons cultivate belief in Arthur's return, they received a new incarnation of the legendary hero when the countess Constance named her son Arthur, contrary to Henry II's plan to give his grandson his own royal name.[3] Constance subsequently fought Henry to protect the independence of Arthur's inheritance.[4] When Richard I recognized Arthur as his heir and Philip II accepted him when Richard died, it probably seemed that the Bretons would indeed drive out the English. John cut these dreams short by sanctioning Arthur's murder in

1203, ensuring that Arthur of Brittany would never restore the realm of Arthur of Britain. Later, in the 1230s, the French duke Pierre de Drieux co-opted indigenous Arthurianism by giving the name to his own short-lived first son.[5] With this gesture, Pierre manifests the colonial lord's impulse to derive power from the mimicry of native culture. Pierre's genealogical strategy, which coincides with the *Gesta*'s composition, recognizes Arthur's potential to unify Breton identity.

In the decades following Arthur of Brittany's death, the Breton lords resisted their French duke. Pierre, a prince of the French royal family, became duke when in 1212 he married Alice (the recognized heir and Arthur's half sister).[6] He arrived in Brittany as a colonial overlord, imposed by the French monarchy and alienated from indigenous culture. Like his aristocratic contemporaries in Champagne and Flanders, however, Pierre resisted his royal patron almost as vigorously as he did his new Breton subjects.[7] For a brief moment in 1225, French and Breton lords rallied around him as Louis VIII blocked his marriage to the countess of Flanders (Louis's opposition demonstrates that he viewed the marriage as a dangerous form of aristocratic collusion). After Louis's death, Pierre courted Henry III as an ally in his rebellion against the French regent Blanche of Castille, but then subsequently turned against his English allies. Pierre continued plotting revolt against Blanche and squared off against Henry again in 1229.[8]

The early 1230s were especially tempestuous for Pierre. When Louis IX marched on the duchy, one by one Pierre's vassals submitted to royal authority. Pierre nonetheless continued to resist royal sovereignty, until Louis finally exacted submission in 1234 (shortly after Thibaut of Champagne's submission).[9] Léon Fleuriot in fact connects this "confiscation" of Brittany directly to the *Gesta*'s anti-French sentiments.[10] Throughout this period, a Breton monk writing for an archbishop would have ample reason to oppose both the English and the French, especially given Pierre's seizures of ecclesiastical wealth and efforts to weaken the Church's political authority.[11] The bishopric of Vannes, moreover, had special ties to Arthurian identity. Cadoc's predecessor, Guethenoc, had championed the Breton cause against the Plantagenets and tutored Arthur of Brittany.[12] The *Gesta* seems to draw on this local attachment to legendary history as a way of resisting the specter of a new "French" Arthur and the injustices of his father Pierre.

In these culturally and politically contentious circumstances, the *Gesta* poet offers an anticolonial epic, succoring Breton pride with a local history to rival those of the Greeks, Trojans, Romans, and Thebans written by Homer, Virgil, Lucan, and Statius (174). The hexameter verse itself claims authority from these exemplary predecessors, while also limiting the poet's expression: he refers to names that cannot be expressed metrically and declares Merlin's prophecies too difficult to versify (116, 148). Within these limits, the *Gesta* represents a regional history of colonial tragedy. The poet does not merely offer an apology or panegyric to the Breton race (he refers only once to "our Britain" [84]). Rather, he intervenes like the Muses he so often evokes to judge, exhort, and admonish historical heroes. Drawing attention to the multiple boundaries that confine and define Breton culture, he prays to find salvation in pious border resistance.

Solis scribo Brittanis

The poet deploys numerous strategies to construct an anticolonial Breton identity capable of withstanding incursions from ethnic cousins, linguistic rivals, and history itself. First, he limits his role in the creative process by invoking Calliope (conventional muse of epic poetry) as the narrative source: "Caliope referas, ut te referente renarrem" (Tell, Calliope, so that I may repeat as you relate) (2); the poet again calls upon Calliope as he begins the arduous task of narrating Arthur (174). The claim to repeat casts the narrator as an ideal colonial poetic subject, who mimics true authority to perfection. Yet with Calliope as author, the poet takes this mimicry beyond coercive power to a timeless, transcendent authority. His "repetition" thus extends a Breton refrain that reclaims ancient Breton territory. The poet defends these historic boundaries by also submitting himself to his bishop: just as Geoffrey gave his text over to Robert, Waleran, and Stephen, so the poet asks Cadioc to correct the work or even destroy it ("lima tollat abusum") if he finds it silly or useless (2). Apparently, the bishop chose not to censure: under ecclesiastical approbation, we can still read this Briton history.

The poet also patrols Breton boundaries by limiting the audience to the bishop and the boys in his monastic care. While the poet is happy to have the bishop read the *Gesta* for entertainment ("post sacre scripture seria") (2), he fears detractors and critics from outside the monastery or Brittany. He insists that he does not seek fame and would rather remain unknown to the Saxons, Romans (Quirites), and Gauls (284). Excluding these foreign readers as inappropriate and undesirable, the poet prefers a puerile audience: "satis est michi si puerorum / Gratus in ore legar" (it is enough for me if I am readily recited by the mouths of children) (284). Indeed, he identifies his intended audience as Breton novitiates:

> Solis hec scribo Britannis,
> Ut memores ueteris patrie iurisque paterni
> Exiliique patrum propriique pudoris, anhelent
> Uocibus et uotis ut regnum restituatur
> Antiquo iuri, quod possidet Anglicus hostis;
> Neue male fidei possessor predia nostra
> Prescribat sumatque bonas a tempore causas.
> At pueri, quibus istud opus commendo, rogate

Pro uestri uatis anima, famaque perhenni
Antistes uestro uiuat Chadiocus in ore.
(286)

[I write this entirely for the Bretons, so that, mindful of their ancient
homeland, their hereditary rights, the exile of their fathers, and their
own shame, they may strive with voice and prayer to restore the
realm to their ancient jurisdiction, which the English enemy now
occupies; and so that the faithless possessor does not lay claim to
our farms and his case gain strength with the passage of time.

Boys, to whom I entrust this work, pray for the soul of your poet,
and let Bishop Cadioc live with eternal fame in your mouths.]

This conclusion calls the young Bretons to action against invaders who
threaten their lands. Only Bretons can properly hear and remember this
history (quite the opposite of Wace's inclusive "ki vult oir et vult saveir"). By
repeating the history, the boys perform their tenancy of the land against
their own colonized heritage. Joining this historiographical refrain to
prayer, they immortalize their poet, their bishop, and their land. Like Laȝamon (his near contemporary), the poet thus purveys a Christian masculine pedagogy that creates and extends dominion through oral repetition.
Readers' partial identification with this subjectivity not only disrupts
the stability of historical, religious, ethnic, and gender differences (as with
Laȝamon), it also unsettles their adulthood. As children, readers are cast
as pliant recipients of the poet's historiographical pedagogy.

The poet materializes the integrity of the historiographical refrain by
turning the *Gesta* into a ship:

Iam mea pene ratis fluctu maris obruta portum
Optatum tangit; et quam nec seua Caribdis
Nec catuli Scille nec terruit equoris unda,
Terrent terrarum fantasmata, terret edacis
Liuoris morsus, tormento seuior omni.
(284)

[Now my ship, almost swamped by the sea waves, touches the port
it longs for, and, although it was not intimidated by cruel Charybdis
nor Scylla's whelps nor the ocean swell, it fears the specters of land,
it fears the bite inflicted by consuming envy, more savage than any
torture.]

The ship metaphor, which draws on the indigenous Breton genre of the
navigatio, as well as on the very classical models the poet has cited elsewhere,[13] tropes mobility in vivid contrast with the genre of the *descriptio*
(scene of colonial encounters). In the navigable border, the ship literally mobilizes resistance, evading the stabilities that sustain colonial domina-

tion. The ship's fear of land (cleverly enmeshed in the *annominatio* of "terreo" and "terra")[14] expresses trepidation about colonization and the loss of historic integrity. The ship's specific fear of landed "fantasmata" overturns the usual poetic trope of navigation, which refers to safe port at a poem's conclusion. Moreover, this dangerous landscape subverts the colonial trope of desirable land that launches the first ship from Greece in the *Gesta*'s first book (and that propels Geoffrey's *Historia*). The *Gesta* itself plies the waves to deny conquest. The poem, an intact ship, thus moves a sacralized, integrated concept of Breton history through waves that undulate with the forces of cultural fragmentation (during the Diocletian controversy, the narrator refers to Christianity as "Petri nauis," Peter's ship [100]). Meanwhile, the ghosts of the past, *fantasmata*, haunt the land and menace the future.

The poetic ship materializes the enduring integrity of Breton identity. Throughout the narrative, the poet carefully seals the seams of history to keep out the water that threatens to submerge native culture. The *Gesta*'s portrayal of Aeneas, for example, conjoins Trojan origins with the Breton claim that the first ruler of Brittany was Aeneas Ledewic of Llysaw.[15] Repeated references to Trojan fathers throughout the *Gesta* bolster the durability of Trojan-Breton memory.[16] Indeed, the Bretons often viewed themselves as the proper heirs of Christian Rome, and the Franks and Saxons as usurpers of their imperial heritage.[17] The poet insinuates continuity almost subliminally through the names of historic rulers that have recurred in recent times (Conanus Hoel, Arthur). The poet also observes the complexity of historic ethnic relations assiduously, underscoring both classical prestige and the immutability of ethnic identity.[18] The poet takes particular care to differentiate Continental Bretons from the Insular populations: he refers consistently to *Armorica* (using *minore Britanniam* only at the moment of conquest) and calls the "Britones" who think that "Pendragon" means "head of a dragon" "stupidum" (168) (in Breton, *pendragon* means "head dragon," that is, "leader" or "chief").[19] The debate between Cadwallo and Salomon reinforces this ethnic difference by identifying the degeneracy of the Insular people and the nobility of the Continentals (262–66). Finally, the poet follows the First Variant in bolstering ethnic legitimacy with an ethic of liberty and in excising genealogical discourses.[20] In Brittany, then, the *Gesta* narrates an always already indigenous history; ethnic resemblances do not leak through the poetic resin that seals the planks of the Breton ship.

To strengthen the difference between the Continental Bretons and the Insular population, the poet promulgates anti-English sentiment. Enjoining Mordred to repent his alliance with the Saxons, for example, he notes that they derive their name from stones ("a saxis") since they are rough and unforgiving (240). Later, as the English flee Ivor, the narrator casts them in the role of the *Historia*'s Welsh, scattering like savages into the wastelands (282). Ivor goes on to rule for thirty-five years, longer than in any other version (284). Finally, the English win no glory from their eventual triumph: the poet enumerates their wickedness and offers an extended etymology of *Angle* that denigrates the English far more than the *Historia* does the Welsh:

> Sed quare Saxones Angli
> Dicuntur michi, Musa, refer, ne nescius errem.
> Respondet sic Musa michi: "Dat patria nomen
> Illud; id euentus nomen facit, Angulus Anglum.
> Anglicus angelicus tamen exponi solet; huius
> Nominis expositor et dictus apostolus Angli
> Gregorius populi respexit ad exteriorem
> Candorem uultus, cum quondam dixerit Anglos
> Angelicos. Tamen angelico peruersa nitore
> Mens caret; angelus est Sathane huius nominis auctor.
> Forte uel inferior determinat angulus Anglos,
> In quo cauda reget; uel id ex 'in-gloria' nomen
> Composita exponit, sine qua gens illa futura est."
> (282–84)

[But tell me Muse, lest I am misled by error, why are the Saxons called *Angles*? The Muse replies to me: "Their homeland gives them the name; from it comes the name, *Anglus* from *Angulus*. *Anglicus*, however, is usually explained as *angelic*. The interpretation of this name comes from Pope Gregory, known as the Apostle of the English people, who had in mind the external brightness of their faces when once he called the English angelic. But their wicked minds lack angelic splendor; the angel of Satan is the instigator of this name. Or perhaps the English are defined by their lower angle, in which they have a stiff tail, or [*Anglos*] may be compounded from *in-gloria*, since that people will be without glory."]

In Bede's *Historia* as in Geoffrey's, Pope Gregory's observations on the Englishmen whom he discovers at his court inspire him to send evangelists to convert the island, thereby legitimizing English dominion and casting them as a chosen people. The *Gesta* here ingeniously subverts Bede's praise, turning divine angels into Satanic power.[21] The equivocation between English deformity and baseness echoes Geoffrey's uncertainty about the origins of the Welsh name, only here there are no honorable possibilities. The Muse's authority thus radically reinterprets the papal text (a rather heterodox maneuver in itself). The poet deploys Her judgment along Armorica's border as an authoritative defense of Breton identity.

Like other historians, the poet sustains English difference by emphasizing the divide between Christians and Pagans. Many small revisions augment the prominence of Christianity. The poet adds, for example, an extended discourse on Christ's birth (86) and then introduces Lucius, the first Christian king, with great rhetorical flourish (92–94). The accession of Constans the monk provokes a clever condemnation of his inconstancy and the illegitimacy of leaving the cloister (122). The Saxons' arrival strengthens the dichotomy between Christians and Pagans (128), as the poet decries Vortigern's marriage to Ronwen (132). During the ensuing battles, he repeatedly identifies the conflict as religious, concluding, as the Britons rout the Saxons: "Christus uincit, Christus regnat et imperat illic" (Christ vanquishes, Christ reigns and rules there) (134). Aurelius later attracts extended praise in biblical terms that assimilate him to crusade heroes.[22] Yet when Augustine brings Christianity to the Saxons, anti-English sentiments override religious confraternity. The poet actually praises Dinoot for refusing to convert the Saxons, adding an extended explanation of God's pleasure in receiving the martyred Briton souls (252–54). After the purported conversion, confrontations between the Britons and the Saxons are still described as clashes of Christians and Pagans (254). Moreover, the discord between Cadwallo and Edwin derives not from Edwin's desire to wear a second crown in the kingdom (he already has his own crown, unlike the case in the *Historia*) but from his request to make Pagan sacrifices (256). Like Robert of Gloucester, then, the poet shifts strategically between ethnic and Christian identification in order to patrol the bounds of Breton identity.

The poet finishes the ship of Breton history with the sands of timelessness, smoothing away signs of historical difference. He consistently eliminates, for example, references to translation that conjure the processes of cultural transmission (56, 66). Likewise, he excises etymologies that refer to chronological changes (72, 90) or reduces them to juxtapositions of original and present practice: the island was "Albion," now "Britannia Maior" (28); Leir's city was called "Kaerleyr," now "Lerecestria" (40). These and many other similar revisions avoid chronological dissonances that disturb historical continuity. Elsewhere, the poet telescopes chronological difference by addressing historical characters in apostrophe, as if he could alter their behavior. Aphorisms universalize historical meaning (40, 48, 80), while anachronisms locate distant history in the contemporary landscape: Ruhudus's city was made famous by Thomas Becket's blood (40); the Roman virgin includes the Normans in her list of Britain's peoples (208). Finally, the poet turns the same Wheel of Fortune as his Continental neighbors, with similar disruptions to linear time (44, 78, 274). In this history beyond the limits of historical difference, the *Gesta* universalizes Breton identity as a sturdy vessel, undaunted by the seas of change. He speaks as the master of this ship, and only to its legitimate Breton crew.

Sanguinis unda ruit

The poet's Breton vessel, propelled by the devoted voices of Breton boys, ferries an anticolonial lament. Whereas Geoffrey generally favors Briton imperialism (with a few shadows of ambivalence), the Breton poet characterizes expansion as intrinsically wrong.[23] Condemning all force as illegitimate, the *Gesta* makes the conquest of Armorica the origin of all Breton ills. Thus while the *Gesta* poet and the First Variant redactors write from conquered cultures with common origins, they take nearly opposite ideological stances. In Wales, post-colonial fantasies embrace force as the grounds for a future restoration; in Brittany, anticolonial convictions display coercion to explain historic losses. These convictions dismiss the aesthetics of landscape and turn the blood of war into rivers that stain the borders of stolen dominions.

Like the First Variant, the *Gesta* founds Briton identity on liberty, not territory. Excising the opening *descriptio* and the generations between Aeneas and Brutus, the poet begins with a lengthy portrait of the Trojans' enslavement and their legitimate demand for freedom (4–6). Within the ethic of liberty, however, the poet promotes pacifism instead of aggression. In the *Historia*, for example, Brutus persuades Anacletus to betray the Greeks by threatening him with a drawn sword; Laȝamon lays a blade right on Anacletus's neck. In the *Gesta*, however, Brutus has no sword: the two men make a peaceful agreement and seal their bond of faith with a kiss (10). And even though the narrator supports the Trojans' liberation, he notes during the second battle that violence does not necessarily lead to justice: "Nemo suo parcit gladio. Fas omne nefasque, / Cuncta licent ensi" (No one spares his sword. Everything both right and wrong is in the power of the sword) (10). He then turns the ensuing carnage into a landscape of horror that delegitimizes force. In a passage not paralleled in the *Historia*, the Greeks themselves become rivers of dead: "Sanguinis unda ruit; quos strauit uulneris ictus, / Hos cruor extinguit et sic leto germinato / Exalant animas" (A current of blood flows; those felled by a wounding blow drown in gore, breathing their last in a double death) 10). Another river of blood later flows from Corineus's sword in Aquitaine 22); Hell itself is frequently represented as the river Styx.[24] These early metaphors color the traditional drowning deaths of Humber (34) and Habren (36), so that illegitimate violence flows along all aquatic boundaries. Coercive desire overrides even the shore when the blood that flows from Caesar's attack mixes the land with the sea (74). Whether the blood flows from illegitimate Roman imperialism or legitimate Trojan freedom, it condemns force. The rivers and oceans that propel conquering vessels thus become dangerous signs of colonial transgression. Like the moralized waters of the prose cycle's *Estoire*, aquatic borders pass judgment.

The threats of Scylla and the ocean swells that menace the narrator's poetic ship also prey on Innogen, Brutus's usually silent Greek wife. As she sets sail for Britain, she makes an impassioned speech to her father and her shore. She complains that she is being carried to her death, with the sea as her tomb; she wonders aloud why she did not die in her mother's womb rather than becoming prey for sea monsters (14). The ocean and the marriage thus both provoke in her a desire to foreclose genealogy, to undo her own birth. Fantasizing the disruption of the continuities that can be bridged across water in a ship or through her body in childbirth, Innogen imagines absolute ends. The poet's invention of this speech sympathizes with resistance to expansionism and anchors its perils in the depths of the sea.

Brutus's settlement of Britain is, of course, suspiciously expansionist, but the poet does his best to minimize its coercive aspects. Diana, for example, does not invoke Troy in her prophecy (18). And when the Trojans arrive at the island, the poet does not mention a "promisa insula" or "amoenus situs" (26–28). Instead, the poet describes the origin of farmlands similar to those the Breton boys are convoked to defend. Overtly feminizing the landscape, the poet describes the first plowing of virgin land, which reacts in amazement ("miratur") to insemination, germination, and the bringing forth of fruit (28). Finally, the poet represents the wrestling match between Corineus and Goemagog through sets of balanced appositions ("Collidunt pectore pectus, / Frontem fronte" [They collide breast to breast, forehead to forehead]) that overlook their differences. In fact, the encounter seems as if it will end in a stalemate, ingeniously expressed as the bind of uncertainty on certainty: "par cum pare certe / Certat in incertum" (certain that each has met his match, each struggles in uncertainty) (28). Once Corineus throws Goemagog's body over the cliff, it falls into pieces, but the poet does not specify where or how, so that the resolution does not return to the liminal space of colonial contact.

Revisions to spatial representations throughout the *Gesta* overlook boundary problems as often as possible. When Brutus's sons divide their inheritance, the poet does not name the divisive rivers. And as in the First Variant, the land is written out of landscape since the brothers divide the *realm*, not the *island* (32). In fact, the crown (*diadema*) and realm (*regnum*) substitute systematically for *insula*. The narrator also describes dominion as a *regio*, shaping *regions* into borders since *regio* connotes a boundary limit. In this formless landscape, architectural monuments become signs of full dominion: if rule can be contained in the crown, it is equally immured in statues, walls, and castles. When the Trojans fortify Tours against the Gauls, for example, Goffar calls their castle a sign of usurpation (24). Hengist later avoids the shore and builds his castle on top of a hill ("montis sublime cacumen") (130), the better to survey and defend. And Belinus's roads do not solve a boundary problem but usefully connect cities. Moreover, their construction materializes the seamless landscape: "Quas omnes ex cementi lapidumque perennat / Coniugic iurique suo rex uendicat illas" (From a lasting marriage of cement and stone, the king builds them all and puts them under his protection) (58). The roads' durable junctures cover the differences that threaten colonial and post-colonial order; they conduct timeless precolonial fantasies. Yet when Aurelius envisions a lasting monument to the massacred Britons, the craftsmen fear God's anger (160). This monument conjures the colonial ambition of Galehot's castle in the *Lancelot*: the craftsmen rightfully fear to submit memories of coercive contact to divine judgment. The stones of the Giants' Ring themselves stand for colonial ambition and illicit magic, even though they commemorate the deaths of men who fought for liberty (159–64).

The *Gesta* turns away from boundaries because they derive from violent efforts to expand dominion. The most severe representation of illegitimate expansion comes with Maximianus's conquest of Armorica. The poet first intimates disapproval of imperial ambition when Maximianus's anchor "bites" the shore ("mordet harenas / Anchora") (106). The narrator himself catalogs the landscape, in an anaphoric sequence that echoes both the First Variant and Wace's *Roman de Brut*:

Rex igitur tot stagna uidens, tot prata, tot amnes,
Tot saltus, tot agros, tot litora, tot nemorosa
Robora, tot frutices, tot fontes, omnia laudat.
(110)

[Seeing all the lakes, all the meadows, all the rivers, all the pastures, all the fields, all the shores, all the wooded forests, all the glades, all the springs, the king praises everything.]

The monotony of the landscape evacuates colonial desire, soon attacked directly in a lengthy apostrophe that merits full citation:

O regnum minime felix! O sanguine fuso
Optentum regale decus! Conane, resigna
Hoc ius iniustum! Prescripcio nulla tueri
Te poterit quoniam dum uixeris intus habebis
Accusatricem que teque tuosque nepotes
Semper mordebit. Non debet predo reatum
Dum tenet ablatum? Res semper erit uiciosa
Que uenit ex rapto, dum raptam predo tenebit;
Predonisque heres, postquam rem nouit ademptam,
In uicium succedit ei. Tecum tua proles
Uerget in interitum penam luitura perhennem,
Dum sic possideat iniuste res alienas;
In sobolem peccata patrum de iure redundant,
Dum soboles effrena patrum peccata sequatur.
Quis putet intrusos Britones uel semen eorum

In male quesitis cum pace quiescere terris
Euentus quis habere bonos se credat in illis
Que male parta tenet? Meritis Deus equa rependit.
Stirps homicidarum totis homicidia uotis
Perpatrare studens reputat dispendia pacem.
Cortinam cortina trahit, sanguisque cruorem.
Inconstans Britonum populus constanter in ipsa
Mobilitate uiget; numquam Ranusia uirgo
Mobiliore rota fertur quam spiritus eius.
O regio, tibi nunc rex presidet; ante ducatus
Aut comitatus eras. Non regnum siue ducatus
Sed comitatus eris; tu, que ducibus dominaris,
Cum seruis domino continget te dominari.
Ecce dies uenient quibus ad sua iura reducti
Tristia sub pedibus Galli tua colla tenebunt.
(112–14)

[O least happy kingdom! O regal power gained by spilled blood! Conanus, surrender your unjust dominion! No prescription will protect you, for, while you live, you will carry within you an accuser that will always gnaw at you and your descendants. Should not a robber be punished while he holds what is stolen? A thing is always sinful that is gained by theft, while the thief holds the spoils — and his heir, after he discovers that the thing is the result of theft, succeeds him in sin. Your descendants will fall to destruction with you, and will suffer eternal punishment while thus they unjustly hold the things of others; the sins of the fathers will rightly be visited on their children for as long as they unrestrainedly repeat their fathers' sins. Who could believe that the usurping Britons and their seed may rest at peace in their ill-gotten lands? Who can expect to enjoy good fortune in respect of things he holds evilly? God will give him what he deserves. The progeny of murderers, thirsting to do murders with all its heart, counts peace as less than nothing. A curtain draws a curtain, blood draws blood. The inconstant Breton people flourishes constantly in its own changeability; like the changing wheel of the Rhamnusian maid, so their spirit ever changes. O region, now a king rules you; before you were a duchy or a county. Neither a kingdom nor a duchy will you be but a county; you, who are ruled by dukes, will serve a master who will rule you like slaves. The day will come when the Gauls will recover their rights and hold your sad neck under their feet.]

This litany of accusations defines the Bretons as thieving usurpers, unjustly holding property taken from native Gauls. The rhetoric of theft directly overturns the *Historia*'s malleable logic of legitimacy. Conanus' transgression continues to haunt the Bretons, and it explains all that they have suffered at the hands of neighbors and foreign invaders. The *Gesta* thus dooms the future of Brittany at the very moment of its creation: the region will never enjoy autonomy because it was founded unjustly. Indeed, the arrival of Duke Pierre in 1212 might seem to fulfill this prophecy of enslavement to the Gauls; his capitulation to Louis IX in 1234 suggests the culmination of the tenurial degeneracy the poet outlines. From the *Gesta*'s perspective, then, Conanus's illegitimate settlement leads directly to Brittany's subsequent subjugation to France. The tragedy of this paradox turns the poet against change (the Breton's greatest fault) altogether.

Although Armorica's settlement, like Britain's, does not inspire an aestheticized landscape, the *Gesta* does proffer one idealized *descriptio*—the island of Avalon. The *descriptio* begins without introduction, immediately after Arthur gives his crown to Constantine. Almost until the end, audiences could imagine that the passage describes Britain itself:

> Cingitur occeano memorabilis insula, nullis
> Desolata bonis: non fur, non predo, nec hostis
> Insidiatur ibi; non nix, non bruma, nec estas
> Immoderata furit. Pax et concordia perpes;
> Uer tepet eternum; nec flos nec lilia desunt
> Nec rosa nec uiole; flores et poma sub una
> Fronde gerit pomus. Habitant sine labe pudoris
> Semper ibi iuuenis cum uirgine. Nulla senectus,
> Nullaque uis morbi, nullus dolor: omnia plena
> Leticie. Proprium nichil hic, communia queque.
> (246)

[The ocean surrounds a memorable island, which lacks no blessing: no thief, no robber, no enemy sets traps there; there is no snow, no mist, nor is summer intemperately hot. There is perpetual peace and harmony; it is eternally warm in spring; no flowers, nor lilies, nor roses, nor violets are lacking; flowers and apples grow together under the apple tree's foliage. There youths ever live with virgins without loss of their chastity. There is no old age, illness has no power, there is no sorrow. All is full of joy. There are no possessions there, everything is held in common.]

This idealized *descriptio* negates imperial landscapes at every turn. The trees grow their own fruit against the genealogical grain (without cultivation, flower and fruit together); the soil bears flowers, not corn; men and women remain chaste. The lack of ordinary production (biological or agricultural) obviates all the tropes of the imperial gaze. Instead, this utopian landscape expresses an ideal inertia, informed by monastic perfection—no thieves, good weather, peace, gardens, youth, virginity, health, and no personal property. Here, Arthur retires when he has finally given up his ancestors' imperial ambitions. This land, beyond time, cannot be settled because it is already fulfilled.

The *Gesta* offers another vision of ideal immobility in the fish of Loch Lomond, where the poet describes boundary formations as immutable and timeless:

> Unum quodque sibi partem tenet appropriatam;
> Nec metam excedens istud genus inuidet illi,
> Sed contentum sorte sua, quam lege perhenni
> Mater ei natura dedit, non se gerit ultra.
> (188)

> [Each type remains in the part appropriate to it; nor does one kind exceed its bounds in envy of another, but, content with its lot (given by the eternal law of Mother Nature), does not claim more.]

Of all the descriptions of this marvel, only the *Gesta* invokes "lege perhenni," affirming the universal value of the status quo.[25] Like the native kings of Gaul, who rule their realms without contention ("sine murmure regna regentes") (22), the fish never trouble their borders. These inert fish perform a preservationist ideal, wherein no group seeks to expand its territorial authority. The allegory implies that if ambitious rulers, like Caesar and Arthur, had been more like the fish, they would not have lost their kingdoms. The poet extends the pool's allegorical force by describing the world itself as "four-cornered" ("quadrangulus orbis") (172). The pool thus contains the shape of the world itself, as well as an anticolonial pedagogy of territorial contentment.

The *Gesta*'s pointed discussions of legitimate dominion ratify this preservationist ideal. In adapting these episodes from the *Historia*, the poet resolves the paradoxes of *inquietatione* in favor of legitimate *quiet*. Once this "external law" is broken, battles drag on indecisively since no transcendent right tips the balance in favor of one side or the other. Ultimately, God punishes the Britons as he has the Bretons, disinheriting them through famine (274); Cadwallader sails away from the island's blood-soaked soil, never to return (278). The poet's apostrophe ratifies the punishment in terms that echo his prophecy of Breton losses:

> O Bruti regio, miserande condicionis
> Insula, plena doli, ueneris domus, hospita martis,
> Sanguinis urna, capax uiciorum sportula: testis
> Fortune stabilis, mendaces esse poetas
> Conuincis, qui stare deam, quam uoluit in orbe
> Orbita, posse negant. Fortunam stare tenaci
> Proposito te teste probas nusquamque moueri:
> Nam qualis tecum cepit persistere, talis
> Perstat adjuc. Regni cepisti nomen habere

Ui gladii; tua cepta tenes, tua cepta tenebis,
Dum poterunt Britones et Saxones arma tenere.
Progenies Priami, fera gens, quam blanda molestat
Pax, quam bella iuuant, que semper uiuis in armis,
Cui semper discors concordia, scismaque concors,
Ecce uenit uindicta Dei dignaque reatus
Punit clade tuos; regni, quod polluis, expers
Huius eris. Tua destituens, aliena sequeris.
(282)

[O region of Brutus, island of unhappy condition, filled with deceit, home of lust, host to war, vessel of blood, spacious basket of sins, you bear witness to the stability of Fortune and convict of false-hood the poets who claim that the goddess, whirled in a circle by her wheel, cannot stand still. You provide evidence of Fortune remaining constant to a fixed purpose and moving nowhere: for just as she first attached herself to you, so she stays to this day. You assumed the name *kingdom* by the sword; you continue as you have begun, and as you began you will continue for as long as Britons and Saxons can hold their weapons. Offspring of Priam, savage race, gentle peace offends you; you delight in war, you live forever amid arms; harmony is ever disrupting to you, and disharmony ever harmonious. Now comes the vengeance of God, punishing your transgressions with just disaster. From this kingdom, which you pollute, you will be disinherited. In your destitution, you will seek another.]

Speaking directly to the *regio* (the region that forms a boundary), the narrator condemns Britain's colonial origins as well as the paradoxes that define its present. The Britons have inherited Priam's blood lust, just as the Bretons have Conanus's theft. Both have disrupted the natural processes of Fortune and attracted God's eternal punishment for founding their kingdoms on force. In the Britons' case, exile paradoxically engenders further thievery. In these closing comments, the poet condemns Britain and Brittany in similar terms, justifying their respective subjugations to later colonizing powers as punishment for their own colonial ambitions. The result is an anticolonial stance that refuses to make peace with the post-colonial present.

Cuius nomine Caliburnus

The poet's anticolonialist ethic converges on Arthur and Caliburn. Within the *Gesta*, where illegitimacy taints all force, Arthur represents a limit case in a long history of compromised historical figures. And his imperial sword embodies a judgment against empire and aggression. Like the *Merlin*, then, the *Gesta* turns Caliburn against the royal hand as it turns history against its imperial heritage. The poet's deployments of Christianity, naturalistic imagery, and the rhetoric of legitimacy all purvey the unequivocal value of peaceful quiet and the transgressive nature of expansionism.

From the first mentions of Arthur, the poet casts shadows of disparagement across his heroic value. Merlin's first allusions to Arthur, for example, cast him out of natural bounds — which is the territory of the illegitimate in the *Gesta*:

> [C]uius preconia fine
> Nullo claudentur, quem semper uiuere credit
> Simplex posteritas, quamuis natura repugnet.
> (146)

> [His praises will be bounded by no limit, and later simpletons will believe that he lives forever, although this is contrary to nature.]

In a world where infractions against nature (such as the sins that disrupt Fortune's natural motion or fish who might dare to cross into their neighbors' aquatic space) define illegitimate action, this assessment of Arthur insinuates criticism. The idea that Arthur exists out of natural bounds ("fine") gains strength at his conception, which takes three nights instead of one (170–72). At the end of the three days, however, Uther takes his own shape right in front of Ygerna (172). Although this innovation resolves all doubts of paternity, the poet remains uneasy about Arthurian value.

Nonetheless, the poet legitimates Arthur's early campaigns by making him a defender of Christian faith. As soon as Arthur is crowned, the narrator notes that he is not corrupted by power and continues to revere Christ (176). Against Cheldric, Arthur defends Christianity, more than territory or ethnicity. The Britons are specifically protected by "clipeo Christi" (Christ's shield) (178–80), and when the Saxons return for the second battle, Arthur exhorts his men against the enemies of the faith and Dubricius makes a more Christianized speech than in the *Historia* (182–84). Arthur's arming reinforces Christ's presence:

> Induit Arturus loricam principe dignam;
> Assumit galeam cuius draco fulgidus auro
> Irradiat conum, clipeum quoque nomine Priduen
> Fert humeris, in quo Christi genetricis ymago
> Fulget; fert gladium, cuius nomine Caliburnus;
> Hastam dextra gerit Ron dictam, cladibus apta.
> (184)

> [Arthur dons a hauberk worthy of a prince; he puts on a helmet on whose crest shines a dragon blazing with gold; a shield named Prid-

wen he bears on his shoulder, on which the image of the Mother of Christ blazes; he bears a sword, whose name is Caliburn; a spear in his right hand he carries named Ron, apt for destruction.]

The poet revises the *Historia*'s structure so that each object is first identified by its common name (the shield and sword descriptions change the most), subtly devaluing the force of their proper names. Moreover, he avoids mentioning Mary by referring to her only in relation to Christ (the poet in fact always invents a Christological reference to Mary [e.g., 86, 188]). Since the poet does not explain how Arthur uses the image on the shield or the origin of Caliburn, the objects lose some of their legitimizing effects. Instead, their power of destruction becomes a force of nature akin to fire ("fulgidus," "fulget"). The blaze will burn the enemy, but it does not specifically augment the hero's stature.

When Arthur meets Cheldric in battle, the *Gesta* represents him as angry (as in the *Historia*), but he does not triumph with the sword:

> Sed cum pars magna diei
> \<Nequiquam\> consumpta foret nec cederet isti
> Aut illi parti uictoria, concitus ira
> Impiger Arturus obstantes fertur in hostes.
> Ut leo, quem stimulant ieiunia uentris inanis,
> In pecudes fertur sternitque et diripit illas,
> Nec stratis sedare famem sed sternere curat,
> Dum quas stare uidet: sic heros marcius hostes
> Impetit et sternit et dissipat; as Stiga solus
> Quingentos mittit.[26]
> (184)

[But when a great part of the day has passed without result and neither side has gained victory, driven by anger the tireless Arthur leaps on the resisting enemy. As a lion, driven by the hunger in its empty belly, leaps on sheep to overthrow and tear them, and does not wish to slake its hunger on the fallen, but rather to overthrow those it sees still standing: so the martial hero attacks, overthrows, and destroys; to the Styx by himself he sends five hundred.]

The extended animal simile replaces Caliburn, and even Arthur's own body. By substituting the lion for Arthur, the poet indicates that a natural desire for blood, rather than legal rights, determines success. Through animalistic simile (which occurs frequently in combat descriptions), the poet weakens the legitimacy of military activity and the ideology of conquest. This particular battle may legitimately defend Insular Christianity, but Arthur does not fight with God's name on his lips. Instead, his success derives from a preternatural hunger that overshadows heroic strength and divine approbation.

The strength of Arthur's anger continues to propel his military success as he confronts Frollo:

> Toto conamine Frollo
> Allidit regis terebrata casside frontem;
> Purpurat arma cruor. Quo uiso flagrat in ira
> Utherides heros et uulneris impete miro
> Impetit auctorem; strictumque tenens Caliburnum
> Adquirit uires extenso corpore toto
> Astantisque uiri galeamque caputque bipertit.
> (194)

[Using all his might, Frollo pierces the king's helmet and strikes his forehead; his armor is purple with blood. At the sight [of it] the heroic son of Uther burns with anger and assaults the author of his wound in a marvelous assault; holding the straight Caliburn he summons his strength with his whole body extended, and he splits his opponent's helmet and head in two.]

The poet takes the occasion to remind the audience of Arthur's genealogy, which also reminds us that Uther never held jurisdiction here. Exceeding his paternal inheritance, Arthur blazes ("flagrat") just as his helmet and shield did in the arming description. The poet's refusal to legitimate force also remains constant, and he overlooks the tempting analogy between this Parisian conquest and the defeat of contemporary Breton enemies. These enemies surface nonetheless in the metaphoric link between wounding and narrative. Arthur's assault on his wound's "author" assigns responsibility for blood; the narrator also authors the blood by describing it. Moreover, the infliction of wounds by the French partly "authors" the *Gesta* itself as a historiography of resistance. And historiography can in fact lead to fatal encounters, as the poet's fear of landing his narrative ship intimates.

While the Briton-Saxon conflict that opens Arthur's reign establishes the bounds between Christian and Pagan, and Frollo's defeat redefines the bounds of Arthur's dominion, the Roman conflict poses the question of right and wrong in legal terms. Here, the limits are more difficult to fix, except that clearly they should not move. Lucius's challenge to Arthur opens the encounter by mobilizing the principle of stability: Lucius suggests that Arthur (like the fish) should be content with his limits: "Sis tantum contentus eo quod iure paterno, / Rex Arture, tenes" (You ought, King Arthur, to be content with the possessions you hold by paternal right) (200). Lucius goes on to denounce Arthur's transgression of established frontiers ("Miratur que fronte tuas excedere"), defining the move as an infraction against justice ("ius"). Finally, Lucius accuses Arthur of illegitimate farming (*gain* in the *Roman de Brut*) and threatens to retaliate with slaughter (200–202). Within the *Gesta*, Lucius's arguments seem valid and irrefutable: Arthur has in fact followed in Conanus's bloody footsteps, illegitimately expanding his territory and cultivating invasive agriculture (which the poet later identifies as a threat to contemporary Breton sovereignty [286]).

Arthur's advisers deploy exactly the same rhetoric to answer these (just) accusations. Hoel invokes *ius* four times in two lines of speech, calling the Roman claim specious and outlining a reversal of the Roman definition of justice without mentioning freedom or enslavement (204). Auguselus continues the argument, invoking the natural laws ("nature . . . legem") offended by the Roman jurisdictional claim; like Caesar, he recalls the terms of ideal action encoded in the fish pool (204). With both sides claiming the same justified authority, legal reasoning itself is shown to be malleable and untrustworthy. Ultimately, the decision to go to war answers to the crowd's plea that Uther's son fight for their freedom ("pro libertate") (206). As in the First Variant, then, freedom becomes the basis for aggressive action. Nonetheless, the entire endeavor is cast into question by the pointed protest of a young Roman woman who watches the men leave for battle (208). The defensive arguments ultimately fail to legitimate themselves, for they rely on always already suspect imperial ambitions.

En route to Rome, the *Gesta* poet, like Wace and Robert of Gloucester, adds Arthur's defeat of the giant of Mont Saint-Michel to the group of battles fought by Caliburn. As in the *Roman de Brut*, the Mont represents an important local border space, and the sword's presence delineates its jurisdictional identity. Although the poet does not name the Mont, the description of the tides leaves no doubt as to the site of the encounter: "cum maris estuat unda, / Insula fit; cum se retrahit, facilis datur illuc / Ingressus pedibus" (when the sea-tide rises, it makes an island; when it retreats, it becomes easily accessible on foot) (210). The horror of the scene, on an island near Brittany, manifests the dangers of colonial invasion. The episode turns the giant into a colonizing figure, instead of the force of indigenous rebellion he represents elsewhere. First, the poet rejects the possibility of colonial contamination by having the nurse comfort herself with the knowledge that Helen died chaste; she repeats to Bedver that Helen died of fright, unviolated (212). Alongside the virginal Helen, the poet casts the giant as a disgrace to nature: he disrupts normal boundaries just like human expansionists. The blood-stained, naked body of the disfigured cannibal conjures a vivid image of preternatural horror, a body from beyond nature disciplined by the sword that reestablishes nature's bounds. When the giant fights Arthur, the noise of the blow he strikes on Arthur's shield fills the shore ("Litora tota replet") (214), signifying the fullness of violence in the border. At his death, the earth itself, his mother, trembles at the forced reimposition of limits (214). Finally, when Arthur recounts his victory over Ritho, Ritho wears the beards of those he has killed and Arthur retaliates by killing him: territorial dominion never enters the discussion. Arthur's victory thus reestablishes original political and natural boundaries. Caliburn, moreover, returns the Mont to its royal Breton origins, as the "Armorican king" founds a church on Helen's grave (216).

As the Armoricans subsequently prepare for battle with the Romans, the poet reiterates the arguments for *quiet*. When Gawain visits the Roman camp, Quintilianus reaffirms that they should be content ("contenti") with the realm of Britain (216). Arthur's preliminary speech repeats that they seek liberty through the sword and defends the honesty of their military tactics, although he concedes that victory may not win them praise even if it brings great rewards (222). Lucius counters with a speech exhorting his men to remember their ancestors and to defend their imperial expansions (224–26). The narrator, however, has the last word in the conflict over legitimation. He apostrophizes to both sides that they will lose everything by exceeding their limits:

> Quis furor, o fortes, pro regno deperituro
> Perdere perpetuum regnum? Perdetis utrumque
> Excedendo modum: contenta Britannia fine
> Debuit esse suo; potuit quoque Roma tributum
> Quod petit iniuste non exegisse.
> (226)

> [What madness, O brave men, drives you to sacrifice the Eternal Kingdom for a transient realm? You will lose both by exceeding the bounds. Britain ought to be content with her own limits; Rome need not have demanded the tribute that she seeks unjustly.]

The ideology articulated in the "contentment" of the fish returns here, as the narrator declares that each side should have stayed within its own "fine" rather than seeking to expand beyond existing borders. The narrator goes on to attribute the conflict to the workings of "hostis / Humani generis" (the enemy of the human race) (226), and to elaborate the various forms of sin; the apostrophe ends by declaring pride the root of the conflict between Britons and Romans (228). The poet's reference to Bellona (230) reinforces Satan's influence, and the fateful battle that can bring no glory begins.

During the battle, the poet attenuates the discourse of legitimation radically. Whereas Arthur's speech to his men in the *Historia* is a rhetorical tour de force of justifications, in the *Gesta* he offers little more than two lines of encouragement to the retreating Armoricans:

> Arturus succurrit eis dicitque: "Fideles
> Et fortes socii, mecum properate; Quirinos

Sternite semimares, titulisque adiungite nostris."
Parent: apparet cui mens adquirere laudem.
(234)

[Arthur succors them and says: "Faithful and bold comrades, hasten with me; overthrow the womanish Quirites and add them to our titles." They prepare: they show which of them has a mind to win glory.]

With no interrogative, no anaphora, and no mention of the sword, the speech focuses only on the acquisition of new titles—and the hollow desire for a glory that the narrator has already judged impossible. As Arthur rushes into the fray, animalistic simile again displaces the sword:

Rex extracto Caliburno
Irruit in Lacios, sternit, ceditque, facitque
Ense uiam; quemcumque semel ferit, ad Stiga mittit;
Sternit equos equitesque simul. Ueluti Iouis ales
Dispergit uolucres, ueluti leo nobilis ire,
Quem stimulat ieiuna fames et uentris inanis
Ingluuie pellente rapax auidusque cruoris,
Se gerit in tauros, rapit hos et dissipat illos:
Sic in Romanos deseuit marcius heros.
Ecce duo reges fato rapiente sinistro
Arturi simul ense cadunt; quoscumque uel hasta
Sauciat aut gladio, uitam cum sanguine fundunt.
(236)

[The king, drawing Caliburn, rushes on the Latins and overthrows and slaughters them and makes a path with his sword; whomever he strikes once, he sends to the Styx; he overthrows horses and horsemen together. As Jupiter's eagle scatters birds, as a lion of noble anger, stimulated by the cravings of hunger and driven by the pangs in its empty belly, fiercely and bloodthirstily hurls himself on bulls, seizing some and tearing others: so the martial hero rages against the Romans. Here two kings are snatched away by an evil fate, both felled by Arthur's sword; whoever is wounded by his spear or sword pours out his life with his blood.]

The reference to the Styx recalls the battle against Cheldric, as does the lion simile. The poet revises his earlier image (and that of the *Historia*) by turning the sheep into bulls, a more formidable foe but still no match for preternatural hunger. Finally, Caliburn has no special role: sword or spear are equally able to generate rivers of blood. As in the *Historia*, the two sides are equally matched and the outcome remains unclear: "quandoque Quirites / Excellunt Britones, illos quandoque Britonni" (sometimes the Quirites excel over the Britons, sometimes the Britons over them) (236). After the nearly accidental Arthurian victory, Arthur marches on Rome: "Sed Deus opposuit tantis sua numina uotis" (but God opposes these lofty ambitions) (238). Although the Roman confrontation began with declarations that force would establish who had the right to Gaul, in the end the sword is impotent as God intervenes to thwart imperial desires.

God punishes Arthur through Mordred's usurpation. The poet never names Guenivere, but the first element of transgression mentioned is the queen's irregular intercourse: "Nam uiolasse thorum regis regnique Britanni / Usurpasse" (He has violated the king's bedchamber and usurped the kingdom of Britain) (238). When the queen then retires to the convent as a widow, the poet criticizes her pretention: "duobus / Nupta tamen uiuisque uiris, incesta secundo" (Yet she remains married to two living men, incestuously to the second) (240). A bigamist adulterer who defies the laws of consanguinity, the queen transgresses spectacularly (presenting a potent lesson for monastic boys). In the spirit of the queen's lawlessness, the final battle displays a complete collapse of stable judgment. As the two sides face off across the river Cambula and brother prepares to fight brother, the narrator observes: "Omnia iura / Natura confusa iacent; concessa uidentur / Fasque nefasque simul, gladio dum uincere captant" (All natural rights lie in confusion; while they wish to conquer with the sword, both right and wrong seem equally legitimate) (240). The confusion of natural rights returns to the limits set out in the fish allegory and reiterated in numerous territorial conflicts. The narrator's apostrophe not only states the judgment explicitly, it exhorts Mordred to repent by offering a history lesson of Briton enslavement and Saxon treachery; weapons themselves are the enemy of honor (240–42). The battle itself resembles originary chaos ("In chaos antiquum") (244), a prehistory devoid of boundaries. Through this confusion of natural limits flows a river of blood:

> Late ruit unda cruoris
> Et fluit in fluuium. Naturam Cambula fontis
> Mutatam stupet esse sui. Transcendit inundans
> Sanguineus torrens ripas et ducit in equor
> Corpora cesorum; plures natare uideres
> Et petere auxilium, quos nondum uita relinquit.
> (244–46)

[A stream of blood spreads wide and flows into the river. The Cambula is amazed that its water is transformed. The swollen, bloody torrent bursts its banks and carries the bodies of the dead to the sea; many whose lives have not yet drained away can be observed swimming and calling for help.]

The description recalls Brutus's defeat of the Greeks (drowned in their own blood) as well as his settlement of the island (amazed at the plow). Unlike the river Achelon, however, the Cambula cannot contain the new river of blood. The fluid that overflows the riparian boundary washes away the lines of difference between the land and the sea, the natural and the monstrous, the legitimate and the transgressive.

In the wake of this dissolution, the boundary of death itself becomes difficult to fix. Indeed, the *Gesta* is elaborately ambiguous in the representation of Arthur's fate. In the prologue to book 9, before Arthur meets Mordred in battle, the poet states clearly that both will die ("Hec causa est utruisque necis") (230). And yet the actual end remains far from clear:

Agmina cuncta fere pereunt regesque ducesque,
Uiuo rege tamen, cui mortia ianua clausa
Creditur, Arturo. Stat et hic pectore uulnus
Letiferum gestans.
(246)

[Almost the whole of the armies and all the kings and dukes are killed, although King Arthur lives, to whom the door of death is believed to be closed. Yet even he stands with a mortal wound in his chest.]

While Arthur has a wound that kills, the poet presents his immortality as only a belief. Leaving Arthur's body in this suspense, the poet begins the idealized *descriptio* of Avalon. The absence of an introduction, however, invites a conflation of Avalon and Britain: one transcends natural differences, and the other erodes them with torrents of blood. The *descriptio*'s culmination casts further doubt on both Arthur's death and his survival:

Regio uirga locis et rebus presidet istis,
Uirginibus stipata suis pulcherrima pulcris
Nimpha, decens uultu, generosis patribus orta,
Consilio pollens, medicine nobilis arte.
Ac simul Arturus regni diadema reliquit
Substituitque sibi regem, se transtulit illuc,
Anno quingeno quadragenoque secundo
Post incarnatum sine patris semine uerbum.
Immodice Iesus Arturus tendit ad aulam
Regis Auallonis, ubi uirgo regia uulnus
Illius tractans, sanati membra reseruat
Ipsa sibi; uiuuntque simul, si credere fas est.
(246–48)

[This place and its benefits are ruled over by a regal maiden: a most beautiful nymph surrounded by comely virgins, she has a pleasing face, is born of noble parents, is wise in counsel, and renowned for her skill in medicine. As soon as Arthur relinquishes the crown of his realm and creates a king in his place, he travels there: it is the five hundred and forty-second year after the Word was made flesh without a father's seed. Badly wounded, he goes to the court of the king of Avalon, where the regal maiden examines his wound and keeps his cured limbs for herself; they live on together, if we are to believe it.]

The poet has no difficulty believing in the maiden's superlative qualities or the island's, only in Arthur's survival. The expanded description may react to the discovery of Arthur's grave at Glastonbury in the late twelfth century,[27] although here the discovery does not lead to certainty about Arthur's death, as it does for Robert of Gloucester. Instead, the poet deftly maintains the certainty of doubt while endowing Avalon with an ordinary political economy. He thus keeps Briton history suspended in the border between past and future, natural and supernatural.

Arthur's liminality nourishes the hope of Briton and Breton restoration, as well as the specter of their transgressions. He exemplifies in every way the *Gesta*'s definitions of illegitimacy: he defies natural limits (at both ends of his life) and expands the realm at sword point. The *Gesta*'s anticolonialism makes Caliburn the emblem of these illegitimate expansions, which in turn justify the Bretons' punishment; the Bretons continue to suffer as a result of their own *inquietatione*. The *Historia*'s Continental itinerary thus concludes on the edge of one absolute certainty force dominates history.

Epilogus historiarum Britanniae

❖

Reactions to the history of forceful domination in Britain have been varied, and continue to be so. I have argued that in the twelfth and thirteenth centuries, a number of these reactions engaged Arthur and his sword. I have maintained, moreover, that these engagements emerged from border regions and that they interrogated relationships among boundaries, coercion, and legitimacy. My investigations have uncovered consistencies that demonstrate that groups on all sides of unequal power share concerns about settlement, reproduction, and historical memory. The different forms of these concerns, meanwhile, testify to unique matrices of regional, ethnic, and social identifications. All of these identifications are "post-colonial" in the sense that they take place after the Norman Conquest of 1066 and are born of the cultural realignments it forced across Europe. Yet the memory of colonial settlement works through historiography in multifarious ways, and its political repercussions were just as varied. Post-colonial Britain, then, sustains malleable and transient discourses of identity, much like more recent postcolonial discourses. This resemblance suggests that the idea of a stable, "precolonial" Middle Ages is as much a fallacy as, say, a precolonial Africa.

My analysis of each narrative began with the representation of topographic and architectural space. For Geoffrey of Monmouth, aestheticized descriptions of Britain and Brittany render them desirable and possessible dominions. Revisions to these descriptions crystallize divergent relations to new dominion. Those who view the island as already in their possession quantify the landscape as a colorless inventory of useful items (the Welsh, Wace, Laȝamon, the Breton poet, Robert of Gloucester). Those who view expansionism negatively moralize topography in order to condemn aggressive authorities (the prose cycle redactors, the Breton poet). Navigable seas surround the settled landscape, and navigable rivers traverse it. Both challenge the stability of boundaries and thus of Insular identity. When Geoffrey defines regional borders along the Severn and the Humber, he grounds dominion in instability. Most subsequent writers dismiss this troubling strategy as they imagine an integrated Insular realm for the benefit of their own regional group (the Welsh, Wace, Laȝamon, Robert). The prose cycle redactors and the Breton poet, however, moralize once again as they pursue critiques of coercive settlement. Once settled, the landscape sustains architectural innovations. In Geoffrey's unstable topography, cities, walls, and monuments reconfigure boundaries and stabilize dominion, usually to the Britons' disadvantage. When topography has been quantified or moralized, architecture signifies established dominion irrespective of boundaries and borders. Indeed, in every subsequent case, the built environment immures the general status of dominion: Hengist's castle leaves the shore to survey Saxon territory (Wace, Laȝamon, the Breton poet, Robert); Stonehenge's colonial histories are long forgotten (Wace, Laȝamon, the prose cycle redactors, the Breton poet, Robert).

Insular settlement extends to the most recent claims of ownership. Each narrative deploys a range of strategies designed to encompass the Britons within new ethnic histories. The universalizing values of strength, craft, and religion all facilitate the crossing of historical boundaries between peoples. Moralization, however, serves divergent ends: the prose cycle tries to dismiss imperial origins but returns to them nonetheless, the *Gesta* condemns them openly, and Robert defends an always already legitimate English dominion. The manipulation of genealogical discourse also patrols the boundaries of ethnic and family identity, constructing historical continuities in the wake of obvious disruptions. Etymology likewise traces ethnic and territorial histories. Geoffrey, equivocal as always, uses language to signify Briton sovereignty as well as its passing. The prose cycle redactors also signify ambivalence through etymology. Meanwhile, other writers emphasize the possessive powers of linguistic interventions (the Welsh, Wace, Laȝamon, the Breton poet, Robert). In each case, histories of *Britain, London,* and *Welsh* codify the dynamics of memory and amnesia in coercive settlement. Finally, translation in general challenges the boundaries of differences while assuming new ones.

The representation of time confronts the limits of memory directly. In Geoffrey's case, the mingling of retrospective commentary with prospective revelations unsettles history's linear progress. Some subsequent writers unravel these equivocations in order to measure progress toward future legitimacy (the Welsh, Wace, Laȝamon, Robert). Others embroil time in further circular confusion in order to critique past and present transgressions (the prose redactors, the Breton poet). Fortune addresses various possibilities—ratifying colonial ambition for Wace, equivocating on expansionist prestige in the prose cycle, and delegitimizing expansion in the *Gesta*. Relations to time address the practice of historiography itself as a boundary mechanism. By rewriting time, historians write their own relation to historical limits and the prospect of the future.

In each narrative, the Arthurian reign opens new historiographical terrain. And in each case, Arthur's relation to his sword defines the nature of legitimate expansion. In Geoffrey's hands, Caliburn signs the prestige of imperial success, in contrast to the story of Briton loss. For the Welsh and Wace, the sword also tracks expansionist values, but with the shade

rs of loss weakened. Laʒamon turns away from Caliburn's military in-
umentality, using the sword to draw Arthur into English dominion.
ne French prose cycle returns to Geoffrey's ambivalence, while demon-
·ating how the sword crosses the border from legitimacy to transgres-
)n. In an anticolonial epic, the *Gesta* turns the sword against imperial
lue, using it as a sign of all that is wrong with expansionism. Finally,
)bert knights the blade, integrating it into the calculation of historical
lue.

The lessons of comparative resemblance suggest that the various dy-
mics activated by coercive contact do not divide neatly along the lines
power. Geoffrey of Monmouth and the French prose cycle redactors,
:hough not invested in the same political structures, manifest similar
ıbivalences toward prestigious authority; they all perform the itiner-
.cy of border subjectivity. Meanwhile, the Welsh and Norman embrace
conquest demonstrates that the colonized and the colonizing often
are more than either would want to admit. Conversely, the Bretons' re-
:tion of force (when compared with their Welsh cousins) reminds us that
·e colonized do not always share what one might think. Finally, the
ıglish assimilation of Briton history shows how confident repossession
n erase historical memory, while leading to divergent judgments of
rce.

Each of these Arthurian histories performs periodic boundary main-
nance for regionalist concepts. As a genealogical narrative of the Insu-
ır landscape, Arthurian historiography can redefine the cultural iden-
:y of topographic spaces and ethnic groups. Border writing does not
erely reflect these processes; it shapes their limits. In this sense, the
rthurian histories' engagements with conflicts over boundaries assim-
ıte them to the narrative struggles that Homi Bhabha identifies as for-
ative for group identity (143). Pierre Bourdieu refers to this same con-
st as the "struggle over representations," whereby narrative has the
)wer to define the mental images that constitute reality, to make and
ımake groups (221). Border writing participates actively in this sym-
)lic struggle, using the story of historical limits to imagine new domin-
ns. Border historiography thus repositions the past in relation to both
·esent and future, teaching the contours of boundaries as it defines them.
he edge, or limit, however, is an ephemeral phenomenon, repeatedly
ritten but never indelibly drawn. In another sense, border writing, like
istoriography in general, buries the past. The repetition of the burial
anslates into a perpetual resurrection. In Arthur's case—"quondam rex
ıturus" (former and future king) (Malory 592)—resurrection in narra-
ve occurs whenever the place or fact of burial becomes culturally sig-
ıficant. The contest over Arthur's body, as well as over boundary for-
ıation in general, embeds violence in the border.

A postcolonialist approach to Arthurian history highlights these coer-
ve encounters and relations between edges and centers in general. The

variability of these dynamics demonstrates vividly that relations amo unequal powers do not progress teleologically from freedom to subjecti to liberation. Indeed, there is nothing inherently colonial, post-coloni or anti-colonial about any particular identification strategy. Mimic: for example, facilitates and resists domination; genealogy and trans: tion perform resemblances and erect intransigent differences. The absen of a clear telos challenges even the notion that the pre-colonial preced the colonial. Contemporary analysts of colonial discourse have in fa demonstrated the fallacy of the "pre-colonial" and of "progress" in mo ern history.[1] By demonstrating that coercive encounters touch and co taminate all parties and that the sacred wholeness of the "pre-colonia is a nostalgic construct of the colonial era, postcolonial studies impli itly deconstruct the myth of a pre-colonial European Middle Ages.[2] Whe for example, Vijay Mishra and Bob Hodge suggest that "the postcoloni is really a splinter in the side of the colonial itself" (411), they open theo to any site of domination. Of course, the frequently political engagemen of postcolonial criticism reasonably demand cultural, historical, and tec nological differentiation. Analogical comparisons run the risk of occlu ing vital contingencies and recolonizing historical subjects. Neverthele: the long history of colonial representation contains numerous contin: ities that quantify and qualify differences.

One clear demonstration of how difference and resemblance confoui colonial teleology comes from an image that rests literally on the edg of pre-colonial, colonial, post-colonial time—Amerigo Vespucci's 149 encounter with indigenes from the "other" side of the sea as produc by Jan van der Straet, Theodor Galle, and Philippe Galle in the 1580s (s figure 3). Since the engraving has become a visual trope of colonial di course analysis over the past twenty-five years,[3] it furnishes an appropi ate site for conclusion. Viewing the image with border eyes, the dynan ics of perennial contamination come into focus. Like Brutus, Amerig stands at the shore, the sails of his ship still billowing with Europe: winds. And like Brutus, he finds inhabited land—only instead of nake male giants, he confronts naked women. He arrives carrying a sword, a astrolabe, and a Christian pennant—which Michel de Certeau has call the "weapons of European meaning" (xxv); Anne McClintock, the "fetis instruments of imperial mastery" (26); and Rosemarie Bank, "metapho for entering history" (41). These artifacts are meant to impose meaning c the female native and her virgin territory. Since de Certeau, critics hav focused on the ambivalences and ambiguities of this erotic encounte Peter Hulme identifies discovery as a ruse of concealment (1), McClii tock exposes its mingling of fears and fantasies about boundary form: tion (26), Louis Montrose draws attention to the ideological implicatioi of the visual oscillation between background and foreground (3–6), Ban speaks of disrupted binaries (42–43), and Margarita Zamora asks wheth the woman rises to greet Amerigo or reclines to invite him onto the han

Figure 3. *America*. Engraving by Theodor Galle, from a drawing by Jan van der Straet. First printed as plate 1 in *Nova Reperta*, 1580. Courtesy of Print Collection, Miriam and Ira D. Wallach Division of Art, Prints, and Photographs, The New York Public Library, Astor, Lenox, and Tilden Foundations; used by permission.

mock (152). I think we can also ask whether she is so naked: her head covering is more elaborate than Amerigo's, she wears some kind of skirt, and she is surrounded by her own instruments of meaning—the leg bracelet, the oar or spear (or scepter?) that rests against the tree, the finely braided hammock (which Tom Conley identifies as a trope of European cartography, squarely connected to Amerigo's astrolabe [307–9]). As with Corineus and Goemagog, then, troubling resemblances weaken the differences between colonizer and colonized (Amerigo even looks a little pregnant).

The natives clearly have their own methods of mastery, as McClintock and Zamora demonstrate by bringing the cannibalistic scene to the fore. As with the giant of Mont Saint-Michel, cannibalism performs a corporeal confusion of differences, linked to colonial aggression. From the background, the newcomer looks more like a fat second course than a new lord. The scene's drama escalates if we cast border eyes across the bounds of Renaissance perspectivalism. In the flat space of medieval perspective, where pointing fingers signify speech, the woman threatens Amerigo with sexual and bodily dismemberment: her gesturing hand points to the skewered thigh that lies on the hill. The severed thigh recalls Laзamon's giant of Mont Saint-Michel and the French prose cycle's Maimed King—along with Geoffrey's Brian, who offers Cadwallader the meat of his own thigh. Long a symbol of phallic sexuality, the thigh conjoins these encounters to both castration and reproduction. The woman's gesture thus speaks the threat of exchange. What's more, in the compressed temporality of medieval iconography, Amerigo replies already: with his phallic sword tucked backward between his legs, he submits.

To see the rest of Amerigo's part in the dialogue, we must return to the drawing that van der Straet actually made (figure 4). Here, Amerigo names the land, the woman, and himself—*America*. Like Brutus's *Britannia*, the feminine form identifies the stakes of exchange and possession. As Amerigo speaks the native, he simultaneously creates and effaces differences of several kinds (gendered, ethnic, corporeal, territorial). When Theodor Galle engraved the image for printing, he silenced this contaminated speech. Yet the preprint image survives, posing a dramatic challenge to postprint epistemology. For in order to produce a properly oriented print, an artist must draw an inverse image. Van der Straet had to imagine, and represent, improper relations (east for west, left for right) before Theodor Galle could engrave it (also improperly) and Philippe Galle could reproduce a proper orientation through printing. In this unsettling process of reversals, van der Straet authorizes himself as artist and Amerigo as historical actor (bottom of figure 4) while simultaneously deforming history. In the engraving process, then, the reversal of conquest precedes conquest itself. Printing—a technology resolutely identified with the progress of modernity—materializes here an intimate relationship with impropriety, illegible history, and unstable power relations.

At the scene of colonization, van der Straet deploys both medieval and modern perspectives; each appears already contaminated with the other. Theodor Galle attenuates some of the resultant ambivalences, successfully blinding most modern critics to the image's "pre-modern" history.[4] Moreover, Galle casts America into the same timeless border as Arthur (always already future) when he replaces the *America* that van der Straet centered on the shore between Amerigo and the native with a rubric at the edge: "Americen Americus retexit & semel vocauit inde semper excitam" (Amerigo repeats *America*, and once he spoke, henceforth was [it/she] always ready) (bottom of figure 3). With "inde semper" (henceforth always), Galle echoes Geoffrey's conclusion about the timeless effects of settlement on the Insular landscape: "brevi tempore ab aevo inhabitatem censere" (after a brief time it seemed to have always been inhabited) (90). Most important, *America* is aroused ("excitam") by repetition ("retexit"), a correction or retextualization that unravels difference: Amerigo originates a colonial refrain already in process. In the rubric, she/it does not even exist as a subject (in "Americen," they are already objects), although her sexuality dominates the naming.

Figure 4. *America*. Drawing by Jan van der Straet (Stradanus), c. 1575. The Metropolitan Museum of Art, Gift of the Estate of James Hazen Hyde, 1959.

Galle's other change, the addition of the southern cross on Amerigo's banner, also obviates origins: Amerigo now arrives already bearing the sign of a knowlege not yet formed. In a subsequent printing as part of Theodor de Bry's collection of European voyages, Galle's rubic was itself removed;[5] since most critics have analyzed this later print, the erasure of paradoxical origins repeatedly dominates colonial discourse analysis.

Comparisons between these images and similar encounter scenes on Britain's shores identify van der Straet and Galle's heteroerotic imagination of colonial contact as historically bounded. In the *longue durée* of colonial representation, this imagination fulfills only one of several colonial desires. Through these perspectives, the "Middle" Ages no longer appear as a subject successfully resisting the "Colonial" Ages that followed. In the "Postcolonial" Ages, colonial discourse analysis can unmoor historical criticism from that epistemological security, setting it adrift among the contentious iterations of history on the edge.

Notes

❖

Prologus historiarum Britanniae

1. Rushdie 343. This initial interpretation of Sisodia emerged from a flurry of cyber-writing as Patricia Clare Ingham and I prepared a panel on colonial Britain for the conference "Comparative Colonialisms" (SUNY Binghamton, October 1997); its authorial origins are in fact long forgotten.

2. Chris Bongie defines the difference between *post-colonial* and *postcolonial* in nearly opposite terms, both situated in a process of linear development toward the liberation of *post/colonial* (12–13); numerous other schemes abound (Trivedi).

3. E.g., Bahri 140–43.

4. Biddick; K. Davis 612–13; Ingham; Warren, "Making Contact" 115–16.

1. Arthurian Border Writing

1. Young 3; Bhattacharyya 15–19.

2. Zumthor 86.

3. Ingham, "Marking Time."

4. Girard d'Albissin 402–3, 407.

5. Alliès 45–69.

6. Schwyzer.

7. *Early Maps*, figs. 6, 8.

8. Quilley.

9. A range of examples appears in Bartlett and MacKay.

10. Lemarignier 79–85.

11. R. Davies, "Frontier" 93–98.

12. Lemarignier 85, 93–95, 101, 143.

13. Whether this insurgency operates outside of fantasy, however, remains uncertain (Fludernik).

14. Klein; Wolf.

15. Holt, *Magna Carta* 43–44.

16. See also Genicot; Spiegel, "Genealogy."

17. Mehrez; Jacquemond.

18. Rollo 123.

19. Bhabha 160–61; Anderson 199–201.

20. De Certeau 85; emphasis in original.

21. Davidson 102–3; Lejeune, "Noms" 142, 150; Oakeshott 14–15.

22. Spitzer, "Name" 50.

23. Davidson 46–48; Oakeshott 5, 54, 57–59.

24. E.g., *Exeter Book* 190–91; O'Curry 254; *Polistorie del Eglise de Christ de Caunterbyre* (cited in R. Fletcher 90).

25. Nichols 200; *Chanson de Roland*, ll. 2297–354.

26. Richardson 174.

27. "The following are the names of military swords:—the sword of Arthur, Caled-vl-wch; the sword of Julius Caesar, Emperor of Rome, Ange glas (*pale death*); the sword of Charles, King of France, Gwdion; the sword of Roland, Durundardd; the sword of Oliver, Llawtyclyr" ("Arthur" 49).

28. *Estoire de Merlin* 231; *Mort le roi Artu* 106.

29. Davidson 10–11; *Chanson de Roland*, l. 2359; *Historia regum Britanniae* 129; *Estoire del saint graal* 522–23.

30. Frantzen 356; Gimeno 54–55; Nichols 199–202.

31. Lejeune, "Noms" 165; Gervase 2:92–93.

32. *Biblia*, "Ad Ephesios" 6:11–17.

33. *Ordines* 28, 43, 54–55; *Pontifical romain* 4:383–84; Ullmann, *Growth* 157, 253.

34. Oakeshott 35, 38, 46, 54, 56, 59.

35. *Pontifical of Magdalen* 92–93; *Benedictional* 144; Jackson; Schramm 20–21; Martindale 225–27.

36. *Sacramentaire* 224; Le Goff 50–56.

37. Flori, *L'essor* 108–11; *Pontifical romain* 3:430, 436, 447, 549.

38. Flori, *Idéologie* 86–99.

39. Culbert; Frantzen; Gimeno; E. Green; Haidu 44–49; Harris; Overing; Van Meter.

40. E.g., Hanning, "Uses of Names" 327–31; Nicole 238; Spitzer, *Linguistics* 41–85.

41. *Biblia*, "Secundum Lucam" 22:38.

42. Field 45–62, 103–78, 200–252; Lecler; Stickler; Ullmann, *Growth* 107, 344–425; Watt.

43. Modern etymologists claim that the Irish *Caladbolg* means "hard notch(er)" (O'Rahilly, l. 4827 n); the Welsh *Caledvwlch*, "strong carving instrument" (*Mabinogion* 1:258); and the French *Durendal*, "strong scythe" (durant dail) (Lejeune, "Noms" 158), "stone master" (Bellamy 273), or "strong flame" (dŭr end'art) (Rohlfs 866–67) (see also Spitzer, "Name").

44. Faral 2:266; e.g., Virgil 8:421, 446; 10:174.

45. Louis 74; Jenkins 12.

46. The modern English *Excalibur* seems to result from the metathesis of the resulting *esc*, rather than from the addition of the prefix *ex*.

47. William of Malmesbury, *De antiquitate* 15.

2. *Historia in marchia*

1. Hanning, *Vision* 145–49. R. Davies characterizes Geoffrey as a "deliberate trader in multiple ambiguities" (*Matter* 6).

2. Courtney 307–9; Hughes 185–96; Tatlock 68–77, 440.

3. E.g., Gillingham, "Context" 100–103, 106–10; Padel 4; Tatlock 396–402.

4. J. Lloyd 460–66.

5. Crick, *Dissemination, Summary; Bern; First Variant*.

6. Remley 460.

7. *Bern* xxxv–xliii, liv–lix.

8. *Bern* xlix; Reeve, review of *First Variant* 124, "Transmission" 107.

9. Dumville 25–29.

10. Davis 12–33.

11. Crouch, *Beaumont*, 38–41.

12. Gillingham, "Context" 114–15.

13. E.g., Gloucester's founding by Claudius (140), Eldol of Gloucester's heroism (184, 206), Eldadus of Gloucester's wisdom (210), and several mentions in Merlin's prophecies (199–201).

14. Amt 30–32.

15. Vine Durling 18.

16. *Brut y Tywysogyon: Red Book* 109–14.

17. Keats-Rohan 65–66.
18. Crouch, *Beaumont* 208.
19. J. Lloyd 465–66.
20. Hanning, *Vision* 142–43.
21. Ibid. 139–40, 164.
22. JanMohamed 103, 114.
23. Lane 16. See also Loxley.
24. Otter 71.
25. Ibid. 71–73.
26. Bloch, *Etymologies* 81.
27. Birns 51.
28. Geoffrey 76.
29. Davies, *Domination* 52–56, 116–17.
30. E. Salter 9.
31. Otter 73.
32. Hanning, *Vision* 149. Jeffrey Cohen insists on this episode's biblical subtext (33–36) and its unifying rather than contaminating effects (61).
33. Otter 74–75.
34. Geoffrey 191.
35. J. Green, "Family" 161–62.
36. Vernon.
37. R. Davies, *Domination* 10, 41–43.
38. Johnson, "Etymologies" 129–30.
39. Gillingham, "Foundations."
40. J. Green, *Aristocracy* 335–42.
41. Mempricius (96), Cunedagius (106), Dunvallo Molmutius (107), Belinus (112), Peredurus (123), Asclepiodotus (149), and Uther (219).
42. E.g., Leir (99–105), five warring kings (109), Belinus and Brennius (109), Ingenius and Peredurus (123), foreigners in the north (205), Gormund (281), and Cadvan (285–86).
43. By rather different means, Shichtman and Finke also link Geoffrey's performance to Merlin's (29).
44. Shichtman and Finke 21–26.
45. Holt, "Politics."
46. Geoffrey 74.
47. Heng suggests that the giant figures the recent trauma of crusader cannibalism (116–26), while Jeffrey Cohen analyzes the episode in terms of bodily containment (37–39).
48. Birns 57–59.
49. Tatlock 279–83.
50. Wright, "Geoffrey of Monmouth and Bede" 36–48, "Geoffrey of Monmouth and Gildas Revisited" 160–62; Flint 453–54.
51. Bhabha 91.
52. Crawford 160 n. 14.
53. Gillingham, "Conquering."
54. R. Davies, *Matter* 11.
55. Flint 457.
56. He divides the north (236), rebuilds towns (237), marches on Rome, and dies at the hand of a close relative.
57. Bern 104 n. 1.
58. Tatlock 308–99; Knight 44–52.
59. Knight 55.
60. Robertson 48–49.
61. Otter 83–84.
62. *First Variant* 192 n. 7.

3. *Ultra Sabrinam in Guallias*

1. Crouch, "March" 261, 263, "Slow Death" 32–36.
2. *Brut y Tywysogyon: Peniarth* 51, 52. Gruffydd's career also inspired a full narrative history, which places him at the multilingual center of international powers (Irish, Danish, and Norman), heir to Trojans, Romans, and noble Hebrews (*History*).
3. Crouch, "March" 276–82, "Slow Death" 34.
4. *Brut y Tywysogyon: Peniarth* 63.
5. R. Davies, *Conquest* 51.
6. Roberts, "Geoffrey."
7. Crick, *Dissemination* 197–98, 214–15; *First Variant* lxxviii–cxiv.
8. *First Variant* lxxvi.
9. Ibid. lxv.
10. R. Davies, *Conquest* 99–100.
11. Leckie 106–7; *First Variant* xlii–xlviii.
12. Geoffrey refers more vaguely to "another name" ("alio nomino" [231]).
13. R. Davies, *Conquest* 181, 200–201.
14. Hammer 18.
15. *First Variant* 192 n. 7.
16. Ibid. lxxiii, lxxix–lxxx.
17. Mempricius rules "regni monarchiam" (20), Cunedagius "tocius regni" (28), Dunvallo "totam Britanniam" (30), Belinus "tocius Britannie" (33), Marius "totum regnum" (63), Octavius "potestas Britannie" (71–72), Maximianus "regum Britanniae" (75) (instead of "regnum Britanniae insulae" [Geoffrey 160]), and Malgo "totam Britanniam" (176); Augustine and Dinoot debate the ecclesiastical *regnum* (178–79).
18. R. Davies, *Domination* 58–65; Lydon 49–51.
19. *Calendar* 86 (a paraphrase and partial citation of the letter, not a complete edition).
20. Cited in D. Lloyd 171.
21. Avent; R. Davies, *Domination* 40–44.
22. Roberts, "Tales" 210–13.
23. Leckie 104–5, 107–8; *First Variant* lxx.
24. Crick, *Dissemination* 197.
25. R. Davies, *Conquest* 57–59, 122–29.
26. Ibid. 18–19.
27. *First Variant* l–liii.
28. Ibid., 4; Geoffrey 76.
29. While Geoffrey explains tersely, "Hortatur Aurelius christianos, monet Hengistis paganos" (207), First Variant redactors elaborate while eliminating religious references: "Hortatur Aurelius *suos ut pro patria et libertate uiriliter pugnent.* Monet Hengistus *Saxones quatinus omni spe fuge postposita fortiter feriant*" (118). Moreover, the narrator does not interject any direct encouragement of the Britons.
30. *First Variant* xxxii.
31. R. Davies, *Conquest* 16–19.
32. *First Variant* lxxi.
33. Ibid. lxiv n. 98; Virgil, 1:313; 12:165.
34. Tilliette 220 n. 17.
35. R. Davies, *Conquest* 66.
36. R. Davies, "Law."
37. *First Variant* 174; Geoffrey 278.
38. R. Davies, *Conquest* 292–307.
39. Ibid. 236–51; *Brut y Tywysogyon: Red Book* 175–239.
40. R. Davies, *Conquest* 308–54.
41. *Brut y Tywysogyon: Peniarth* 110.
42. *Brut y Tywysogyon: Red Book* 247–57; *Brut y Tywysogyon: Peniarth* 114.

43. *Brut y Tywysogyon: Red Book* 257–58; *Brut y Tywysogyon: Peniarth* 115.
44. *Brut y Tywysogyon: Red Book* 263.
45. Ibid. 267–69; *Brut y Tywysogyon: Peniarth* 120–21; *Annales Monastici* 2:401–2.
46. Thornton 10–12, 18.
47. *Registrum* 2:435–92, 3:774–78.
48. Roberts, ed., xxxiv–xxxvi.
49. Reiss 107.
50. *Brut y Brenhinedd* 193, 199–200. Ian Wood argues that stories of Augustine's difficulties originated in Wales (although without refering to the *Brut*).
51. *Brut y Brenhinedd* 163.
52. Roberts, ed., 57–61.
53. Jesus College LXI 536.
54. Brutus arrives at the island 1,200 years after the Flood (22), Madoc dies 1,274 years after (27), and so on.
55. R. Davies, *Conquest* 16–19. Llywelyn's genealogy testifies to this shift.
56. Reiss 102.
57. *Cyfranc* 8–9; *Trioedd* 84.
58. I cite from the translation in *Brut y Brenhinedd*; a similar version is translated in Jesus College LXI 302–6.
59. *Cyfranc* xxxii–xxxiii; *Troiedd* 84–86.
60. *Cyfranc* 1.
61. Ibid. 5; Jesus College LXI 304.

4. *Here to Engelonde*

1. Allen, "Implied" 137.
2. Laȝamon, ll. 4775, 8071, 8100–225, 8290, 8340, 9535, 13580, 15478, 15618 ff.
3. Robert of Gloucester, ll. 2679 ff., 7722–8911, 9925, 10560, 11138 ff.
4. Mason 162–63; Robert, l. 10559.
5. Prestwich 81; Robert, ll. 10561, 10655, 11786.
6. Howell 49–70, 168–70; Prestwich 84–90; Robert, ll. 10986–1005.
7. Turville-Petre 9.
8. Laing identifies the Otho dialect as more southerly (46). The text is edited on the pages facing the Caligula manuscript text in Brooke and Leslie's edition; on dating, see Bryan, *Collaborative* 183–90.
9. Watson; Bryan, *Collaborative* 48–50; Cannon 203.
10. Bryan, *Collaborative* 64–65, 77–78, 92–94.
11. E.g., Donoghue 544.
12. Mercatanti Corsi 302–3; E. Salter 66–70; Weinberg summarizes the complete range of regionalist evidence.
13. Le Saux, "Laȝamon's Welsh" 389–93; Tatlock 501. On English-Welsh bilingualism, see Bullock-Davies and Richards. An earlier version of the *Brut* may even have been copied in Wales (Le Saux, "Listening").
14. Everett 24–25, 45; Rampolla 190; E. Salter 68–69; Stanley, "Laȝamon's Antiquarian" 30.
15. Allen, "*Eorles*" 15–16.
16. Allen, "Implied" 136.
17. E.g., generosity of kings with food (ll. 3025, 3259, 4040, etc.); food and kitchen items at Arthur's feast (ll. 9945 ff.); children's quarrels (l. 7776); Brian as wine merchant (ll. 15311–19); payment for services (ll. 9441–43); Vortimer's promises to the land tillers (l. 7409); and the role of peasants in wars (ll. 7300, 10730, 15151).
18. Laȝamon, ll. 1309–15, 1897–906, 7575, 8840, 12730, 13924, 14180; 2140 ff.; 5815–25, 9795.

19. Ibid., ll. 3246–49, 9335, 11189–93, 13094–100, 14225.
20. Johnson, "Reading" 152; Allen, trans, l. 13526.
21. Gillingham, "Beginnings" 393; Short.
22. E. Salter 39–66; Stanly, "Laȝamon's Un-Anglo-Saxon."
23. E. Salter 33–34; Turville-Petre 60. Tiller emphasizes the violence of this conquest (19–21, 143, 152).
24. Carruthers 165–70.
25. Bryan, *Collaborative* 37–46.
26. Laȝamon, ll. 4964–75; the Otho redactor suppresses the runes.
27. Gaimar, ll. 6429–525. Since the Arthurian portion has not survived, I have not studied Gaimar here.
28. Herbert 4:15, 61–62, 372.
29. Turville-Petre 74.
30. E.g., Robert, ll. 1631, 6517, 7323, 10628.
31. Ibid., ll. 624–25, 859–60.
32. Ibid., ll. 1329–32, 1358–61.
33. Gransden, *Historical Writing* 1:432–38; Robert, ll. 8886–909, 11581–95. Local references are too numerous to catalog here.
34. Robert 1:xv–xxxii; Turville-Petre 76.
35. E.g., the *commendacio hybernie* that accompanies the settlement of Ireland (ll. 997–1014) and the dating of Caesar's arrival in England as sixty years before Christ's birth (l. 1068).
36. Robert's own reviser used the English *Brut* as an additional source (Robert 1:xxxiii–xxxvii).
37. Turville-Petre 142.
38. E.g., Laȝamon, ll. 478–79, 560–63, 1011.
39. E.g., ibid., ll. 662, 4435.
40. Robert, ll. 1044, 2223, 3190.
41. Laȝamon, ll. 7087, 7089; Wace gives no topographical description.
42. Ibid., ll. 8577–80, 8622–23.
43. Ibid., ll. 144337, 14668–75.
44. Ibid., ll. 8471, 8568, 8570, 8899, 8903.
45. For Robert, "round table" is not an object but a social event, as much chivalric as imperial (ll. 3881, 3889, 3902, 3916).
46. Robert, ll. 9275–77, 10980–85, 11484–85, 11618–21.
47. Allen, trans., xxvii; Brewer 204.
48. E.g., Kirby 53–55; Allen, trans., l. 7. Interestingly, both the oldest and the newest translations accept Laȝamon's radical view (Madden; Barron and Wienberg).
49. Robert later narrates the founding of Bath and Stonehenge (ll. 660–75, 3060 ff.).
50. Robert, ll. 445, 660, 1762, 2379, 3047, 3056, 3106, 7464, 8436.
51. Le Saux, *Laȝamon's "Brut"* 39. The Otho redactor takes the process a step further, shifting focus to territory and away from regnal genealogy (Bryan, *Collaborative* 85–94).
52. Le Saux, "Relations."
53. Laȝamon, ll. 12930, 12957; Bryan, "Laȝamon's Four Helens" 70.
54. Robert, ll. 1057–67, 1886–94, 1989–238. When Caesar decides to warn the Britons of his intent to conquer, he does cite chivalric courtesy ("hende") rather than fear of offending his ancestors.
55. Vincent, Albanus, and Christine appear in the *South English Legendary* (25–31, 238–40, 315–26); Albanus, Foy, and Vincent, in the *Early South-English Legendary* (67–70, 83–86, 184–89).
56. Laȝamon, ll. 7255–57, Robert, ll. 2945–48.
57. Robert, ll. 2535–36, 2541–42, 2560–64.
58. Laȝamon, ll. 13635–70, 14115–22; Robert, ll. 4522, 4528.

59. Laȝamon, ll. 16670–78; Allen, trans., 466.
60. Laȝamon, ll. 15614, 15781; the Otho redactor again substitutes "England" (l. 15781) (there is no line corresponding to l. 15614).
61. Le Saux, *Laȝamon's "Brut"* 166.
62. Johnson, "Reading" 155–56.
63. Laȝamon, l. 15870; Bryan, "Laȝamon's Four Helens" 72.
64. Laȝamon, ll. 15969–70, 15974–77.
65. Le Saux, *Laȝamon's "Brut"* 229; Wright likewise dismisses the idea that Laȝamon distinguishes Angles from Saxons ("Angles").
66. E.g., Robert, ll. 56, 2121 ff., 2935ff., 7324.
67. Turville-Petre 94.
68. Stein 108–9.
69. Turville-Petre 89–91.
70. Robert, ll. 8068–547, 9866 ff., 8520, 8808–17, 9075 ff., 9640 ff., 9735 ff., 9866 ff., 9947 ff., 10150 ff.
71. Ibid., ll. 7876–8000, 8580–673.
72. Ibid., ll. 8800–817, 8510–46.
73. E.g., ibid., ll. 10165–91, 10645.
74. Ibid., ll. 9909–23, 10245, 10972, 11634–41, 11935–40.
75. Ibid., ll. 5150–51, 5199–5200, 5210–15.
76. Turville-Petre 19 n. 47.
77. Robert, ll. 7250, 8064, 8635–51, 8938–79; Turville-Petre 18–19, 93.
78. Turville-Petre 94–95.
79. Robert, ll. 7566–71, 7631, 7638, 7645, 8065, 8730–51.
80. Turville-Petre 98.
81. Robert, ll. 9121, 9993–95, 10112–23.
82. Maddicott 5, 75–76, 229–32, 361–63.
83. Ibid. 161, 317–18.
84. Short 259.
85. Turville-Petre 20–21.
86. Stanley, "Laȝamon's Antiquarian" 30–33; Donoghue 546–50.
87. E.g., *Pendragon* (l. 9090), *Cernel* (ll. 14809–17).
88. Laȝamon, ll. 6950–55 (the Otho redactor heightens the effect by giving each day a half line and presenting them in chronological order); Robert, ll. 2431 ff., 4699 ff.
89. E.g., Allen, trans. l. 3547; Barron and Weinberg, l. 3547.
90. Le Saux, *Laȝamon's "Brut"* 83–92.
91. Gillingham, "Beginnings" 398.
92. E. Salter 34–35. Walter Map describes Gilbert Foliot as a man versed in Latin, French, and English (18); Roger Bacon affirms that English, French, and Latin are spoken in England (1:433).
93. Laȝamon, l. 13099; the Otho redactor reverses the order of the languages.
94. Gillingham, "Beginnings" 396.
95. Laȝamon, ll. 4505, 4581; e.g., Robert, ll. 475–77, 4898, 10548.
96. E.g., Laȝamon, ll. 960, 5410, 5815, 5895.
97. E.g., Robert, ll. 10825, 10857, 11069, 11249.
98. Le Saux, "Narrative Rhythm" 47.
99. Turville-Petre 73.
100. Robert, ll. 190–205, 478–82.
101. E.g., ibid., ll. 645–47, 893–900, 946–52.
102. Ibid., ll. 1068, 1093–94, 1522–24, 4732–38, 7515, 8664–69.
103. Ibid., ll. 1368–71, 1405–9.
104. E.g., ibid., ll. 1525, 3373, 4136, 4681, 4753, 5890, 6482, 6497, 10524.
105. E.g., ibid., ll. 2815, 3190–94, 3201–4, 3849, 4701, 6741, 7285, 7301, 7925, 9345.
106. Donoghue 554.

107. Laȝamon, ll. 10543–45; Allen, trans., 446–47.
108. Everett 36; Le Saux, *Laȝamon's "Brut"* 197–200.
109. Le Saux, "Narrative Rhythm" 69.
110. Laȝamon, ll. 14055–59, 14065–66, 14082–83.
111. Allen, trans., 461; Barron and Weinberg 887–88.
112. Laȝamon, ll. 9405–19, 11500–517, 14277–82, 14288–97.
113. Le Saux, *Laȝamon's "Brut"* 230.
114. Donoghue 563.
115. Le Saux, *Laȝamon's "Brut"* 230.
116. Robert, ll. 5538–43, 8148, 9450, 9787.
117. "Elegy" 82, 92.
118. Robert, ll. 3881, 3889, 3902, 3916.
119. Ibid., ll. 4093, 4378, 4452, 5793; Geoffrey 272.
120. Ibid., ll. 4685, 4692, 4736–37.
121. Riddy 326.

5. *L'enor d'Engleterre*

1. Cited in Richard 37–38.
2. Hollister 17–57.
3. Potts, "*Atque*"; Crouch, "Normans" 59.
4. Bates "Normandy," "Rise"; Crouch, "Normans," "Robert"; J. Green, "Unity."
5. Crick, *Dissemination* 180–81, 187–88, 204–5, 214; Crick, *Summary* 125, 127, 150.
6. *Bern* xxxv–xliii, lix; Dumville 22–25.
7. *Bern* liv–lix.
8. Wace, *Roman de Brut*, ll. 3849–54, 9761–72, 10107–32, 11141–52.
9. Ibid., ll. 795, 12190, 13927.
10. Knight 38–66; Ingledew 685.
11. Caldwell; Leckie 116; *First Variant* liv–lxx.
12. Wace, *Roman de Brut*, ll. 21 ff., 2478 ff., 3287 ff., 6040 ff., 11192–238, 12061–64.
13. Wace, *Roman de Rou*, ll. 5305–12.
14. Francis 83–84.
15. Houck 163–64, 207–8, 219–28; Blanchet.
16. Wace, *Roman de Brut*, ll. 1532–34.
17. Ibid., ll. 7539–40, 9015–16, 9787–98, 10286, 13275, 13282–90, 13291–93.
18. Marcia likewise translates with great "engin" (ibid., ll. 3335–48); Vine Durling 27–30.
19. Rollo 144–45.
20. Hanning, *Individual* 12–13.
21. He loses his patron's support before finishing the work (Gouttebroze).
22. Wace, *Roman de Brut*, ll. 3822, 5173–84.
23. Schmolke-Hasselmann, "Round Table" 61–62.
24. Holmes 61.
25. Tyson 194–95.
26. White.
27. Amt 21, 26–28.
28. Lejeune, "Rôle" 45; Legge 139.
29. *Recueil* 3:4–9.
30. Broich 43–54; Haskins 74.
31. Ransford.
32. Ingledew 693–94.
33. Ritchie 347–48.
34. Broich 54–63; Haskins 75.

35. Lejeune, "Rôle" 52–53.
36. Ibid. 25.
37. Wace, *Roman de Rou*, ll. 5311, 5313–16.
38. Green, "Unity" 129–32.
39. Blacker, *Faces* 97.
40. Cingolani.
41. Wace, *Roman de Brut*, ll. 1667, 2044, 2316, 2599, 3559–60.
42. Ibid., ll. 3315–26, 3289–92.
43. Variants underscore the equivalence between cultivated land and inheritance: for *desertee*, two redactors substitute *desheritez* and one *desgastee*.
44. Shopkow.
45. Wace, *Roman de Brut*, ll. 1829–34, 9781–84, 12485–94, 13036.
46. Ibid., ll. 5153–60, 5199–208, 11753–58; 4888–90, 5102–6.
47. Hanning, *Individual* 105–38.
48. One redactor identifies the equal legitimacy of force and deception explicitly: "Engin et force deit l'en faire" (Wace, *Roman de Brut*, l. 363 n.).
49. Wace, *Roman de Brut*, ll. 2403–4, 2420–22.
50. *Bern* 92; *First Variant* 125; Wace, *Roman de Brut*, ll. 8147–50.
51. *Bern* 3, *First Variant* 3.
52. Reynolds 254–55.
53. Searle 161–75.
54. Searle 167–77.
55. Wace, *Roman de Brut*, ll. 3834–38, *Roman de Rou* 1:12, l. 304.
56. Blacker, "Transformations" 67.
57. Wace, *Roman de Brut*, ll. 2183–84, 2207–10.
58. Ibid., ll. 2890, 3903–60, 5048, 9611–40, 10171, 11132, 13631–42, 14381–90, 14609–16, 14401–2.
59. Ibid., ll. 4855–76, 13842–64.
60. Ibid., ll. 9516–21, 13461–62.
61. Ibid., ll. 946, 1597, 2310, 5086, 5093, 10360; Vine Durling 19, 26.
62. Some redactors resist these effects by revising lines 7–8: one specifies the language of the source ("Cil reconte la verité / Qui lo Latin a translaté") and another the result ("Del livre oez la verité / Qui en romanz est translaté").
63. Rollo 112.
64. One Insular redactor rehistoricizes the account by amending the name to *Engellonde* (l. 1198 n.).
65. I discuss Cernel's etymology at length in "Memory."
66. Wace, *Roman de Brut*, ll. 1223–30, 1233–35, 1521–24.
67. Brosnahan lists the proverbs exhaustively.
68. Blacker, "Transformations" 62.
69. Leckie 111–12.
70. Schmolke-Hasselmann, "Round Table" 47–49.
71. Wace, *Roman de Rou*, 1:3, ll. 5–6, 45–46.
72. Holt, "Politics"; W. Warren 332–33.
73. Whether the silence has anything to do with the shame of crusader cannibalism (Heng 140) is another matter. Finke and Shichtman also link the episode to boundary issues, but in rather general terms that cast the giant as a figure of the purely foreign.
74. Potts, "Normandy."
75. Dufief 98–99.
76. Ibid. 81–101.
77. One redactor extends the litany of aggression by inserting two additional lines between ll. 11726 and 11727: "Et par bataille la tandra / Et par bataille la randra" (And by battle he'll hold it, and by battle he'll take it).

6. *En la marche de Gaule*

1. Micha 87; *Lancelot* 7:2 (subsequent citations from this edition).
2. Burns, *Arthurian* 114.
3. *Estoire del saint graal* xi–xiv, lvi–lix; Stones.
4. Lot 140–51 and Frappier 22–23 (Champagne); Micha 294 (Berry); Bloch, *Medieval* 44.
5. Putter.
6. Benton, "Collaborative" 52; Bur, "Comtes" 32; Stirnemann 204–6, 212.
7. Frappier 151–72; Stirnemann 204–9. Another early manuscript, however, seems to have originated in Paris (Stones). Perhaps it witnesses a royal appropriation of an aristocratic form, similar to the royal French prose chronicles (Spiegel 269 ff.).
8. Crick, *Dissemination* 210–13.
9. Bur, "Comtes" 25–27.
10. Bur, *Formation* 283–92, "Comtes" 29.
11. Bur, "Quelques" 347.
12. Bur, "Comtes" 30–32.
13. Baldwin 101–25.
14. Bur, "Rôle" 244–45; Evergates.
15. D'Arbois de Jubainville 4.1:101–7; Lemarignier 156, 166–67.
16. Bur, *Formation* 504, "Comtes" 32.
17. Bloch, *Etymologies* 198–227, *Medieval* 8–12, 25–28, 202–10; Schmolke-Hasselmann, *Arthurische*.
18. Spiegel, *Romancing* 126; Brandsma 64–65; Hanning, "Arthurian" 356–57; Kennedy; Lagorio 1–2; Méla 386; Hartman.
19. Burns, *Arthurian* 11–12; *Estoire del saint graal* xi–xil.
20. Kittay and Godzich 179–83.
21. Baumgartner, "Choix" 13; Kittay and Godzich 34, 53–58; Nimis 402; Perret 175.
22. Kittay and Godzich 183.
23. Ibid. 125.
24. Burns, "*Voie*" 166.
25. Kittay and Godzich 207.
26. Spiegel, *Romancing* 158–59, 269 ff.; Bloch, *Medieval* 224–58; Boutet, "Arthur" 50.
27. Cited in Kennedy 82–83.
28. Shell 28–29.
29. Todorov 129; Leupin 153.
30. Baumgartner, *L'arbre* 146–54; Lagorio.
31. Berthelot 471–88; Burns 7–54; Leupin 25–53.
32. Leupin 25–30.
33. Lepick 520–24.
34. Ibid. 525.
35. Türk 159–60.
36. Baumgartner, "Espace" 109–10.
37. Türk 162, 168–69.
38. Benton, "Court" 576; Map, *De nugis* 225–26.
39. E.g., Narrow March (*Lancelot* 8:272), Beyond the Marches (*Lancelot* 7:96), Marcoise (*Queste* 145); Micha 278; Méla 334.
40. *Estoire* 3, 53–60.
41. E.g., *Estoire* 187–95, 249–57; *Queste* 93–115; Szkilnik, *Archipel* 8, 20–21.
42. *Estoire* 22, 40–42.
43. D'Arbois de Jubainville 4.1:110–95.
44. *Estoire* 98; *Mort* 205–7.
45. Baumgartner, "Joseph" 11.
46. *Estoire* 453–72, 484, 513–24, 545, 549; Baumgartner, "Joseph."
47. *Lancelot* 1:3, 8:128–30.

48. *Merlin* 175, 229, 286, 370, passim.
49. Pickford.
50. Baumgartner, "Lancelot" 28–31.
51. Bloch, *Etymologies* 219.
52. Ibid. 219–21, 224–25.
53. Baumgartner, "From Lancelot" 16.
54. Morris argues that these and other resistances derive from nationalistically "French" interests ("King Arthur" 122–29).
55. Burns, *Arthurian* 45.
56. Leupin 71.
57. Bloch, *Etymologies* 209–10; Méla 369–71; Leupin 86, 174.
58. *Lancelot* 1:1; Leupin 116; Plummer; Mieszkowski.
59. Citation in Leupin 90; Bloch, *Etymologies* 210–12.
60. Leupin 48.
61. *Estoire* 73, 155, 261, 562.
62. Banitt, *Étude* 191, "Poterim"; Levy; Signer xxii; Lambert and Brandin; Strong 56; Blondheim 2:48; Spitzer, Review 128.
63. William of Malmesbury, *Polyhistor* 62.
64. Isidore 31, 33; Bloch, *Etymologies* 39–41; Dahan 239–40; Sapir Abulafia 96–97, 133; Jordan 15.
65. Jordan 16; Dahan 520–27; Trachtenberg.
66. Hugh 32; Jeremy Cohen, "Scholarship" 319.
67. Grabois 629; Dahan 276; Pakter 71.
68. Jeremy Cohen, "Scholarship" 326, *Friars*; Dahan 258–63; Chazan, *Daggers, Medieval* 124–33.
69. Stow 241.
70. Grayzel, "Papal."
71. Stow 238–51; Synan 103–6; Chazan, *Medieval* 149.
72. Stow 235–38; Chazan, *Medieval* 101–39; Taitz 147–81.
73. Jeremy Cohen, "Scholarship" 324.
74. Stow 98–99, 278; Chazan, *Medieval* 69–70; Menache.
75. Taitz 150.
76. Chazan, *Medieval* 75; Jordan 38–39, 69.
77. Jordan 88; Grayzel, *Church* 351–56; Taitz 166.
78. Jordan 97.
79. Chazan, *Medieval* 107; Taitz 167–68.
80. Jordan 101.
81. Ibid. 133.
82. E.g., *Estoire* 28, 39, 47, 188–95, 327, 349, 366, 411, 484, 551; 546; Halász 180–84.
83. *Queste* 280; *Mort*, 263.
84. *Estoire* 23, 69; *Merlin* 96.
85. Bloch, *Etymologies* 1–5, 212–15.
86. Chase 129–32; Rockwell 187–228.
87. Micha 91–93.
88. Burns, *Arthurian* 44–45.
89. Ibid. 85–112; Méla 342 ff.
90. Baumgartner, *L'arbre* 94–95, 137.
91. Todorov 141–42.
92. Burns, *Arthurian* 172.
93. *Estoire* 346; *Mort* 221, 226–27, 243, 247.
94. *Queste* 211; Hanning, *Individual* 106.
95. The twelve manuscripts that witness this episode transmit the *Merlin* in conjunction with both the *Estoire* and the *Lancelot* (Pickens 108), firmly establishing their mutual entanglements.

96. Benoît, *Roman de Troie*, ll. 980–1023.
97. Vielliard 7.
98. Jung 504.
99. Later, Arthur grants Merlin complete dominion over himself and his lands (378).
100. Beaune 344–47.
101. Flori, "L'épée."
102. *Lancelot* 8:234–35, 388, 416; 1:111.
103. Leupin 74 n. 15.
104. Ibid. 137.
105. Williams 395.
106. *Lancelot* 2:218–19, 261.
107. Williams 396.
108. Warren, "Marmiadoise" 145.
109. The final battle, for example, begins at least three times (118, 125, 142).
110. *Mort* 3, 61–65, 107–10; McCracken 105–8.
111. Vinaver 519–25.
112. Frappier 152–64.
113. Grisward 300–304; citation in Burns, *Arthurian* 164.
114. Boutet, *Charlemagne*, e.g., 171, 603; Boutet, "La fin" 45–46.
115. Lepick 518; Burns, *Arthurian* 167.

7. *In Armoricam*

1. Montigny 177–79.
2. *Gesta regum* xcix–ciii.
3. William of Newburgh 1:235.
4. Hillion.
5. Montigny 137.
6. Chédeville and Tonnerre 104.
7. Galliou and Jones 199–200.
8. Montigny 143–61.
9. Ibid. 162–68, 170–75.
10. Fleuriot, "Histoires" 100.
11. Montigny 188–209.
12. Chédeville and Tonnerre 97.
13. Fleuriot, "Prophéties" 161–64; Curtius 128–29.
14. *Gesta regum* liii–liv.
15. Brett 17.
16. E.g., Hector (18), Priam (100, 282), and Brutus (236, 282).
17. Fleuriot, "Histoires" 107.
18. E.g., Sabines, Latins, Italians, Quirites, and Romans—all from Rome (38, 218, 220).
19. W. Smith 95.
20. E.g., the narrator accuses Androgeus of selling the Britons into Roman slavery (80–82), Conanus's speech is eliminated (116), and the archbishop does not reason genealogically with Aldroenus of Armorica (120).
21. *Gesta regum* liv, lix.
22. *Gesta regum* xlviii–xlix.
23. Morris, "*Gesta*" 71.
24. E.g., *Gesta regum* 20, 22, 180, 236.
25. Morris notes, without reference to the fish, "The idea that each nation should remain within its natural boundaries . . . is at the root of the *Gesta*" ("*Gesta*" 98).
26. The angle brackets indicate the editor's emendation.
27. Morris, "*Gesta*" 95.

Epilogus historiarum Britanniae

1. Appiah; McClintock; Suleri; Young 164–65.

2. Ingham, " 'In Contrayez Straunge.' "

3. E.g., de Certeau (1975); Hulme (1986); Montrose (1991); Rabasa (1993); Zamora (1993); McClintock (1995); Conley (1996); Bank (1999). The first printing, by Philippe Galle, is reproduced in Stegman.

4. Hulme (268 n. 8) and Montrose (35 n. 5) both mention the drawing in passing; only Rabasa compares the two images, analyzing the perspectival effects of rubrication (23–48).

5. Rabasa 23, 29, 37.

Bibliography

❖

Primary Sources

Abbreviations

BH   *British History and the Welsh Annals.* Ed. and trans. John Morris. London: Phillimore, 1980.

EETS   Early English Text Society

HRB   *The "Historia regum Britannie" of Geoffrey of Monmouth.* Ed. Neil Wright. 5 vols. Cambridge: Brewer, 1985–91.

PL   *Patrologia Latina.* Ed. J.-P. Migne.

RB   Rerum Britannicarum Medii Aevi Scriptores

Vulgate   *The Vulgate Version of the Arthurian Romances.* Ed. Oskar Sommer. Washington, D.C.: Carnegie Institute, 1908–16.

Aelred of Rievaulx. *Opera Omnia. PL* 195 (1855).

Alfred. *King Alfred's West-Saxon Version of Gregory's Pastoral Care.* Ed. Henry Sweet. EETS o.s. 45. London: Oxford University Press, 1871.

André. "Le roman des franceis." In *Études de langue et de littérature du moyen âge offertes à Félix Lecoy,* ed. Anthony J. Holden, 213–33. Paris: Champion, 1973.

Annales Cambriae. In *BH,* 44–49, 85–91.

Annales Monastici. Ed. Henry Richards Luard. RB 36. London, 1865.

"Arthur and His Knights." *Archaeologia Cambrensis* 1 (1847): 48–49.

Bacon, Roger. *Opera.* Ed. J. S. Brewer. RB 76. London: Longman, 1859.

Bede. *Bede's Ecclesiastical History of the English People.* Ed. and trans. Bertram Colgrave and R. A. B. Mynors. Oxford: Clarendon Press, 1969.

The Benedictional of Archbishop Robert. Ed. H. A. Wilson. London: Harrison and Son, 1903.

Benoît de Sainte-Maure. *Chronique des ducs de Normandie.* Ed. Francisque Michel. Paris: Imprimerie Royale, 1836–44.

———. *Le roman de Troie.* Ed. Léopold Constans. Paris: Firmin Didot, 1904–12.

Beowulf. Ed. and trans. Michael Swanton. Manchester: Manchester University Press, 1978.

Bern, Burgerbibliothek, MS 568. HRB. Vol. 1. 1985.

Biblia sacra. Stuttgart: Württembergische Bibelanstalt, 1969.

Bleddyn Fardd. "Elegy for Llywelyn ap Gruffudd." In *Welsh Verse,* trans. Tony Conran, 165–66. Bridgend, Glamorgan: Poetry Wales Press, 1986.

Brenhinedd y Saesson; or, The Kings of the Saxons. Ed. and trans. Thomas Jones. Cardiff: University of Wales Press, 1971.

Brut Dingestow. Ed. Henry Lewis. Cardiff: University of Wales Press, 1942.

Brut y Brenhinedd: Cotton Cleopatra Version. Ed. John J. Parry. Cambridge: Medieval Academy of America, 1937.

Brut y Tywysogyon; or, The Chronicle of the Princes: Peniarth Ms. 20 Version. Trans. Thomas Jones. Cardiff: University of Wales Press, 1952.

Brut y Tywysogyon; or, The Chronicle of the Princes: Red Book of Hergest Version. Ed. and trans. Thomas Jones. Cardiff: University of Wales Press, 1955.

Calendar of Ancient Correspondence concerning Wales. Ed. J. Goronwy Edwards. Cardiff: Cardiff University Press, 1935.

La chanson de Roland. Ed. and trans. Ian Short. Paris: Librairie générale française, 1990.

Crispin, Gilbert. "Disputatio Iudei et Christiani." *PL* 159 (1854): 1005–36.

Cyfranc Lludd a Llefelys. Ed. Brynley F. Roberts. Dublin: Dublin Institute for Advanced Studies, 1975.

"Description of England." Ed. Alexander Bell. In *Anglo-Norman Anniversary Essays,* ed. Ian Short, 38–47. London: Anglo-Norman Text Society, 1993.

Dudo de Saint-Quentin. *De moribus et actis primorum Normanniae ducum.* Ed. J. Lair. Caen: F. Le Blanc-Hardel, 1865.

The Early South-English Legendary. Ed. Carl Horstmann. EETS 87. London: Trübner, 1887.

"Elegy on the Death of Edward I." In *Anglo-Norman Political Songs,* ed. Isabel S. T. Aspin, 79–92. Oxford: Blackwell, 1953.

L'estoire del saint graal. Ed. Jean-Paul Ponceau. Paris: Champion, 1997.

L'estoire de Merlin. Vulgate. Vol. 2. 1908.

The Exeter Book. Ed. George Krapp and Elliott Dobbie. New York: Columbia University Press, 1936.

First Variant Version: A Critical Edition. HRB. Vol. 2. 1988.

Gaimar, Geffrei. *L'estoire des Engleis.* Ed. Alexander Bell. Oxford: Blackwell, 1960.

Geoffroi de Villehardouin. *La conquête de Constantinople.* Ed. and trans. Edmond Faral. Paris: Belles Lettres, 1938–39.

Geoffrey of Monmouth. *Historia regum Britanniae.* In Faral, vol. 3.

Gerald of Wales. *Opera.* RB 21. London: Longman, 1867.

Gervase of Canterbury. *The Historical Works.* RB 73. London: Longman, 1880.

Gesta Normannorum ducum. Ed. and trans. Elisabeth M. C. Van Houts. Oxford: Clarendon Press, 1992.

Gesta regum Britannie. HRB. Vol. 5. 1991.

Gesta Stephani. Ed. and trans. K. R. Potter. Oxford: Clarendon Press, 1976.

Gildas. *The Ruin of Britain and Other Works.* Ed. and trans. Michael Winterbottom. London: Phillimore, 1978.

Guillaume de Saint-Pair. *Der Roman du Mont Saint-Michel.* Ed. Paul Redlich. Marburg: Elwertsche, 1894.

Henry of Huntingdon. *Historia Anglorum.* Ed. and trans. Diana Greenway. Oxford: Clarendon Press, 1996.

Historia Brittonum. In *BH,* 9–43, 50–84.

The History of Gruffydd ap Cynan. Ed. and trans. Arthur Jones. Manchester: Manchester University Press, 1910.

Hue de Rotelande. *Ipomédon.* Ed. Anthony J. Holden. Paris: Klincksieck, 1979.

Hugh of St. Victor. "Adnotationes elucidatoriae in Pentateuchon." *PL* 175 (1854): 30–86.

Isidore of Seville. *Etymologiae sive origines, IX.* Ed. and trans. Marc Reydellet. Paris: Belles Lettres, 1984.

Jesus College LXI [*Brut y Brenhinedd*]. Trans. Robert Ellis Jones. In Griscom.

John of Marmoutier. "Historia abbreviata consulum Andegavorum." In *Chroniques d'Anjou,* ed. Paul Marchegay and André Salmon, 1:351–63. Paris: Jules Renouard, 1856.

Lancelot. Ed. Alexandre Micha. Geneva: Droz, 1978–83.

Laȝamon. *Brut.* Ed. G. L. Brooke and R. F. Leslie. EETS 250, 277. London: Oxford University Press, 1963–78.

Le livre de Lancelot del lac. Vulgate. Vol. 5. 1912.

Mabinogion. Trans. Gwyn Jones and Thomas Jones. New York: Dutton, 1968.

Malory, Thomas. *Caxton's Malory.* Ed. James Spisak and William Matthews. Berkeley: University of California Press, 1983.

Map, Walter. *De nugis curialium.* Ed. M. R. James. Oxford: Clarendon Press, 1914.

La mort le roi Artu. Ed. Jean Frappier. Geneva: Droz, 1964.

Die "Ordines" für Weihe und Krönung des Kaisers und der Kaiserin. Ed. Reinhard Elze. Hanover: Hahnsche Buchhandlung, 1960.

Osbert of Clare. "Dux illustris Normannorum." In *Epistolae Herberti de Losinga,* ed. Robert Anstruther, 205–11. New York: Franklin, 1969.

The Pontifical of Magdalen College. Ed. H. A. Wilson. London: Harrison and Sons, 1910.

Le pontifical romain au Moyen-Age. Ed. Michel Andrieu. Vatican City: Biblioteca Apostolica Vaticana, 1938–40.

La queste del saint graal. Ed. Albert Pauphilet. Paris: Champion, 1984.

Ralph of Coggeshall. *Chronicon Anglicanum.* Ed. Joseph Stevenson. RB 66. London: Longman, 1875.

Recueil des actes de Henri II. Ed. Léopold Delisle and E. Berger. Paris: Imprimerie nationale, 1909–27.

Registrum epistolarum fratris Johannis Peckham. Ed. Charles Trice Martin. RB 77. London: Longman, 1882–85.

Robert de Boron. *Merlin: Roman du XIIIe siècle.* Ed. Alexandre Micha. Geneva: Droz, 1980.

———. *Le roman de l'estoire du graal.* Ed. William A. Nitze. Paris: Champion, 1983.

———. *Le roman du graal: Manuscrit de Modène.* Ed. Bernard de Cerquiglini. Paris: Union générale d'édition, 1981.

Robert de Clari. *La conquête de Constantinople.* Ed. and trans. Alexandre Micha. Paris: Christian Bourgeois, 1991.

Robert of Gloucester. *The Metrical Chronicle.* Ed. William Aldis Wright. RB 86. London: Eyre and Spottiswoode, 1887.

Le roman d'Enéas. Ed. Jean-Jacques Salverda de Grave. Paris: Champion, 1983–85.

Le roman de Thèbes. Ed. and trans. Francine Mora-Lebrun. Paris: Librairie générale française, 1995.

Roman van Walewein. Ed. and trans. David F. Johnson. New York: Garland Press, 1992.

Rufinus. *Summa decretorum.* Ed. Heinrich Singer. Paderborn: Schoningh, 1902.

Rushdie, Salman. *The Satanic Verses.* New York: Viking, 1988.

Sacramentaire et martyrologie de l'abbaye de Saint-Remy. Ed. Ulysse Chevalier. Paris: Picard, 1900.

The South English Legendary. Ed. Charlotte D'Evelyn and Anna J. Mill. EETS 235, 236, 244. London: Oxford University Press, 1956–59.

Troiedd Ynys Prydein. Ed. Rachel Bromwich. Cardiff: University of Wales Press, 1961.

Virgil. *The Aeneid of Virgil.* Ed. R. D. Williams. London: Macmillan, 1972.

Wace. *Le roman de Brut.* Ed. Ivor Arnold. Paris: Société des anciens textes français, 1938–40.

———. *Le roman de Rou.* Ed. A. J. Holden. Paris: Picard, 1970–73.

Walter of Guisborough. *Chronicle.* Ed. Harry Rothwell. London: Camden Society, 1957.

William of Malmesbury. *De antiquitate glastonie ecclesie.* Ed. and trans. John Scott. Woodbridge: Boydell Press, 1981.

———. *Polyhistor: A Critical Edition.* Ed. Helen Testroet Ouellette. Binghamton: Center for Medieval and Early Renaissance Studies, 1982.

William of Newburgh. *Chronicles of the Reigns of Stephen, Henry II, and Richard I.* Ed. Richard Howlett. RB 82. London: Longman, 1884.

Secondary Sources
Abbreviations

AL	*Arthurian Literature*
ANS	*Anglo-Norman Studies*
British	*The British Isles, 1100–1500: Comparisons, Contrasts, and Connections.* Ed. R. R. Davies. Edinburgh: John Donald Press, 1988.
CCM	*Cahiers de civilisation médiévale*
CMCS	*Cambridge Medieval Celtic Studies*
EHR	*English Historical Review*
England	*England and Normandy in the Middle Ages.* Ed. David Bates and Anne Curry. London: Hambledon Press, 1994.
Essential	*Essential Papers on Judaism and Christianity in Conflict.* Ed. Jeremy Cohen. New York: New York University Press, 1991.
Family	*Family Trees and the Roots of Politics.* Ed. K. S. B. Keats-Rohan. Woodbridge: Boydell Press, 1997.
Imagining	*Imagining Nations.* Ed. Geoffrey Cubitt. Manchester: Manchester University Press, 1998.
JEGP	*Journal of English and Germanic Philology*
JMH	*Journal of Medieval History*
Lancelot-Grail	*The Lancelot-Grail Cycle: Text and Transformations.* Ed. William W. Kibler. Austin: University of Texas Press, 1994.
Lancelot-Lanzelet	*Lancelot-Lanzelet: Hier et aujourd'hui.* Ed. Danielle Buschinger and Michel Zink. Greifswald: Reineke, 1995.
LSE	*Leeds Studies in English*
MA	*Medium Aevum*
Mort	*La mort du roi Arthur ou le crépuscule de la chevalerie.* Ed. Jean Dufournet. Paris: Champion, 1994.
NMS	*Nottingham Medieval Studies*
PQ	*Philological Quarterly*
Rethinking	*Rethinking Translation: Discourse, Subjectivity, Ideology.* Ed. Lawrence Venuti. London: Routledge, 1992.
Roques	*Mélanges de linguistique et de littérature romanes offerts à Mario Roques.* Geneva: Slatkine, 1974.
SM	*Studi Medievali*
Text and Intertext	*Text and Intertext in Medieval Arthurian Literature.* Ed. Norris Lacy. New York: Garland, 1996.
Text and Tradition	*The Text and Tradition of Laȝamon's "Brut."* Ed. Françoise Le Saux. Cambridge: Brewer, 1994.
Welsh	*Welsh Society and Nationhood.* Ed. R. R. Davies and Glanmoor Williams. Cardiff: University of Wales Press, 1984.

Allen, Rosamund. "*Eorles* and *Beornes*: Contextualizing Lawman's *Brut.*" *Arthuriana* 8, no. 3 (1998): 4–22.

———. "The Implied Audience of Layamon's *Brut.*" In *Text and Tradition*, 121–39.

———, trans. *Brut.* By Lawman. New York: St. Martin's Press, 1992.

Alliès, Paul. *L'invention du territoire.* Grenoble: Presse universitaire de Grenoble, 1980.

Amt, Emilie. *The Accession of Henry II in England.* Woodbridge: Boydell Press, 1993.

Anderson, Benedict. *Imagined Communities.* 2nd ed. London: Verso, 1991.

Appiah, Kwame Anthony. "Is the Post- in Postmodernism the Post- in Postcolonial?" *Critical Inquiry* 17 (1991): 336–57.

Armstrong, John. *Nations before Nationalism.* Chapel Hill: University of North Carolina Press, 1982.

Avent, Richard. *Cestyll Tywysogion Gwynedd (Castles of the Princes of Gwynedd)*. Cardiff: Her Majesty's Stationery Office, 1983.

Bahri, Deepika. "Coming to Terms with the 'Postcolonial.'" In *Between the Lines: South Asians and Post-Coloniality*, ed. Deepika Bahri and Mary Vasudera, 137–64. Philadelphia: Temple University Press, 1996.

Baldwin, John W. *The Government of Philip Augustus*. Berkeley: University of California Press, 1986.

Banitt, Menahem. *L'étude des glossaires bibliques des juifs de France au Moyen Age*. Jerusalem: Israel Academy of Sciences, 1967.

———. "Les *Poterim*." *Revue des études juives* 125 (1966): 21–33.

Bank, Rosemarie K. "Meditations upon Opening and Crossing Over: Transgressing the Boundaries of Historiography and Tracking the History of Nineteenth-Century American Theatre." In *Of Borders and Thresholds: Theatre History, Practice, and Theory*, ed. Michal Kobialka, 30–69. Minneapolis: University of Minnesota Press, 1999.

Barron, W. R. J., and S. C. Weinberg, eds. and trans. *Brut, or Hystoria Brutonum*. Harlow, Essex: Longman, 1995.

Barth, Fredrik. Introduction to *Ethnic Groups and Boundaries*, ed. Fredrik Barth, 9–38. Boston: Little, Brown, 1969.

Bartlett, Robert, and Angus MacKay, eds. *Medieval Frontier Societies*. Oxford: Oxford University Press, 1989.

Bate, Keith. "La littérature latine d'imagination à la cour d'Henri II d'Angleterre." *CCM* 34 (1991): 3–21.

Bates, David. "Normandy and England after 1066." *EHR* 104 (1989): 853–61.

———. "The Rise and Fall of Normandy, c. 911–1204." In *England*, 19–36.

Baudrillard, Jean. *Le système des objets*. Paris: Gallimard, 1968.

Baumgartner, Emmanuèle. *L'arbre et le pain: Essai sur "La queste del saint graal."* Paris: Société d'édition d'enseignement supérieur, 1981.

———. "Le choix de la prose." *Cahiers de recherches médiévales* 5 (1998): 7–13.

———. "Espace du texte, espace du manuscrit: Les manuscrits du *Lancelot-Graal*." In *De l'histoire de Troie au livre du Graal*, 379–404. Orléans: Paradigme, 1994.

———. "From Lancelot to Galahad: The Stakes of Filiation." In *Lancelot-Grail*, 14–30.

———. "Joseph d'Arimathie dans le *Lancelot en prose*." In *Colloque sur Lancelot*, ed. Danielle Buschinger, 7–15. Göppingen: Kümmerle, 1984.

———. "Lancelot et le royaume." In *Mort*, 25–44.

Beaune, Colette. "L'utilisation politique du mythe des origines troyennes en France à la fin du moyen âge." In *Lectures médiévales de Virgile*, 331–55. Rome: École française de Rome, 1985.

Bellamy, James A. "Arabic Names in the *Chanson de Roland*: Saracen Gods, Frankish Swords, Roland's Horse, and the Olifant." *Journal of the American Oriental Society* 107 (1987): 267–77.

Benton, John F. "Collaborative Approaches to Fantasy and Reality in the Literature of Champagne." In *Court and Poet*, ed. Glyn S. Burgess, 43–57. Liverpool: Francis Cairn, 1981.

———. "The Court of Champagne as a Literary Center." *Speculum* 36 (1961): 551–91.

Berthelot, Anne. *Figures et fonctions de l'écrivain au XIIIe siècle*. Montreal: Institut d'études médiévales, 1991.

Bhabha, Homi K. *The Location of Culture*. London: Routledge, 1994.

Bhattacharyya, Gargi. "Cultural Education in Britain: From the Newbolt Report to the National Curriculum." *Oxford Literary Review* 13 (1991): 4–19.

Biddick, Kathleen. *The Shock of Medievalism*. Durham, N.C.: Duke University Press, 1998.

Binns, Alison. *Dedications of Monastic Houses in England and Wales, 1066–1216*. Woodbridge: Boydell, 1989.

Birns, Nicholas. "The Trojan Myth: Postmodern Reverberations." *Exemplaria* 5, no. 1 (1993): 45–78.

Blacker, Jean. *The Faces of Time: Portrayal of the Past in Old French and Latin Historical Narrative of the Anglo-Norman "Regnum."* Austin: University of Texas Press, 1994.

———. "Transformations of a Theme: The Depoliticization of the Arthurian World in the *Roman de Brut.*" In *The Arthurian Tradition: Essays in Convergence,* ed. Mary Flowers Braswell and John Bugge, 54–74, 204–9. Tuscaloosa: University of Alabama Press, 1988.

Blanchet, Marie-Claude. "Maistre Wace, trouvère normand." *Marche Roman* 9 (1959): 149–58.

Bloch, R. Howard. *Etymologies and Genealogies.* Chicago: University of Chicago Press, 1983.

———. *Medieval French Literature and Law.* Chicago: University of Chicago Press, 1977.

Blondheim, David. *Les gloses françaises dans les commentaires talmudiques de Raschi.* Paris: Champion, 1937.

Bongie, Chris. *Islands and Exiles: The Creole Identities of Post/colonial Literature.* Stanford: Stanford University Press, 1998.

Bourdieu, Pierre. "Identity and Representation: Elements for a Critical Reflection on the Idea of Region." In *Language and Symbolic Power,* ed. John B. Thompson, trans. Gino Raymond and Matthew Adamson, 220–28. Cambridge: Harvard University Press, 1991. Originally published as "La force de la représentation," in *Ce que parler veut dire: L'économie des échanges linguistiques,* 135–48 (Paris: Fayard, 1982).

Boutet, Dominique. "Arthur et son mythe dans la *Mort le roi Artu*: Visions psychologique, politique, et théologique." In *Mort,* 45–65.

———. *Charlemagne et Arthur ou le roi imaginaire.* Paris: Champion-Slatkine, 1992.

———. "La fin des temps arthuriens, du *Roman de Brut* au *Lancelot-Graal*: Critique esthetique et critique historique." In *Lancelot-Lanzelet,* 39–52.

Brandsma, Frank. "The Eyewitness Narrator in Vernacular Prose Chronicles and Prose Romances." In *Text and Intertext,* 57–69.

Brandt, William J. *The Shape of Medieval History.* New York: Schocken Books, 1973.

Brett, Caroline. "Breton Latin Literature as Evidence for Literature in the Vernacular, A.D. 800–1300." *CMCS* 18 (1989): 1–25.

Brewer, Derek. "The Paradox of the Archaic and the Modern in Laȝamon's *Brut.*" In *From Anglo-Saxon to Early Modern English,* ed. Malcolm Godden, Douglas Gray, T. F. Hoad, and Eric Gerald Stanley, 188–205. Oxford: Clarendon Press, 1994.

Broich, Ulrich. In *Studien zum literarischen Patronat im England des 12. Jahrhunderts,* by Walter F. Schirmer and Ulrich Broich. Cologne: Westdeutscher Verlag, 1962.

Brosnahan, Leger. "Wace's Use of Proverbs." *Speculum* 39 (1964): 444–73.

Bryan, Elizabeth J. *Collaborative Meaning in Medieval Scribal Culture: The Otho Laȝamon.* Ann Arbor: University of Michigan Press, 1999.

———. "Laȝamon's Four Helens: Female Figurations of Nation in the *Brut.*" *LSE* 26 (1995): 63–78.

Bullock-Davies, Constance, and Melville Richards. "The Population of the Welsh Border." *Transactions of the Honourable Society of Cymmrodorian* 20 (1976): 29–40.

Bur, Michel. "Les comtes de Champagne et la 'Normanitas': Sémiologie d'un tombeau." *ANS* 3 (1980): 22–32, 202–3.

———. "De quelques champenois dans l'entourage français des rois d'Angleterre aux XIe et XIIe siècles." In *Family,* 333–48.

———. *La formation du comté de Champagne, v.950–v.1150.* Nancy: Université de Nancy, 1977.

———. "Rôle et place de la Champagne dans le royaume de France au temps de Philippe Auguste." In *La France de Philippe Auguste,* ed. Robert-Henri Bautier, 237–54. Paris: Centre national de la recherche scientifique, 1982.

Burns, E. Jane. *Arthurian Fictions: Rereading the Vulgate Cycle.* Columbus: Ohio State University Press, 1985.

———. "Of Arthurian Bondage: Thematic Patterning in the Vulgate Romances." *Medievalia et Humanistica* n.s. 11 (1982): 165–76.

——. "*La voie de la voix*: The Aesthetics of Indirection in the Vulgate Cycle." In *The Legacy of Chrétien de Troyes*, ed. Norris J. Lacy, Douglas Kelly, and Keith Busby, 2:151–67. Amsterdam: Rodopi, 1988.

aldwell, Robert A. "*Wace's Roman de Brut* and the Variant Version of Geoffrey of Monmouth's *Historia regum Britanniae.*" *Speculum* 31 (1956): 675–82.

annon, Christopher. "The Style and Authorship of the Otho Revision of Laȝamon's *Brut.*" *MA* 62 (1993): 187–209.

arruthers, Mary. *The Book of Memory: A Study of Memory in Medieval Culture.* Cambridge: Cambridge University Press, 1990.

aspary, Gerard E. *Politics and Exegesis: Origen and the Two Swords.* Berkeley: University of California Press, 1979.

hase, Carol. "'Or dist li contes': Narrative Interventions and the Implied Audience in the *Estoire del Saint Graal.*" In *Lancelot-Grail*, 117–38.

hazan, Robert. *Daggers of Faith: Thirteenth-Century Christian Missionizing and Jewish Response.* Berkeley: University of California Press, 1989.

——. *Medieval Jewry in Northern France.* Baltimore, Md.: Johns Hopkins University Press, 1973.

hédeville, André, and Noël-Yves Tonnerre. *La Bretagne féodale, XIe–XIIIe siècle.* Rennes: Ouest-France, 1987.

heyfitz, Eric. *The Poetics of Imperialism.* Oxford: Oxford University Press, 1991.

ingolani, Stefano Maria. "Filologia e miti storiografici: Enrico II, la corte plantageneta e la letteratura." *SM* 32 (1991): 815–32.

lanchy, M. T. *From Memory to Written Record: England, 1066–1307.* 2nd ed. Oxford: Blackwell, 1993.

lark, John. "Trinovantum: The Evolution of a Legend." *JMH* 7 (1981): 135–51.

ohen, Jeffrey Jerome. *Of Giants: Sex, Monsters, and the Middle Ages.* Minneapolis: University of Minnesota Press, 1999.

ohen, Jeremy. *The Friars and the Jews: The Evolution of Medieval Anti-Judaism.* Ithaca, N.Y.: Cornell University Press, 1982.

——. "Scholarship and Tolerance in the Medieval Academy: The Study and Evaluation of Judaism in European Christendom." In *Essential*, 310–41.

onley, Tom. *The Self-Made Map: Cartographic Writing in Early Modern France.* Minneapolis: University of Minnesota Press, 1996.

oss, Peter. *Lordship, Knighthood, and Locality: A Study of English Society, c. 1180–c. 1280.* Cambridge: Cambridge University Press, 1991.

ourtney, Paul. "The Norman Invasion of Gwent: A Reassessment." *JMH* 12 (1986): 297–313.

rawford, T. D. "On the Linguistic Competence of Geoffrey of Monmouth." *MA* 51 (1982): 152–62.

rick, Julia. *Dissemination and Reception in the Later Middle Ages.* HRB. Vol. 4. 1991.

——. *A Summary Catalogue of the Manuscripts.* HRB. Vol. 3. 1989.

rouch, David. *The Beaumont Twins: The Roots and Branches of Power in the Twelfth Century.* Cambridge: Cambridge University Press, 1986.

——. "The March and the Welsh Kings." In *The Anarchy of King Stephen's Reign*, ed. Edmund King, 255–89. Oxford: Clarendon Press, 1994.

——. "Normans and Anglo-Normans: A Divided Aristocracy?" In *England*, 51–68.

——. "Robert, Earl of Gloucester, and the Daughter of Zelophehad." *JMH* 11 (1985): 227–43.

——. "The Slow Death of Kingship in Glamorgan, 1067–1158." *Morgannwg* 29 (1985): 20–41.

ulbert, Taylor. "The Narrative Functions of Beowulf's Swords." *JEGP* 59 (1960): 13–20.

urtius, Ernst R. *European Literature and the Latin Middle Ages.* Trans. Willard R. Trask. Princeton, N.J.: Princeton University Press, 1953.

ahan, Gilbert. *Les intellectuels chrétiens et les juifs au moyen âge.* Paris: Cerf, 1990.

D'Arbois de Jubainville, H. *Histoire des ducs et des comtes de Champagne.* Paris: Aubr 1865.

Davidson, Hilda Ellis. *The Sword in Anglo-Saxon England.* Woodbridge: Boydell Pres 1994.

Davies, R. R. *Conquest, Coexistence, and Change: Wales, 1063–1415.* Oxford: Clarendc Press, 1987.

———. *Domination and Conquest: The Experience of Ireland, Scotland, and Wales, 110(1300.* Cambridge: Cambridge University Press, 1990.

———. "Frontier Arrangements in Fragmented Societies: Ireland and Wales." In Bartle and MacKay, 77–100.

———. "Law and National Identity in Thirteenth-Century Wales." In *Welsh,* 51–69.

———. *The Matter of Britain and the Matter of England.* Oxford: Clarendon Press, 1996.

Davies, Wendy. *Patterns of Power in Early Wales.* Oxford: Clarendon Press, 1990.

Davis, Kathleen. "National Writing in the Ninth Century: A Reminder for Postcoloni Thinking about the Nation." *Journal of Medieval and Early Modern Studies* 28 (1998 611–37.

Davis, R. H. C. *King Stephen.* 3rd ed. London: Longman, 1990.

de Certeau, Michel. *The Writing of History.* Trans. Tom Conley. New York: Columbia Un versity Press, 1988.

Deleuze, Gilles, and Félix Guattari. *A Thousand Plateaus: Capitalism and Schizophreni* Trans. Brian Massumi. Minneapolis: University of Minnesota Press, 1987.

Dictionary of Medieval Latin from British Sources. Ed. R. E. Latham. London: Oxfo University Press, 1975–.

Donoghue, Daniel. "Laȝamon's Ambivalence." *Speculum* 65 (1990): 537–63.

Duby, Georges. *The Chivalrous Society.* Trans. Cynthia Postan. London: Edward Arnol 1977.

Dufief, André. "La vie monastique au Mont Saint-Michel pendant le XIIe siècle (1085 1186)." In *Millénaire monastique du Mont Saint-Michel,* ed. J. Laporte, 1:81–12(Paris: Lethielleux, 1966.

Dumville, David N. "An Early Text of Geoffrey of Monmouth's *Historia regum Britar niae* and the Circulation of Some Latin Histories in Twelfth-Century Normandy." *A* 4 (1984): 1–33.

Early Maps of the British Isles, A.D. 1000–A.D. 1579. Ed. G. R. Crone. London: Royal G(ographical Society, 1961.

Everett, Dorothy. "Laȝamon and the Earliest Middle English Alliterative Verse." In *Essay in Middle English Literature,* ed. Patricia Kean, 23–45. Oxford: Oxford University Pres 1955.

Evergates, Theodore. *Feudal Society in the Bailliage of Troyes under the Counts of Char pagne, 1152–1284.* Baltimore, Md.: Johns Hopkins University Press, 1975.

———, ed. and trans. *Feudal Society in Medieval France: Documents from the County (Champagne.* Philadelphia: University of Pennsylvania Press, 1993.

Faral, Edmond. *La légende arthurienne: Études et documents.* Paris: Champion, 1929.

Field, Lester L., Jr. *Liberty, Dominion, and the Two Swords: On the Origins of Wester Political Theology (180–398).* Notre Dame, Ind.: University of Notre Dame Press, 1998

Finke, Laurie, and Martin Shichtman. "The Mont St. Michel Giant: Sexual Violence an Imperialism in the Chronicles of Wace and Laȝamon." In *Violence against Wome in Medieval Texts,* ed. Anna Roberts, 56–74. Gainesville: University of Florida Pres 1998.

Fletcher, Angus. *Allegory: The Theory of a Symbolic Mode.* Ithaca, N.Y.: Cornell Unive sity Press, 1964.

Fletcher, Robert. "Gawain's Sword in the *Polistorie del Eglise de Christ de Caunterbyre.* *Publications of the Modern Language Association* 18 (1903): 89–90.

Fleuriot, Léon. "Histoires et légendes." In *Histoire littéraire et culturelle de la Bretagne* ed. Léon Fleuriot and Auguste-Pierre Ségalen, 1:97–129. Paris: Champion, 1987.

———. "Prophéties, navigations et thèmes divers." In *Histoire*, ed. Fleuriot and Ségalen, 1:153–172.

Flint, Valerie J. "The *Historia regum Britanniæ* of Geoffrey of Monmouth: Parody and Its Purpose. A Suggestion." *Speculum* 54 (1979): 447–68.

Flori, Jean. "L'épée de Lancelot: Adoubement et idéologie au début du treizième siècle." In *Lancelot-Lanzelet*, 147–56.

———. *L'essor de la chevalerie, XIe-XIIe siècles*. Geneva: Droz, 1986.

———. *Idéologie du glaive: Préhistoire de la chevalerie*. Geneva: Droz, 1983.

Fludernik, Monika. "The Constitution of Hybridity: Postcolonial Interventions." In *Hybridity and Postcolonialism: Twentieth-Century Indian Literature*, ed. Monika Fludernik, 19–53. Tübingen: Stauffenburg, 1998.

Francis, E. A. "Notes sur un terme employé par Wace, avec quelques observations sur la chronologie de ses oeuvres." In *Roques*, 2:81–92.

Frantzen, Allen J. "Writing the Unreadable Beowulf: 'Writan' and 'Forwritan,' the Pen and the Sword." *Exemplaria* 3 (1991): 327–57.

Frappier, Jean. *Étude sur "La mort le roi Artu."* Geneva: Droz, 1972.

Galliou, Patrick, and Michael Jones. *The Bretons*. Oxford: Blackwell, 1991.

Genicot, Léopold. *Les généalogies*. Turnhout: Brepols, 1975.

Gillingham, John. "The Beginnings of English Imperialism." *Journal of Historical Sociology* 5 (1992): 392–409.

———. "Conquering the Barbarians: War and Chivalry in Twelfth-Century England." *Haskins Society Journal* 4 (1992): 67–84.

———. "The Context and Purposes of Geoffrey of Monmouth's *History of the Kings of Britain*." *ANS* 13 (1990): 99–118.

———. "Foundations of a Disunited Kingdom." In *Uniting the Kingdom? The Making of British History*, ed. Alexander Grant and Keith J. Stringer, 48–64. London: Routledge, 1995.

Gimeno, Joaquín. "Las espadas del Cid en el *Poema*." *Mester* 9 (1980): 49–56.

Girard d'Albissin, Nelly. "Propos sur la frontière." *Revue historique de droit français et étranger* 47 (1969): 390–407.

Godefroy, Frederic. *Dictionnaire de l'ancienne langue française*. Paris: Viewig, 1881–1902.

Gouttebroze, Jean-Guy. "Henry II Plantagenêt: Patron des historiographes anglo-normands de langue d'oil." In *La littérature angevine médiévale*, ed. Georges Cesbron, 91–105. Angers: Hérault, 1981.

———. "Pourquoi congédier un historiographe, Henri II Plantagenêt et Wace (1155–1174)." *Romania* 112 (1991): 289–311.

Grabois, Aryeh. "The *Hebraica veritas* and Jewish-Christian Intellectual Relations in the Twelfth Century." *Speculum* 50 (1975): 613–34.

Gransden, Antonia. *Historical Writing in England*. Ithaca, N.Y.: Cornell University Press, 1974–82.

Grayzel, Solomon. *The Church and the Jews in the Thirteenth Century*. New York: Hermon Press, 1966.

———. "The Papal Bull *Sicut Judeis*." In *Essential*, 231–59.

Green, Eugene. "Power, Commitment, and the Right to a Name in *Beowulf*." In *Persons in Groups*, ed. Richard C. Trexler, 133–40. Binghamton, N.Y.: Medieval and Renaissance Texts and Studies, 1985.

Green, Judith A. *The Aristocracy of Norman England*. Cambridge: Cambridge University Press, 1997.

———. "Family Matters: Family and the Formation of the Empress's Party in South-West England." In *Family*, 147–64.

———. "Unity and Disunity in the Anglo-Norman State." *Historical Research* 63 (1989): 128–33.

Griffiths, Ralph A. "Medieval Severnside: The Welsh Connection." In *Welsh*, 70–89.

Griscom, Acton, ed. *The "Historia regum Britanniæ" of Geoffrey of Monmouth*. London: Longmans, Green, 1929.

Grisward, Joël H. "Le motif de l'épée jetée au lac: La mort d'Artur et la mort de Batradz." *Romania* 90 (1969): 289–340, 473–514.

Haidu, Peter. *The Subject of Violence: The "Song of Roland" and the Birth of the State.* Bloomington: Indiana University Press, 1993.

Hailpern, Herman. *Rashi and the Christian Scholars.* Pittsburgh: University of Pittsburgh Press, 1963.

Halász, Katalin. "The Representation of Time and Its Models in the Prose Romance." In *Text and Intertext,* 175–86.

Hammer, Jacob, ed. *Historia regum Britanniæ.* Cambridge, Mass.: Medieval Academy of America, 1951.

Hanning, Robert W. "Arthurian Evangelists: The Language of Truth in Thirteenth-Century French Prose Romances." *PQ* 64 (1985): 347–65.

———. *The Individual in Twelfth-Century Romance.* New Haven, Conn.: Yale University Press, 1977.

———. "Uses of Names in Medieval Literature." *Names* 16 (1968): 325–38.

———. *The Vision of History in Early Britain: From Gildas to Geoffrey of Monmouth.* New York: Columbia University Press, 1966.

Harris, Anne Leslie. "Hands, Helms, and Heroes: The Role of Proper Names in *Beowolf.*" *Neuphilologische Mitteilungen* 83 (1982): 414–21.

Hartman, Richard. *La quête et la croisade: Villehardouin, Clari, et le "Lancelot en prose."* New York: Postillion Press, 1977.

Harvey, P. D. A. *Medieval Maps.* Toronto: University of Toronto Press, 1991.

Haskins, Charles H. "Henry II as a Patron of Literature." In *Essays in Medieval History Presented to T. F. Tout,* ed. A G. Little and F. M. Powicke, 71–77. Manchester: [Subscribers], 1925.

Heng, Geraldine. "Cannibalism, the First Crusade, and the Genesis of Medieval Romance." *Differences* 10, no. 1 (1998): 98–174.

Herbert, N. M., ed. *A History of the County of Gloucester.* Oxford: Oxford University Press, 1988.

Hillion, Yannick. "La Bretagne et la rivalité Capétiens-Plantagenêts: Un exemple: La duchesse Constance (1186–1202)." *Annales de Bretagne et des Pays de l'Ouest* 92 (1985): 111–45.

Hilton, Rodney H. *A Medieval Society: The West Midlands at the End of the Thirteenth Century.* London: Weidenfeld and Nicolson, 1966.

Hollister, C. Warren. *Monarchy, Magnates, and Institutions in the Anglo-Norman World.* London: Hambledon Press, 1986.

Holmes, Urban T., Jr. "Norman Literature and Wace." In *Medieval Secular Literature,* ed. William Matthews, 46–67. Berkeley: University of California Press, 1967.

Holt, James C. *Magna Carta and Medieval Government.* London: Hambledon Press, 1985.

———. "Politics and Property in Early Medieval England." *Past and Present* 57 (1972): 3–52.

Houck, Margaret. *Sources of the "Roman de Brut" of Wace.* University of California Publications in English 5 (1940–44): 161–356.

Howell, Margaret. *Eleanor of Provence.* Oxford: Blackwell, 1998.

Hughes, Kathleen. "British Museum MS. Cotton Vespasian A. xiv (*Vitae sanctorum Wallensium*): Its Purpose and Provenance." In *Studies in the Early British Church,* ed. Nora K. Chadwick, 183–200. Cambridge: Cambridge University Press, 1958.

Hulme, Peter. *Colonial Encounters.* London: Methuen, 1986.

Ingham, Patricia Clare. " 'In Contrayez Straunge': Colonial Relations, British Identity, and *Sir Gawain and the Green Knight.*" *New Medieval Literatures* 6 (2000).

———. "Marking Time: Branwen, Daughter of Llyr, and the Colonial Refrain." In *The Postcolonial Middle Ages,* ed. Jeffrey Jerome Cohen. New York: St. Martin's Press, 2000.

Ingledew, Francis. "The Book of Troy and the Genealogical Construction of History: The Case of Geoffrey of Monmouth's *Historia regum Britanniae.*" *Speculum* 69 (1994): 665–704.

Jackson, Richard A. *"Ordines Coronationis Franciae"*: *Texts and "Ordines" for the Coronations of Frankish and French Kings and Queens in the Middle Ages*. Philadelphia: University of Pennsylvania Press, 1995.

Jacquemond, Richard. "Translation and Cultural Hegemony: The Case of French-Arabic Translation." In *Rethinking*, 139–58.

JanMohamed, Abdul R. "Wordliness-without-World, Homelessless-as-Home: Toward a Definition of the Specular Border Intellectual." In *Edward Said: A Critical Reader*, ed. Michael Sprinker, 96–120. Oxford: Blackwell, 1992.

Jenkins, T. Atkinson. "Old French *Escalibor*." *Modern Philology* 10 (1912–13): 449–50.

Johnson, Lesley. "Etymologies, Genealogies, and Nationalism (Again)." In *Concepts of National Identity in the Middle Ages*, ed. Simon Forde et al., 125–36. Leeds: Leeds Texts, 1995.

———. "Reading the Past in Laȝamon's *Brut*." In *Text and Tradition*, 141–60.

Jordan, William Chester. *The French Monarchy and the Jews*. Philadelphia: University of Pennsylvania Press, 1989.

Jung, Marc-René. *La légende de Troie en France au moyen âge*: Tübingen: Francke, 1996.

Kay, Sarah. "Adultery and Killing in *La Mort le roi Artu*." In *Scarlet Letters: Fictions of Adultery from Antiquity to the 1990s*, ed. Nicholas White and Naomi Segal, 34–44. London: Macmillan, 1997.

Keats-Rohan, K. S. B. "The Bretons and Normans of England, 1066–1154: The Family, the Fief, and the Feudal Monarchy." *NMS* 36 (1992): 42–78.

Kennedy, Elspeth. "Intertextuality between Genres in the *Lancelot-Grail*." In *Text and Intertext*, 71–90.

King, Edmund. "Stephen and the Anglo-Norman Aristocracy." *History* 59 (1974): 180–94.

Kirby, Ian J. "Angles and Saxons in Laȝamon's *Brut*." *Studia Neophilologica* 26 (1964): 51–62.

Kittay, Jeffrey, and Wlad Godzich. *The Emergence of Prose*. Minneapolis: University of Minnesota Press, 1987.

Klein, Kerwin Lee. "In Search of Narrative Mastery: Postmodernism and the People without History." *History and Theory* 34 (1995): 275–98.

Knight, Stephen. *Arthurian Literature and Society*. London: Macmillan, 1983.

Köhler, Erich. *Ideal und Wirklichkeit in der höfischen Epik*. 2nd ed. Tübingen: Max Niemeyer, 1970.

Kopytoff, Igor. "The Cultural Biography of Things: Commoditization as Process." In *The Social Life of Things*, ed. Arjun Appadurai, 64–91. Cambridge: Cambridge University Press, 1986.

Lagorio, Valerie M. "The Apocalyptic Mode in the Vulgate Cycle of Arthurian Romances." *PQ* 57 (1978): 1–22.

Laing, Margaret. "Anchor Texts and Literary Manuscripts in Early Middle English." In *Regionalism in Late Medieval Manuscripts and Texts*, ed. Felicity Riddy, 27–52. Woodbridge: Brewer, 1991.

Lambert, Mayer, and Louis Brandin. *Glossaire hébreu-français du XIIIe siècle*. Geneva: Slatkine, 1977.

Lane, Dorothy. *The Island as Site of Resistance*. New York: Peter Lang, 1995.

Leckie, R. William, Jr. *The Passage of Dominion: Geoffrey of Monmouth and the Periodization of Insular History in the Twelfth Century*. Toronto: University of Toronto Press, 1981.

Lecler, Joseph. "L'argument des deux glaives." *Recherches de science religieuse* 21 (1931): 299–339; 22 (1932): 151–77, 280–303.

Legg, Leopold G. W., ed. *English Coronation Records*. Westminster: Constable, 1901.

Legge, M. Dominica. "The Influence of Patronage on Form in Medieval French Literature." In *Stil- und Formprobleme in der Literatur*, 136–41. Heidelberg: Winter, 1959.

Le Goff, Jacques. "A Coronation Program for the Age of Saint Louis: The Ordo of 1250." In *Coronations: Medieval and Early Modern Monarchic Ritual*, ed. János M. Bak, 46–57. Berkeley: University of California Press, 1990.

Lejeune, Rita. "Les noms d'épées dans la *Chanson de Roland.*" In *Roques*, 1:149–66.

———. "Rôle littéraire d'Aliénor d'Aquitaine et de sa famille." *Cultura Neolatina* 14 (1954): 5–57.

Lemarignier, Jean-François. *Recherches sur l'hommage en marche et les frontières féodales.* Lille: Bibliothèque universitaire de Lille, 1945.

Le Patourel, John. *Feudal Empires Norman and Plantagenêt.* London: Hambledon Press, 1984.

Lepick, Julie Ann. "History and Story: The End and Ending of *La mort le roi Artu.*" *Michigan Academician* 12 (1980): 517–26.

Le Saux, Françoise. *Laȝamon's "Brut": The Poem and Its Sources.* Cambridge: Brewer, 1989.

———. "Laȝamon's Welsh Sources." *English Studies* 67 (1986): 385–93.

———. "Listening to the Manuscript: Editing Laȝamon's *Brut.*" In *Orality and Literature in Early Middle English*, ed. H. Pilch, 11–20. Tübingen: Narr, 1996.

———. "Narrative Rhythm and Narrative Content in Laȝamon's *Brut.*" *Parergon* 10 (1992): 45–70.

———. "Relations familiales et autorité royale: De l'*Historia regum Britanniae* au *Brut* de Layamon." *Sénéfiance* 26 (1989): 215–31.

Leupin, Alexandre. *Le graal et la littérature.* Lausanne: L'Age d'Homme, 1982.

Leviant, Curt, ed. and trans. *King Artus: A Hebrew Arthurian Romance of 1279.* New York: Ktav, 1969.

Lévi-Strauss, Claude. *La pensée sauvage.* Paris: Plon, 1962.

Levy, Raphaël. "The Use of Hebrew Characters for Writing Old French." In *Mélanges de langue et de littérature du Moyen Age et de la Renaissance offerts à Jean Frappier*, 2:645–52. Geneva: Droz, 1970.

Lloyd, D. Myrddin. "The Poets of the Princes." In *A Guide to Welsh Literature*, ed. A. O. H. Jarman and Gwilym Rees Hughes, 1:157–88. Swansea: Christopher Davies, 1976.

Lloyd, John E. "Geoffrey of Monmouth." *EHR* 57 (1942): 460–68.

Lot, Ferdinand. *Étude sur le "Lancelot en prose."* Paris: Champion, 1954.

Louis, René. "Le préfixe inorganique es- dans les noms propres en ancien français." In *Festgabe Ernst Gamillscheg*, 66–76. Tübingen: Max Niemeyer, 1952.

Loxley, Diana. *Problematic Shores: The Literature of Islands.* London: Macmillan, 1990.

Lydon, James. "Lordship and Crown: Llywelyn of Wales and O'Connor of Connacht." In *British*, 48–63.

Madden, Frederic, ed. and trans. *Layamon's Brut; or, Chronicle of Britain.* London: Society of Antiquaries, 1847.

Maddicott, J. R. *Simon de Montfort.* Cambridge: Cambridge University Press, 1994.

Martindale, Jane. "The Sword on the Stone: Some Resonances of a Medieval Symbol of Power (The Tomb of King John in Worcester Cathedral)." *ANS* 15 (1992): 199–241.

Mason, Emma. "St. Wulfstan's Staff: A Legend and Its Uses." *MA* 53 (1984): 157–79.

McClintock, Anne. *Imperial Leather.* London: Routledge, 1995.

McCracken, Peggy. *The Romance of Adultery.* Philadelphia: University of Pennsylvania Press, 1998.

Mehrez, Samia. "The Subversive Poetics of Radical Bilingualism: Postcolonial Francophone North African Literature." In *The Bounds of Race: Perspectives on Hegemony and Resistance*, ed. Dominick LaCapra, 255–77. Ithaca, N.Y.: Cornell University Press, 1991.

———. "Translation and the Postcolonial Experience: The Francophone North African Text." In *Rethinking*, 120–38.

Méla, Charles. *La reine et le graal.* Paris: Seuil, 1984.

Menache, Sophia. "The King, the Church, and the Jews: Some Considerations on the Expulsions from England and France." *JMH* 13 (1987): 223–36.

Mercatanti Corsi, Gloria. "L'idendità del poeta Layamon: Tentativo di chiarificazione." *SM* 25 (1984): 301–14.

Micha, Alexandre. *Essais sur le cycle du Lancelot-Graal.* Geneva: Droz, 1987.

Middle English Dictionary. Ed. Hans Kurath. Ann Arbor: University of Michigan Press, 1952–.

Mieszkowski, Gretchen. "The Prose *Lancelot*'s Galehot, Malory's Lavain, and the Queering of Late Medieval Literature." *Arthuriana* 5, no. 1 (1995): 21–51.

Mignolo, Walter D. "Linguistic Maps, Literary Geographies, and Cultural Landscapes: Languages, Languaging, and (Trans)nationalism." *Modern Language Quarterly* 57, no. 2 (1996): 181–96.

Mishra, Vijay, and Bob Hodge. "What Is Post(-)Colonialism?" *Textual Practice* 5 (1991): 399–414.

Mitchell, W. J. T. "Imperial Landscape." In *Landscape and Power,* ed. W. J. T. Mitchell, 5–34. Chicago: University of Chicago Press, 1994.

Montigny, Jean-Loup. *Essai sur les institutions du duché de Bretagne à l'époque de Pierre Mauclerc et sur la politique de ce prince (1213–1237).* Paris: La Nef de Paris, 1961.

Montrose, Louis. "The Work of Gender in the Discourse of Discovery." *Representations* 33 (1991): 1–41.

Morris, Rosemary. "The *Gesta regum Britanniae* of William of Rennes: An Arthurian Epic." *AL* 6 (1986): 60–123.

———. "King Arthur and the Growth of French Nationalism." In *France and the British Isles in the Middle Ages and Renaissance,* ed. Gillian Jondorf and David N. Dumville, 115–29. Woodbridge: Boydell Press, 1991.

Nelson, Janet L. *Politics and Ritual in Early Medieval Europe.* London: Hambledon Press, 1986.

Nichols, Stephen G., Jr. *Romanesque Signs: Early Medieval Narrative and Iconography.* New Haven, Conn.: Yale University Press, 1983.

Nicole, Eugène. "L'onomastique littéraire." *Poétique* 54 (1983): 233–53.

Nimis, Steve. "The Prosaics of the Ancient Novels." *Arethusa* 27 (1994): 387–411.

Noble, James. "Laȝamon's 'Ambivalence' Reconsidered." In *Text and Tradition,* 171–82.

Oakeshott, R. Ewart. *Records of the Medieval Sword.* Woodbridge: Boydell Press, 1991.

O'Curry, Eugene. *On the Manners and Customs of the Ancient Irish.* Ed. W. K. Sullivan. London: Williams and Norgate, 1873.

O'Rahilly, Cecile, ed. *The Stowe Version of the Táin Bó Cúailnge.* Dublin: Dublin Institute for Advanced Studies, 1961.

Otter, Monika. *Inventiones: Fiction and Referentiality in Twelfth-Century English Historical Writing.* Chapel Hill: University of North Carolina Press, 1996.

Overing, Gillian R. "Swords and Signs: A Semiotic Perspective on *Beowulf.*" *American Journal of Semiotics* 5 (1987): 35–57.

Padel, O. J. "Geoffrey of Monmouth and Cornwall." *CMCS* 8 (1984): 1–28.

Pähler, Heinrich. *Anglistik: Strukturuntersuchungen zur "Historia regum Britanniae" des Geoffrey of Monmouth.* Bonn: Rheinische Friedrich Wilhems-Universität, 1958.

Pakter, Walter. *Medieval Canon Law and the Jews.* Ebelsbach: Rolf Gremer, 1988.

Patterson, Lee. *Negotiating the Past.* Madison: University of Wisconsin Press, 1987.

Pauphilet, Albert. *Études sur la "Queste del saint graal" attribuée à Gautier Map.* Paris: Champion, 1921.

Perret, Michèle. "De l'espace romanesque à la matérialité du livre: L'espace énonciatif des premiers romans en prose." *Poétique* 50 (1982): 173–82.

Pickens, Rupert T. "Autobiography and History in the Vulgate *Estoire* and the Prose *Merlin.*" In *Lancelot-Grail,* 98–116.

Pickford, Cedric E. "The River Humber in French Arthurian Romances." In *The Legend of Arthur in the Middle Ages,* ed. P. B. Grout et al., 149–59, 247–48. Cambridge: Brewer, 1983.

Plummer, John F. "Frenzy and Females: Subject Formation in Opposition to the Other in the Prose *Lancelot.*" *Arthuriana* 6, no. 4 (1996): 45–51.

Potts, Cassandra. "*Atque unum ex diversis gentibus populum effecit*: Historical Tradition and Norman Identity." *ANS* 18 (1996): 139–52.

———. "Normandy or Brittany? A Conflict of Interests at Mont Saint Michel (966–1035)." *ANS* 12 (1989): 135–56.

Pratt, Mary Louise. *Imperial Eyes: Travel Writing and Transculturation.* London: Routledge, 1992.

Prestwich, Michael. *English Politics in the Thirteenth Century.* New York: St. Martin's Press, 1990.

Putter, Ad. "Knights and Clerics at the Court of Champagne: Chrétien de Troyes's Romances in Context." In *Medieval Knighthood,* ed. Stephen Church and Ruth Harvey, 5:243–66. Woodbridge: Boydell Press, 1995.

Quilley, Geoff. "'All Ocean Is Her Own': The Image of the Sea and the Identity of the Maritime Nation in Eighteenth-Century British Art." In *Imagining,* 132–52.

Rabasa, José. *Inventing A-m-e-r-i-c-a: Spanish Historiography and the Formation of Eurocentrism.* Norman: University of Oklahoma Press, 1993.

Rampolla, Mary Lynn. "'A Pious Legend': St. Oswald and the Foundation of Worcester Cathedral Priory." *Oral Tradition in the Middle Ages,* ed. W. F. H. Nicolaisen, 187–210. Binghamton, N.Y.: Medieval and Renaissance Texts and Studies, 1995.

Ransford, Rosalind. "A Kind of Noah's Ark: Aelred of Rievaulx and National Identity." In *Religion and National Identity,* ed. Stuart Mews, 137–46. Oxford: Blackwell, 1982.

Reeve, Michael D. Review of *First Variant. CMCS* 18 (1989): 123–25.

———. "The Transmission of the *Historia regum Britanniae." Journal of Medieval Latin* 1 (1991): 73–117.

Reiss, Edmund. "The Welsh Versions of Geoffrey of Monmouth's *Historia." Welsh History Review* 4 (1968–69): 97–127.

Remley, Paul. "Geoffrey of Monmouth: In His Own Words?" *Peritia* 5 (1986): 452–61.

Reynolds, Susan. *Kingdoms and Communities in Western Europe, 900–1300.* Oxford: Clarendon Press, 1984.

Richard, Charles. *Notice sur l'ancienne bibliothèque des échevins de la ville de Rouen.* Rouen: Alfred Peron, 1845.

Richardson, Miles. "The Artefact as Abbreviated Act: A Social Interpretation of Material Culture." In *The Meaning of Things: Material Culture and Symbolic Expression,* ed. Ian Hodder, 172–77. London: Unwin Hyman, 1989.

Riddy, Felicity. "Reading for England: Arthurian Literature and National Consciousness." *Bibliographical Bulletin of the International Arthurian Society* 43 (1991): 314–32.

Ritchie, R. L. Graeme. *The Normans in Scotland.* Edinburgh: Edinburgh University Press, 1954.

Roberts, Brynley F. "Geoffrey of Monmouth and the Welsh Historical Tradition." *NMS* 20 (1976): 29–40.

———. "Tales and Romances." In *A Guide to Welsh Literature,* ed. A. O. H. Jarman and Gwilym Rees Hughes, 1:203–43. Swansea: Christopher Davies, 1976.

———, ed. *Brut y Brenhinedd: Llanstephan MS. 1 Version.* Excerpts. Dublin: Dublin Institute for Advanced Studies, 1971.

Robertson, Kellie. "Geoffrey of Monmouth and the Translation of Insular Historiography." *Arthuriana,* 8, no. 4 (1998): 42–57.

Rockwell, Paul Vincent. *Rewriting Resemblance in Medieval French Romance: "Ceci n'es pas un graal."* New York: Garland, 1995.

Rohlfs, Gerhard. "Ci conte de Durendal l'espee." In *Mélanges offerts à Rita Lejeune,* 2:859–69. Gembloux: J. Duculot, 1969.

Rollo, David. *Historical Fabrication, Ethnic Fable, and French Romance in Twelfth-Century England.* Lexington, Ky.: French Forum, 1998.

Rosenberg, Daniel. "'A New Sort of Logick and Critick': Etymological Interpretation in Horne Tooke's *The Diversions of Purley."* In *Language, Self, and Society: A Social History of Language,* ed. Peter Burke and Roy Porter, 300–329. Cambridge: Polity Press, 1991.

Sack, Robert David. *Human Territoriality: Its Theory and History.* Cambridge: Cambridge University Press, 1986.

Said, Edward W. "Yeats and Decolonization." In *Nationalism, Colonialism, and Literature*, 69–95. Minneapolis: University of Minnesota Press, 1990.

Salter, Elizabeth. *English and International: Studies in the Literature, Art, and Patronage of Medieval England*. Ed. Derek Pearsall and Nicolette Zeeman. Cambridge: Cambridge University Press, 1988.

Salter, H. E. "Geoffrey of Monmouth and Oxford." *EHR* 34 (1919): 382–85.

Sapir Abulafia, Anna. *Christians and Jews in the Twelfth-Century Renaissance*. London: Routledge, 1995.

Schirmer, Walter F. *Die frühen Darstellungen des Arthurstoffes*. Cologne: Westdeutscher Verlag, 1958.

Schmolke-Hasselmann, Beate. *Der arthurische Versroman von Chrestien bis Froissart*. Tübingen: Max Neimeyer, 1980.

———. "The Round Table: Ideal, Fiction, Reality." *AL* 2 (1982): 41–75.

Schramm, Percy Ernst. *A History of the English Coronation*. Trans. Leopold G. Wickham Legg. Oxford: Clarendon Press, 1937.

Schwyzer, Philip. "Purity and Danger on the West Bank of the Severn: The Cultural Geography of *A Masque Presented at Ludlow Castle, 1634*." *Representations* 60 (1997): 22–48.

Searle, Eleanor. *Predatory Kinship and the Creation of Norman Power, 840–1066*. Berkeley: University of California Press, 1988.

Shell, Marc. *Money, Language, and Thought: Literary and Philosophical Economies from the Medieval to the Modern Era*. Berkeley: University of California Press, 1982.

Shichtman, Martin. "Gawain in Wace and Layamon: A Case of Metahistorical Evolution." In *Medieval Texts and Contemporary Readers*, ed. Laurie A. Finke and Martin B. Shichtman, 103–19. Ithaca, N.Y.: Cornell University Press, 1987.

Shichtman, Martin, and Laurie Finke. "Profiting from the Past: History as Symbolic Culture in the *Historia regum Britanniae*." *AL* 12 (1993): 1–35.

Shopkow, Leah. *History and Community: Norman Historical Writing in the Eleventh and Twelfth Centuries*. Washington, D.C.: Catholic University of America Press, 1997.

Short, Ian. "Patrons and Polyglots: French Literature in Twelfth-Century England." *ANS* 14 (1991): 229–49.

Signer, Michael Alan, ed. *Expositionem in Ezechielem*. Turnholt: Brepols, 1991.

Smith, Anthony D. *The Ethnic Origins of Nations*. Oxford: Blackwell, 1986.

Smith, J. Beverley. "The Succession to Welsh Princely Inheritance: The Evidence Reconsidered." In *British*, 64–81.

Smith, Jonathan. "The Lie that Blinds: Destabilizing the Text of Landscape." In *Place/Culture/Representation*, ed. James Duncan and David Ley, 78–92. London: Routledge, 1993.

Smith, W. B. S. "De la toponymie bretonne: Dictionnaire étymologique." *Language* 16, no. 2, supplement (1940): 1–136.

Southern, R. W. "Aspects of the European Tradition of Historical Writing: The Sense of the Past." *Royal Historical Society Transactions*, 5th ser., 23 (1973): 243–63.

Spiegel, Gabrielle. "Genealogy: Form and Function in Medieval Historical Narrative." *History and Theory* 22 (1983): 43–53.

———. *Romancing the Past: The Rise of Vernacular Prose Historiography in Thirteenth-Century France*. Berkeley: University of California Press, 1993.

Spitzer, Leo. *Linguistics and Literary History*. New York: Russell and Russell, 1962.

———. "The Name of Roland's Sword." *Language* 15 (1939): 48–50.

———. Review *Glosarios latino-españoles de la edad media*, by Américo Castro. *Modern Language Notes* 53 (1938): 122–46.

Stanley, E. G. "Laȝamon's Antiquarian Sentiments." *MA* 38 (1969): 23–37.

———. "Laȝamon's Un-Anglo-Saxon Syntax." In *Text and Tradition*, 47–56.

Stegman, André, Guy Demerson, and Michel Reulos, eds. *Nova Reperta*. By Jan van der Straet. Tours: Bienvault, 1977.

Stein, Robert M. "Making History English: Cultural Identity and Historical Explanation in William of Malmesbury and Laȝamon's *Brut.*" In *Text and Territory: Geographical Imagination in the European Middle Ages*, ed. Sylvia Tomasch and Sealy Gilles, 97–115. Philadelphia: University of Pennsylvania Press, 1998.

Stickler, A. M. "Il 'gladius' negli atti dei concili et dei RR. Pontefici sino a Graziano e Bernardo di Clairvaux." *Salesianum* 13 (1951): 414–45.

Stirnemann, Patricia. "Some Champenois Vernacular Manuscripts and the Manerius Style of Illumination." *The Manuscripts of Chrétien de Troyes*, ed. Keith Busby, Terry Nixon, Alison Stones, and Lori Walters, 1:195–226. Amsterdam: Rodopi, 1993.

Stones, Alison. "The Earliest Illustrated Prose *Lancelot* Manuscript?" *Reading Medieval Studies* 3 (1977): 3–44.

Stow, Kenneth. *Alienated Minority: The Jews of Medieval Latin Europe.* Cambridge: Harvard University Press, 1992.

Streuver, Nancy. "Fables of Power." *Representations* 4 (1983): 108–27.

Strong, James. "A Concise Dictionary of the Words in the Hebrew Bible." In *Exhaustive Concordance of the Bible*, 1–169. 1890. Reprint. Nashville: Abingdon Press, 1986.

Sturm-Maddox, Sara. "'Tenir sa terre en pais': Social Order in the *Brut* and in the *Conte del Graal.*" *Studies in Philology* 81 (1984): 28–41.

Suleri, Sara. *The Rhetoric of English India.* Chicago: University of Chicago Press, 1992.

Swanson, R. N. "Two Swords." In *Dictionary of the Middle Ages*, ed. Joseph Strayer, 12:233–35. New York: Scribner's, 1982–89.

Synan, Edward A. *The Popes and the Jews in the Middle Ages.* New York: Macmillan, 1965.

Szkilnik, Michelle. *L'archipel du graal.* Geneva: Droz, 1991.

———. "*Loiauté* et *traïson* dans la *Mort le roi Artu.*" *Op. Cit.: Revue littérature française et comparée* 3 (1994): 25–32.

Taitz, Emily. *The Jews of Medieval France: The Community of Champagne.* Westport, Conn.: Greenwood Press, 1994.

Tatlock, J. S. P. *The Legendary History of Britain.* Berkeley: University of California Press, 1950.

Thornton, David Ewan. "A Neglected Genealogy of Llywelyn ap Gruffudd." *CMCS* 23 (1992): 9–23.

Thorpe, Lewis, trans. *The History of the Kings of Britain.* By Geoffrey of Monmouth. London: Penguin, 1966.

Tiller, Kenneth Jack. *Performing History: Historiography and the Role of the Translator in Laȝamon's "Brut."* Ph.D. diss., University of Notre Dame, 1996.

Tilliette, Jean-Yves. "Invention du récit: La 'Brutiade' de Geoffroy de Monmouth." *CCM* 39 (1996): 217–33.

Todorov, Tzvetan. *Poétique de la prose.* Paris: Seuil, 1971.

Trachtenberg, J. *The Devil and the Jews.* New Haven, Conn.: Yale University Press, 1943.

Trivedi, Harish. "India and Post-colonial Discourse." In *Interrogating Post-colonialism: Theory, Text and Context*, ed. Harish Trivedi and Meenakshi Mukherjee, 231–47. Rahtrapati Nivas, Shimla: Indian Institute of Advanced Study, 1996.

Türk, Egbert. *Nugae Curialium: Le règne d'Henri II Plantagenêt (1145–1189) et l'éthique politique.* Geneva: Droz, 1977.

Turville-Petre, Thorlac. *England the Nation: Language, Literature, and National Identity, 1290–1340.* Oxford: Clarendon Press, 1996.

Tyson, Diana B. "Patronage of French Vernacular History Writers in the Twelfth and Thirteenth Centuries." *Romania* 100 (1979): 180–222.

Ullmann, Walter. *The Growth of Papal Government in the Middle Ages.* New York: Barnes and Noble, 1956.

———. "On the Influence of Geoffrey of Monmouth in English History." In *Speculum historiale*, ed. Clemens Bauer, Johannes Sporl, Laetittia Boehm, and Max Müller, 257–76. Munich: Freiburg, 1965.

Van Meter, David C. "The Ritualized Presentation of Weapons and the Ideology of Nobility in *Beowulf*." *JEGP* 95 (1996): 175–89.

Vernon, James. "Border Crossings: Cornwall and English (Imagi)Nation." In *Imagining*, 153–72.

Vielliard, Françoise, ed. *Le roman de Troie en prose*. Cologny-Genève: Martin Bodmer, 1979.

Vinaver, Eugène. "King Arthur's Sword; or, The Making of a Medieval Romance." *Bulletin of the John Rylands Library* 40 (1958): 513–26.

Vine Durling, Nancy. "Translation and Innovation in the *Roman de Brut*." In *Medieval Translators and Their Craft*, ed. Jeanette Beer, 9–39. Kalamazoo: Western Michigan University, 1989.

Ward, Charlotte. "Arthur in the Welsh *Bruts*." In *Celtic Languages and Celtic Peoples*, ed. Cyril Bryne, Margaret Rose Harry, and Padraig O'Siadhail, 383–90. Halifax: St. Mary's University, 1992.

Warren, Michelle. "Making Contact: Postcolonial Perspectives through Geoffrey of Monmouth's *Historia regum Britannie*." *Arthuriana* 8, no. 4 (1998): 115–34.

———. "Marmiadoise of Greece: The Force of Ancient History in the *Estoire de Merlin*." *Romance Languages Annual* 9 (1997): 141–48.

———. "Memory out of Line: Hebrew Etymologies in Medieval French Literature." *Exemplaria* 12, no. 2 (2000).

Warren, W. L. *Henry II*. Berkeley: University of California Press, 1973.

Waswo, Richard. "Our Ancestors, the Trojans: Inventing Cultural Identity in the Middle Ages." *Exemplaria* 7, no. 2 (1995): 269–90.

Watson, Jonathan. "Affective Poetics and Social Reperformance in Lawman's *Brut*: A Comparison of the Caligula and Otho Versions." *Arthuriana* 8, no. 3 (1998): 62–75.

Watt, J. A. "Spiritual and Temporal Powers." In *Cambridge History of Medieval Political Thought, c. 350–c. 1450*, ed. J. H. Burns, 367–423. Cambridge: Cambridge University Press, 1988.

Weinberg, Carole. " 'By a noble church on the bank of the Severn': A Regional View of Laȝamon's *Brut*." *LSE* 26 (1995): 49–62.

Weiner, Annette. *Inalienable Possessions: The Paradox of Keeping-While-Giving*. Berkeley: University of California Press, 1992.

White, Graeme J. "The End of Stephen's Reign." *History* 75 (1990): 3–22.

Williams, Andrea M. L. "The Enchanted Swords and the Quest for the Holy Grail: Metaphoric Structure in *La queste del saint graal*." *French Studies* 48 (1994): 385–401.

Wood, Ian. "The Mission of Augustine of Canterbury to the English." *Speculum* 69 (1994): 1–17.

Wolf, Eric R. *Europe and the People without History*. Berkeley: University of California Press, 1982.

Wright, Neil. "Angles and Saxons in Laȝamon's *Brut*: A Reassessment." In *Text and Tradition*, 161–70.

———. "Geoffrey of Monmouth and Bede." *AL* 6 (1986): 27–59.

———. "Geoffrey of Monmouth and Gildas." *AL* 2 (1982): 1–40.

———. "Geoffrey of Monmouth and Gildas Revisited." *AL* 4 (1985): 155–63.

Young, Robert J. C. *Colonial Desire: Hybridity in Theory, Culture, and Race*. London: Routledge, 1995.

Zamora, Margarita. *Reading Columbus*. Berkeley: University of California Press, 1993.

Zumthor, Paul. *La mesure du monde: Représentation de l'espace au moyen âge*. Paris: Seuil, 1993.

Index

Michelle R. Warren teaches French and medieval studies in the Department of Foreign Languages and Literatures at the University of Miami, Coral Gables, Florida.